INNOVATIONS IN TEACHING AND LEARNING

INNOVATIONS IN TEACHING AND LEARNING

Research Methodologies and Project Management in Higher Education

Prof. Ram Chandra

KALPAZ

First Published, 2020

Published by

Kalpaz Publications
C-30, Satyawati Nagar,
Delhi – 110052
Ph.: 011-47034999, 9811692060
www.kalpazpublications.com
E-mail: kalpaz@hotmail.com

Printed at: G. Print Process, Delhi

Cataloging in Publication Data—DK
Courtesy: D.K. Agencies (P) Ltd. <docinfo@dkagencies.com>

Chandra, Ram *(Professor)*, **author.**
Innovations in teaching and learning, research methodologies and project management in higher education / Prof. Ram Chandra.
pages cm
Includes bibliographical references.
ISBN 9789353240851 (HB)

1. Education, Higher—India. 2. Educational innovations—India. I. Title.

LCC LA1153.I56 2019 | DDC 378.54 23

Contents

Foreword

The book entitled "Innovations in Teaching and Learning, Research Methodologies and Project Management in Higher Education" written by Prof. (Dr.) Ram Chandra has come at the time when higher education is rapidly changing across the globe because of several reasons.

The universities are evolving innovative methods of teaching and learning for the benefit to the students as well as to the society. This in turn requires tremendous change in the higher education system. The book has dealt several teaching and learning strategies and different study skills.

The learning skills which are suitable today may not be appropriate tomorrow; the learning skills in the near future are going to be dominated by technological innovations, critical thinking and research (what and how people are willing to learn). This requires a basic understanding of research methodologies and to think of a project, develop it and execute it. This in turn will require a detailed understanding of project and all related issues. The book has rightly emphasized the need of industries and academic institutions joining hands and developing suitable course curriculum where training, research and projects are an integral part of the education.

The book is divided into seven chapters covering higher education system, teaching and learning in higher education, innovations in integrated model of higher education, academia and industry interaction, research methodologies, project management and field training.

The book will be useful for the teachers and students who are engaged in teaching and learning, doing research and writing and conducting projects and training.

Er. Awadhesh Kumar
Managing Director
Buddha Group of Institutions
Gaya (Bihar)

Preface

The higher education is changing at a very fast pace across the globe because of several reasons. One important reason is that the course curriculum of any programme needs to be changed on regular intervals so as to meet the requirements of the nation and also to match with technology (Industry 5.0) and communication (5G). This in turn requires adequate training of the faculty members. Another important reason is that higher educational system of the country should meet the manpower requirements of the society in general and the country in particular.

The universities need to evolve new and alternative methods of teaching and learning based on lectures, seminars, group discussions, assignments etc. This is because it is going to be beneficial not only to the students but also to the society. This in turn requires tremendous change in the higher education system. The institutions have to design their programmes and their objectives and learning outcomes by keeping in mind the diversity among the students. The institutions have to realize that if students can't learn the way we teach, we should teach them the way they learn. This in turn requires good teaching, reading, learning, writing and presentation skills.

We have discussed teaching and learning strategies and different study skills. The strategies and techniques that enable students to make the most efficient use of their time, resources, and academic potential are referred to as study skills. The efficient use of time will enable any one to get more work done in less time. Students will also be able to make their learning easier and help retain what you have learned for longer.

The learning skills which are suitable today may not be appropriate tomorrow. Most likely, the learning skills in the near future are going to be dominated by (1) technological innovations (use of digital resources including innovations), (2) critical thinking (building new solutions through novel combination of given information) and (3) research (what and how people are willing to learn).

Another important aspect of teaching and learning is to inculcate the habit of doing research for several purposes like reading, learning, latest information about a subject etc. This requires a basic understanding of research methodologies. Another significant aspect of teaching and learning is to think of a project, develop it and execute it. This in turn will require a detailed understanding of project and all related issues.

The education world is changing at an alarming rate. The ever-rising higher skill expectations and changing structure of the employment sector have posed numerous challenges for higher education providers. This has become more important and relevant because of increasing competitive environment in business and service sectors. This has resulted a mismatch between students seeking employment and industries requiring skilled employees. Therefore, there is no other way to resolve this, but to align education especially higher education with necessary skills. The industries and academic institutions need to join hands and develop suitable course curriculum where training, research and projects are an integral part of the education.

This book has been written for the teachers and students who are engaged in teaching and learning, doing research and writing and conducting projects and training and want to improve their study skills as per the guidelines of regulatory bodies.

Prof. Ram Chandra

Acknowledgement

First and foremost, I would like to thank all the researchers whose work has been cited in the book. I would also like to thank the authorities of Cavendish University Zambia, Mewar University, Monad University, IGNOU where a lot of understanding of the subject was obtained and practiced.

Last but not the least, I would like to thank my family members: my wife Smt. Vimla Devi and sons Deepak, Udit and Peyush and grand children (Naman and Aanya) for their patience and moral support.

Prof. Ram Chandra

List of Tables

List of Figures

1

Higher Education System

....education is not what the teacher gives:
education is a natural process spontaneously
carried out by the human individual.
It is acquired not by listening to words,
but by experiences upon the environment.

Maria Montessori

Education

Education is a field which is needed by each and every individual as well as by all the nations. Education is a process by which knowledge, character and behavior of a person is changed in a positive and productive direction. Education is a vital process for human resource development, nation building, national development and transformation of the society. Education is a powerful tool to generate knowledge for a technology based society.

There are several definitions available in the literature. Some of them are cited below:

- Education is the key to success in life, and teachers make a lasting impact in the lives of their students. **Solomon Ortiz**
- Education is the passport to the future, for tomorrow belongs to those who prepare for it today. **Malcolm X**
- Education is the most powerful weapon which you can use to change the world. **Nelson Mandela**
- Knowledge is power. Information is liberating. Education is the premise of progress, in every society, in every family. **Kofi Annan**
- The function of education is to teach one to think intensively and to think critically. Intelligence plus character - that is the goal of true education. **Martin Luther King, Jr.**

Higher Education System

The higher education system of any country, India is no exception to this, mainly falls under the following two categories:

(1) Conventional System of Education

(2) Open and Distance Education System

A brief description of these educational systems is given below:

Conventional System of Education

The conventional system of education has the following limitations/ disadvantages (Gadiya and Chandra 2014), see Fig. 1.1:

- It is a costly system and is available to only those who can afford it.
- The number of institutions available for providing quality education is inadequate and is centralized to big cities.
- The system is very rigid. The duration of study, courses, examination are fixed.
- The system is teacher centered. This means that teacher decides what to teach, how to teach and how to evaluate the performance of the students.
- The system has no fixed parameters to standardize the parameters for quality education.
- There are as many standards as the institutions and teachers in them.

Open and Distance Education System

The conventional education system was not able to provide education to all those who need it. To overcome this problem and to remove some of the rigidities of conventional system, open and distance education system was evolved in different phases. The first phase was correspondence education as shown in Fig. 1.2 (Chandra and Singh 2004).

In the correspondence education system, an effort was made to standardize the study material but the students were left alone to study and write examination. There was no contact between students and their teachers. In other words, this education system was without any student support. In open and distance education system, student support services were added; and, therefore, it became a popular system (Fig. 1.3).

Some of the student support services are given below:

- Each and every student is attached to a learner support centre (study centre) established in well reputed universities/institutions.

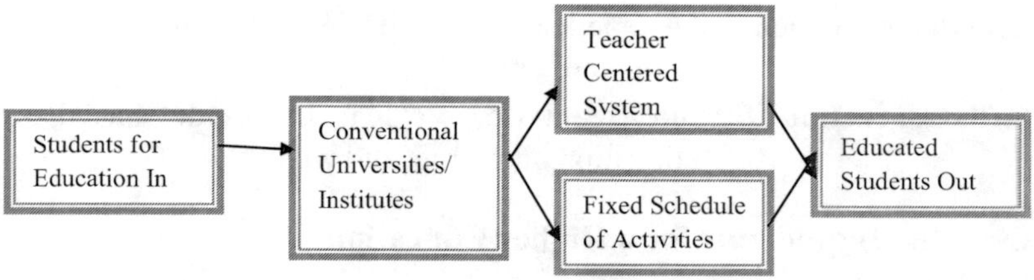

Fig. 1.1: Teacher Centered Conventional System of Education

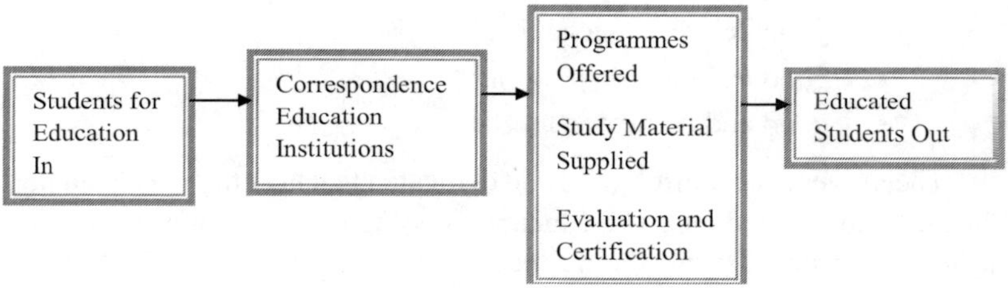

Fig. 1.2: Correspondence System of Education

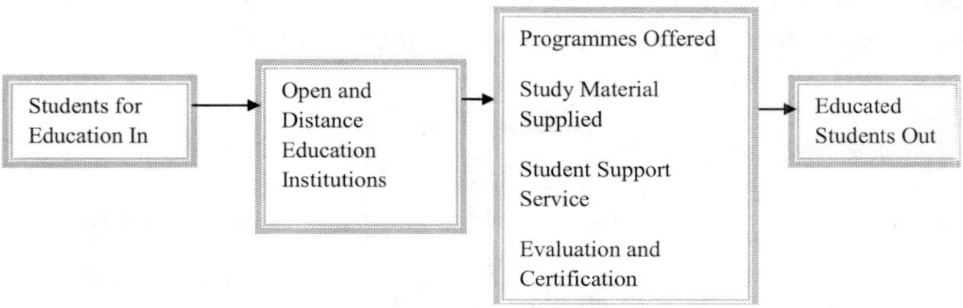

Fig. 1.3: Open and Distance Education System

- Students will get all academic support like submission of the assignments, counselling and feedback, library facilities, facilities to write examinations etc. at the study centres.
- Students are able to contact their teachers and peer groups.

The open and distance education system evolved during the years is shown in Fig. 1.4. There are five generations of this system.

First Generation : Correspondence model based on printed study material only.

Second Generation : Multimedia model based on printed study material and A/V system.

Third Generation : Tele learning model based on telecommunication.

Fourth Generation : Flexible learning model based on online delivery using internet.

Fifth Generation : Intelligent flexible learning model based on utilization of internet and web.

Essential Ingredients for a Higher Education

The essential ingredients for a higher education are:

- good course curriculum
- good delivery mechanism
- good training programmes
- good and dedicated teachers

The university requires good and dedicated teachers to provide quality education to the students. The educational system of any country, whether developed or developing, should meet the manpower requirements of the society in general and the country in particular. A country requires engineers, doctors, nurses, administrators, technicians, biologists, physicists, lawyers and so on. At the same time, we must also spare a thought for our society such that all these classes of people are full of nationality (Fig.1.5).

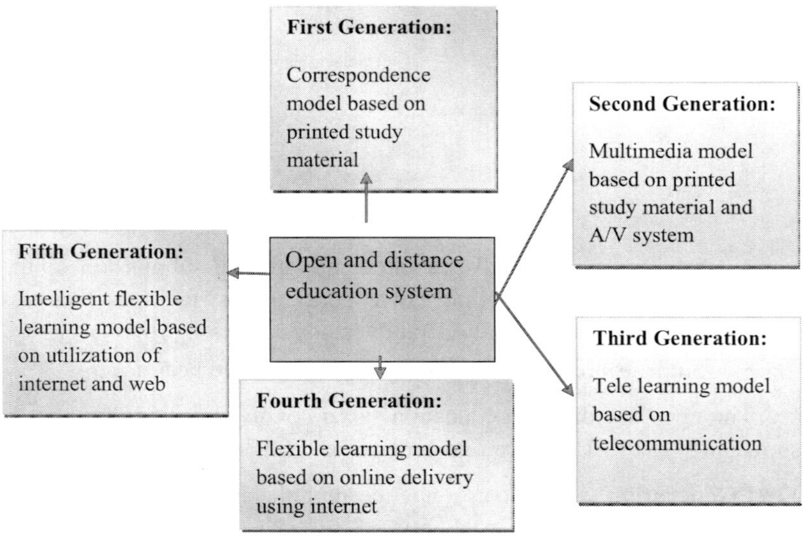

Fig. 1.4: Evolution of Open and Distance Education System

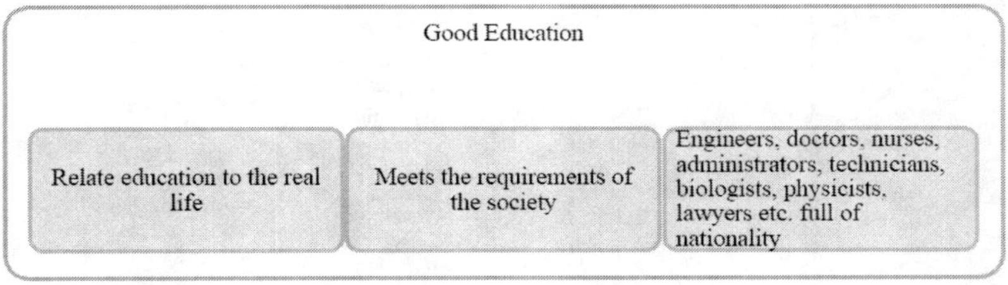

Fig. 1.5: An Ideal Higher Education

Education is what survives when what has been learned has been forgotten. It is the supreme art of the teacher to awaken joy in creative expression and knowledge. We should always see and recognise that knowledge is increasing but the question is whether happiness is increasing? We know that colleges and universities are multiplying but again the question is whether happy homes are multiplying? Therefore, education should be related to life, and not be an academic study alone. This in turn requires an integral education in which humanism is blended with the spiritual ideal. Education must teach students to stand up as soldiers of the ideal. Unfortunately, this is not happening in many universities.

An ideal higher education requires dedicated teachers, good infrastructure and an adequate industry-academia interaction. There are several definitions available in the literature. A very good and most appropriate definition of education could be as follows:

Education improves the lives of people. Education ultimately modifies society, country and world better than you find them today. Education is the power to think intelligently, the power to act well and the power to appreciate life.

The next question which arises is to understand higher education in broader perspective.

In a society full of diversity, ideologies and opinions, higher education means different things to different people. Even then, one can categorise higher education among the four prominent concepts as shown in Fig. 1.6.

Education is a choice. We don't become educated by watching television, and we don't learn a whole lot having similar conversations with the same people day after day. Our education comes from pushing up against boundaries, from taking risks that may seem at first to be overwhelming, and by persevering past the first disappointments or shortfalls until we reach a point at which actual learning takes place. Determination and

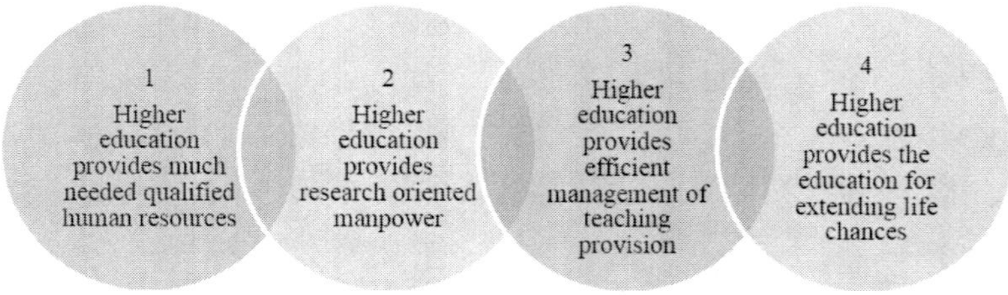

Fig. 1.6: Four Concepts of Higher Education

perseverance are absolutely vital to developing a true education—rarely, if ever, do we learn the most valuable lessons in the first few steps of the journey.

Higher Education Requires Integrating Teaching

With so many options, the higher education may be possible by integrating teaching only. The way of connecting skills and knowledge from multiple sources and experiences or applying skills and practice in various settings is integrated teaching. It simply means bridging connections between academic knowledge and practical knowledge.

This alternative method of teaching based on lectures, seminars, and assignments is believed to be beneficial to the student community and would be the ideal approach because of the following reasons:

- System wise teaching (block wise)
- Integration along with case oriented approach
- Student centered (learners oriented)
- Promotes interdepartmental collaboration
- Students learn to apply their knowledge to daily life experiences

It is well known fact that not all students learn at the same pace. Students are unique in their own ways, including the way they read, learn and write. Since not all students learn in the same way, it is essential that teachers recognize the learning style differences of their students and teach in a manner in which all learning styles are considered.

Need of Great Teachers

This is only possible provided we have the great teachers in higher education. You may be wondering who the great teachers are. In fact there are three classes of teachers as defined below:

1. **An average teacher**: This class of teachers only instructs the students.
2. **A good teacher**: This class of teachers guides the students. A good teacher is like a candle which consumes itself to light others. Good teachers are those who know how little they know. Bad teachers are those who think they know more than they don't know.
3. **A great teacher**: This class of teachers not only instructs and guides the students but also inspires the students.

The characteristics of teachers are just as diverse as those of the students. We know that the learning style, teaching style, and personality style of teachers have implications for student learning. A good book covering all necessary study skills for diverse group of students is a must. Individuals have the basic capability to learn and to teach; however, they are not able to learn and teach effectively in the same exact way. It has been observed that not only do students learn in considerably different ways, but certain students succeed only through selected teaching methods.

Role of Higher Education Institutions

There is going to be tremendous change in the higher education system. The institutions have to design the programmes and their objectives and learning outcomes by keeping in mind the diversity among the students. We will discuss the issue of diversity among the students.

Diversity Among Students

The diversity among students should be kept in mind by the teachers to plan strategically in order to reach the needs of diverse learners of higher education. The diversity varies from language, to families, to cultural backgrounds, to economics and experiential background. There is large number of published work having the following conclusion:

- No two students are alike.
- No two students learn in the same way.
- Each student likes its own environment. An enriched environment for one student is not necessarily enriched for another.
- Each student learns and thinks differently and therefore students should learn to think for themselves.
- ***If students can't learn the way we teach, we should teach them the way they learn."***

What Teachers Should Know About the Learners?

It is for the benefit for the educational planners, especially for the teachers, to consider all the elements for differentiating learners. All teachers should build their instructional strategies so flexible and diverse so that they can adjust the learning for a group of learners. Some of the strategies are:

- **Knowing the learner:** It is very essential. We need to know the learner so that we can make sure that the curriculum fits. It will still be better if we know how students access, process, and express information. At the top of these, we need to know their learning styles and their thinking styles.
- **Assessing the learner:** There is need to pre-assess the learner so that we can find out what they already know. We need to assess during the learning through class assignments and after the learning through multiple choice questions (Bloom's Taxonomy) and through short answer, medium answer and long answer questions.
- **Curriculum approaches:** Curriculum can be delivered in many ways so that it will appeal to individual learners.
- **Instructional strategies:** The use of variety of instructional strategies adds novelty, choice, and individuality to learning. A true and inspiring teacher always does this. All teachers should build their appropriate instructional strategies, suitable for the learning for a group of learners.
- **Flexible assignments:** This is very crucial for the teachers. All teachers should help students focus on essential skills and understanding key concepts, recognizing that they may be at different levels of readiness. A true teacher must reach at the level of students' mind so that students have the opportunity to develop essential skills and understanding at his or her appropriate level of challenge.
- **Ambience in the classroom**: All inspiring teachers believe that all students are capable of learning and to become successful in their studies. This could be possible if teachers create a climate where all students feel included and feel that there is potential in each learner.

Teachers Need to Understand Paradigm Shift in Education

There is definite paradigm shift in higher education. Whether it is in curriculum, instruction, or environment, the students have to become independent, active, self-organizing, responsible and empowered. Table 1.1 gives what is conventional and what is emerging in curriculum, instruction and environment.

For example, if we see the curriculum, conventionally the focus is on content whereas the new emphasis should be balancing the content and process of its delivery. The largely teacher-centered approach of instruction is being shifted to student centered. Also, multiple resource-based learning and multiple approaches to instruction are being given due emphasis. The competitive approach is being replaced by cooperative approach. Another important factor is that supervision of learners is being overtaken by empowerment of learners.

Table 1.1: Paradigm Shift in Education

Category	*Conventional Approach*	*Evolving or Emerging Approach*
Curriculum	• Major focus is on content • Content acquisition • Lock step progress	• Content & process are balanced • Learning to learn is emphasized • Continuous progress is planned
Instruction	• Largely teacher-centered approach • Single textbook recommended by the teacher • Single instructional approach largely by lecture • Passive learning; students remain passive during learning process	• Student –centered approach • Multiple resource-based learning • Multiple approaches to instruction • Active learning: students are always active by asking questions, group discussion etc.
Environment	• Competitive approach • System level management • Supervision of learners • Hierarchical structures	• Cooperative approach • Institution-site management • Empowerment of learners • Professional/collegial structures

e-learning as Evaluator

We are living in the era of information and communication technology (ICT). With the use of ICT, open and distance education is going to be greatly benefitted. Traditional method of teaching is not found suitable by most of the modern students. The teachers are not serious enough to teach and evaluate the students in the way, it should have been done.

We have proposed a unique system of e-learning after discussing with larger sections of the students and taking their feedbacks. The system will work like this. Imagine a course is divided into 5 sections. The learning process will take place in 5 steps.

- Firstly, the students will go through the course material of section 1. At the end of the duration, the system will ask the students whether they are ready for the exam. If yes, the system will give a set of question paper. The students will attempt the question paper, submit it, the system will evaluate and place the marks obtained in the student's data bank. Then system will allow them to move to section 2.

- The student will go through the course material of section 2. The step 1 will be repeated.
- The students will go through the course material of step 3. The step 1 will be repeated. In case the system finds that students have not fared well, the system may refer the students to the desired section backwards. The students will do the set activities there and then moves upwards.
- The system will declare the final result of the students after clearing the section 5. The students will reach the final stage only if they have cleared all the previous sections.

The proposed system will remove majority of the anomalies with respect to evaluation process. It will be uniform for all the students. The course material will be student friendly. Many universities have already started in converting the study material into e-learning having above mentioned unique features and is going to introduce these courses.

Once implemented, a comparison may be made with the system of manual delivery and evaluation of the programmes. Based on the feedback, the system may be improved further. In order to make the concept popular and acceptable to the students, the universities are also going to introduce the concept of mobile e-learning support centres wherein a van fitted with computers with e-learning resources will move from one place to another to provide on the spot support to the desired students.

e-learning is going to be the next phase of teaching and learning process. However, for a developing country like India, this is going to be a challenge. If we have to march along with other fast-moving countries, then we have to adopt e-learning for both face to face as well as open and distance education. However, it is open and distance education which will be greatly benefitted. This is because traditional method of teaching is not found suitable by the modern students and teachers are not serious enough to teach and evaluate the students. These issues will be addressed through e-learning.

Evolution of e-learning

1. In the conventional education, the teacher decides what to teach and how to teach. The teacher also decides how to evaluate. It is,

therefore, said that in conventional education, there are as many standards as the number of teachers.

2. In open and distance education, at least the study material is standardized and made available to each and every student. The evaluation, however, still remained a challenge.
3. All the above constraints could be resolved if the concept of e-learning is adopted.

e-learning refers to the use of electronic media and information and communication technologies (ICT) in education. e-learning includes numerous types of media that deliver text, audio, images, animation, and streaming video, and includes technology applications and processes such as audio or video tape, satellite TV, CD-ROM, and computer-based learning, as well as local intranet/extranet and web-based learning.

It is cost effective, can be accessed from anywhere/anytime (portability), device Independence (PC/Laptop/Tablets/iPads/Phone), self-paced, delivers a consistent message, easy maintenance (content updation), localization (in any other language), better retention with learners, easy management of learner's progress, evaluation and records.

Process of e-learning

There are several steps for creating e-learning contents. These are:

- Content is created
- Required graphics are created
- Programmer integrates all to make an eLearning module
- Module is hosted on a Web Server (Learning Management System, LMS) and assigned to learners
- Learners view the content
- Learners take the online exam
- LMS grades the learner
- Certificate of completion is assigned to learners

Typical Features of an e-learning Module

Typically, an e-learning module consists of the following:

- Text/Graphics/Audio/Video/Animations/Simulations
- Assessment Questions/End-of-Course Assessment/Exam
- Try-Me Exercises

- Course Menu
- Glossary/External Resource Links (additional reference content links)
- Navigational Buttons (Next/Back)
- Audio/Video Transcript (subtitles/Closed Captioning)
- Progress Indicators

Implementing e-learning

e-learning requires both software and manpower. A Learning Management System (LMS) is a software application for the administration, documentation, tracking, reporting and delivery of eLearning courses or training programs. The manpower requirements and their functions are given in Table 1.2.

Table 1.2: Manpower Requirement and their Functions

Type of Manpower	*Functions*
LMS Administrator	• Hosting and managing eLearning courses • Managing Learners' profiles • Managing and taking required Reports • Manages the backend Database
Project Manager	• Manages a team of Instructional Designers, Graphic Designers, Programmers, and Quality Checkers. • Manages Schedule, creates Plan and Delivers the final product • Owns the product and is responsible for Quality, relevance of content and smooth delivery of content to learners • Take feedback and implement improvements/suggestions to content and modules
Instructional Designer (ID)/Content Writer	Instructional Designers creates the instructional experiences which make the acquisition of knowledge and skill more efficient, effective, and appealing to learners. They take the raw content and present it in a manner that ensure faster, better and long-lasting learning. They are also responsible to guide Graphic Designers and Programmers to design and program in a certain way.
Graphic Designer	A graphic designer is a professional within the graphic design and graphic arts industry who assembles together images, typography or motion graphics to create a piece of design. They follow IDs' instructions and create the required graphics.
Programmer/Integrator	A programmer or integrator specializes in bringing together content and graphics into a complete working module. He/she creates the interactivities, examinations and programs the flow of navigation within a module.
Quality Control (QC) Executive	A QC Executive is a person who reviews the quality of all factors involved in production of an eLearning module. This person usually works as an internal client who first looks at the complete module from a third person's perspective. The student/She is responsible for quality in all departments, ID/GD/Programming.
IT Security Manager	An IT/Cyber Security Manager is someone who protects information systems and computer networks from cyber-attacks, intrusions, malware and various types of data breaches. He keeps networks running smoothly and protecting sensitive data takes constant monitoring and proper cyber security management.

Global University in the Knowledge Societies

As noted in the UNESCO Report on Knowledge Societies (2005), there is a general agreement on the appropriateness of the expression" knowledge societies". We have to ask which type of knowledge we are talking about. There is a need for a new global strategy for promoting the role of information and communication technology (ICT) in different fields of the working life in the emerging knowledge societies and developing educational and training approaches on how to learn the use of ICT and become digitally literate in the spirit of sustainable development.

According to the UNESCO International Institute for Educational Planning, higher education institutions worldwide face significant challenges related to providing increased access, while containing or reducing costs. Meeting increasing and increasingly varied demand for quality higher education is an important consideration in policy debate and institutional development in many countries. New developments in higher education from virtual universities and cross-border education to e-learning, blended learning and open educational resources – all speak of the efforts on the part of the traditional higher education community, as well as new providers, to address the challenges they face in increasing provision.

The Global University System (GUS) is a worldwide initiative to create satellite/wireless telecommunications infrastructure and educational programmes for access to educational resources across national and cultural boundaries for global peace. The GUS helps higher educational institutions in remote/rural areas of developing countries to deploy broadband Internet in order for them to close the digital divide and act as the knowledge centre of their community for the eradication of poverty and isolation. The GUS has task forces working in the major regions of the globe with partnerships of higher education and healthcare institutions. Learners in these regions will be able to take their courses, via advanced broadband Internet, from member institutions around the world to receive a GUS degree. These learners and their professors from participating institutions will form a global forum for the exchange of ideas and information and for conducting collaborative research and development.

Challenges Confronting Higher Education: A Case for Understanding Innovation

Tierney et. al. have discussed challenges confronting higher education. If the intensity with which global forces are compelling change is exceptional, innovative responses are needed. To maintain their relevance in contemporary society, many universities will need to carefully cultivate their respective identities while responding to turbulent external and internal pressures in which inherited philosophical beliefs and organizational structures are likely to be challenged. There are explicit developments in the higher education landscape for worthy of consideration when thinking about innovation.

(1) The Emergence of the Knowledge-Intensive Economy

Prior to 2008, two types of cross-border trade were vital to global economic development: (1) labor intensive ows from nations with developing economies and (2) commodity-intensive ows from nations with developed economies. The main drivers of globalization, however, have changed dramatically since the 2008 nancial crisis. Today, knowledge-intensive services are indispensable to workforce development. In a knowledge-based economy, human resource not only need to cultivate specialized skills, but they must be creative, work in teams, and adapt to rapidly-evolving technologies and innovations.

(2) The Need to Train a Creative and Innovative Workforce

The effects of outsourcing jobs related to manufacturing and services have been well documented in the literature. However, the training of the manpower as per the changing needs of the industry is of prime importance.

Innovation in Higher Education

Peilin Li (2016) has studied innovation in education and e-learning. Innovation is very important in education. The new concept of learning online is becoming a trend, people learn from different digital platforms, using various online services to attain knowledge, and the learning is not restricted in classrooms. The methodology of teaching in a classroom is to help students who are slower at their pace to catch up with other students. The question is, how about the students who are naturally faster at learning?

In fact, the e-learning is helping more people to educate themselves, even without paying too much and having an absence on a regular basis at college/university. The students can take additional courses according to their interests to fulfil the requirements of their free elective studies. What is more interesting, is that there are many institutions/universities offering online based programmes. In the fast-growing digitalization of social activities, people are spending more time online, people are creating digital information all the time. There is an increasing significance of online education platforms, the MOOCs, SWAYAM are providing course information and updates.

There seems to be several points which should be kept in mind. Some of them are:

- What are the key terms defining innovation in higher education?
- What is disruptive technology and what does it mean in successful implementation of a disruptive breakthrough in higher education?
- What are the current solutions and applications for e-learning in higher education?
- Are there any problems facing in e-learning and what are the possible countermeasures for improving the methods?

Even though, traditional learning continues as a mainstream adoption; disruptive technologies such as MOOCs, SWAYAM are the favourite hype now, since it is disruptive in ways that enables the university courses (open as well as traditional) to be available. Some new features are added to it, highly valued content from famous universities around the world also appreciated professors deliver learning materials for everyone who have enrolled to the course.

Higher Education and Disruptive Technology

An innovation in higher education is in enhancing innovative thinking among the graduates so that they could generate innovation practices as benefit to the nation and humankind. The higher education should not only use innovations in learning nevertheless able to produce new generation that could create future innovations.

When we try to understand disruptive innovation, we have to consider the following questions:

- What we mean by disruptive technology?
- What does it disrupt?
- Should it be implemented? If yes, how?
- What are its benefits?
- What are the issues connected with it?
- What is it that is essentially sought to be achieved by higher education institutions?

One definition of disruptive technology is the disruption of markets when new entrants find ways of making a product which is simpler than the existing product, performs the same functions, and is more affordable.

Since it is perceived as a better and more user-friendly product at a lower price, it disrupts the market for the existing product.

Another definition of disruptive technology is in the field of education where disruptive technology is essentially the use of ICT to deliver education:

- Whether conventional online education
- Massive Open Online Courses (MOOCs)
- Cloud Computing
- Any other mode

These courses/modes are usually free and cover a wide range like Computer Science, Life Science, Pure Science, Engineering, Business Management etc. These are seen by the people as an opportunity to get new knowledge and skills or updates the ones they already have. They are need based and flexible. They are modular in nature and hence do not have to follow a sequence as in conventional education.

Conceptual Framework of Disruptive Technology

Disruptive technology is impacting all walks of life. There are two phases of disruption as shown in Fig. 1.7.

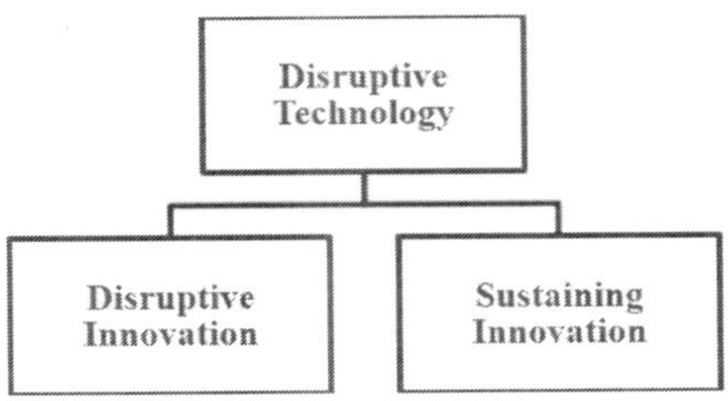

Fig. 1.7: Two Phases of Disruption

Examples of Disruptive Technology

Few examples of disruptive technology are shown in Fig. 1.8. Let us discus disruptive and sustaining innovation.

Disruptive Innovation

A disruptive innovation helps create a new market and value network, and eventually disrupts an existing market and value network (over a few years or decades), displacing an earlier technology. It creates substantial growth by offering a new performance trajectory – "a game changer" -

that, even if initially inferior to the performance of existing technologies, has the potential to become a superior.

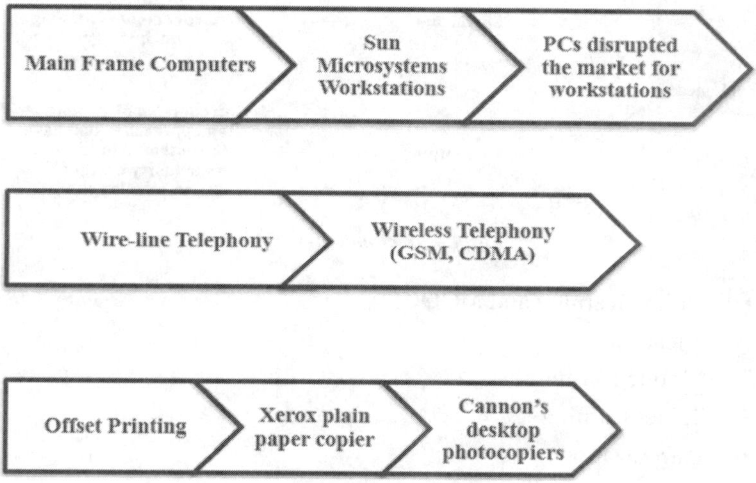

Fig. 1.8: Examples of Disruptive Technology

Sustaining Innovation

Sustaining innovations are typically innovations in technology, whereas disruptive innovations change entire markets. For example, the automobile was a revolutionary technological innovation, but it was not a disruptive innovation, because early automobiles were expensive luxury items that did not disrupt the market for horse driven vehicles. The market for transportation essentially remained unchanged until the debut of the lower priced Ford Model T in 1908. The mass-produced automobile was a disruptive innovation, because it changed the transportation market. The automobile, by itself, was not.

Technologies Spectrum

The technologies spectrum is shown in Fig. 1.9. The sustaining technologies are steady, linear improvement of existing technology. The disruptive technologies are completely new approaches that have the potential to create a new industry or transform an existing one.

Innovation in Education

Innovations in education are important because education plays a crucial role in creating a sustainable future. The disruptive innovations have a direct bearing on education as it has also become a business.

Some Innovations are:

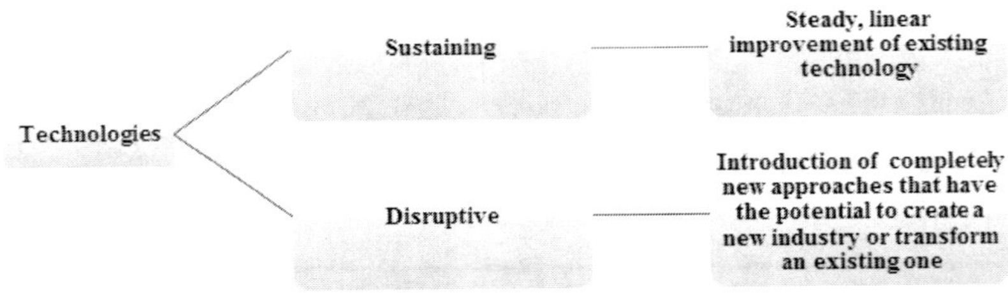

Fig. 1.9: Technologies

- Online learning and MOOCs
- e-learning
- Mobile learning
- Tablet learning
- Patronization
- Learning analytics
- 3D learning

Online Learning and the MOOC

Massive Open Online Courses are free courses available for online to enroll. MOOCs provide an affordable and flexible way to learn new skill with no limit on attendance, advance one's carrier and deliver quality experience. MOOCs offer a large number of students the opportunity to study high quality courses online with prestigious universities, often at no cost. MOOCs do not always lead to formal qualifications. There are no entry requirements. Video-based, they offer interaction either through peer review and group collaboration or automate feedback through objective, online assessments. "Anytime, any place, any pace" are the watch words of online learning.

e-learning/Online Learning

This is a non-traditional approach to teaching, which has been experimented in many universities. With appropriate infrastructure, e-leaning is a boon to those students who are not in a position to undergo face-to-face learning. A detailed discussion of e-learning will be presented in this chapter elsewhere.

Mobile Learning

Using portable computing devices such as iPads, laptops, smart phones or tablet computers provide continuous assess to be learning process anywhere, anytime. Educational applications are the second most downloaded of all categories. The mobile market is expected to consist of about 7 billions accounts. Mobile traffic on the internet is expected to surpass desktop traffic.

Tablet Computer

The portability of the tablets facilitates personalized learning environment, with all resources and tools on a single device. This portable PC with a mobile operating system and LCD touch screen display processing circuitry and a rechargeable battery is a gift of technology to learners. Tablets facilitate real time data mining needed to support learning analytics to offering a plethora of game-based learning apps.

Patronization and Customization

Privatization is a key customer requirement. In personalization, we address the needs and interests of the learner.

Learning Analytics

This is measurement, collection, analysis and reporting of data about learners and their contexts, for the purpose of understanding and optimizing learning and the environments in which it occurs. This is useful in the design of personalized and online platforms.

3 D Learning

This is an exciting developing area of the e-learning industry. This allows learning through practice. Students can visualize equipment, procedures and tasks in a unique practical way. This can make learning a fun.

Indeed, to evolve strategies for building successful universities of the future the universities have to be Door Openers in a rapidly globalizing world. It is important to follow the emerging 5 Technological Trends that are shaping the educational landscape in the next few years.

1. Augmented Reality (AR)

The absolute Matrix is already there through a really low-level version. As an example of AR's educational applications, the Art gallery, to view each place through our phone (such as the Samsung VR Gear Handset) to juxtapose the real-life artwork with a complementary price of art stored in the cloud is possible now.

2. The Web

The web has evolved tremendously since its creation, having moved incrementally from Web 1.0 to where we are today, Web 4.0 and everything is going to be connected.

3. Extreme BYOD

The driving force behind the movement of **b**ring **y**our **o**wn **d**evice (BYOD) is that actually "everybody wants their own individualized workspace." As educators, we need to support students on their BYOD possessions, also helping them make distinctions between their real lives and their digital levels.

4. Transmedia

Transmedia story telling is underutilized in education, as the greatest portal into the multi universe we have. If used properly, transmedia would give educators and students the opportunity to tell stories in a variety of ways and span the gap between critical thinking and creative thinking, forming a new and exciting" critical thinking".

5. Big Data

Big data combined with predicative analytics, has great potential to personalize learning and bring students up to in exactly the areas where they're falling behind.

The likely impact of disruption in higher education is given in Table 1.3.

Table 1.3: Impact of Disruption in Higher Education

S,No	*Technology*	*Impact on Higher Education*
1	Mobile Internet	Increasingly inexpensive and capable mobile computing devices and internet connectivity
2	Automation of Knowledge	Intelligent software systems that can perform knowledge work tasks involving unstructured companies
3	Internet of Things	Networks of low cost sensors and actuators for data collection, monitoring, decision making and process optimization

(Contd...)

4	Cloud Technology	Use of computer hardware and software resources delivered over a network or the internet, often as a service
5	Advanced Robotics	Increasingly capable robots with enhanced sensors and intelligence used to automate tasks or argument humans
6	Autonomous Vehicle	Vehicle that can navigate and operate with reduced or no human intervention
7	Energy Storage	Devices or systems that store energy for later use
8	3D Printing	Techniques to create objects for printing layers of materials based on digital models
9	Advanced Materials	Materials designed to have superior characteristics (strength, weight, conductivity etc.)
10	Advanced Gas and Oil Exploration	Exploration and recovery techniques that make extraction of oil and gas economical
11	Renewable Energy	Generation of electricity from renewable sources with reduced environmental emissions
12	Next Generation Genomics	Fast, low-cost gene sequencing, advanced big data analytics and synthetic biology

University of Tomorrow

The universities of tomorrow have to respond to various reforms and also have to come forward to take the responsibility of several key components of higher education as shown in Fig.1.10. As for as reforms in education are concerned, there are several areas which are needed as reforms in education. Some of them are:

- To endeavor to relate it to the life
- Needs and appreciations of the people,
- Powerful instrument of social, economic and cultural transformations
- Knowledge based in the universities and industries

On the other hand, education in India has been reduced to meet simply the functions of the business without any or very less linkages to the national goal.

Fig. 1.10 shows that universities have to be in a dynamic process by which tomorrow of an individual and that of a nation is shaped in a proper perspective towards development and excellence. All the six areas have to be built in carefully and to be developed in close collaboration and interaction amongst themselves.

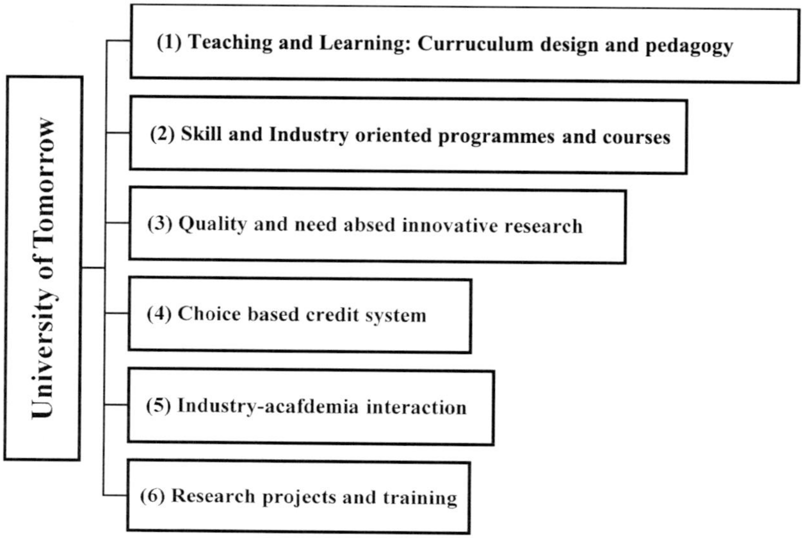

Fig.1.10: Characteristics of University Tomorrow

Ranking of the Universities

In the competitive world today, quality of education is gaining importance. For this, several rankings have been developed. The most important world university rankings are:

(1) Time Higher Education (THE)
(2) Quacquarelli Symonds (QS)
(3) Academic Ranking of World Universities (ARWU)

These rankings are considered to be indicative on comprehensive performance or achievements of universities. The ranking of top 25 universities during 2017-18 is given in Table 1.4. The representative countries of these 25 top ranking universities are given in Table 1.5. The majority of these universities are more than 100 years old. It is rightly said that best institutions/universities are not created in a year or so but it takes 100 of years to do so. It seems that USA and UK have taken due care to offer quality education and research.

The quality and relevance of higher education in India is largely average to mediocre. Let us take an example of the NAAC accreditation in the first cycle on 2nd November, 2018. The list was having 6 universities, 4 autonomous colleges, 106 affiliating colleges. The data shows the following trend:

Table 1.4: Top 25 Universities in 2017-18

S.No.	*Times Higher Education (THE)*	*Quacquarelli Symonds (QS)*	*Academic Ranking of World Universities (ARWU)*
1	University of Oxford, UK	Massachusetts Institute of Technology, USA	Harvard University, USA
2	University of Cambridge, UK	Stanford University, USA	Stanford University, USA
3	California Institute of Technology, USA	Harvard University, USA	University of Cambridge, UK
4	Stanford University, USA	California Institute of Technology, USA	Massachusetts Institute of Technology, USA
5	Massachusetts Institute of Technology, USA	University of Cambridge, UK	University of California, Berkeley, USA
6	Harvard University, USA	University of Oxford, UK	Princeton University, USA
7	Princeton University, USA	University College of London, UK	University of Oxford, UK
8	Imperial College London, UK	Imperial College London, UK	Columbia University, USA
9	University of Chicago, USA	University of Chicago, USA	California Institute of Technology, USA
10	ETH Zurich, Switzerland	ETH Zurich, Switzerland	University of Chicago, USA
11	University of Pennsylvania, USA	Nanyang Technological University, Singapore	University of California, Los Angeles, USA
12	Yale University, USA	EPFL-EcolePolytechniqueFederale de Lausanne	Cornell University, USA
13	Johns Hopkins University, USA	Princeton University, USA	Yale University, USA
14	Columbia University, USA	Cornell University, USA	University of Washington, USA
15	University of California, Los Angeles, USA	National University of Singapore	University of California, San Diego, USA
16	UCL UK	Yale University, USA	University of Pennsylvania, USA
17	Duke University, USA	Johns Hopkins University, USA	University College London, UK
18	University of California, Berkeley, USA	Columbia University, USA	Johns Hopkins University, USA
19	Cornell University, USA	University of Pennsylvania, USA	Swiss Federal Institute of Technology, Zurich, Switzerland
20	Northwestern University, USA	The Australian National University, Australia	Washington University, St. Louis, USA
21	University of Michigan, USA	Duke University, USA	University of California, San Francisco, USA
22	National University of Singapore	University of Michigan, USA	University of Tokyo, Japan
23	University of Toronto, Canada	King's College, London	University of Toronto, Canada
24	Carnegie Mellon University, USA	The University of Edinburg, UK	Imperial College London, UK
25	London School of Economics and Political Science, UK	Tsinghua University, China	Northwestern University, USA

Table 1.5: Representative Countries in the Top 25 and Top 100 Universities during 2017-18

Country	*THE*		*QS*		*ARWU*	
	Top 25	Top 100	Top 25	Top 100	Top 25	Top 100
USA	17	43	13	31	18	48
UK	5	12	6	16	4	9
Germany	0	10	0	3	0	4
The Nederland	0	7	0	2	0	4
Australia	0	6	1	8	0	6
Canada	1	4	9	4	1	4
Sweden	0	3	0	2	0	3
Switzerland	1	3	2	4	1	5
Hongkong	0	3	0	5	0	0
Japan	0	2	0	5	1	3

- All the universities and law college got below average Grade B+. This was the case for 90 percent Arts, Science or Commerce College, 70 percent of the Management Institutions, and 57 percent Engineering Institutions.
- 22 percent and 32 percent of the colleges received the bottom C and B grade respectively.
- There was not a single institution in A++ Grade in the list of 106 institutions.

Widening Scope of Education

A Massive Open Online Course (MOOC) is a web-based platform which provides unlimited number of students worldwide. It was established back in 2008 and gained momentum in 2012 as a popular learning tool. Many MOOCs have communities that have interactive sessions and forums between the student, professors and Teaching Assistants (TAs) along with the study/course material and video lectures.

There are various notable institutions, both non-profit and commercial, that offer these courses worldwide with the help of MOOC providers. A few of these are listed below:

- **NPTEL (India):** Indian Institutes of Technology (IITs) and Indian Institute of Science (IISc.) offer online courses through this platform which require no registration and are free of cost.
- **WizIQ (India and USA):** IIT Delhi, India offers this course through this platform which requires registration and fees to study courses offered by them.

- **Open2Study:** The headquarters of this platform for online courses is based in Australia.
- **Coursera:** The headquarters of this platform for online courses is based in USA.
- **edX:** The headquarters of this platform for online courses is based in USA.
- **udemy:** The headquarters of this platform for online courses is based in USA.

MOOC Programme in India

The University Grants Commission (UGC) along with the MHRD (Ministry of Human Resource Development) has launched the MOOC programme in India for higher secondary, bachelors and master's degrees. This covers a wide range of subjects that may or may not be taught in regular campus studies.

A new portal for MOOCs named **Study Webs of Active-Learning for Young Aspiring Minds (SWAYAM)** is said to present students with an opportunity to study anything from a list of more than 2000 courses out of which more than 200 are currently available for registration. Audio-visual medium, illustrations, research and case studies with self-assessment are few of the mediums chosen to approach the study of these courses.

MOOC cannot replace the traditional approach of classroom learning but it can be used as an alternative method to bridge the gap between various schools of learning. It has been said however that MOOC has certain limitations which are listed below:

- Although digitalization is a must now, there are many nations that are unable to provide the basic necessities to enrol for MOOCs, hence the spread of MOOCs is limited.
- It is not always certain that all MOOCs provide degrees, certificates and/or diplomas which limits the number of candidates that enrol for these courses as many companies ask for records of the education levels achieved and candidates are unable to provide them.
- A student's life is confined to one room that has internet access and a laptop or a computer which allows little or no interaction with the outside world.
- Since MOOCs are web-based, there is no monitoring of the candidates/students, which carries a risk of plagiarism or cheating.

Arya (2017) has given very good update of MOOCs in India. The term "MOOC" was coined in 2008 by Canadian academician named David Cormier whereas first MOOC was taught by George Siemens and Stephen Downes in University of Manitoba, Canada where a class of 25 regular students was extended online to teach 1500 students. In this technological development, traditional teaching methods are substituted by the online interaction between the teachers and students, entirely or partially.

MOOC could be considered as an extension of "Open Educational Resources" movement which contribute positively to all forms of classroom types available – distance education, online learning and traditional classroom session". MOOCs are the new medium of education through online teaching. Some experts term the MOOC as a disruptive technology i.e. the technology which demolishes the traditional structure of pedagogy and creates a new platform of learning.

Types of MOOCs

There are two types of MOOCs: (1) cMOOC and (2) xMOOC.

cMOOC: cMOOC stands for connectivist MOOC. It is based on the connectivist theory of education where connectivism, openness, and participatory teaching are the principles (Conole, 2013). Participants share their views, resources etc. on a particular topic and send it to the instructor. The latter sorts the material and organizes it into a sharable e-mail with embedded HTML links and send it to all the participants. This builds a "connective ecosystem" of the learning resources under a common platform.

xMOOC: xMOOC (extended MOOC) method revolves around the traditional college teaching model with video recorded lectures along with quizzes and other evaluation assignments and verifiable certificates or "statement of accomplishment" delivered online through some MOOC providing website. xMOOC is more of a behaviourist approach (Conole, 2013). The xMOOC uses the open source LMS (learning management system) for course management.

The "Innovation Pedagogy Report 2014" by Open University describes ten pedagogies which might transform education. These are – MOOCs, badges to accredit learning, learning analytics, seamless learning, crow learning, digital scholarship, geo- learning, learning from gaming, maker culture and citizen inquiry.

Mooc$_s$ Initiatives by Educational Institutes

Twenty-two of the top 25 US universities in US News World Report rankings are now offering courses online for free (Shah, 2014). India is very slow in catching up with the MOOC wave as high education regulators like University Grants Commission and All India Council for Technical Education didn't match up with the trend. However, reputed Indian institutes have come forward with their offerings on specialties. IIT-B has recently collaborated with Massachusetts Institute of Technology (MIT) and Harvard to launch MOOCs through its websites to all interested students for free (Bhattacharyya, 2013). IIT Delhi has started offering MOOC in partnership with coursera, a US based largest MOOC provider. Private players have also helped in contributing to this education cause. Arya (2017) studied the MOOCs under the heads, online courses, massive open online courses (MOOC), open courseware (OCW), online education and video lecture.

Performance Indicators

In contemporary knowledge societies, performance indicators are an indispensable element of sustainable quality management and enhancement through monitoring and evaluating quality performance of higher education institutions. It is argued that learning and teaching quality in higher education should be approached in a holistic way, namely across the four subdomains of learning and teaching environment:

- teaching processes
- learning processes
- learning outcomes
- learning assessment

Performance indicators related to these areas must align with a synoptic understanding of learning and teaching comprising behavioural, information processing, cognitive, social (constructivism) and humanistic theories of learning.

Faced with the rapid pace of knowledge expansion, higher education institutions are challenged to raise the efficacy of learner education, overcoming the traditionally rigid teaching-centred approach, and shifting the focus instead towards learning, while preparing competent professionals who are able to self-manage knowledge. There are research studies which have outlined the impact that quality assurance processes on teaching and learning processes from the perspectives of their main stakeholders: students, teachers and academic authorities. There are indications that it is still early to ascertain the direct impact that these transformations will have on learning outcomes.

The quality management of research, development and innovation (RDI) activities of universities is an area largely neglected in studies of quality in higher education. In fact, little is known about it as most of the attention is traditionally placed upon quality management and evaluation of education (Kajaste 2018).

Many universities policies are increasingly developed with reference to students' learning experiences, with a focus on the concept of the 'student voice'. Yet the 'student voice' is difficult to define and emphasis is often placed on numerical performance indicators. A diverse student population has wide-ranging educational experiences, which may not be easily captured within the broad categories provided by traditional survey tools, which can drown out the rich, varied and gradual processes of individual development. There is no single tool that can be used to measure students' experiences.

Arkorful and Abaidoo (2015) investigated the effectiveness of using e-learning in teaching in tertiary institutions. In institutions of higher education, the issue of utilizing modern information and communication technologies (ICTs) for teaching and learning is very important. The definitions of e-learning and the role that e-learning plays in higher educational institutions in relation to teaching and learning processes, and the advantages and disadvantages of its adoption and implementation are very important.

The Concept and Definition of e-learning

The Internet has made available resources for research and learning for both teachers and students to share and acquire information (Richard and Haya 2003). Technology-based e-learning encompasses the use of the internet and other important technologies to produce materials for learning, teach learners, and also regulate courses in an organization (Fry, 2001). e-learning refers to the use of information and communication technologies to enable the access to online learning/teaching resources.

e-learning as a concept covers a range of applications, learning methods and processes (Rossi, 2009). It is therefore difficult to find a commonly accepted definition of e-learning. The following questions arise in the mind (Dublin, 2003).

- Is e-learning an on-line coursework for students at a distance?
- Does it mean using a virtual learning environment to support the provision of campus-based education?
- Does it refer to an on-line tool to enrich, extend and enhance collaboration?
- Does it a totally on-line learning or part of blended learning?

Some of the definitions of the term e-learning as given by different researchers and institutions are reviewed below.

- **European Commission (2001)**: e-learning is the use of new multimedia technologies and the Internet to increase learning quality by easing access to facilities and services as well as distant exchanges and collaboration.
- **Abbad et al (2009)**: e-learning is any learning that is enabled electronically.
- **LaRose et al, (1998): Keller and Cernerud, (2002)**: e-learning is any learning that is internet-enabled or web- based.
- **Maltz et al (2005)**: e-learning is applied in different perspectives, including distributed learning, online-distance learning, as well as hybrid learning.
- **OECD (2005):** e-learning is defined as the use of information and communication technologies in diverse processes of education to support and enhance learning in institutions of higher education, and includes the usage of information and communication technology as a complement to traditional classrooms, online learning or mixing the two modes.
- **Wentling et al (2000):** e-learning refers to the attainment and use of knowledge that are predominantly facilitated and distributed by electronic means. e-learning depends on computers and networks, but it is likely it will progress into systems comprising of a variety of channels such as wireless and satellite, and technologies such as cellular phones.
- **Gotschall (2000), Liu and Wang (2009)**: e- learning is proposed based on distance learning, thus a transmission of lectures to distant locations by way of video presentations.
- **Liaw and Huang (2003):** e-learning is defined based on its characteristics. (1) a multimedia environment, (2) incorporating several kinds of information, (3) e-learning systems support collaborative communication, whereby users have total control over their own situations of learning (4) e-learning support networks for accessing information and (5) e-learning allows for the systems to be implemented freely on various kinds of computer operating systems.
- **Tao et al (2006):** this new environment for learning that is centered on electronic networks has allowed learners in universities to receive individualized support and also to have learning

schedules that is more suitable to them as well as separate from other learners. This facilitates a high interaction and collaboration level between instructors or teachers and peers than traditional environment for learning.

- **Borstorff and Lowe (2007):** e-learning can empower students at higher educational levels to acquire their education in while at the same time perusing their personal objectives as well as maintaining their own careers, with no need to attend be subjected to rigid schedule.
- **Algahtani (2011):** categorized the definitions of e-learning from three different perspectives: the distance learning perspective (Alarifi, 2003; Holmes and Gardner, 2006), the technological perspective (Nichols, 2003) and also from the perspective of e-learning as pedagogy (Khan, 2005).

Types of e-learning

Algahtani (2011) divided e-learning into two basic types, consisting of computer-based and the internet based e-learning.

The computer-based e-learning: It comprises the use of a full range of hardware and software generally that are available for the use of Information and Communication Technology and also each component can be used in either of two ways: computer-managed instruction and computer-assisted-learning. In computer assisted- learning, computers are used instead of the traditional methods by providing interactive software as a support tool within the class or as a tool for self-learning outside the class. In the computer-managed-instruction, however, computers are employed for the purpose of storing and retrieving information to aid in the management of education.

The internet-based e-learning: It is a further improvement of the computer-based e-learning, and it makes the content available on the internet, with the readiness of links to related knowledge sources. Zeitoun (2008) classified this by the extent of such features use in education, mixed or blended more, assistant mode, and completely online mode. The assistant mode supplements the traditional method as needed. Mixed or blended mode offers a short-term degree for a partly traditional method. The completely online mode, which is the most complete improvement, involves the exclusive use of the network for learning (Zeitoun, 2008).

There is another way of classification of e-learning as mentioned below:

- Synchronous e-learning
- Asynchronous e-learning

Synchronous learning involves interaction of students with a teacher via WWW in real time. For example, virtual class rooms that are nothing else but real classrooms online.

The advantages of synchronous e-learning are:

- Ability to track learning activities.
- Continuous monitoring and correction
- Possibilities of global connectivity and collaboration oppor-tunities among learners.
- Ability to personalize learning for each learner.

Asynchronous e-learning allows the participants to learn at their own pace, without live interaction with the teachers. The major advantage is that this kind of e-learning offers the learners the information they need whenever they need it.

The advantages of asynchronous e-learning are:

- Available for instant learning and reference.
- Flexibility of access from anywhere at any time.
- Ability to simultaneously reach an unlimited number of employees.
- Uniformity of content and one-time cost of production.

The use of e-learning in Education

The development of multimedia and information technologies, as well as the use internet as a new technique of teaching, has made radical changes in the traditional process of teaching (Wang et al. 2003). Development in information technology has generated more choices for today's education. Colleges, universities, and other institutions of higher learning race to advance online course capability in a speedily developing cyber education market (Love and Fry 2006). e-learning, has come to be more and more important in institutions of higher education. The introduction and expansion of a range of e-learning tools has been initiating several changes in higher education institutions, particularly when it comes to their educational delivery and support processes.

There are different ways of employing the technique in education. Algahtani, (2011) discovered three distinct models of using e-learning in education.

(1) **Adjunct e-learning**: It is the situation which e-learning is employed as an assistant in the traditional classroom providing relative independence to the learners or students.

(2) **Blended e-learning**: In this way of using e-learning, the delivery of course materials and explanations is shared between traditional learning method and e-learning method in the classroom setting.

(3) **Online e-learning**: In this form of usage, the e-learning is total so that there is maximum independence of the learners or students.

Advantages of e-learning

The adoption of e-learning in education, especially for higher educational institutions has several benefits and e-learning is considered among the best methods of education. Some of the advantages of e-learning in education are:

- It is flexible when issues of time and place are taken into consideration. The adoption of e-learning provides the institutions as well as their students or learners the much flexibility of time and place of delivery or receipt of according to learning information.
- e-learning enhances the efficacy of knowledge and qualifications via ease of access to a huge amount of information.
- e-learning helps eliminate barriers that have the potential of hindering participation including the fear of talking to other learners.
- e-learning motivates students to interact with other, as well as exchange and respect different point of views.
- e-learning eases communication and also improves the relationships that sustain learning.
- e-Learning makes available extra prospects for interactivity between students and teachers during content delivery.
- e-learning is cost effective in the sense that there is no need for the students or learners to travel. It is also cost effective in the sense that it offers opportunities for learning for maximum number of learners with no need for many buildings.
- e-learning takes into consideration the individual learners differences. Some learners, for instance prefer to concentrate on certain parts of the course, while others are prepared to review the entire course.

- e-learning helps compensate for scarcities of academic staff, including instructors or teachers as well as facilitators, lab technicians etc.
- The use of e-learning allows self-pacing.

Disadvantages of e-learning

e-learning, in spite of advantages it has when adopted in education, also has some disadvantages (Hameed et al, 2008; Akkoyuklu and Soylu, 2006; Dowling et al, 2003). Disadvantages of e-learning include:

- e-learning as a method of education makes the learners undergo contemplation, remoteness, as well as lack of interaction or relation. It therefore requires a very strong motivation and time management skills in order to reduce such effects.
- With respect to clarifications, explanations, and interpretations, the e-learning method may be less effective that traditional methods of learning. The learning process is much easier face-to-face with instructors or teachers.
- When it comes to improvement of learner's communication skills, e-learning may have a negative effect. Though learners might have an excellent academic knowledge, they may not possess the needed skills to deliver their acquired knowledge to others.
- Since tests and assessments in e-learning are frequently supervised by proxy, it may be difficult, if not impossible, to control or regulate activities such as cheating.
- e-learning may also be subject to piracy, plagiarism, cheating, inadequate selection skills, and inappropriate use of copy and paste.
- e-learning may negatively impact socialization skills and limit the role of instructors as directors of the educational process.
- Not all disciplines can effectively use e-learning in education. For instance, scientific fields that require hands-on practical experiences may be more difficult to study through e-learning.
- e-learning may also lead to congestion or heavy use of some websites. This may bring about unanticipated costs both in time and money.

Emotional Intelligence in Learning

There exist several definitions of e-learning as already discussed. e-learning is aggregation of all kind of learning which use the computer for medial support of the learning process. e-learning is the general term for all kind of software supported learning.

Many researchers have seen e-learning where all real business process of learning, teaching and organization has been migrated into the digital environment. According to Rosenberg (2001) e-learning depends on internet technology and is typically a networked form of learning based on a more general concept of learning which transcends the traditional paradigms. We suggest the following definition to emphasise the new and different aspects of e-learning as compared with traditional learning:

> We will call e-learning all forms of electronic supported learning and teaching, which are procedural in character and aim to effect the construction of knowledge with reference to individual experience, practice and knowledge of the learner. Information and communication systems, whether networked or not, serve as specific media (specific in the sense elaborated previously) to implement the learning process (Tavangarian et. al. 2004).

Tavangarian et. al. (2004) have identified the following four issues about the requirements e-learning systems must meet to support individual in the learning process.

- How can the teacher be supported in producing teaching material for standardized profiles?
- How should the material be presented to learner and which kind of interaction with the material will support learning?
- Which kind of feedback is useful and possible?
- How should teachers and co-learners be represented within the system?

We are living in the technological advanced era where each and every section of the society is being dominated by the technology. The teaching and learning is no exception to this. For example, e-learning is projected to grow fifteen-fold, accounting for about 30 percent of all educational provisions over the next few years.

We are moving to a situation where learning anywhere and at any time is possible. In order to make it possible, research activities have to resolve the following points:

- The technology should have made teaching more student centered.
- The social media has to come forward to take the ownership of learning.

- The students have to increase ownership of knowledge.
- The teachers have to upgrade their skills in order to move in pace with time.
- These steps have to take artificial intelligence and emotions of the teachers in to account.

The subject of Artificial Intelligence (AI) and Emotional Intelligence (EI) is emerging as an important area of research in recent years. The research on EI is not done in detail from two the following two perspectives:

1. to know the EI patterns of students
2. to know the EI patterns of faculty members.

Therefore, all the issues need to be studied carefully so that they are included in AI based systems for learning including e-learning and evaluation.

The functions and activities of emotional intelligence are shown in Fig. 1.11. The recognition and understanding of human emotions is of great importance for artificial emotional intelligence systems.

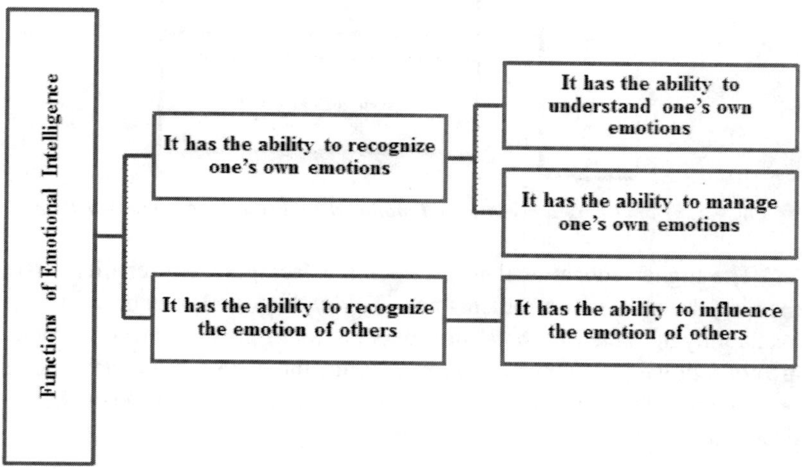

Fig. 1.11: Functions of Emotional Intelligence

It is possible to communicate emotional data of a person to a machine in several different ways. Some of them are shown in Fig. 1.12. Thus, understanding emotions of large section of the faculty members will help in artificial intelligence for future machines including e-learning and evaluation. Universities can have teaching methodologies through an optimum combination of trained teachers, adequate labs, Open Educational Resources (OER), Massive Open Online Courses (MOOCs) and e-learning.

The evaluation process also needs a thorough re-consideration. Better training is possible through the training programmes in house as well as at the leading training institutions and industrial establishments. This will expose the students about the latest training components relevant to their streams. Better placement is possible by adopting multiple approaches.

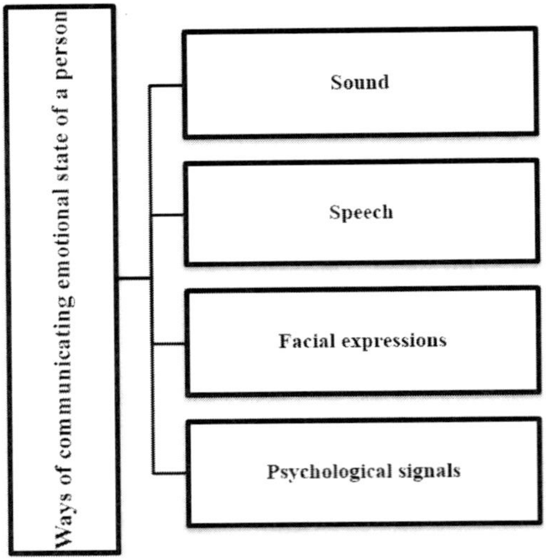

Fig. 1.12: Data Communicating the Emotional State of a Person to a Machine

The higher educational institutions are facing several challenges in meeting the above requirements and in providing quality education. The availability of trained teachers and guidelines for evaluation and certification are not followed by many institutions. In fact, there are as many procedures or standards of teaching and certification as the number of teachers in higher education.

This problem could be addressed to some extents if the programmes include open educational resources (OER) and on-line learning (e-learning) and evaluation systems as an integral system. Each and every conventional university has its own method of teaching and evaluation. These activities are by and large teacher centered. Open and distance educational universities, on the other hand, have the systems which are student centered. Each one of these approaches has some advantages and disadvantages. The recent advances in educational technologies and innovations necessitates constant changes not only in course curricula but also in teaching and evaluation methodologies.

The innovations in these areas have been undertaken widely. These include the following learning mechanisms (Smith, 2005):

- self-directed learning
- problem based learning
- integrated teaching

The integrated teaching is a way of connecting skills and knowledge from multiple sources and experiences.

The alternative method of teaching based on lectures, seminar, and assignments is believed to be beneficial to the students and would be the ideal approach because of the following reasons:

- System wise teaching
- Integration along with case oriented approach
- Student centered
- Interdepartmental collaboration
- Learn to apply the knowledge to daily life experiences

It is proved beyond doubt that the delivery of online courses enhances student learning in several respects. The e-learning material and open educational resources could be utilized properly and extensively provided they are suitably re-designed as per the needs of the hour. Mishra (2017) has rightly observed that Open Educational Resources (OER) have emerged as one of the most innovative teaching and learning practices as well as cost-effective mechanisms to improve the quality of educational offerings by optimizing the use of available resources to improve the cost efficiency. Several authors have observed that OER have the capacity to transform teaching and learning practices in all possible educational settings (Kanwar et. al. 2010).

For example, OER can be used for the following purposes:

- to reduce the time to develop courses and programmes
- to facilitate knowledge sharing
- to preserve the disseminate indigenous knowledge
- to improve educational quality at all levels for teachers and students
- to provide access to global content that can be localized without restrictions

- to give them more choices about learning resources
- to create inclusive learning communities

e-learning is gaining importance as the powerful source of teaching-learning process. If we see the literature, e-learning (web based courses) have several unique characteristics. They are characterized by a predominance of several activities replacing classroom interaction between the students, teacher and the study material. The technology is advancing at such a rapid pace that in the time to come, it is quite possible that e-learning term may disappear from the literature. This may happen because technology will appear invisible to both the learners and the teachers.

The future e-learning technologies should allow for a learning environment having human touch (Virginio et. al. 2004). This is exactly where emotions will enter in the teaching-learning and even evaluation process. The affective states are identified in the literature as anger, sadness, fear and pleasure. The emotions experienced online are fear, frustration, anxiety, apprehension, shame, excitement and pride. Rha and Sung (2005) concluded that six emotional expressions elements like pleasure, concern, disappointment, anger, pride and delightfulness are useful.

This indicates that emotions of the teachers as well as of the students have to be studied very seriously for their applications in artificial intelligence, e-learning and evaluation. It has also been suggested that teachers usually feel anger, fear and sympathy while students feel fear, anger and pleasure.

New age teaching and learning online like e-learning, OER, MOOCs etc. have been growing as a mainstream educational approach. This is because these technologies lead to maximizing access and interactions with various knowledge sources (Lee, 2002). It gives new opportunities not only for learners but also for the teachers.

Emotions play a critical role in understanding the learning and performance of human beings. Several authors have extensively analysed all the major issues related to emotions, emotional intelligence and e-learning (Lee 2011, 2012); Callahan, 2004; Dirkx, 2006; Yang 2009; Rowe 2005; Kim 2008; Kang & Goo, 2007; Kang et. al., 2011; Lee & Song, 2007; Park et. al. 2008; Yang and Kim 2010; Jung 2006; Pekrun 2006; Armory and Vuilleumier 2013).

The studies have been carried under the following major heads:

- e-learning, emotion and emotional intelligence
- emotion in e-learning

- emotional intelligence in e-learning
- emotionally sensitive instructional strategies and design

Rha and Sung (2005) advised four different emotionally sensitive strategies in e- learning as shown in Fig. 1.13. These include:

- Communication tools
- Appropriate emotion delivery mechanism
- Online learning space
- Online learning community

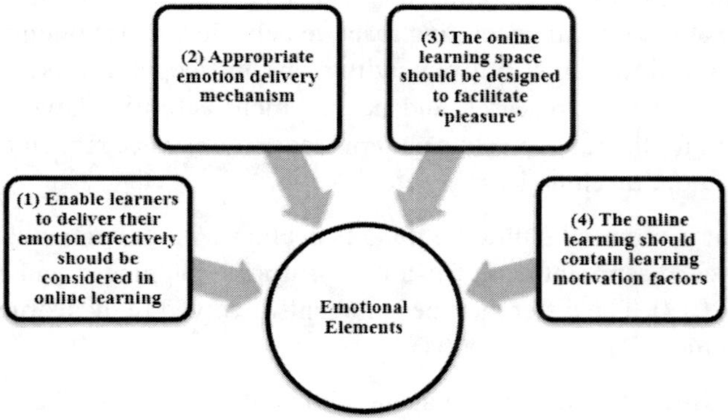

Fig. 1.13: Emotionally Sensitive Strategies for e-learning

Astleitner (2000) and Astleitner and Leutner (2000) have discussed several strategies to control emotions like reduce fear, envy and anger and to increase sympathy and pleasure.

Learner Model

Loizou *et. al.* (2012) developed a model for incorporating anger, sadness, anxiety and fear into intelligent agents. A special pedagogical agent is used in e-learning systems to guide and motivate students (Ivanovic *et. al.* 2011, Heidig and Clarebout 2011). Existing computational models of emotions (based on different psychological theories) share common properties and emotional processes. Experiments have indicated high application potential for such systems. The synthetic character helps students to overcome learning obstacles in face to face communication. Various synthetic characters have the potential to expose emotions by recording user's emotions and reacting accordingly in improving e- learning processes.

Arroyo *et. al.* (2011) studied gender issues and the reactions of male and female students to the presence of animated pedagogical agents that provided emotional and motivational support. The authors did the experiments with the Intelligent Tutoring System for Mathematics. The system improved affective outcomes of all students.

Rodrigo *et. al.* (2012) analyzed the effects of the affective states exhibited by students using an intelligent tutoring system with and without an interactive software agent. A behavior decision model of an intelligent agent based on emotion psychology and artificial emotion was presented. The model incorporates emotions, motivations and behavior decision.

A mind model for life-like agents should have the features like expressing emotion, generating behavior based on motivation, learning, selective attention and generating reactive behavior. AI is not only limited to learning algorithms, but expanding fast in deeper levels of human consciousness. The research and development activities have made AI successful for the functions like pattern recognition, voice recognition, face identification, machine learning etc.

What is required still to be done is dealing with emotions like anger, impatience, disappointment, frustration, surprise, happiness, and gratitude (Mikko 2017). The different types of agents involved in the learner model are (Pasquier and Paulmaz 2004):

- **Tutor Agent**: It is the agent who is responsible for the managing the courses and cognitive status of the e-learner.
- **Style Agent**: It is the agent who is responsible to determine the suitable learning style of the e-learner.
- **Emotional Agent**: It is the agent who determines the emotional status of the e-learner using the results of voice analysis and the feedback.

These are shown in Fig. 1.14. The information could be recognized through major recognition processes like text, speaker, language and emotion.

Mostafa *et. al.* (2005) have studied and defined e-learning based on the following three components:

(1) Motivation

(2) Lesson

(3) Assessment

Therefore, assessment should be considered as an important parameter for e-learning.

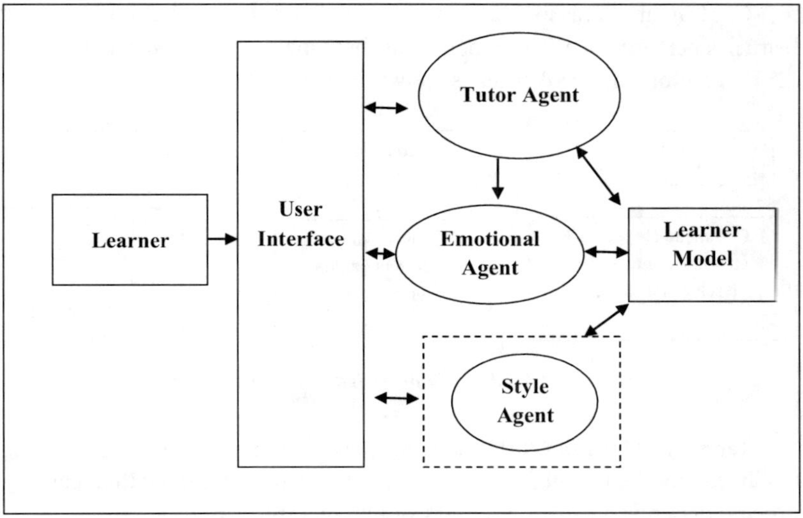

Fig. 1.14: Agents involved in the Emotions

Kort *et. al.* (2001) concluded that machines are going to recognize human behavior and studied characteristics of the software agent by several functional outputs. Some of them are as follows:

- Friendliness
- Expressiveness
- Encouragement
- Pedagogy
- Loving
- Pleasantness
- Politeness
- Confidence
- Funny

Fatahi and Aghaee (2010), in a significant study, concluded that personality and emotions are effective parameters in learning process. They developed a new e-learning model. Their model was based on following two agents:

- **Virtual Tutor Agent (VTA):** VTA selects suitable learning style for the learners based on their personality
- **Virtual Classmate Agent (VCA):** VCA acts as an intelligent agent having its own personality

Chaffar and Frasson (2004) had proposed a model for improving learner's performance. Their model has three main components; (1) Central (2) Perception and (3) Action as shown in Fig. 1.15.

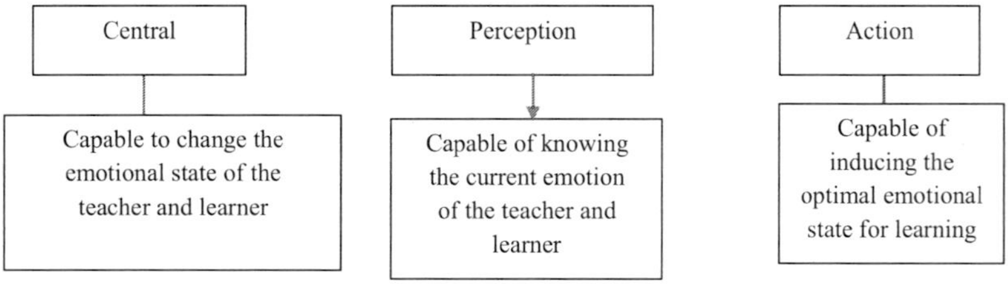

Fig. 1.15: A Model to improve learner's performance

Tang and Mccalla (2002) have proposed an adaptive and an evolving e-learning model useful for the students. It may be mentioned that learning process depends on several factors shown in Table 1.6.

Table 1.6: Learning Process Areas for Students

Learning	Learning to study and learn effectively and efficiently
	Learning as a student
	Learning as an adult
	Active learning
	Action learning
Learning with others	Collaborative learning
	Group learning through projects
	Learning through case studies
	Learning through experts
Classroom learning	Preparing for the classes
	Classroom discussions
	Taking effective notes
	Problem based learning
	Guided notes learning
Online learning	e-learning
	Distance learning
	Mobile learning
Online evaluation	Advanced e-learning to learn anywhere and at any time with built in evaluation

When students are learning something in classroom, they need to reinforce the knowledge that they learn in the classroom at home by doing assignments and other related learning activities like e-learning. These assignments and other related learning activities allow for extra practice, so that they can refine their skills and knowledge in a particular area.

It is really unfortunate that as a University students take several subjects but most of them are never really taught how to study effectively. The key is that students should be able to develop effective study skills so that they can study effectively. If students adopt effective study methods and tools, they will find that studying is less time-consuming and more useful.

There has been extensive research on how effectively the students are learning a particular subject. However, the main finding which emerges is that study is a very personal matter and each student must develop his/her own methods which they find most effective. It is e-learning which can help the students in this mission.

Fatahi and Aghaee (2010) have developed a learning model with the following important goals:

- to determine learner's group based on personality questionnaire on emotions and other relevant aspects
- to recognize learner's emotions based on personality
- to recognize teacher's emotions based on personality
- to change teaching style based on personality
- to change evaluation style

The model includes following modules:

- Module of personality identification
- Module of choosing a teaching style matching with learner's personality
- Module of choosing virtual classmate agent
- Module of education and learning
- Module of emotion evaluation
- Module of choosing behavior and updating style of teaching

The research and development activities in the recent years have made it possible to include emotions into machine intelligence. It should be possible to develop a model that allows the machine to recognize human feelings, advanced e-learning and evaluation.

i^{2}OER: An Approach For Teaching, Learning and Certification in Higher Education

Academic Institutions are supposed to deliver higher education that is able to create industry specific and future ready professionals. This concept will require two major shifts:

- A realistic approach for better teaching, training during teaching and placements drives
- A realistic framework of academic programmes having a suitable combination of courses: core courses, elective courses, skill development courses and open educational resources

Universities can have better teaching through an optimum combination of trained teachers, adequate labs, best study material and highly motivational evaluation process. Any Institution/University has to adopt a unique approach towards these aspects. Better training is possible through the training programmes in house as well as at the leading training institutions and industrial establishments. This will expose the students about the latest training components relevant to their streams. Better placement is possible by adopting multiple approaches.

The higher educational institutions are facing several challenges in meeting the above requirements and in providing quality education. The availability of trained teachers and guidelines for evaluation and certification are not followed. In fact, there are as many procedures or standards of teaching and certification as the number of teachers in higher education. This problem could be addressed to some extents if the programmes are made of a combination of core courses, elective courses, skill development courses and open educational resources (OER). The demand of OER could be substantially increased by adopting i^2OER, a revolutionary approach, which is described for the first time in this paper. The approach will lead to multiple advantages not only for the students but also for universities.

Open Education Resources (OER)

OER are educational materials which are freely available. One key difference between OER and other educational resources is that OER have an open license, which allows adaptation and reuse without having to request the copyright holder. This definition looks at OER as content or product. OER penetration in the developing world has been slower than in industrialized countries, with the exception of China, India, Japan, Vietnam and Indonesia. Yet there are emergent examples which give an indication of how OER are being used in low-resource contexts. The reasons are obvious. There are no proper guidelines for the students.

The IITs, in partnership with the government, have made their engineering and technology courses available as OER. These are being used in over 600 institutions, most of them in remote locations with very limited resources. Both teachers and students are using the free IIT resources to improve the quality of their teaching and learning. The number of institutions making their courses available as OER has increased substantially. Developing countries have emerged as major players. India, a large Commonwealth country and Antigua and Barbuda, a small island state, have recently developed national OER policies.

Mishra (2017) has rightly observed that Open Educational Resources (OER) have emerged as one of the most innovate teaching and learning practices as well as cost-effective mechanisms to improve the quality of educational offerings by optimizing the use of available resources to improve the cost efficiency. Kanwar et. al. (2010) have observed that OER have the potential to transform teaching and learning practices in all educational setting. OER can be used for the following:

- to reduce the time to develop courses and programmes
- to facilitate knowledge sharing
- to preserve the disseminate indigenous knowledge
- to improve educational quality at all levels
- to provide access to global content that can be localized without restrictions
- to give them more choices about learning resources
- to create inclusive learning communities (Butcher, 2011).

India has about 900 universities but the use of OER still is not common. However, the potential for OER both to improve the quality of teaching and learning and to achieve cost efficiency is enormous. India as a developing country seems to have a growing appetite for openness in education, including the creation and dissemination of OER. The country has a National, Repository of Open Educational Resources (NROER) for K-12 educational students. In 2008, the Indian government's National Knowledge Commission (NKC) called for a "National E-Content and curriculum initiative" to stimulate the creation, adaption and utilization of OER by Indian institutions and the leveraging of OER produced outside India (Perryman & Seal, 2015). The Commonwealth Educational Media Centre for Asia (CEMCA) has assisted several organizations to develop content.

To promote the use of OER and contribute to their production, more effectors are needed to build capacity, develop OER and use them in appropriate instructional design models for reaching and learning. It is authors' strong view that with i^{2}OER, there will be strong demand for OER in the country as well as abroad.

i^2OER: Step 1: Course Curriculum Structure

The course curriculum of the programmes has to be designed so as to have the following components:

- Core courses related to the main stream
- Elective courses related to emerging technologies
- Foundation courses which may be common to all related streams
- Training related courses relevant to the chosen streams
- Industry internship
- OER

The credit distribution of a given programme could be as follows:

- Core courses : 60 percent
- Elective courses : 15 percent
- Foundation courses : 8 percent
- Training related courses : 2 percent
- Industry internship : 5 percent
- OER/MOOCs/SWAYAM : 10 percent

i^2OER: Step 2: Guiding Manual for Selecting Suitable OER

The students are not properly advised how to choose appropriate OER for their chosen stream/programme/course. There must be a guiding book, may be called as Programme Guide, which should guide the students properly. This guide should have all the necessary details for how to choose material, how to read, how to prepare for the examination and how to write right answers. There must be proper guidelines for the teachers as well for designing the question paper and marking the answer scripts. As is evident, this step ultimately become teacher oriented and therefore is not suitable much though it has the potential for reducing the requirement of a teacher and resource material.

i^2OER: Step 3: iOER (interactive OER)

In the interactive OER, the system will evaluate the performance of the students. This requires modification of existing OER as shown in Fig. 1.16.

The methodology of how students will read, learn and how the system will evaluate the performance is described below:

(1) Get Started

- Students enter the Lab housing necessary infrastructure for OER reading etc if they want to read and then to be evaluated by the system.
- Otherwise they can read at anytime and anywhere.

(2) Start Reading

- After identification of the students, they are allowed to download the material of Unit 1
- Students read the material as per their convenience within the allotted time (1 to 8 hrs).

(3) Get Examined

- After one hour or so the system will ask the students whether they would like to be tested for Unit 1. The students will respond with either Y or N.
- In case of Y, the system will open a new screen containing 5 or 10 objective type questions. The students will attempt the questions and would submit their answers. The system will immediately evaluate the performance.
- In case of N, the students will continue to read the same unit until they clear it.

(4) Clear the Course

- In case the students are satisfied with their performance, the system will allow them to move to the Unit 2.
- The same procedure will continue till the end.
- At the end when students have cleared all the Units, the system will print their award list and also will send the same to the Exam Cell of the concerned university.

The entire process is described in Fig. 1.17.

i^{2}OER: Step 4: i^{2}OER (interactive and intelligent OER)

This is most difficult but most ideal if we want that OER are used in a big way. It contains several steps as elaborated below:

(1) Existing OER, suppose a course of 4 Credits (40 Hrs of study), needs to be modified substantially.

(2) Any new OER is also to be written in this way.

(3) The OER has to be re-written in such a way that entire course is divided into 10 difficulty levels in the increasing order, level 1 being least difficult and level 10 the most difficult.

Difficulty Level 1	Difficulty Level 2	Difficulty Level 3	Difficulty Level 4	----------	Difficulty Level 8	Difficulty Level 9	Difficulty Level 10

Thereafter all the action points of step 3 are repeated till the student clears all the difficulty levels and his performance is declared by the system. In case the student wants to improve his performance, the system can allow it but within the total time allotted for a course

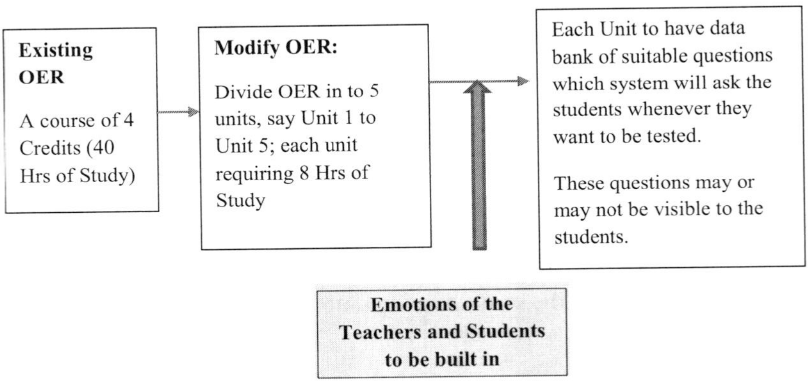

Fig. 1.16: Modification of Existing OER

E-learning and Emotional Intelligent Models

The e-learning environments has now started to consider the emotional state of the teachers as well as learners for enhancing their capabilities and performance. The emotions, if built in the e-learning and evaluation process, will help in a big way not only the students but also the teachers and the institutions.

We have proposed an advanced evolving e-learning system originally developed by Tang and Mccalla (2002).

The architecture of the proposed system having all the necessary components as described above is shown in Fig. 1.18.

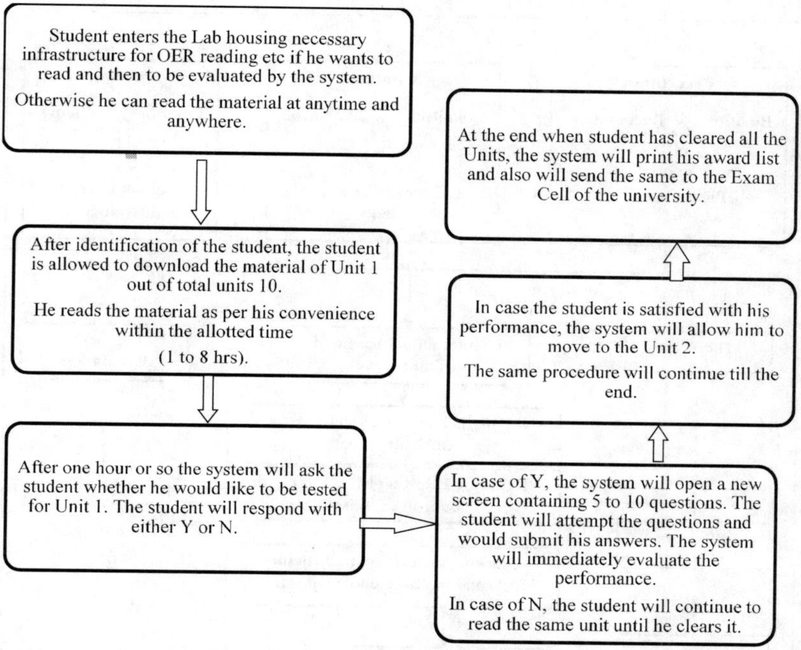

Fig. 1.17: Operational Scheme for Advanced e-learning

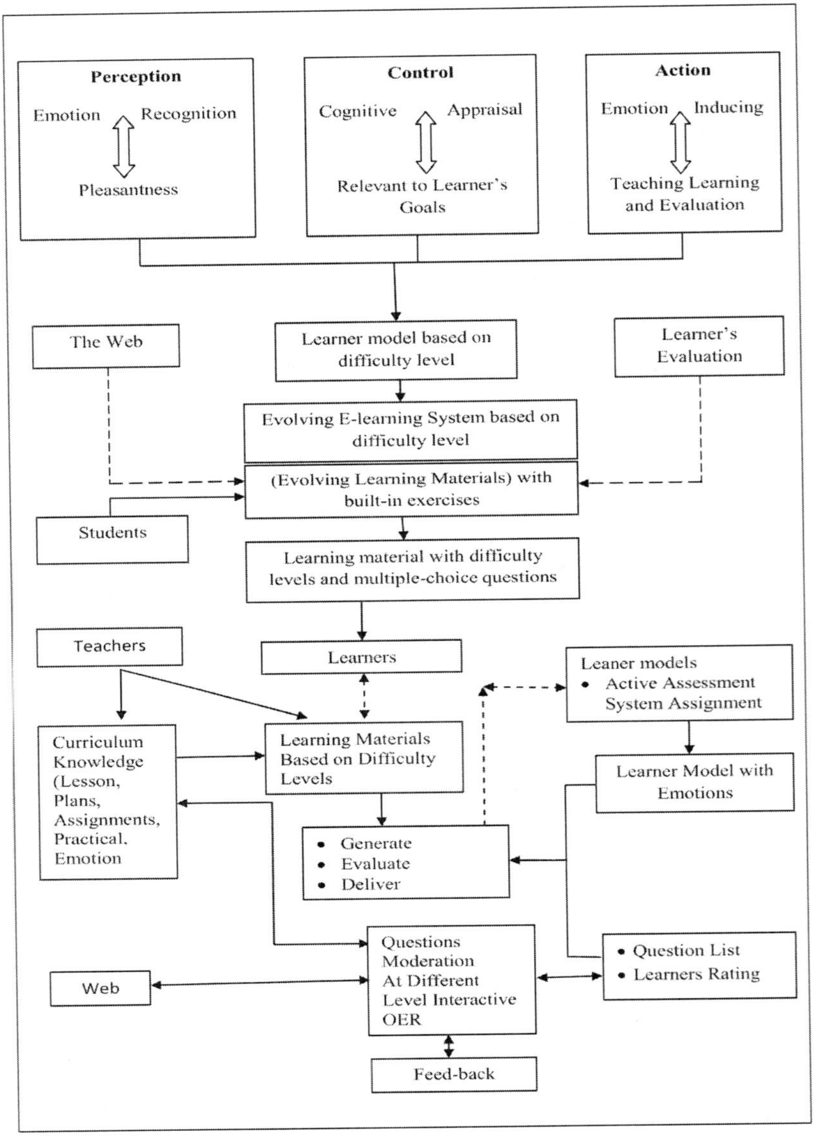

Fig. 1.18 Architecture of Proposed System

2

Teaching and Learning in Higher Education System

The capacity to learn is a gift
The ability to learn is a skill
The willingness to learn is a choice

Brian Herbert

Teaching and Learning Skills

Teaching and learning in higher educational institutions/universities is a wide subject and needs careful analysis of all its vital components. We have touched upon certain aspects of teaching and learning in higher education. Gadiya and Chandra (2014) have extensively studied the teaching and learning skills in a university system. Each and every conventional university has its own method of teaching and evaluation. These activities are by and large teacher centred. Open and distance educational universities, on the other hand, have the systems which are student centred. Each one of these approaches has some advantages and disadvantages (Gadiya and Chandra 2014, Salati and Chandra 2014).

The emphasis is also shifting from conventional teaching to integrating teaching (Smith 2005). The way of connecting skills and knowledge from multiple sources and experiences or applying skills and practice in various settings is integrated teaching. It simply means bridging connections between academic knowledge and practical (Huber and Hutchings 2004). Thus, alternative method of teaching based on lectures, seminar, and assignments is believed to be beneficial to the student community at the institution and seems to be the ideal approach. Large undergraduate courses in any university offer a challenge to those involved in both their development and their delivery, to ensure that the best possible learning outcomes are achieved in the most efficient way possible. When these students represent a combination of internal and distance students, and domestic and international, the challenge to achieve these outcomes become even more complex (Kehoe et.al. 2004).

Online and technology-based modes of study have been identified as a useful addition to classroom-based, traditional teaching methods (Light et al, 2000). The delivery of online courses enhances student learning in some respects, researchers have also caution against using the technology without adequate regard for the learning outcomes being sought (Buckley, 2003; Lawther & Walker, 2001; Willett, 2002). In fact, teaching should drive technology and not vice versa (Petrides, 2002).

It has been observed that not all students learn at the same pace. Students are unique in their own ways, including the way they learn. Since not all students learn in the same style, it is essential that teachers recognize the learning style differences of their students and teach in a manner in which all learning styles are considered. The characteristics of teachers are just as diverse as those of the students. Garger and Guild (1984) suggested that the learning style, teaching style, and personality style of teachers have implications for student learning. The teachers teaching styles may or may not be consistent with their learning styles. The teachers teach the way they learned. However, Koppleman (1980) commented that there is a lack of research concerning the influence of a person's learning style on their teaching style. Heimlich (1990) in an attempt to describe an individual's teaching style, defined two domains, sensitivity and inclusion. The sensitivity domain is based on the ability of the teacher to sense the shared characteristics of the learners. The inclusion domain is based on the teacher's willingness and ability to utilize instructional strategies that take advantage of the group's characteristics.

The students are directly in touch with their lecturers, programme leaders and also to the deans. All these three class of academics derive necessary guidelines from university authorities. A constant interaction and feedback on the entire teaching and learning process is very important. We need to know how students feel about teaching and learning, what they know about learning, what is their learning styles, how they feel about good grades and good learning. Equally important is the issue whether our teachers are able to orient themselves to satisfy the learning requirement of each and every student.

Usually it is asked how we could envision engaging with our students for our further understanding of higher education contexts and how we can utilise their responses for improving our teaching and learning process. This we have done by asking several questions.

Students' Response in Teaching and Learning

We have taken the views of 500 students of Monad University and have analysed their responses. We administered a questionnaire to the students. Almost all the students to whom the questionnaire was administered responded. The distribution of the students among various faculties is given in Table 2.1. We have taken a sample of 500 students spread among five broad disciplines. We have analysed the student responses with reference to each of these disciplines.

Table 2.1: Student Sample For Knowing Their Views on Teaching and Learning

Sr. No.	*School of Study*	*Student Number*	*% of Students*
1	Management and Business	100	22
2	Social Sciences	50	10
3	Applied and Life Sciences	50	8
4	Engineering Science and Technology	200	40
5	Agricultural Science and Technology	100	20
	Total	500	100

Before we proceed to know about teaching and learning, it is equally important to know why students are studying. We wanted to know how the students want to shape their future, whether they are able to think ahead or just take the study as it comes to them from their parents. When we analysed the responses received from the students, many innovative things emerged. Some of these are discussed below:

Why are you studying?

We asked the students "Why are you studying"? We wanted to know how the students want to shape their future, whether they are able to think ahead or just take the study as it comes to them from their parents. We gave the students following options:

- For getting good job
- For getting promotion in the existing job
- For increasing knowledge (moving to higher degree)
- For becoming an entrepreneur
- For getting good life partner

The responses of the students are shown in Fig. 2.1. The results show that most preferred option of the students is that they are studying for increasing their knowledge meaning thereby that they want to continue their study for higher degree. On an average, about 50 percent of the students opted for this. The next highest option preferred by the students is that they are studying for getting good job. On an average, about 23 percent of the students preferred this. About 10 percent said that they want to become an entrepreneur. The response to the option that they are studying to get a good life partner was not significant. About 2 percent students opted for it.

Do you know the difference between studying and learning?

Now it makes sense to go further and see whether students know the difference between studying and learning or not. At the higher educational level, it must be very clear in the minds of the students the basic difference between studying and learning. We have seen various definitions of studying and learning in the literature given by the eminent educationalists but what the younger generation of 21st centaury feels about studying and learning is equally important. We asked the students do they know the difference between studying and learning and if their response is yes, then define them. On an average, about 71.2 percent of the students (Fig. 2.2) said that they know the difference between studying and learning.

Their definition of studying and learning is shown in Fig. 2.3 and 2.4 respectively. Broadly speaking, we can group the student's responses in to five major groups as shown in Table 1 and Table 2. Majority of the students (67.78 percent) have defined "studying" as "the application of mind to the acquisition of knowledge by reading, investigation or reflection". The definitions of learning were having wide variations but the most preferred definition given is "Learning is the modification of behaviour through practice, training or experience".

What is Your Learning Strategy?

In higher education, we need to understand the students' learning styles or strategy. When teachers are asked to cater for individual student needs,

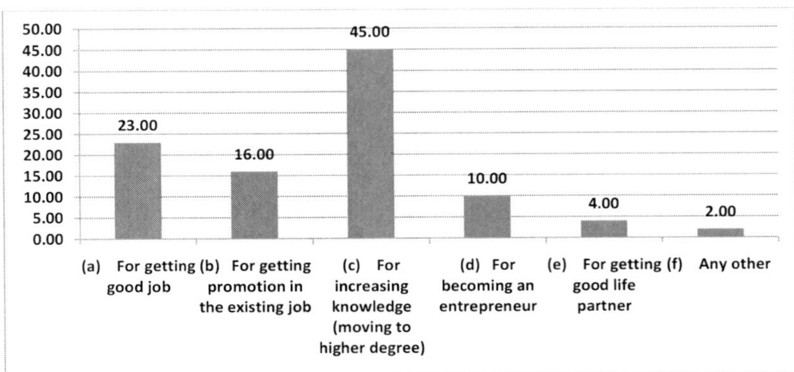

Fig. 2.1: Why Are You Studying?

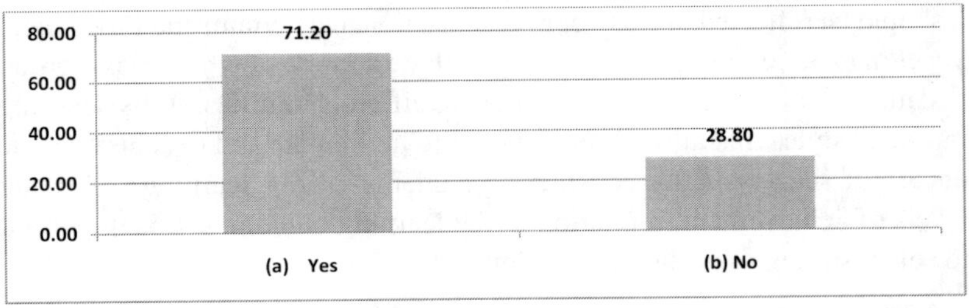

Fig. 2.2: Students Responses for the difference between Studying and Learning

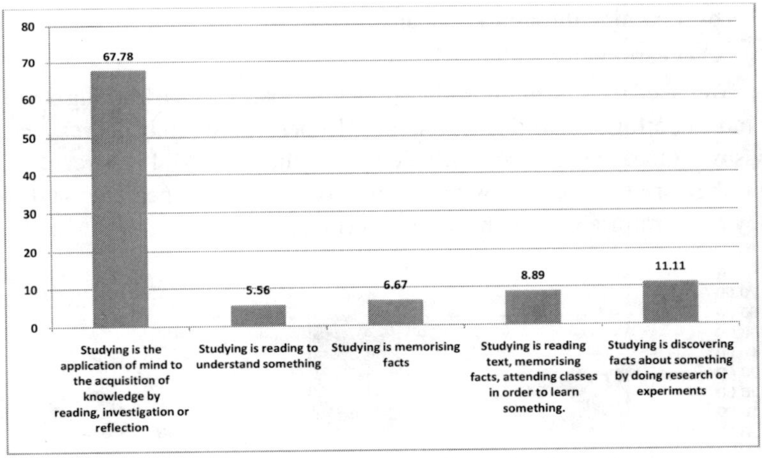

Fig. 2.3: Students Responses for Studying

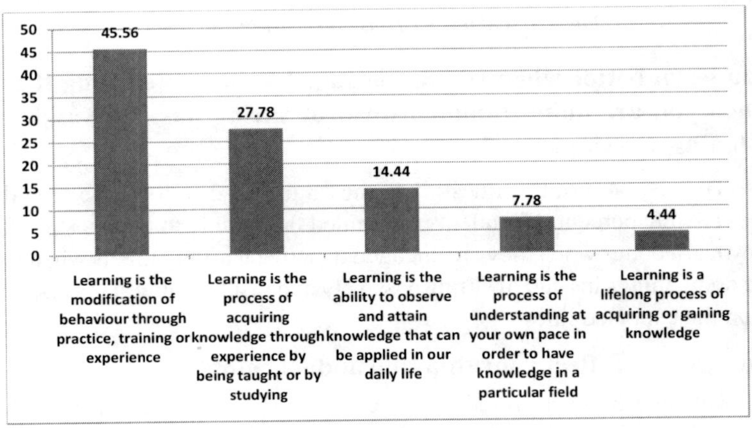

Fig. 2.4: Students Responses for Learning

it should be reflected in classroom organisation, curriculum and instruction. Teaching and learning strategies can include a range of whole class, group and individual activities to accommodate different abilities, skills, learning rates and styles that allow every student to participate and to achieve some degree of success. After considering students' needs, learning styles and levels of achievement in relation to the learning outcomes, it is important to select strategies (www.ceo.wa.edu.au).

We know the three broad classes of learning strategies as given below:

(a) Learning through audio aids

(b) Learning through visual aids

(c) Learning through moving aids

We asked the students how they prefer to learn or which learning strategy is most comfortable to them. About 33.13 percent of students responded by saying that they are comfortable with audio aids, 61.45 percent said that they are comfortable with visual aids while 5.42 percent said that they are comfortable with moving aids (Fig.2.5).

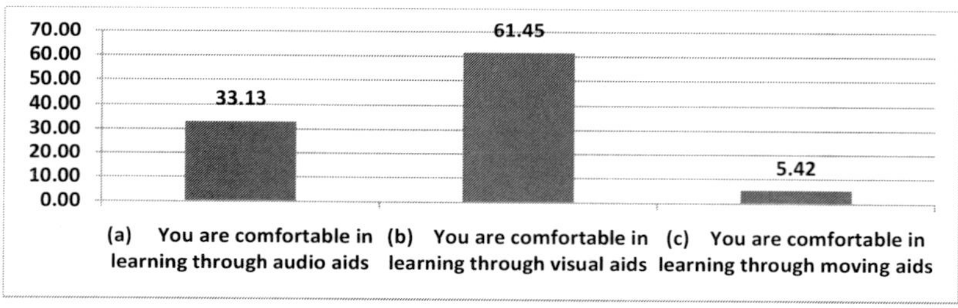

Fig. 2.5:Students Response forLearning Strategy

You learn better when you are engaged in active learning that is when you are doing things instead of sitting passively and just listening. Do you agree?

The response of this question is shown in Fig. 2.6. It can be seen that about 89.88 percent of students responded favourably to the question that they learn better when they are engaged in active learning that is when they are doing things instead of sitting passively and just listening. This response is on the expected lines.

How grades reflect your thinking and learning?

This question was asked to probe the minds of the students how they link good grades to their thinking and learning level. We gave them three options as indicated below:

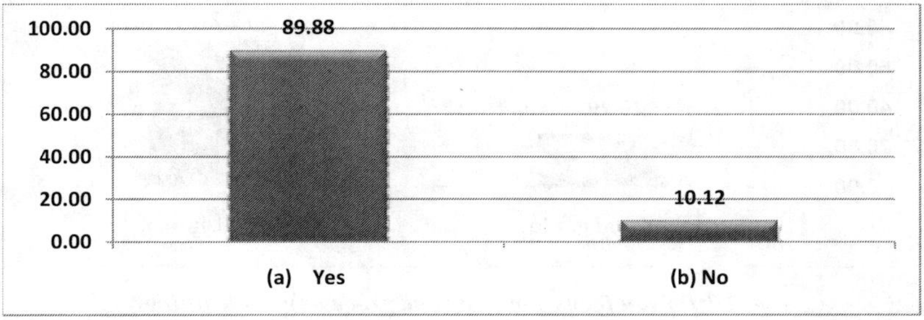

Fig. 2.6: You learn better when you are engaged in active learning that is when you are doing things instead of sitting passively and just listening

- Good grades indicate that you are capable of thinking intelligently.
- Good grades indicate that you have learned the module satisfactorily.
- Good grades indicate that your knowledge in the subject has increased.

The response of the students is shown in Fig. 2.7. It is interesting to observe that about 64.88 percent of the students responded by saying that good grades indicate increase in their knowledge in the subject. About 21.43 percent of the students said that good grades indicate that they have learned the module satisfactorily. About 13.69 percent of the students were of the view that good grades indicate that they are capable of thinking intelligently.

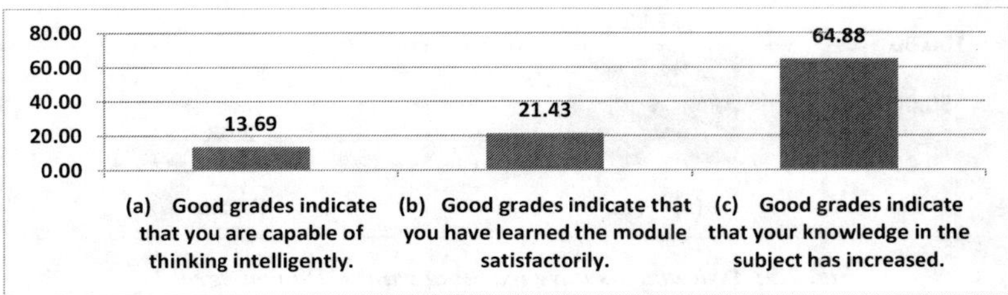

Fig. 2.7: How grades reflect your thinking and learning?

Do you focus more on good grade or good learning?

We continued to further probe on the good grades and asked the students whether they focus more on good grade or on good learning. The response of the students is shown in Fig. 2.8. It can be seen that about 73.21 percent of the students gave importance to good learning rather than good grades. This clearly indicates that today's young generation is more concerned to the learning rather than getting good grades.

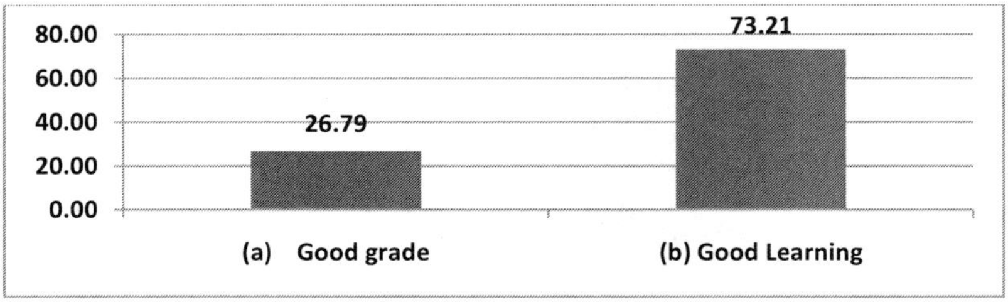

Fig. 2.8:Do you focus more on good grade or good learning?

Assignments have teaching values. Do you agree?

We have seen that many students do not write assignment responses on their own, instead they try to copy either from their fellow students or from web. Under such circumstances, assignments have no teaching values but become simply a means of scoring good marks. We have seen many cases where students have scored good marks (more than 75 percent) in assignments but very low marks (below 40 percent) in semester end examinations and vice versa.

We therefore asked the students whether assignments have teaching values or not. The response is shown in Fig. 2.9. To our great satisfaction, about 97.02 percent of the students said that assignments have teaching values.

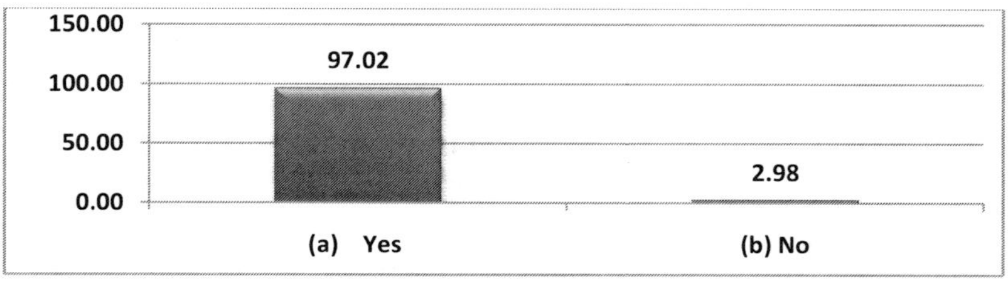

Fig. 2.9: Assignments have teaching values. Do you agree?

In your view, how your learning outcome of a subject/course/ module can be evaluated by your teacher?

Nowadays, there are so many techniques available for testing the outcome of learning activity. We wanted to know how students view this. We gave them following four options:

- By assignments and their presentations
- By surprised class tests

- By asking multiple choice questions in the exam
- By case studies and questions based on them

The response of the students is shown in Fig. 2.10. The students responded to all the options. About 44.31 percent were of the view that learning outcome can be best evaluated through assignments and their presentations. The next preferred option was case studies and questions based on them. This option was given by about 29.94 percent of the students. About 15.57 percent of the students were of the view that surprised test could be the best alternative to test their learning outcome. About 10.18 percent of the students favoured multiple choice alternatives.

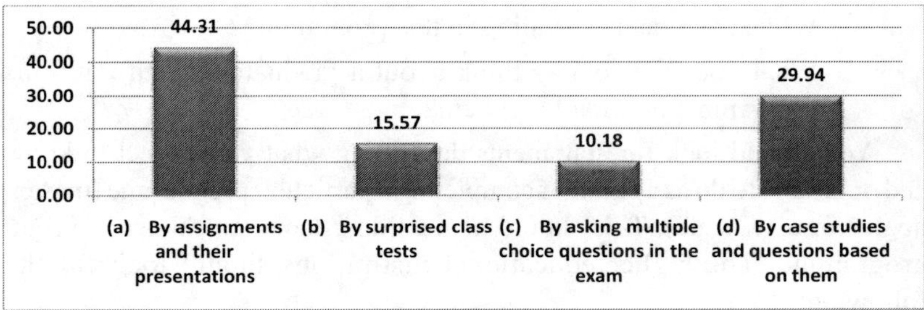

Fig. 2.10:How your learning outcome of a module can be evaluated by your teacher?

Conclusion

- It was observed that majority of the students are studying for increasing knowledge (moving to higher degree).
- About 88.55 percent of the students know the difference between studying and learning.
- About 61.45 percent of the students responded by saying that they are comfortable in learning through visual aids.
- About 89.88 percent of the students feel that they learn better when they are engaged in active learning that is when they are doing things instead of sitting passively and just listening.
- About 64.88 percent of the students feel that good grades indicate that their knowledge in the subject has increased.
- About 73.21 percent of the students focus on good learning rather than good grades.
- More than 97 percent of the students feel that assignments have teaching values.

- Majority of the students said that their learning outcome of a module can be evaluated by assignments and their presentations.

Skills for Developing Programme Learning Outcomes

In order to have proper teaching and learning environment in a university system, there is strong need of developing skills for programme learning. Developing skills for programme learning outcomes is very important for the students as well as for the teachers. When students plan to join a programme, the obvious questions which should emerge in their mind should be the following:

- What is essential to this programme?
- Why are students enrolling in this programme?
- What does the society think about a graduate student with this programme is suitable to them?

You should look for statements describing what you expect to know and or be able to do as a result of completing a particular programme (master, degree or certificate). This should be a guiding factor to choose the right programme. The higher educational institutions should look for the following:

- Modify and improve programmes based on the research inputs
- Evaluate programmes based on the requirements of the society
- Assist in meeting accreditation requirements
- Refer to the models of best practices

Each and every programme to be offered by the higher education institutions should answer the following questions:

- Why a particular programme is being offered?
- Why the students should enroll in this course?
- What knowledge and/or skills will students gain after clearing this course?

Those teachers, who are responsible for developing a programme, must ensure that three things are given. These are programme overview, objectives and outcome.

- **Overview of a programme:** This describes the relevance and the need of the programme for the society and the country.
- **Objectives:** Objectives are more a list of the content that will be covered in a particular programme.

- **Programme learning outcomes:** This can be measured based on the skills students will get and also based on the concepts; (1) skilled students will master in the class in speaking in a group and outlining a speech and analyzing the speaking situation and (2) concepts like delivery, audience analysis and language

Skills for Writing Learning Outcomes

The teachers should ensure that leaning outcomes are able to address the following:

- Is learning outcome measurable?
- Is learning outcome meaningful?
- Is learning outcome manageable?
- Who is the target audience of learning outcome?
- Who would know if my learning outcome has been met?
- How will I know if learning outcome has been met?
- Will learning outcome provide me with evidence that will lead me to make a decision for continuous improvement?

Some of the examples of writing learning outcomes are discussed below:

(a) Educational Counselling Learning Outcomes

At the end of this counselling session, students will be able to understand:

- Their responsibility in creating their own academic, personal, and professional successes.
- How to utilize the necessary information, resources, and options available for them to make sound educational and lifelong decisions.
- Need to do to achieve their desired goals.

(b) Energy Audit Learning Outcomes

At the end of this session, students will be able to understand:

- The definition of energy audit
- To distinguish between walk through energy audit, preliminary energy audit and comprehensive energy audit
- To prepare an energy balance of the audit exercise.
- To determine energy wastage areas
- To recommend energy conservation measures

Assessment Strategy

We need to ask ourselves if students are learning the skills and knowledge that they will need, to be successful in a career for a particular degree. Students need to understand the expectations of the level of learning and also how they are assessed. Assessment is the systematic basis for making inferences about the learning and development of students. Assessment is one component of programme evaluation.

A good assessment is more of giving right kind of questions rather than giving right kind of answers.

The tools for assessments may include the following:

- assignments and their presentations in the class
- surprised class tests
- asking multiple choice questions in the examination
- case studies and questions based on them
- seminar presentations
- student debates

The author has carried detailed analysis of student's preferences of their assessment. We asked the students how their learning outcome of a module/unit/course/programme can be evaluated by their teachers. The response of the students is shown in Fig. 2.11. About 44.31 percent of the students were of the view that learning outcome can be best evaluated through assignments and their presentations. The next preferred option was case studies and questions based on them. This option was given by about 29.94 percent of the students. About 15.57 percent of the students were of the view that surprise test could be the best alternative to assess their learning outcome. About 10.18 percent of the students favoured multiple choice alternatives. It clearly indicates that higher education institutions have to adopt a mix of technologies to evaluate the learning outcome.

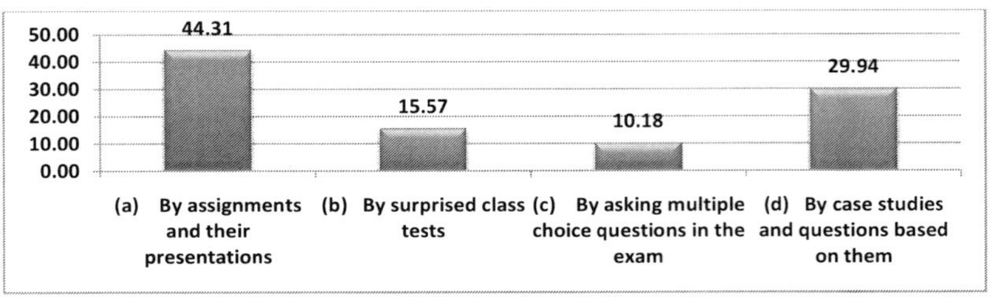

Fig. 2.11:How your learning outcome of a module can be evaluated by your teacher?

Stages of the Assessment Process

The assessment process contains several steps. The most important is establishing objectives. It is very essential to establish clear programme goals and objectives because objectives drive the assessment process and assessment methods are based on the objectives that are being measured.

Objectives provide the following:

- Both teachers and students worked towards a common goal – teacher knows what and how to teach, students know what is expected of them
- A means for assessing student success: well-written objectives will dictate how success is measured and criteria for determining if success has been achieved

> A good assessment is more of giving right kind of questions rather than giving right kind of answers.

- Allow for self-evaluation: objectives provide the means for determining program success as well; framework for collecting and providing evidence of accountability

Bloom's taxonomy is a tool for writing subject matter objectives – a guide to classify objectives according to their level of complexity.

Learning Skills at a Glance

All the important learning skills (study skills) can be combined into four major categories as shown in Fig. 2.12.

Time Management

- You should start using a planner or task list at the start of the semester.
- Write down important dates for exams, assignments and other projects on a planner.
- Make a weekly or monthly schedule to get an overall picture of when you'll be busiest and when you have free time.
- Make a task list to keep track of things you need to do on a daily basis.
- Use short breaks in your daily schedule (such as an hour between classes) wisely. Schedule appointments on campus, check email or review your class notes.

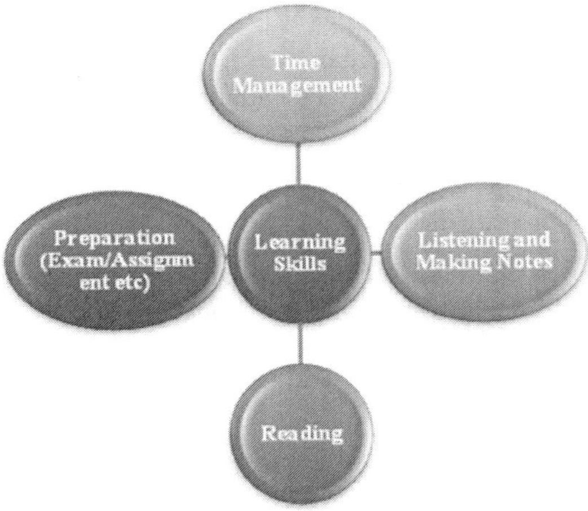

Fig.2.12: Learning Strategies

- Divide large tasks into smaller pieces that can be completed within a few hours (or even a few minutes).
- No one can - or wants to - study all the time! Plan your time to include doing things that you enjoy.
- Be patient and flexible. If certain time management strategies don't work for you, try a different strategy.

Listening and Note Making

- Always attend classes on regular basis.
- Find out how you'll be evaluated on the material from lectures.
- Come prepared to class by bringing lecture notes.
- Do assigned readings before the lecture in order to participate in class discussion, better follow the lecture, and ask meaningful questions.
- Disconnect your internet connection in class or leave your laptop at home.
- Listen actively by comparing what you hear in the lecture to what you learned in the last lecture.
- Concentrate to get the most out of the lectures. Sit where you can hear and see everything you need to.
- Organize your notes after the lecture by identifying main topics and key terms, underlining or using different colours for important

points, and making diagrams or concept maps to illustrate relationships.

- Update your notes on a regular basis in order to fill in missing information and identify what you know and what's unclear.
- Review your notes on a weekly basis to prepare in advance for exams.

Reading

- Find out how you'll be evaluated on your knowledge of the readings.
- Think carefully about reading strategies and techniques that will help you the most in each course. SQ3R is a good choice.
- Break long readings up into shorter, smaller chunks, depending on how long you can concentrate in that subject area. No one can read for hours at a time and remember details well.
- Find a quiet, comfortable place to read. Your body associates your bed with sleeping, so it's probably not the best place!
- Preview the reading by noting the subtitles and headings, looking at diagrams and skimming through the introduction and summary.
- Reflect on the content as you read and take notes. How the reading is connected to the course lectures? In what way does it connect to the main ideas in the course?
- Pay attention to your attention span. Take a quick break if you can't remember what you just read.
- Summarize and take notes in your own words to help you understand and retain information. Don't rely on highlighting as your main method of note-taking.
- If you tend to read the textbook after a lecture, review your lecture notes before you read, and don't take additional notes on the material already well explained in your lecture notes.
- Review the notes from your readings on a regular basis to keep them fresh in your memory.

Preparation (Assignments/Exam/Charts/Models/Project Reports)

- Locate one or two good study places with few distractions or interruptions.

- Review the course outline for information about what your teacher expects you to learn in the course.
- Review previous assignments, papers, labs, etc. to pinpoint where you've had difficulty in the course. Make sure you understand that material since you may see it again in the next exam.
- Learn by doing. Do practice questions based on old exams, or create and answer your own test questions.
- Write practice exams under exam-like conditions (timed and with your books closed).
- Study in small chunks of time when possible. Two-hour blocks with a 15-minute break work well for many students.
- Keep a regular schedule. Be sure to eat right, get enough sleep, and take time to exercise.
- During the exam, focus on what you do know rather than what you wish you had spent more time studying.

Teaching Learning Styles in Higher Education Institutions

There are several methods and strategies through which students are learning in universities/colleges/institutions. Some of the important ones are given in Table 2.2. These are lectures, seminars, tutorials, practical work, group work and case study. Students have to concentrate on acquiring knowledge and skills from all these strategies.

There are flaws in the present teaching strategies adopted by the teaching community; some important ones are given below:

- Students are passive listener in the class
- Students are not advised to be innovative and for critical thinking
- Students are not encouraged for active learning
- Students are not given practical examples correlating day to day experiences
- Students are discouraged from learning

Students can overcome all these obstacles provided they adopt right kind of study skills (see Fig. 2.13).

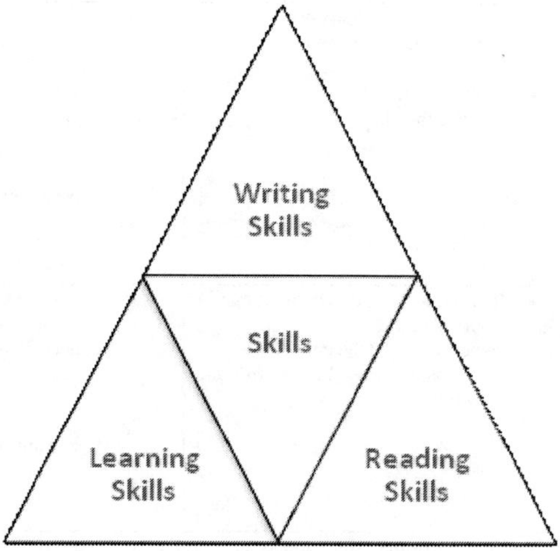

Fig. 2.13: Skills Domain

Table 2.2: Teaching and Learning Methods and Strategies

Methods and Approaches	*Characteristics*	*How you can derive the best*
Lectures	• The teacher picks up a portion of subject matter, prepares talk and delivers in the class room • The teacher explains difficult ideas but may not be able to give what you need to know. • The teacher provides students with common material as the starting point for further study. • A lectureformat maybe entertainingandefficientdeliveryof information,but it may not facilitatethebestway to learn	• You are expected to read further on the subject to clear your difficult areas. • You are supposed to read the study material provided by your teacher • Put your mind in the highest state of concentration. This means listen carefully what the teacher is saying. **(Concentration of Mind)**
Seminars	• The traditional lectures may and may not be supported by seminar.	• Form a group of students and talk through ideas, questions etc and discuss all aspects of the subject. **(Confidence Building)**

(Contd...)

Tutorials	The tutorials help you in many ways: • You can ask questions • You can check your understanding of the subject. • You can discuss work assignments individually	• Always list the difficult points of subject matter • Discuss these points in the tutorial hour and get the answer **(Active notes are the key)**
Laboratory and Practical Work	• The students of practical oriented courses need to test experimentally the concepts and methods introduced in lectures and tutorials.	• These are very good tools for understanding the theoretical concepts and also to get hands on training. **(Learning while doing)**
Group Work	• In group work, you collaborate with other students in the overall guidance of yourteacher on any topic/project. • This will make you ready to take up new assignments. The ability to work effectively in groups is much sought after by employers.	• Your participation will give you enough confidence to take different roles (e.g. leading a group), share expertise and tackle tasks that you would not be able to undertake alone. **(Multi Skilled Learner)**
Independent Study	• Independent reading and study based on thelecturers is very important.	• This will enable you to prepare for an assignment: a coursework essay, a presentation or preparation for an exam. **(Highly confidential and motivated person)**

Non-Traditional Strategies of Teaching and Learning

You might have observed that many universities/colleges/institutions follow traditional teaching approaches which may not provide you with valuable skills or knowledge that lasts much beyond the end of the term. To enhance the quality of teaching and learning in the classroom non-traditional strategies such as active, cooperative, collaborative and problem-based learning can be utilized. Even if, you are not given this type of teaching, you can still do the best by adopting right kind of skills.

Bloom and Krathwohl (1956) have excellently described the link between strategies and learning objectives to assist the teachers in developing and directing students in logical steps of learning. This is given in Table 2.3.

Knowledge, comprehension and application are passive modes where activities are more or less teacher centred. Knowledge and comprehension focus on a recall of facts that you can attain by reading the course material and attending lectures. The evaluation strategies are through true/false and multiple-choice questions for knowledge and short essays for comprehension. In the application category, you use previously learned information in new and concrete situations to solve problems that have single or best answers.

Table 2.3: Strategies and Learning Objectives

Cognitive Domain	*Feature*	*Outcomes*	*Learning Outcome*
Knowledge	Passive	Recall of specificfacts	know common terms, know specific facts, know methods and procedures, know basic concepts, know principles
Comprehension	Passive	Grasping or under standing meaning of informational study materials	understand facts and principles, interpret verbal material, interpret charts and graphs, translate verbal material to mathematical formulae, estimate the future consequences implied in data, justify methods and procedures
Application	Passive	Makeuse of the knowledge	apply concepts and principles to new situations, apply laws and theories to practical situations, solve mathematical problems, construct graphs and charts, and demonstrate the correct usage of a method or procedure
Analysis	Active	Taking apart the known & identifying relationships among them	recognize unstated assumptions, logical fallacies in reasoning, distinguish between facts and inferences, evaluate the relevancy of data, analyse the organizational structure of a work.
Synthesis	Active	Putting thing stoge therin a creative manner	write awell-organized theme, gives a well-organized speech, writes a creative short story, propose a plan for an experiment, integrate learning from different areas into a plan for solving a problem, formulates a new scheme for classifying objects.
Evaluation	Active	Makes judgments about the value of materials or methods	judge the logical consistency of written material, judge the adequacy with which conclusions are supported by data, judge the value of a work by the use of internal criteria, judge the value of a work by use of external standards of excellence

The analysis, synthesis and evaluation are the characteristics of teaching and learning that engage you the most because they are active. These categories deal with the issues that inspire you to learn and reveal the creative. You assume responsibility for acquiring the knowledge necessary to respond creatively and evaluate outcomes. This is the basis for developing skills, attitudes and values. This will lead you to engage in higher order of thinking such as analysis, synthesis, and evaluation.

Let us see some of the non-traditional learning strategies:

Case-Based Learning

The significance of case-based learning is that it links theory and application to real or possible circumstances. The questions are created to guide you through appropriate analysis, synthesis and evaluation.

- Let us take a simple case study: Why the tyers of all vehicles are always black?
- The students are discussing possible reasons and arrive at a suitable answer.
- It is because of the Physics law of black body radiation. All black bodies (tyer is a black body) absorb the heat radiation at the same rate at which they radiate the heat. In absence of this, the tier will become so hot that they can burst any point of time.

Discussion based Learning

Topics of discussion are important and are generally conceived to utilize group discussions in a manner that will move you from knowledge of facts to the evaluation of outcomes. This will help you to develop the skills necessary for becoming a critical thinker and assesses the student's learning based on six different levels specified in Table 2.3.

Debate based Learning

Classroom debate will involve the students in researching, teaching, and recognizing alternative points of view. The benefits of a formal classroom debate include:

- enhancing skills for research and analysis
- promoting logical and critical thinking
- increasing oral communication skills
- motivating
- building effective team work skills

Let us take a simple example. A question is raised for the discussion. How to determine the height of a tower? The students are debating and are giving possible answers (see Fig.2.14) which may and may not be there in the text books, study materials or even the teacher might have not explained that procedure. Both teacher and the students have to be innovative all the time.

Problem-Based Learning and Problem-Solving Learning

The problem-based learning and problem-solving learning are two different things. The basic difference is given in Table 2.4.

How to determnine the height of a tower?

Answer1:I will take a rope and a stone. I will climb the tower and after tieing the stone at the one end of the rope will send the rope down till it touches the ground. I will measure the length of the rope which is the height of the tower.

Answer 2: I will take a watch and a pendulum. I will determine the value of g (acceleration due to gravity) at the top of the tower. I know the value of g at the ground. By the difference, I will calculute the height of the tower.

Answer 3: I will measure the shadow of the tower at two different times and then using the properties of the triangles, measure the height of the tower.

Answer 4: I will throw a stone from the top of the tower and will measure the time it takes to reach the ground. Then by using the Newton's formula, will determine the height of the tower.

Fig. 2.14 An Example of Discussion

The problem-solving is referred to arriving at decisions based on prior knowledge and reasoning. The following are the basic steps:

- Start
- State what we need to know/problem
- Learn it
- Give an example how to use it.

The problem-based learning is referred to the process of acquiring new knowledge based on recognition of a need to learn. The following are the basic steps:

- Start
- State the problem
- Identify what we need to know
- Learn it
- Apply it

Table 2.4: Problem-Based Learning (PBL) and Problem-Solving Learning (PSL)

	Problem Solving	***Problem Based Learning***
Educational strategy	Traditional discipline-based	Integrated systems-based
Main characteristics	The focus is on preparatory learning prior to exposure to the problem. Theteacher sets the problems and students attempt to resolve them using previously taught related content.	The problem comes first without advance readings, lectures, or preparation. The problem serves as a stimulus for the need to know. The students basedontheirpriorknowledgeandtheidentifiedgapsinthatknowledgedeterminethelearningissueswithintheirowngroup. Theythenidentifyanduse a varietyoflearningresourcestostudytheseissues. Theyreturntothegrouptodiscussandsharewhattheyhavelearned.
Role of the teacher	Content expert	Tutor/Facilitator
Learning environment	Passive, teacher-centered	Learning becomes dependent upon the self-directed efforts of the small group. This method creates a more active, student-centered learning environment
Who is responsible for directing the learning activities	Teacher	The student decides what he/she needs to learn

The rationale for PBL lies in its comparability with modern educational principles. Its approach is based on principles of adult education and self-directed learning. The principles of adult learning are based on the fact that adults are motivated in deciding the programme, place of study, pace of study etc. The key elements of self-directed learning are based on the fact that the learner takes the initiatives for identifying learning needs, formulating goals, identifying resources, implementing appropriate activities and evaluating outcomes.

This has the roles for both teachers and students.

The Role of Teachers

- Develop real-world, complex and open-ended problems which as might be faced in daily life.
- Act as facilitators, making sure that the students are finding the resources they need.
- Raise questions to student groups that help in making the concepts clear.
- Strike a balance between providing direct guidance and encouraging self-directed learning.

The Role of Students

- Address the problem, identifying what students need to learn in order to develop a solution and where to look for appropriate learning resources.
- Collaborate to gather resources, share and synthesize their findings, and pose questions to guide further learning tasks for the group.

Example: PBL tutorial process

(1) Case presentation: The teacher provides the student group with some introductory "power information" about a manufacturing company, say X.

Manufacturing company X is using coal and electricity to produce different kinds of paper. The efficiency of the company is 50 percent. The management wants to increase the efficiency to 70 percent.

(2) Identifying key information: The quality of coal, the type of boiler, the purpose of boiler to heat the water, or to generate steam, peak electricity demand etc.

(3) Generate an enquiry strategy: What additional information is required? For example, annual power consumption, annual paper production, whether energy audit of the plant has been done or not.

(4) Defining learning objectives: Once the students have adequate knowledge about the problem, they can think for the following questions to further their understanding of the underlying process, and their ability to suggest the measures to increase the efficiency:

- What students know?
- What they do not know?
- What they need to know?

The students may identify gaps in their knowledge.

(5) Reporting back

- In the follow-up session, students reconvene to report on their self-directed study and share and integrate new knowledge.
- All students should contribute to the report-back and their unique perspectives are incorporated into the process of knowledge buil-ding. The exchange and debate of ideas

promotes the consolidation and elaboration of new knowledge and understanding

(6) Integrating new knowledge

- Based on the principle that knowledge is consolidated more readily in context, students, guided by the teacher, and should relate new knowledge.
- Students are required also to extend their discussion covering all aspects.

How to get started with PBL?

Efforts should be made to develop problems that capture students' interest by relating to real-world issues. This is the key to relate learning to the real world problems. Identify students' previous learning and experience on the chosen problem and then integrate content objectives with problem-solving skills followed by some independent research to gather all information relevant to the problem.

The following key points should be kept in mind while PBL construction:

- The content of the problem should be comparable to students' prior knowledge.
- There should be a clear connection with one or more of the objectives of the subject matter.
- The problem should be sufficiently complex and relevant for initial discussion and for generating learning issues.
- The problem should be structured in such a way that it offers enough opportunities for discussion in the group.
- The problem should be multidisciplinary and be clear to students.
- The problem should include of all the relevant information that is needed for identifying learning issues.

Problem-based learning links theory and practice where you are engaged in real life problems. The purpose of the problem is to motivate you to learn by providing a real- world context for examining the issues involved. It has been observed that learning is more meaningful and enjoyable when it occurs in small self-directed active groups. This in turn will encourage you to take responsibility for their own learning and that of their learning group.

You may be the student either of conventional education or open and distance education. It would be better if you know their characteristics.

Preparing the Right Kind of Workforce

The current model of higher education caters to the needs of the society of the second industrial revolution. However, it is important to create new paradigms/models of higher education that focus on creating capabilities powered by innovation, inclusively and concern for sustainability rather than merely creating informed and trained manpower. The shifting employment landscape has significant implications for companies, education systems, governments and society. Business leaders and policy makers will need to have a cohesive approach as they seek to foster high employment levels while promoting productivity.

Bringing Quality to Technology Enhanced Learning

Learning in a digital age includes using the tools usually employed daily and should encompass, and teaching in an age includes facilitating learners that are digital natives. Five years ago, many business schools were bracing of massive online open courses, or MOOCs. This surge in the use of new technologies in higher education often described as 'mediatization of the higher education ecosystem', and the type about the perils and pitfalls of MOOCs has moves the discussion on to thinking about the changes and benefits of refining pedagogical approaches that incorporate new learning technologies.

The design and delivery of technology enhanced learning (TEL) demands specific skills and capabilities in web design and the preparation of a wide array of learning materials and learning technologies. Furthermore, new roles have emerged such as e-tutor, discussion leader and content specialist. Because of the nature of the learning experience, careful design of the range of materials and technologies used or proposed is needed.

Learning in a digital age includes using the digital tools we employ daily and should encompass our new digital habits/behaviors. Teaching in a digital age includes facilitating learners that are digital age includes.

Channels of Learning and Delivery in Open University System

There could be several strategies which may be adopted by any open university system for delivery of academic programmes. Every student may be attached to a Learning Support Centre. The Learner Support Centre provides accesses to all learning resources (course material, counselling sessions, tutorial support, assignments and examinations). In addition to this, special facilities (computing, laboratories) whenever required are also arranged with the help of Learning Support Centers. This approach is bound to help the university in many ways. For instance, the Learning Support Center provides the local face of a university to its students. However, these centres may have some limitations as discussed below:

The Limitations of Learning Support Centres

In an open university, following situation may arise. The enrolment may increase, programmes may get multiplied and the specialized nature of facilities required began to get diversified. The process of such a growth will throw up several new issues and concerns. The growth in enrolment may not be uniform across all programmes; attachment of a small number of students with Learning Support Centers may make some of these centers non-viable. This may lead to delays in services reaching students. The university has to provide certain facilities (equipment and furniture) and staff. This cost is fixed and has to be incurred whether or not there are students availing the facilities. The Learning Support Centers have to be equipped with the capacity to provide all the services even if they are not fully utilized. There is always, therefore, a gap between the provision and its utilization.

Thus, the Learning Support Centre approach alone cannot take education at the door-steps of the students. It is, therefore, necessary to rationalize and diversify the existing Learning Support Centre and add new alternative channels of delivery.

Alternate Learning Channels

On the basis of place, facilities, resources, etc. we may identify the alternate learning channels as shown in Fig. 2.15.

Home Based Learning (personalized learning)

This channel consists of printed self instructional material, A/V material, textual referral material, enrichment reading, educational Radio/TV Broadcast/ On-line computer network services.

There are certain constraints in the extensive use of this channel in the present context. For instance, every home may not be equipped with all the facilities; in fact, most of the houses will be without higher-end communication faculties. However, such facilities are likely to be available in many houses.

Open University (OU) can deliver its materials and academic counselling/tutoring through the media mentioned above. One simple way is to offer counselling through interactive audio channel. The experts may device different ways of counseling and helping students at their living or working place to reach the goal of 'education at year door-step'. Communication Technology (CT) will make OU task quite easy.

Work-place Based Learning (Experiential Learning)

This channel includes field work/observations, experimentation/project work, product development, group learning and action research etc.

Community Based Learning (Societal Learning)

This channel includes group problem solving (self-help groups, women, youth circles), group learning, participation in related community service/ development activities, learning at community/peoples' learning where multi-media learning facilities are available.

A dynamic and developed community is the foundation for empowerment and enrichment of any nation. Hence, these channels are the most important for democratization of education and for developing a learning society. Learning here is through observation, participation in activities, and collective or group action.

Resource Centre Based Learning

This channel includes counselling/tutoring, lectures, lab based practical work and learning, training (face-to-face), group discussions/group problem solving), Multi-media internet, A/V conferencing. Recourse Centre (RC) will provide many facilities of learning and 'closeness' of the RC will ensure access to the learner.

Special Resource Centre Based Learning

This channel is conceived when a learner wants to acquire knowledge and/or skills at the highest level by interacting with the best physical and intellectual resources available at the institution. This could be through intensive training, workshops, seminars, attachments, etc. The approach should be to develop a partnership with such specialized institutions through open education mode. The institutes having specialized facilities and expertise in professional and specialized subject can be used as a Special Resource Centre for learning/training in specialized topics and programmes.

Alternate Delivery Channels

The purpose of the delivery system is to support learners in their learning activities by making available materials, facilities and expert services through diversified communication media (Multi Media) and interactive processes. The academic services through counseling, tutoring, expert advice etc. help learners, individually and group-wise, to assimilate more knowledge and reach higher levels.

We may conceive broadly three types of delivery channels as shown in Fig. 2.16:

Direct to Learners

The University could reach directly the learners at their place of living and working through print materials, A/V material, broadcast of programmes (Radio, TV, ITV etc.), on-line computer network and Distance Learning Facilities (DLFs) or Mentors of coordinators. When enrolment is low, but learner distribution is wide, a group of 30-35 students may be attached to a Distance Learning Facilitator (DLF), who may secure various services for the learners through learner support centres.

Through Resource Centers

Diversified study approach and public and private support could be used to establish Resource Centers with various types of learning resources. Different types of Resources Centers could be:

- Learner Support Centres
- Partnership with special intuitions/organizations with one-window operation
- Multi-Media Learning Centers established by public or private institutions to offer learning services, mainly of electronic communication type.
- Local Institutions/Organizations taking responsibility of offering total services as per university norms.

Through Extension Activities

This could be in partnership with Government, non-Government organizations and local people's organizations.

Information and Communication Technologies

The role of information and communication technologies is rapidly expanding in all processes of value addition. As value addition in human resource development is a function of education, these technologies can mediate between the educational providers and their students located

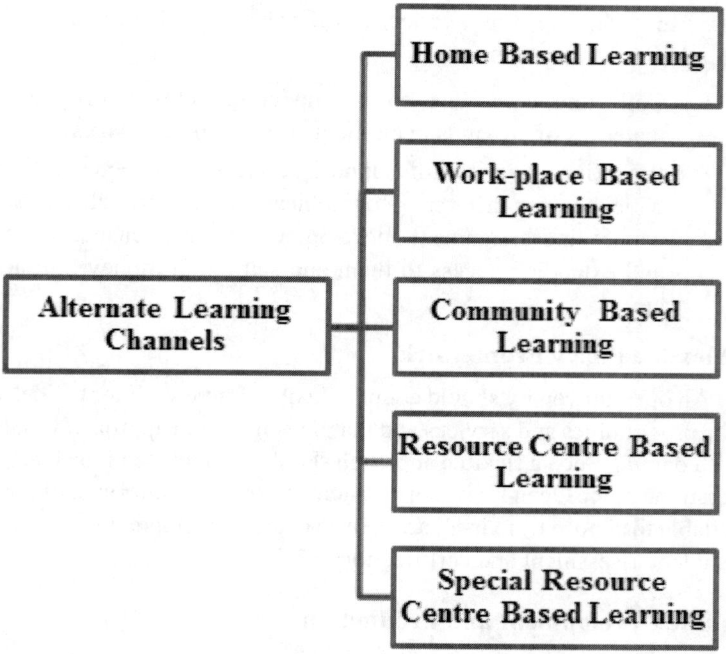

Fig. 2.15: Alternate Learning Channels

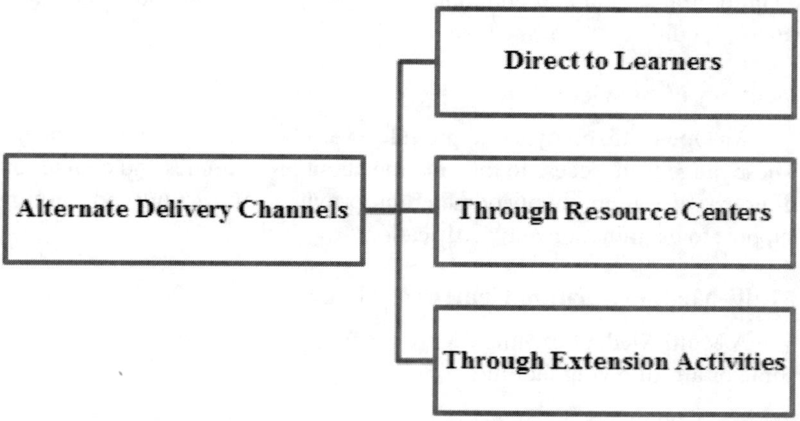

Fig. 2.16: Alternate Delivery Channels

anywhere in the world in a variety of different ways. For instance, these technologies can be used for.

- Collecting, compiling, editing, updating and transforming study materials of all kinds in all media (print, voice, images).
- Providing a variety of support services to students dispersed widely across different geographical regions through interactive counselling, assignments, development and maintenance of records and extending access to them and setting all money transaction etc.

A Flexible Policy Framework

An open university should adopt a flexible framework for the delivery of its programmes and services and that no single rigid approach should be insisted upon. Such a flexible approach should in fact extend to all areas of operations of the Open University System. There is a wide range of options available to choose from in all areas form course development and delivery to student assessment and certification.

Course Development and Production

There can be several modes like in house development and production with support from external experts, use of available material by adoption/adaption/translation and communicating the preparation and production, revision, editing, etc. of the texts.

Delivery of Services

An Open University has to provide a variety of services to its students. These range from access to information about programmes and courses on offer to registration, supply of materials, provision of teaching and learning support to examination and certification.

Multi-Media Learning Centre (MMLC)

A Multi-Media Learning Centre is conceived as a resource centre with some or all following facilities:

- Computers
- Internet connectivity
- E-Mail/Fax
- Infrastructure for accessing library resources.
- Electronic library facilities.

- Receiving/recording tele counseling.
- Multi-coping of audio/video tapes.

These centres will be provided access to University technology networked support systems. They can access materials and provide them to students on demand. They can also serve as information accessing points and providers of electronic media support of all facilities which are available on the network.

The provision of services through the MMLC could be in two ways:

(a) There could be a set of programmes delivered only through this mode.

(b) For the remaining programmes this could be an additional facility that students can avail of an payment.

Capacity Building of Teachers for Quality Education

You can teach a student a lesson for a day; but if you can teach him to learn by creating curiosity, he will continue the learning process as long as he lives. Rriya (2017) has rightly pointed out that teacher is one of the most demanding professional in the world and in order to fulfill their professional responsibility in an excellent way teachers need training, motivation as well as regular mental, emotional and spiritual rejuvenation.

The importance given to teaching profession in any country is often evading by the resources spent on teacher capacity building. However, the issues often have been about building an efficient model and mechanism that would develop and enhance the teachers, capacity and provide them avenues for professional development.

The training needs of teachers in India are truly daunting. The pre-service training curriculum followed in the country in often outdated and does not develop teachers who can handle the challenges of their role. Given this scenario, the in-service teacher education and professional development document reports the following lacunae in in-service teacher education and professional development:

- The current training approach is fragmented, often leading to a situation that teachers repeatedly attend the same training programme year after year.
- Training often does not lead to capacity enhancement or content enrichment, or result in enhancing motivation levels of teachers to bring about changes in classroom practices.

- The practice of developing an overall Training Plan, which delineates details of different training modules, does not exist, and needs to be introduced.
- Focus needs to be given to introduce and sustain interactive, participatory and democratic training methods/processes.

Understanding the Concept of Capacity Building

The concept of capacity building has to do with the allocation of, and investment in the following resources:

- physical
- intellectual
- human

The benefits of capacity building are consequential, "in the short term, to the specific individuals and institutions that are their recipients, but the ultimate beneficiaries are future members of society, whose interests cannot be clearly determined in the present". Crucially, for capacity building to be effective, it must respond to the growth and development needs of the teachers as well as those of the relevant institutions. For all practical purposes, building teacher capacity is, ultimately, engendering development, growth and excellence within an educational system (Delaney, 2002).

Role of Teachers and Concerns

There is a definite range of personal competence that makes a difference to the quality and effectiveness of teaching. These are:

- sound subject knowledge
- communication skills
- ability to relate to individual students
- self-management skills
- organizational skills
- classroom management skills
- problem-solving skills
- a range of teaching methods
- teamwork skills
- research skills

In the Indian context, most of these competencies are not adequately addresses in the curriculum of teacher education. As for pedagogical knowledge, the teacher training curriculum needs to encompass a clear focus on understanding of learning and teaching, including concepts of how students' progress in the subject, how they acquire key concepts, and importantly an understanding of misconceptions and how they arise.

We conducted a survey among the faculty members about the seven important questions given in Table 2.5. The possible answers are also given. The response of the faculty members is given in Fig. 2.17 and Fig. 2.18. The teachers of higher education should differentiate between lecturing and tutoring. This is because, the course contents are delivered through a scheme called LTPC (Lecture, Tutorial, Practical; C stands for a Credit). About 74.73 percent of the teachers were found to be aware about the difference between lecturing and tutoring. As regards to the difference between case based learning, problem based learning and outcome based learning, the status was very poor. Only about 26.37 percent of the faculty members were able to differentiate.

In higher education, there are class assignments (CA) questions which help the student in learning. On the other hand, the questions in semester end examination are used for assessing the students. It was really disappointing to observe that about 9.89 percent of the faculty members were aware about this.

The academic pedagogy of any university is very important and each and every faculty member should be aware about this. However, only about 56.04 percent of the faculty members were found to be aware about this.

To understand the credit of a course is very important for the faculty members. It is because the lesson plan, teaching schedule etc are linked with it. The credit of a course is based on the weekly load of a course. A course may be theoretical as well as theoretical and practical. The course has to be delivered through lectures (L), Tutorials (T) and Practical (P). The credit C=L+T+P/2. Only about 5.49 percent of the faculty members were aware about the credit of a course.

The faculty members were asked to differentiate between a course, programme and subject. About 35.16 percent of the faculty members were aware about the difference between a course, programme and subject. The about mentioned survey indicates that there is strong need of faculty development programmes for any university.

Effective Teacher Development Programme

For the teacher, professional development programmes to be effective in improving the teacher's classroom performance, the following must be ensured;

Table 2.5: Questions used in the Faculty Survey

<table>
<tr><th>S.No.</th><th>Question</th><th>Answer</th></tr>
<tr><td>1</td><td>Differentiate between lecturing and tutoring.</td><td>Lecturing:<ul><li>The teacher picks up a portion of subject matter, prepare talk and delivers in the class room</li><li>The teacher explains difficult ideas but may not be able to give what students need to know.</li><li>Students are expected to read further on the subject.</li></ul>Tutoring:<ul><li>It is meant to solve student's problems regarding difficult concepts</li></ul></td></tr>
<tr><td>2</td><td>Differentiate between case based learning, problem based learning and outcome based learning.</td><td>Problem Based Learning<ul><li>Links theory and practice by engaging students in real life problems.</li><li>Motivate students to learn by providing a real- world context for examining the issues involved.</li><li>Learning becomes more meaningful and enjoyable in small active groups.</li><li>Encourages students to take responsibility for their own learning and that of their learning group.</li></ul>Case Based Learning<ul><li>Utilizes real or imagined scenarios to teach students about their field of study.</li><li>Links theory and application to real or possible circumstances.</li><li>The questions are created to guide the students through appropriate analysis, synthesis and evaluation.</li></ul>Outcome Based Learning (OBL)<ul><li>OBL is focused not on what the teacher intends to teach but rather the emphasis is on what is the outcome from the learner of that teaching is intended to be.</li><li>The basic premise of OBL is that the teaching and learning activities and assessment methods are constructively aligned with the intended learning outcomes for the course.</li><li>In other words, the outcomes determine the curriculum content, the teaching methods and strategies, and the assessment process.</li><li>The outcomes also provide a framework for curriculum evaluation.</li></ul></td></tr>
<tr><td>3</td><td>Differentiate between questions given in CA and SEE.</td><td>Questions in CA help the student in learning. Questions are used to teach students rather than to just test students

Questions in SEE are for assessing the students.</td></tr>
</table>

(Contd...)

4	Explain the Academic Pedagogy of the University.	• The University follows Semester System of education. • The Programme and Courses are creditised. • The University adopts multidimensional delivery approach. • Evaluation is based on Class Assignments (30% weightage) and Semester End Examination (70%). • For clearing a course, the students should get 40% in CAs and 40% in Semester End Exam/On Demand Exam; however, the total marks should be equal to or more than 50%. • In case the students have failed in CAs, they can resubmit it after making payments as per norms of the University. • The University conducts exam twice a year (June and December). The students have to apply for writing Exam as per schedule announced by the University. • The University conducts On Demand Examination (ODE) as and when required. The students, who have failed in Semester End Exam, are eligible for ODE. • The last semester of all the programmes is devoted to industrial attachment/dissertation/projects.
5	Define and explain credit of a course.	Credit of a course is based on the weekly load of a course. A course may be theoretical as well as theoretical and practical. The course has to be delivered through lectures (L), Tutorials (T) and Practical (P). Credit C=L+T+P/2
6	Differentiate between a course, programme and subject.	**Programme**: Like B.Tech, BBA, M.Sc etc **Course**: A programme consists of several courses each of fixed credits **Subject**: A course contains several subjects (topics) which are covered in the class based on lesson plan (D day)

- Some accountability system by which the teacher accepts responsibility for the quality of student learning.
- Periodic Student and Teacher Assessment that evokes an emotional response that may help stakeholders to act on it. The assessment would provide data based inputs on progress and gaps.
- Targeted teacher trainings that focus on the actual learning gaps found in students (and also among teachers) and how to overcome them – the problem has to be understood first before the solution.
- Training modules that are well structured and include motivational workshops as well as building strength in content and pedagogy.

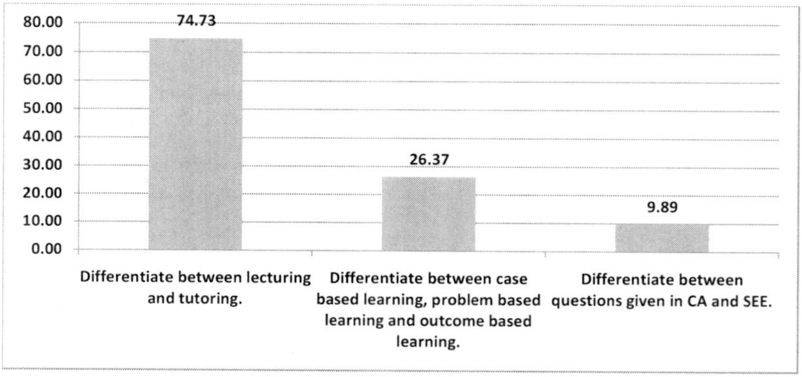

Fig. 2.17: Faculty Response

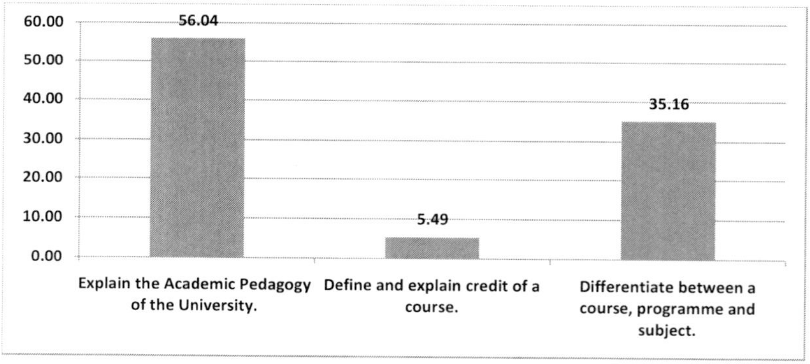

Fig. 2.18: Faculty Response

- The entire training approach to be one of moving the system from role learning to learning with understanding.
- A training plan for the year that is made visible and transparent, so that teachers can apply and get selected based on their needs.
- A teacher professional development system built with teacher mentors and master trainers who are constantly updated in knowledge and skills.
- Research and development of innovative methods involving experts in the field to further the professional development of teachers.
- Capacity building methods that are participatory and develops a culture of shared learning.
- Use of technology to attain scale and provide individual attention to teacher needs.

Need Analyses

Needs Analysis should be done through different methods to identify and determine the type capacity that needs to be built in teachers. Teacher needs for capacity building could be established in the following ways:

Student Assessment

Assessment is an integral part of learning. It helps to determine whether the goals of curriculum are being met or not. Well-designed assessment not only helps leaners to demonstrate what they have learnt, but also enables the teachers to understand:

- Are we teacher what we think we are teaching?
- Are students learning what they are supposed to be learning?
- Is there a way to teach the subject better, for promoting better learning?

Teacher Assessment

- Teachers need insights on where, what and how to improve their own abilities in order to function with effectiveness.
- Teacher assessments would identify common strengths or weaknesses among teachers, provide feedback to individual teachers on their strengths and weakness and improvement areas, and recommend interventional for improvement based on the above.

Background Questionnaires

Along with teacher assessments, information can be collected through background questionnaires, where teachers can be asked to provide their perception of what they most require to effectively enhance their performance.

Focus Group Meetings

Focus group discussions with teachers, students, parents and school management, can be carried out to identify needs.

Class Room Observations

Class room observations are undertaken to understand the following:

- interactions between the teacher and the class
- the class environment, to capture how the tone is set at the beginning of the class

- classroom management
- lesson planning
- any specific teacher activities
- nonverbal behavior of the teacher, and such other factors.

These enable the identification of areas that the teacher is strong in and areas that need improvement.

Best Ways for Capacity Building

Finding the best ways for enhancing capacity of the teachers is to practice research lessons which help the professionals in the following way:

Individual Professional Development

Young teachers many times struggle with problems in the classroom. Their more experienced colleagues can quickly help them with. The practice of observation and feedback provides an effective way of professional development.

Teachers Learning to See Students

A tremendous impact of research lessons is that teachers start to understand how their students think and behave in a classroom. Such an understanding helps developing parameters by which teachers can judge the status of their class. In research lessons, data is often collected on student eagerness, student interaction, even aspects like moments of surprise in the students or excitement. This understanding is probably the most critical aspect of teaching for understanding. Research lessons help the teacher build this understanding steadily through observation and discussion.

Understanding and Designing Assessments

Today's students need to know not only the basic reading and arithmetic skills, but also skills that will allow them to face a world that is continually changing. They must be able to think critically, to analyze, and to make inferences.

It is essential to understand the need for assessment and the role assessment plays in understanding student learning, the link between assessment and instruction, different types of assessment and the criteria for a scientifically designed assessment.

Well-designed assessments are built using good questions. A good question is one that challenges and stimulates students to think deeply and to apply concepts learnt. The ability to ask questions that make students think – both at the time of instruction and assessment, is the hallmark of a good teacher. A good question, correctly framed, can help a teacher understand the through processes of students and how well a student has internalized a concept or mastered a skill.

The types of questions teachers ask influence what and how students study, read, practice, etc. The questions teachers ask should match what the students are expected to learn. That is, assessment should be linked to the goals of a unit, and should be used by the teacher for feedback.

Using Assessment Data for Classroom Progress

Student, teachers and educational planning often have to take decisions without being supported by analysis of authentic data on student learning. However, data from a large scale, scientifically designed and well administered test can be extremely reliable and authentic in developing insights about the status of misconceptions.

Technology Solutions to Capacity Building

Technology solutions enable providing access to professional development activities for a large number of teachers at their convenience. These could be 'e-teacher': The idea is to create a bank of videos of good teachers teaching at least basic and key topics and make them widely available so that they can be used by a large number of teachers.

Need for Having Universities for Teacher Training

Majority of higher educational institutions are not producing industry-specific manpower. They are simply producing bookish diploma holders, graduate, post- graduates, engineers without having the necessary skill or industry- specific knowledge. The result is a huge gap between demand and supply of skilled manpower, industry- specific manpower in the country. The universities have to come forward for meeting demand of skilled manpower.

Our universities and institutions have to develop graduates which are skilled and industry- specific. The vocational training institutions which are having world- class infrastructure may be allowed to join hands with the universities to produce industry- specific graduates. There is a clear gap between Academia-Industry-University.

There are institutions which may be providing best teaching; others may be concentrating on best practices in training while some may be concentrating on placement issues. But, there are very few universities/ institutions which are concentrating on all these aspects holistically. Only a handful of universities can be counted which are having course curriculum as per industry requirement. We do not have sufficient number of universities which can provide higher education as per the industry requirement. There are no clear-cut guidelines available from the regulatory bodies directing the universities to orient their course curriculum as per the need of the hour.

The possible solution could be that our universities start working hand-in- hand with industries and provide industry- specific education. This is only possible when universities go out from their campuses to the industries as well as those vocational training institutions which boast of world- class infrastructure. This will serve twin purpose. The universities will be able to provide industry-specific graduates on one hand, and on the other hand, the existing infrastructure available in such institutions will be utilized to their full potential.

With an objective to impart best teaching to its students, Universities need to have well trained teachers. At present the scenario is as follows:

- There are no specific training institutes/universities which can train the teachers for teaching in higher educational institutes/ universities.
- There are as many methodologies for teaching in higher education as the number of teachers.
- A fresh graduate is employed to teach the students at Diploma level.
- A fresh M.Sc/M.Tech/MBA is employed to teach the students at B.Sc/B.Tech/BBA level.
- A similar scenario is there in all areas.
- The end result is that quality of higher education always remains questionable.

Awareness of the Faculty Members about the Essential Components of Teaching and Learning

We conducted a survey from the faculty members about various aspects of teaching and learning in higher education. 50 questions were administered and the response was collected. Faculty members were told that out from the four options given, only one option is correct. The results are discussed in the following section:

Question 1: For a teacher teaching a class with large strength, which of the techniques is best?

(a) Debate, discussions, practical, (b) Group work with a lecture, (c) Lecture and class notes, (d) Self-study and asking questions?

The faculty exposure to various questions seems to be in the poor state. For example, for question 1, out of the four options given, only 17.96 percent of the faculty members have opted for option (c) which is the correct answer. The teachers could not apply their mind that debate, discussion and practical i.e. option (a) cannot be implemented in a class of large strength, 28.21 percent teachers opted for option (a). Surprisingly, 41.03 percent of teachers opted for option (b) i.e. for group work with a lecture. They forgot to realize that group work and lecture cannot go simultaneously. Even 1.28 percent of the faculty members opted for option (d) and 11.54 percent faculty members could not attempt the question. This is shown in Fig. 2.19.

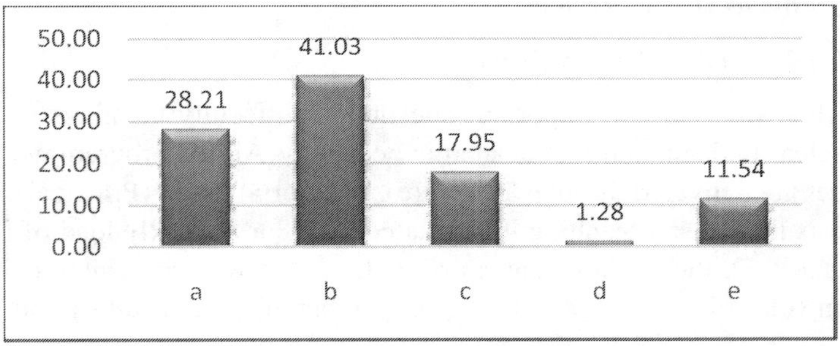

Fig. 2.19: Best Technique for Teaching (percent)

Question 2: Talking and indiscipline in classroom is an indication of—?

(a) Indisciplined students, (b) Boredom caused by repetitiveness, (c) Confusion about things taught, (d) Not summarizing lecture points

Question 2 was very important and deals with the indiscipline in classroom which has become a common feature nowadays. Usually, students get bored in the classroom if the same thing is repeated many times. Though re-enforcement is also necessary but within permissible limits. Thus the right option was (b) but it was opted by only 11.54 percent of the faculty members. It may be seen that about 55.13 percent of the faculty members opted for option (c) which says "Confusion about things taught"; 11.54 percent of the faculty members opted for option (d) and 19.23 percent faculty members opted not to answer the question, meaning thereby they are not clear about the problem. This is shown in Fig. 2.20.

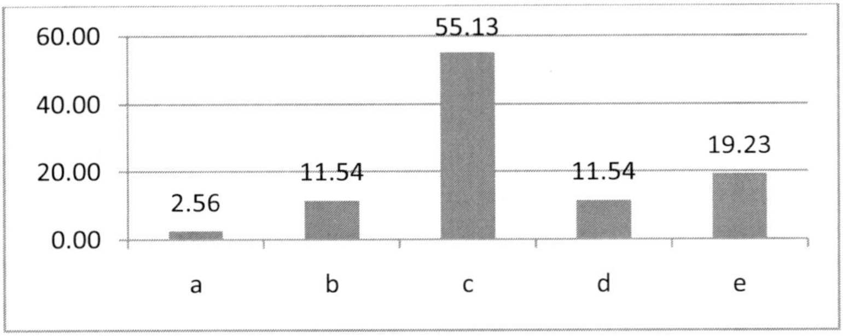

Fig. 2.20: Talking and Indiscipline in Classroom

Question 3. A course has weekly teaching load of L=2, T=0, P=2, the credit of this course is

(a) 4, (b) 2, (c) 3, (d) None

This was again an important question. The faculty members should have clear understanding of academic pedagogy. All the programmes and courses are delivered through L (lecture), T(Tutorial) and P(Practical). The credit is the weekly teaching load of a course. For a weekly load of L=2, T=0 and P=2, the credit of the course is L+T+P/2 which is equal to 3 i.e. option (c) which was opted by 91.03 percent of the faculty members.

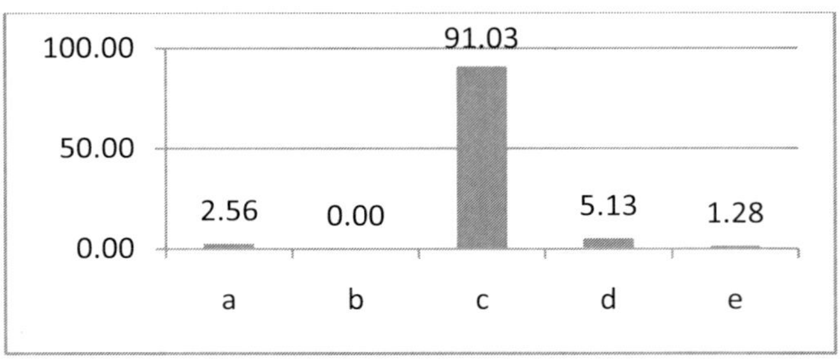

Fig. 2.21: Credit of a Course

Remaining about 9 percent of the faculty members either opted for option (a), (d) or even not opted for any option. This is shown in Fig. 2.21.

Question 4. Which subject explains and appreciates the contribution of the past to the present?

(a) Economics, (b) Geography, (c) History, (d) Sociology

Question 4 was related to linking the past knowledge to the present one. Obviously, the correct option was (c) i.e History and it was opted by about 67.95 percent of the faculty members. About 10.26 percent of the faculty members opted for option (d) which has nothing to do with the

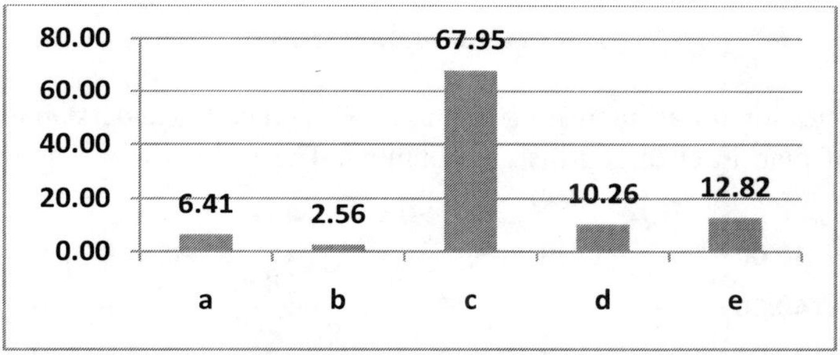

Fig. 2.22: Contribution of the Past to the Present

contribution of the past to the present. It is suspiring that about 6.41 percent of the faculty members opted for (a) i.e. economics, 12.82 percent of the faculty members remained neutral i.e. they don't have clear choice. This is shown in Fig. 2.22.

Question 5. What is the use of study material in a class?

(a) To achieve learning objectives, (b) To delimit what is to be taught, (c) To explain ideas and concepts, (d) Set new standards

The use of study material for the teachers as well as for the students in the class is very important. The teachers should have clear ideas. The teachers gave different options as shown in Fig. 13.5. About 44.87 percent of the faculty members gave the option (a) i.e. "to achieve learning objectives" which is true. About 25.64 percent of the faculty opted for option (c) i.e. "to explain ideas and concepts". About 16.67 percent of the faculty members gave no option. This is shown in Fig. 2.23.

Question 6. Which subject tries to understand the role of man in changing his environment?

(a) Biology, (b) Geography, (c) History, (d) Political Science

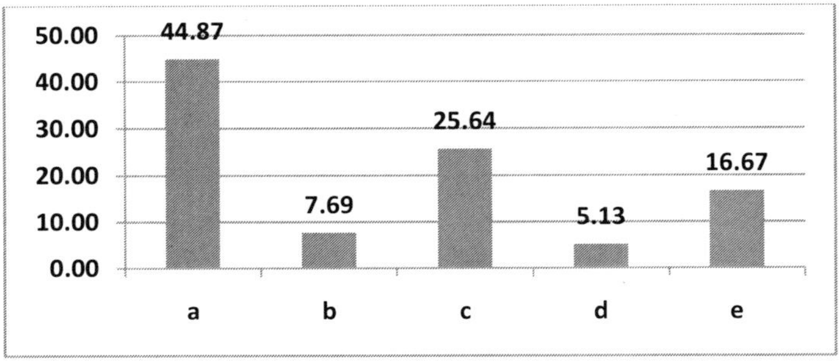

Fig. 2.23: Use of Study Material

Question 6 was interesting because it was related to understanding the role of man in changing his environment. The right option was (b) i.e.

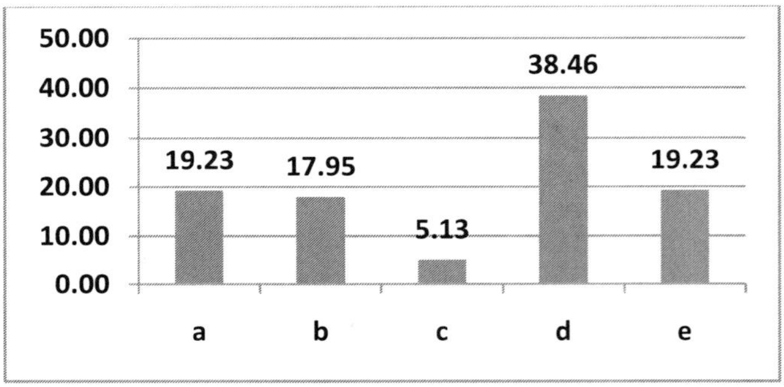

Fig. 2.24: Role of man in changing his environment

geography and it was opted by about 17.95 percent of the faculty members only. About 38.46 percent of the faculty members opted for option (d) i.e. Political Science, about 19.23 percent of the faculty members for option (a) i.e. biology and 19.23 percent of the faculty members remained neutral. This is shown in Fig. 2.24.

Question 7. Why is faculty development programme necessary?

(a) Increase teaching skills, (b) Understand methods of university organization, (c) Upgrade knowledge of content, (d) All the above

The faculty members seems to be aware about faculty development programme and its need. About 88.46 percent teachers opted for option (d) which is correct because FDP is necessary for (a), (b) and (c). This is shown in Fig. 2.25.

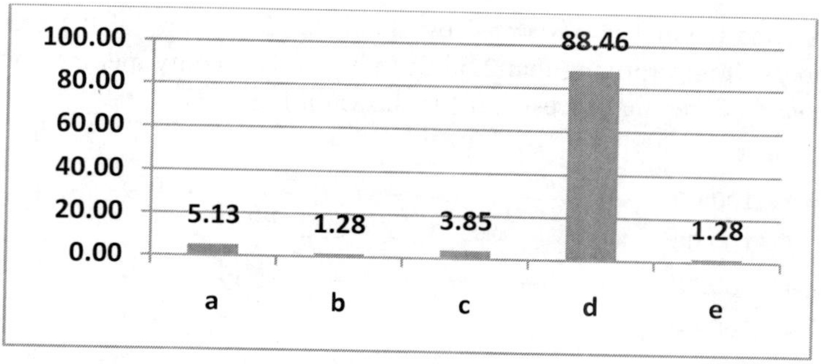

Fig. 2.25: Faculty Development Programme

Question 8. Study of _______ improves a student's ability to experiment and analyse the subject

(a) History, (b) Language, (c) Mathematics, (d) Science

This question was related to test the faculty about a subject which improves students ability to experiment and analyses. The right option was (d) i.e. science and it was opted by about 76.92 percent of the faculty members; 11.54 percent of the faculty members opted for option (b) i.e. language and 2.56 percent of the faculty members gave no answer. This is shown in Fig. 2.26.

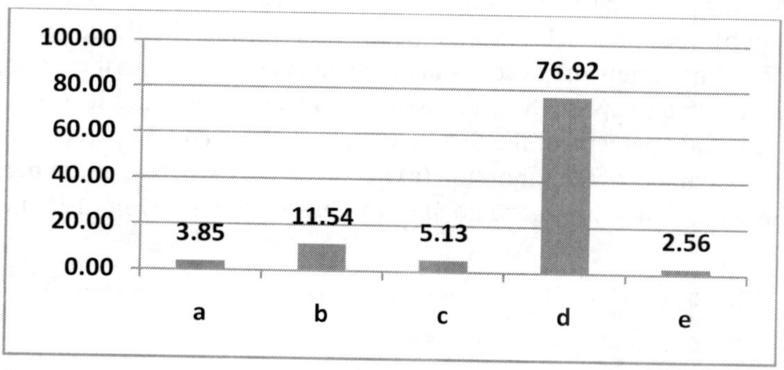

Fig. 2.26: Study of Science

Question 9. Learning

(a) Starts at 10 years of age, (b) Starts at 30 years of age, (c) Starts at 50 years of age, (d) is life long process

This question was asked to have an idea about faculty's views over learning process. We know that learning is a lifelong process; the right option was (d) and it was opted by about 96.15 percent of the faculty members. It is surprising that 2.56 percent of the faculty members were not aware of leaning process. This is shown in Fig. 2.27.

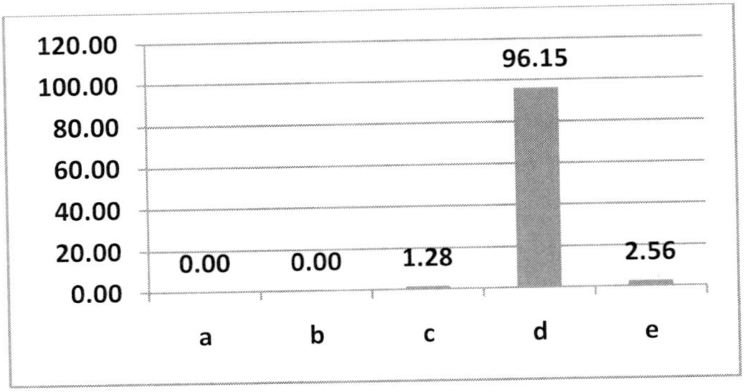

Fig. 2.27: Learning Process

Question10. Having variety of questions in a question paper increases its —

(a) Objectivity, (b) Reliability, (c) Validity, (d) Difficulty

This question was related to identify a suitable way for testing the students. There are several types of question papers. Why we should have variety of questions in a question papers, the faculty should have a clear concept. The variety of questions in a question paper increases the reliability of the question paper. Thus, the option (b) was correct and it was opted only by 25.64 percent of the faculty members. About 42.31 percent of the faculty members opted for option (a) i.e. objectivity whereas 23.08 percent of the faculty members gave no answer. This is shown in Fig. 2.28.

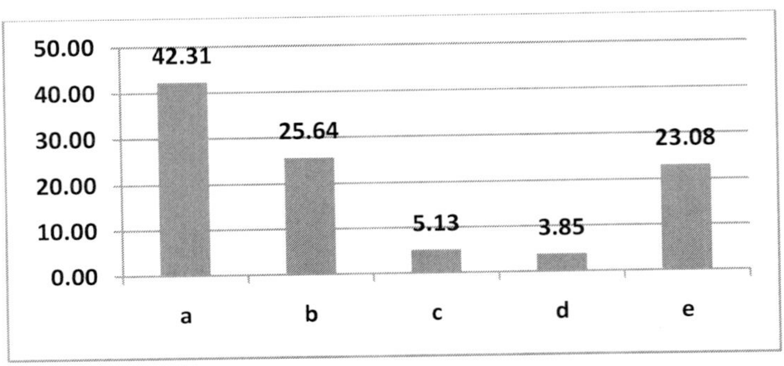

Fig. 2.28: Variety of Questions in a Question Paper

Question 11. — is the quality of a good teacher.

(a) Control over emotions, (b) Good command over the subject, (c) Physical strength, (d) Sense of humour

The faculty members should be aware about the qualities of a good teacher. A good teacher should have good command over the subject and at the same time the relationship with the students should be cordial and academic. It is nice to see that about 71.79 percent of the faculty members used the option (b) i.e good command over the subject. About 16.67 percent of the faculty members said that sense of humor is more important whereas 2.56 percent of the faculty members said that control over emotions is the good quality. This is shown in Fig. 2.29.

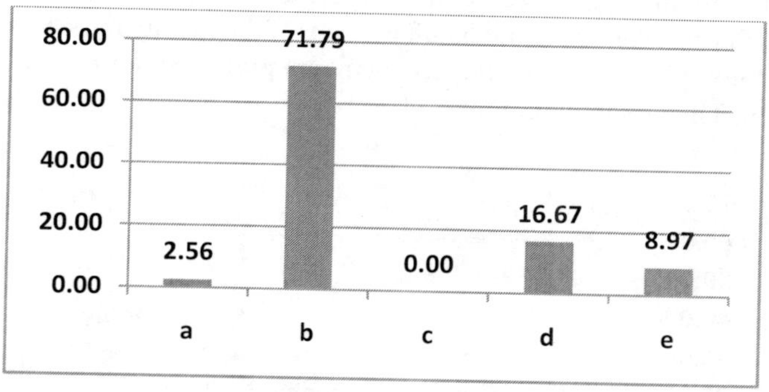

Fig. 2.29: Quality of a Good Teacher

Question 12. Which of the following is true about the ways of learning for students?

(a) Speed of learning is same for all students, (b) Each student has a unique learning style, (c) Students follow the way other students learn, (d) All students immediately follow teacher's instruction

The faculty members of higher education need to understand the different ways of learning for students. Each student has a unique learning style and this was stated by about 83.33 percent of faculty members. This is shown in Fig. 2.30. About 11.54 percent of the faculty members could not express their views.

Question 13. How should a teacher be related to his peers?

(a) Should copy other teacher's style, (b) Follow independent views, (c) Should not intervene in other's work, (d) Suggest each other the effective ways to teach

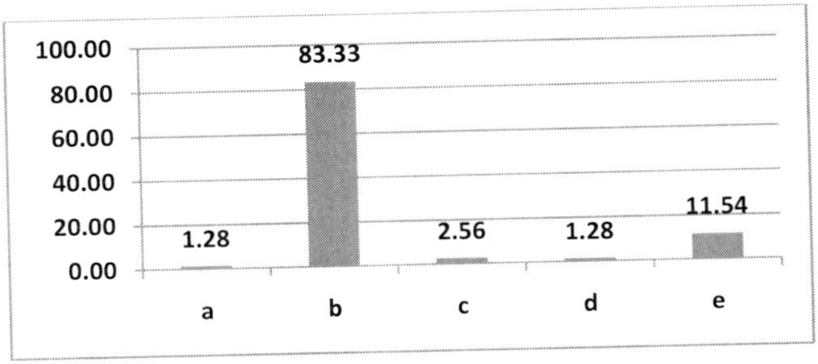

Fig. 2.30: Ways of Learning for the Students

How should a teacher be related to his peers is very important. The teachers should suggest each other the effective ways to teach, i.e option (d) which was given by about 65.38 percent of the faculty members. Here, about 29.49 percent of the faculty members preferred not to answer this question. This is shown in Fig. 2.31.

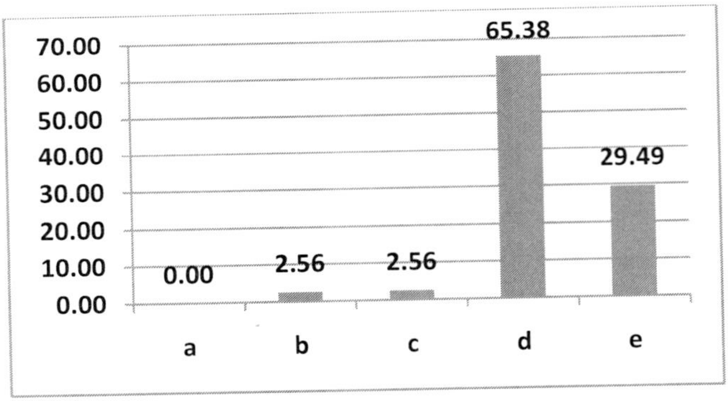

Fig. 2.31: Teachers behavior to his Peers

Question 14. A teacher should encourage the students to

(a) Score best grades in the class, (b) Improve their own capabilities, (c) Obey teacher's command, (d) Submit home-work on time

This question was related to asking the faculty members to answer the question "A teacher should encourage the students to .....". Infect, there could be several options but we gave only four options. Option (a) was "to score best grades in the class" which is the true option. This was opted only by 8.97 percent of the faculty members. The option (b), "to improve that own capabilities" was opted by about 83.33 percent of the faculty members.

About 5.13 percent of the faculty members opted for option (c) i.e. "obey teacher's command". This is shown in Fig. 2.32.

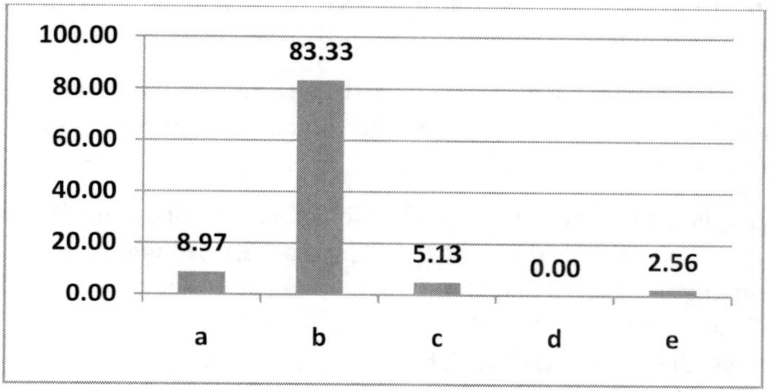

Fig. 2.32: A Teacher Should Encourage the Students

Question 15. How can a teacher develop creativity in himself and in the students?

(a) By giving new up-to-date information, (b) By playing thought provoking games, (c) By praising any creative work, (d) Set new tasks

This question was related to asking teachers 'how can a teacher develop creativity in himself and in the students?. About 39.74 percent of the faculty members opted for option (c) i.e. "by praising any creative work" which is not the correct option. About 2.56 percent of the faculty members opted for the option (b), i.e. "by playing thought provoking games" which is correct option. About 20.51 percent of the faculty members said that "setting new tasks", option (d) is the right choice whereas about 23.08 percent of the faculty members opted for option (a) i.e. "by giving new up-to-date

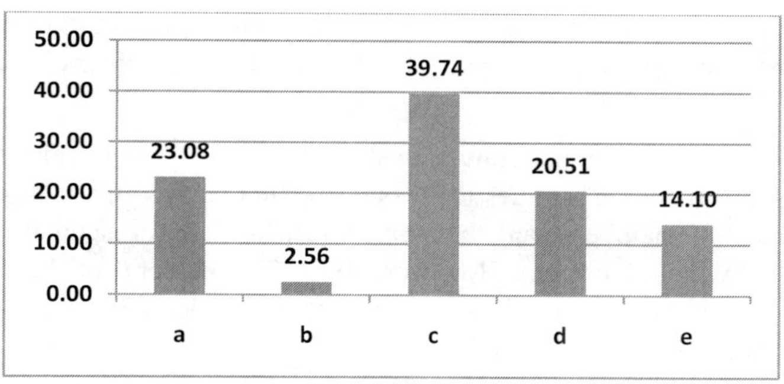

Fig. 2.33: Development of Creativity

information" which is correct. Thus, there seems to be no clarity among the faculty members. This is shown in Fig. 2.33.

Question 16. What is the best way for a teacher to resolve the problems in a class?

(a) Ask for other teacher's opinion, (b) Depends on one's own opinion, (c) Think on suggestions offered by the students and implement the good ones, (d) None of the above

What is the best way for a teacher to resolve the problems in a class? This type of question is daily faced by the teachers of higher education. It is heartening to observe that about 73. 08 percent of the faculty members opted for option (c), i.e. "think on suggestions offered by the students and implement the good ones" which is correct. About 8.91 percent of the faculty members said that none of the options given are correct whereas about 16.67 percent of the faculty members gave no response (Fig. 2.34).

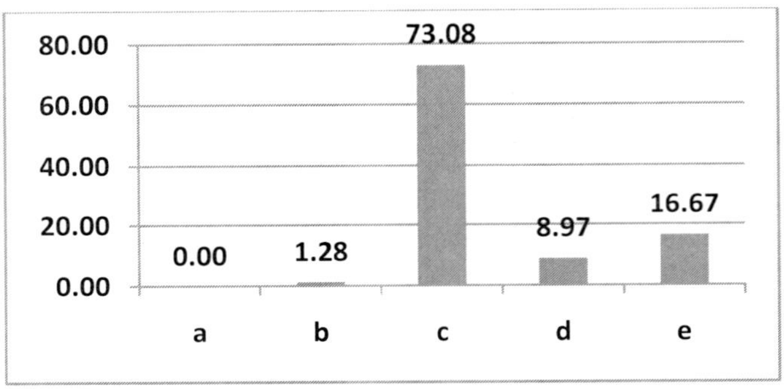

Fig. 2.34: Ways to Resolve Problems in Class

Question 17. How would you make your students independent?

(a) Give responsibility to everyone, (b) Giving orders and expecting obedience, (c) Ignoring their petty fights, (d) Solving their problems for them

The students of higher education should be developed as independent responsible citizens. This question was related to this. About 89.74 percent of the faculty members said that option (a), i.e. "give responsibility to everyone" which is correct. However, about 5.13 percent of the faculty members said that option (d) i.e. "solving their problems for them" is the right option. This is shown in Fig. 2.35.

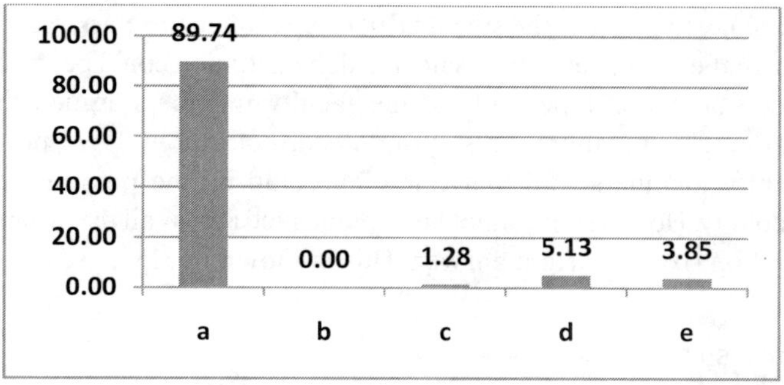

Fig. 2.35: Ways of Making Students Independent

Question 18. Why is 'learning by doing' important?

(a) It develops interest among students, (b) It maintains discipline, (c) It keeps students busy, (d) It promotes meaningful learning

The question "why is learning by doing important" is very important About 58.97 percent of the faculty members opted for option (a)., i.e. "it develops interest among students", which is correct option. About 33.33 percent of the faculty members also opted for option (d) i.e. it promotes meaningful learning. This is shown in Fig. 2.36.

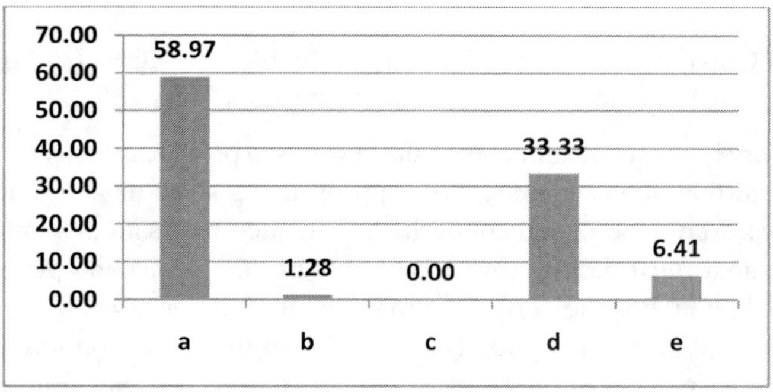

Fig. 2.36: Learning by Doing

19. You want to ensure participation of more students in class. Which of the following methods of teaching would you adopt?

(a) Demonstration, (b) Discussion, (c) Recitation, (d) Role-play

One of the serious problem being faced by the higher educational institutions is that students are not coming to attend the classes. There could be several reasons for this. We asked the faculty members the teaching methodology to increase the students' participation in the class. About 15.38 percent of the faculty members said that demonstration could be the possible method. About 20.51 percent of the faculty members argued that it is discussion which matters. This option is correct. About 39.74 percent of the faculty members said that role-play could be the possible teaching methodology. However, it cannot be implemented across all the programmes. Thus option (b) is the right answer. This is shown in Fig. 2.37.

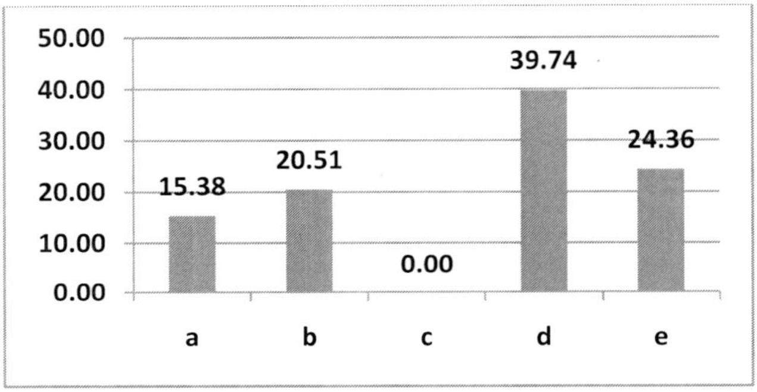

Fig. 2.37: Increasing Student's Participation in Class

20. To make learning effective, a goal must be meaningful in terms of ?

(a) Objectives of the curriculum, (b) Intellectual ideas, (c) Standards of others, (d) The needs and purposes of students

Every higher educational institution wants to provide effective learning. We asked the faculty members the appropriate goal to make the learning effective. About 34.62 percent of the faculty members said that option (d), i.e. the goal must be meaningful in terms of "the needs and purposes of students", which is the correct option. About 19.23 percent of the faculty members opted for the option (a) which is not the correct option whereas about 34.62 percent of the faculty members gave no answer (Fig. 2.38).

21. Which of the following items of information are important about students to motivate them for studies?

(a) Learning style, (b) Personality, (c) Socio-cultural background, (d) All of the above

If a teacher wants to motivate his students for studies, he should know the students' learning style, personality and socio-cultural background. The right option was therefore (d) and it was opted by 57.69 percent of the

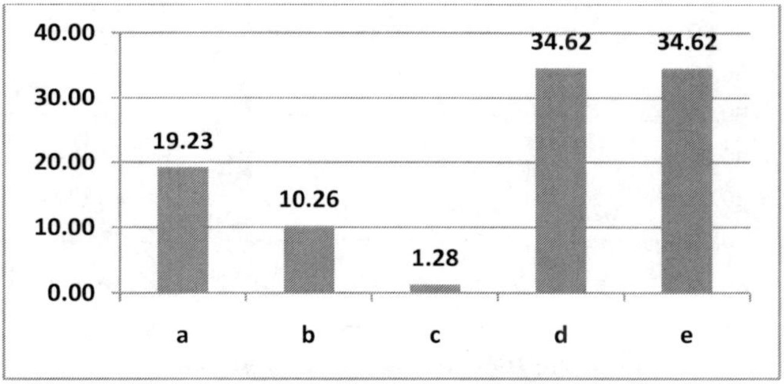

Fig. 2.38: Making Learning Effective

faculty members. About 19.23 percent of the faculty members said that it is the learning style only which is important whereas about 20.51 percent of the faculty members gave no answer. This is shown in Fig. 2.39.

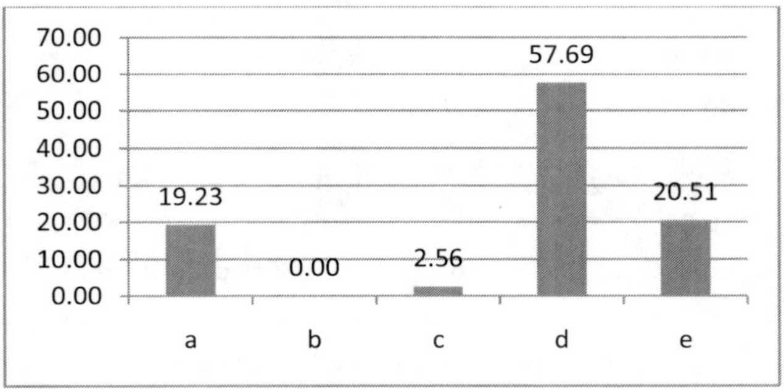

Fig. 2.39: Student's Motivation for Study

22. Which of the following is highest academic qualification?

(a) MA, (b) M. Sc., (c) M. Phil, (d) Ph. D

Majority of the faculty members (92.31 percent) rightly said that option (d) is correct. This is shown in Fig. 2.40.

23. _______ is the apex institution involved in the planned and coordinated development of the teacher education in the country.

(a) UGC, (b) NCERT, (c) NCTE, (d) AICTE

In our country, NCTE is the apex institution involved in the planned and coordinated development of the teacher education. About 84.62 percent of the faculty members rightly opted for option (c). However, about 8.97

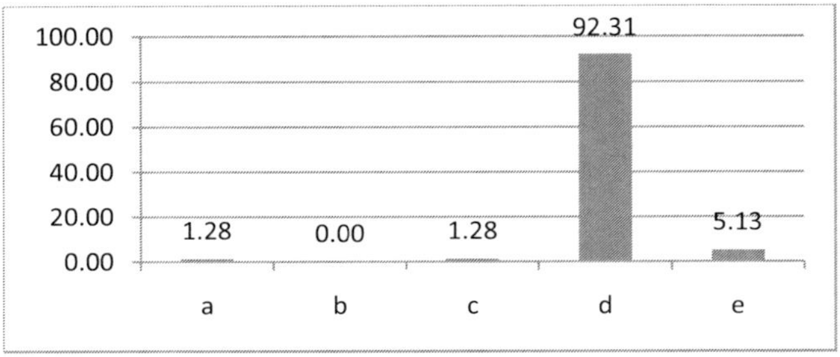

Fig. 2.40: Highest Academic Qualification

percent of the faculty members opted for option (b). This is shown in Fig. 2.41.

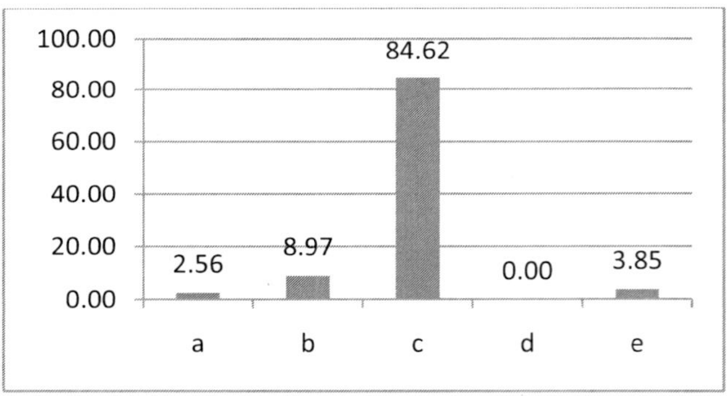

Fig. 2.41: Teacher Education Authority

24. You want to develop cooperation and team spirit in students. Which activities would you propose?

(a) Art, (b) Debate, (c) Project work, (d) Quiz

Faculty members should be aware about the activities which are able to develop cooperation and team spirit among the students. About 82.05 percent of the faculty members rightly opted for option (c), i.e. project work (Fig. 2.42).

25. Why environment awareness is necessary at all stages of education?

(a) Important for human survival, (b) Environment varies from region to region, (c) Man must control and change environment, (d) None of the above

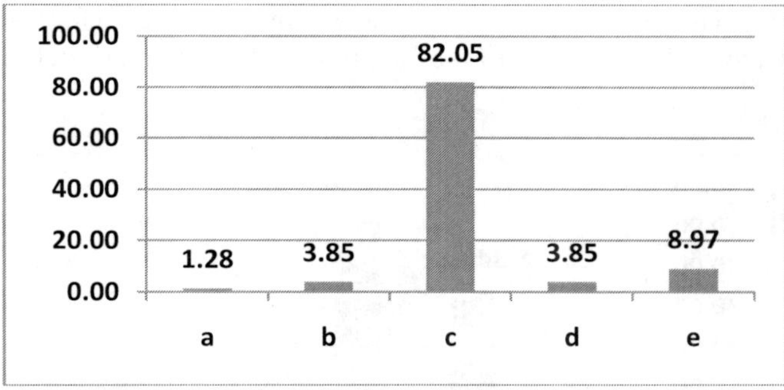

Fig. 2.42:Cooperation and Team Spirit in Students

The environmental education has become very important for the teachers as well as for the students. The question why environment awareness is necessary at all stages of education was not correctly answered by any faculty member. About 61.54 of the faculty members opted for the option (a) i.e. it is "important for human survival", which is not true option. About 14.10 percent of the faculty members opted for the option (c) i.e. "man must control and change environment", which is again wrong option. The correct option was (b) i.e. "environment varies from region to region" and hence the environmental awareness is necessary at all stages of education (Fig. 2.43).

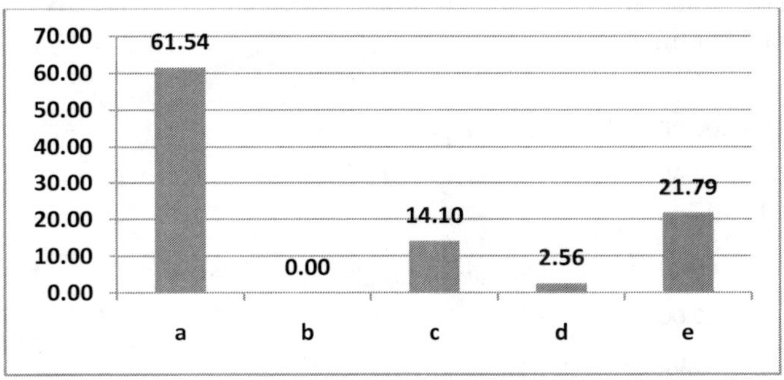

Fig. 2.43: Environmental Awareness

26. Which of the following is Doordarshan's Educational Television Channel?

(a) Gurukul, (b) Gyan Bharati, (c) Gyan Darshan, (d) Vidya

The correct option for this question was option (c) i.e. Gyan Darshan and about 52.56 percent of the faculty members opted for this (Fig. 13.26).

However, about 34.62 percent of the faculty members opted for the option (b) and about 11.54 percent of the faculty members remained neutral (Fig. 2.44).

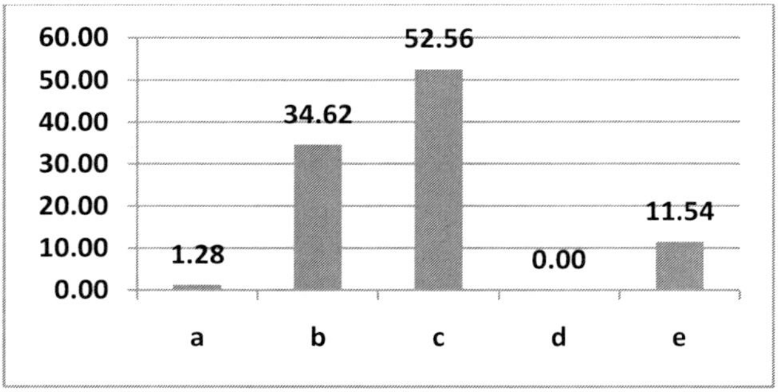

Fig. 2.44: Doordarshan's Educational Television Channel

27. SWOT stands for

(a) Survey, Weakness, Open, Trends, (b) Strength, Weakness, Opportunities, Threats, (c) Summer, Winter, Offspring, Trends, (d) Solar, Water, Operation, Table

It was expected that all the faculty members are aware of SWOT. However, about 84.62 percent of the faculty members opted for the correct option (b) as shown in Fig. 2.45. About 8.97 percent of the faculty members remained neutral.

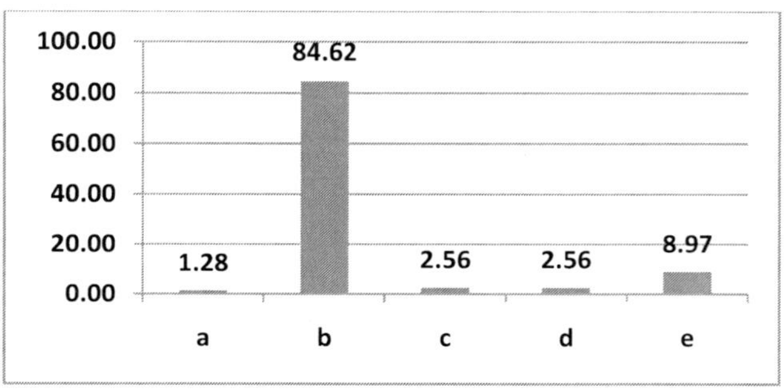

Fig. 2.45: SWOT Analysis

28. For __________, experimentation is the standard procedure to know the truth.

(a) Public Administration, (b) Geography, (c) Archeology, (d) Science

This was a straight question to know the scientific view of the faculty members. About 62.82 percent of the faculty members opted for the correct option (d) whereas about 10.26 percent of the faculty members opted for the option (a) i.e. public administration. It is not understood how public administration can tell us the truth. About 19.23 percent of the faculty members remained neutral (Fig. 2.46).

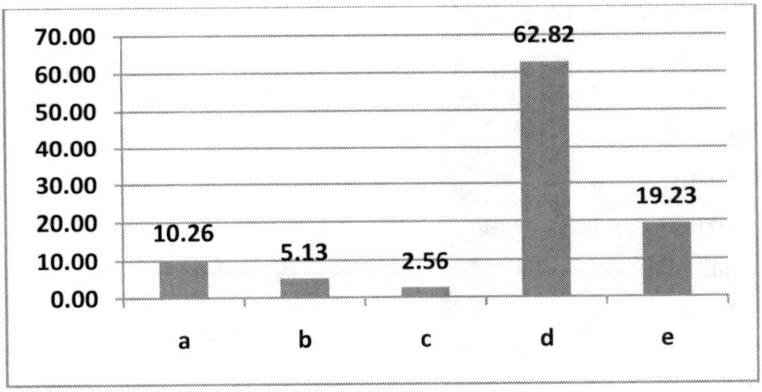

Fig. 2.46: Experimentation for Truth

29. Monad University is a _________

(a) Employment University, (b) Rural University, (c) Private University, (d) State University

Monad University is a private university and all faculty members should be aware of this. However, only about 89.74 percent of the faculty members were aware of this because they opted for option (c). About 9 percent of the faculty members gave wrong option which is a serious issue (Fig. 2.47).

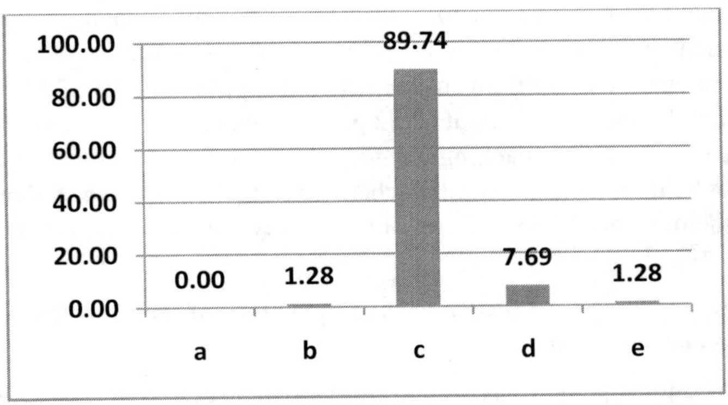

Fig. 2.47: Monad University

30. Which of the following is not a type of university?

(a) Central, (b) Crown, (c) Deemed, (d) State

It is expected from each and every faculty members that they are aware about the types of the universities in the country. There are universities designated as Central, Deemed and State. But there are no Crown universities. About 96.15 percent of the faculty members gave the right option (b) as shown in Fig. 2.48.

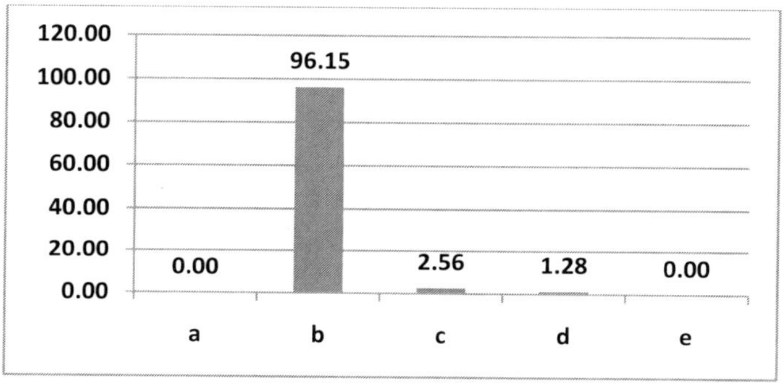

Fig. 2.48: Types of Universities

31. The most important elements in teaching is

(a) Relationship between teachers and students, (b) Subject matter, (c) Teaching techniques and aids used (d) Student's knowledge

There are three important elements in teaching and learning; Teachers, Students and Subject Matter. All these are interrelated. The teachers should have a solid understanding and command of the subject matter. The students should have the right attitude for learning. But, the important link is between the student and teachers. They should have a strong academic relationship. Thus option (a) was the right answer which was opted by only 17.95 percent of the faculty members. About 62.82 percent of the faculty members opted for the option (c) i.e. teaching techniques and aids used (Fig. 2.49). This will not help the students until teachers go to the level of the students and teach them. About 15.38 percent of the faculty members remained neutral (Fig. 2.49).

32. ____________ tests measure the extent of students learning in a given content area.

(a) Achievement Tests, (b) Aptitude Tests, (c) Diagnostic Tests, (d) Readiness Tests

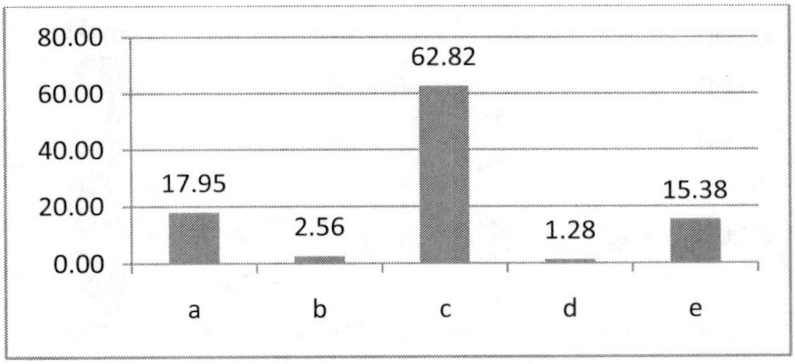

Fig. 2.49: Important Elements in Teaching

There exist several methods for the certification of the students. This question was related to which test measures the extent of students learning in a given content area. The right answer was option (a), i.e. achievement tests and this was opted by about 12.82 percent of the faculty members only. About 38.46 percent of the faculty members opted for the option (b) i.e. aptitude tests whereas about 42.31 percent of the faculty members just ignored the question (Fig. 2.50).

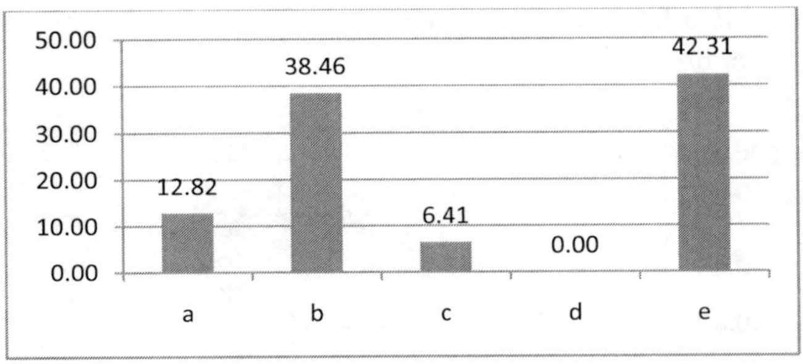

Fig. 2.50: Student Learning in a given Area

33. _______ is the degree to which a test measures what it is supposed to measure?

(a) Objectivity, (b) Reliability, (c) Validity, (d) Usability

This was a difficult question and even science and engineering faculty members could not give the right answer. About 56.41 percent of the faculty members just ignored the question. Only about 7.69 percent of the faculty members gave the right option (c). About 20.51 percent of the faculty members opted for option (a) i.e. objectivity (Fig. 2.51).

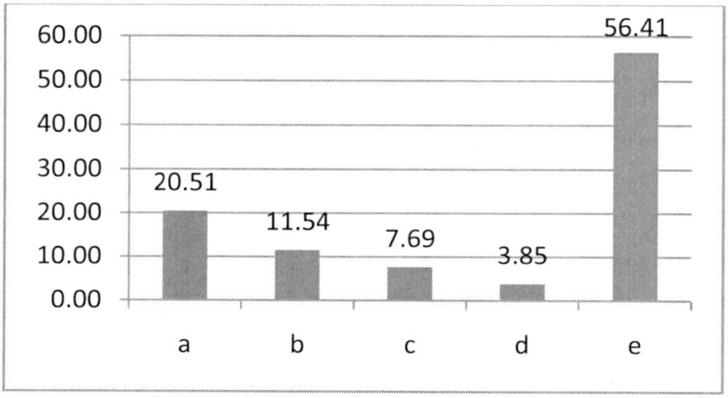

Fig. 2.51: Degree of Test Measurement

34. SQ3R stands for

(a) System, Quality, Recall, Review, Read, (b) Summarise, Question, Read, Review, Recall, (c) Syllabus, Question, Review, Recall, Read, (d) Survey, Question, Read, Recall, Review

SQ3R is an important technique for teaching and learning in higher education. Majority of the faculty members (91.03 percent) gave the right answer i.e. option (d) as shown in Fig. 2.52.

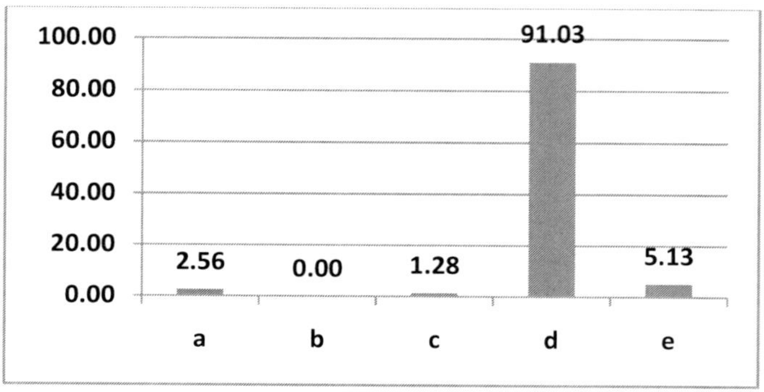

Fig. 2.52: SQ3R

35. The highest thinking level is

(a) Comprehension, (b) Application, (c) Synthesis, (d) Evaluation

The Bloom's Taxonomy is very important and useful for teaching and learning. It deals with 6 thinking levels, 3 are passive ones and remaining 3 are active ones. The sequence of thinking levels is knowledge, comprehension, application, analysis, synthesis and evaluation. This means that knowledge is the lowest thinking level and evaluation is the highest level of thinking. About 60.26 percent of the faculty members gave the right option (d). About 15.38 percent of the faculty members gave option (a) which is not correct while 16.67 percent of the faculty members remained neutral (Fig. 2.53).

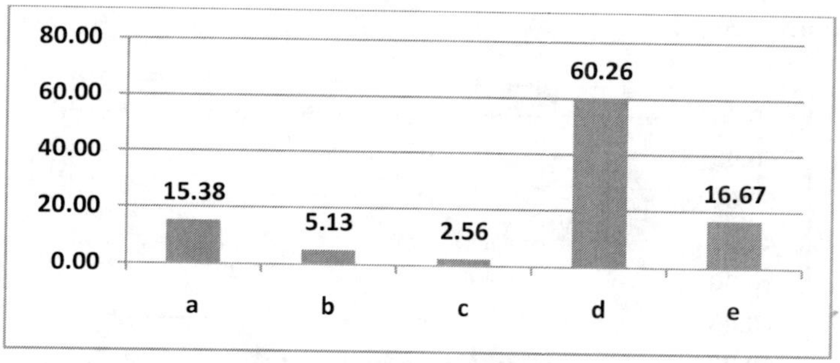

Fig. 2.53: Highest Thinking Level

36. The learning via knowledge is able to

(a) Recall, (b) Restate, (c) Remember, (d) All the above

This is related to the study skills. We are aware that learning via knowledge is able to recall, restate and remember. About 62.82 percent of the faculty members gave the right answer by choosing option (d). However, about 20.51 percent of the faculty members opted for the option (c) whereas 12.82 percent of the faculty members could not answer (Fig. 2.54).

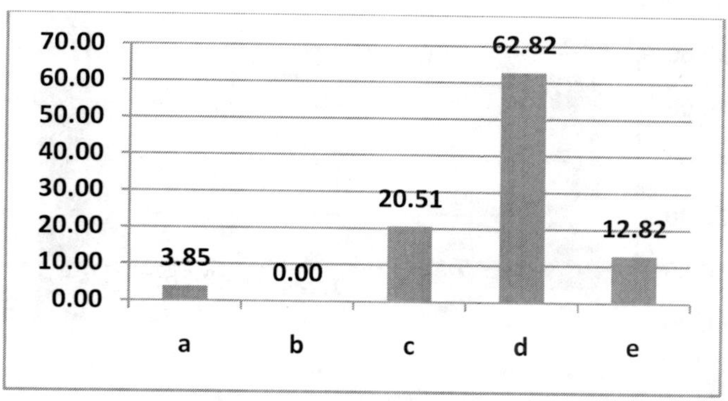

Fig. 2.54: Learning via Knowledge

37. The lowest thinking level is

(a) Knowledge, (b) Comprehension, (c) Synthesis, (d) None of these

As explained in question no 35, the lowest thinking level is knowledge. About 57.69 percent of the faculty members opted for the option (a) which is correct. About 24.36 percent of the faculty members said none of the option is correct whereas about 12.82 percent of the faculty members remained neutral (Fig. 2.55).

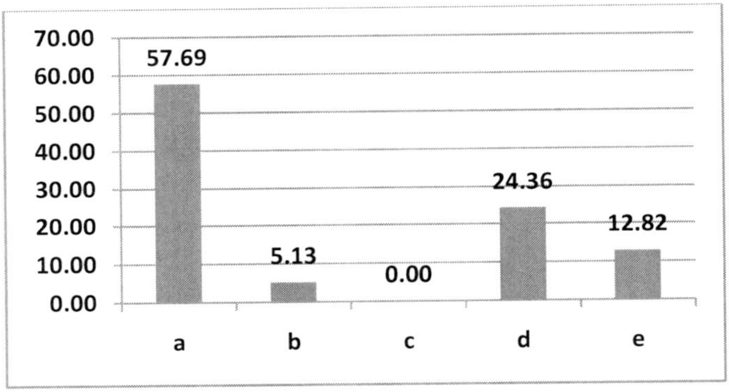

Fig. 2.55: Lowest Thinking Level

38. Which of the following research types aims at immediate application?

(a) Action Research, (b) Conceptual Research, (c) Empirical Research, (d) Fundamental Research

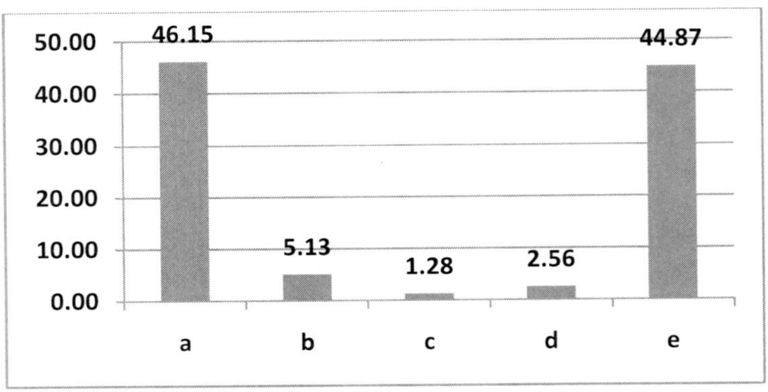

Fig. 2.56: Research for Immediate Application

In higher education institutions, especially the Universities, the faculty members are supposed to do research (research for improving teaching and course curriculum and research for academic publications). They should be aware about which type of research will give immediate results. The right answer was option (a), i.e. application research. Surprisingly, about 44.87 percent of the faculty members gave no answer (Fig. 2.56).

39. Mind mapping refers to:

(a) An action plan for an adventure, (b) A technique to enhance comprehension, (c) Drawing the picture of mind, (d) Studying the functions of mind

Faculty members should be able to read the minds of the students. The answer to this mind mapping question was option (b), i.e. " a technique to enhance comprehension". This was opted by about 50 percent of the faculty members. About 38.46 percent of the faculty members ignored this question (Fig. 2.57).

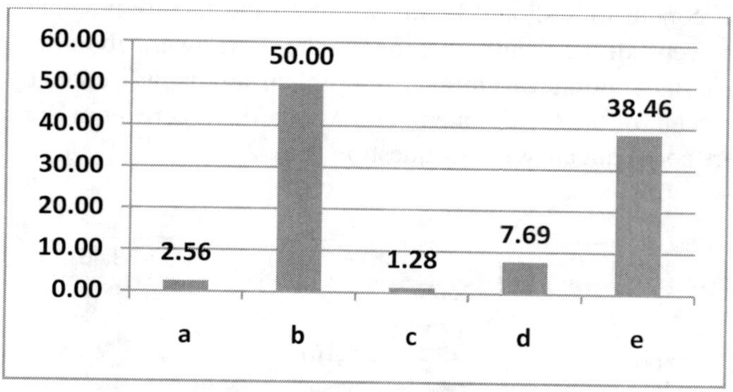

Fig. 2.57: Mind Mapping

40. What does curriculum mean?

(a) A collection of all the curricular activities, (b) A collection of the experiences that university wants students to learn, (c) A list of compulsory and optional subjects, (d) None of these

Faculty members should be aware about the course curriculum, its development and objectives. However, about 15.38 percent of the faculty members could give the correct option (b). On the contrary, about 46.15 percent of the faculty members opted for the option (a), i.e. "a collection of all the curricular activities". About 23.08 percent of the faculty members gave no option (Fig. 2.58).

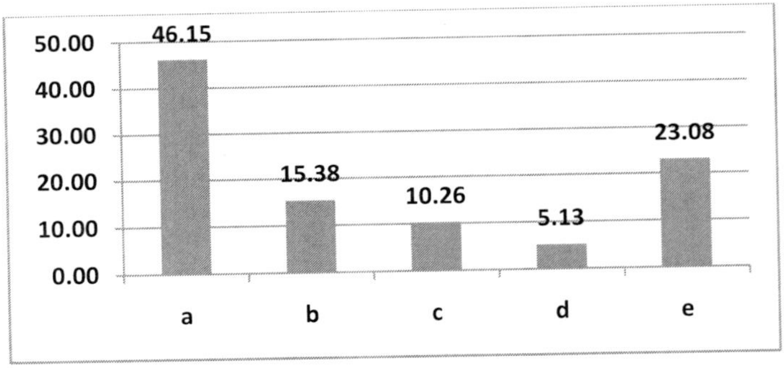

Fig. 2.58: Curriculum

41. Through which activity do we transform available information to reach conclusions?

(a) Motivating, (b) Problem solving, (c) Reasoning, (d) Thinking

The activities through which we can transform available information to reach conclusions should be known to all the faculty members. Only 14.10 percent of the faculty members seem to be aware about it because they gave right option (c). Option (b), problem solving was opted by about 30.77 percent of the faculty members. About 38.46 percent of the faculty members could not answer this question (Fig. 2.59).

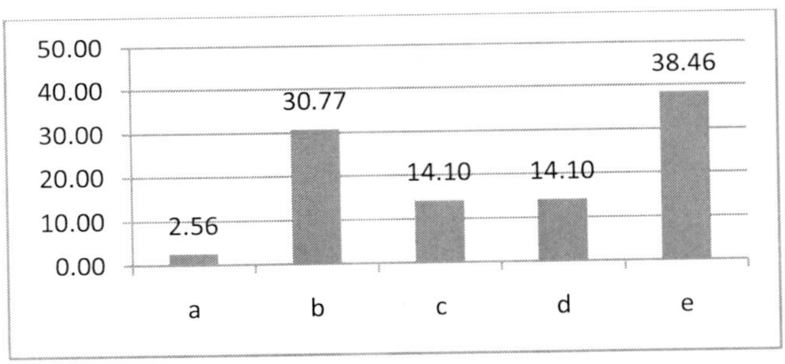

Fig. 2.59: Activity for Transforming Available Information To Conclusions

42. Which of the following would you use to shape the habits?

(a) Tutoring, (b) Teaching, (c) Training, (d) None of these

The mechanism for shaping the habits should also be known to the faculty members. About 52.56 percent of the faculty members gave the correct option (c) i.e. training. About 32.05 percent of the faculty members gave no option (Fig. 2.60).

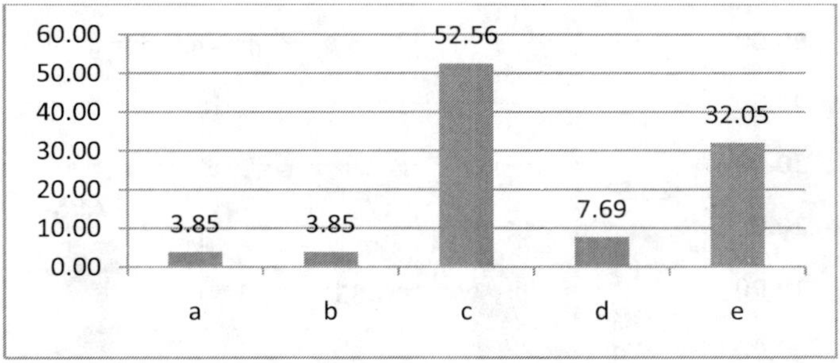

Fig. 2.60: Shaping the Habits

43. A consultant conducts the evaluation process in a particular way, which of the following decides that?

(a) Business analysis, (b) Quality management, (c) Project management, (d) Terms of reference

It is widely known that if a consultant conducts the evaluation process in a particular way, only terms of reference can decide that. Only 2.56 percent of the faculty members could answer this question. A majority of the faculty members (62.82 percent) gave no answer (Fig. 2.61).

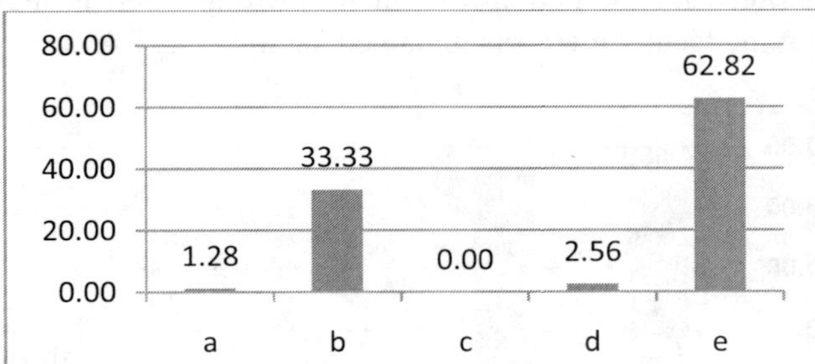

Fig. 2.61: Factors for the Evaluation Process

44. A teacher should be _______ towards his students?

(a) Tolerant, (b) Outspoken, (c) Supreme, (d) Sympathetic

A teacher should be tolerant towards the students. About 20.51 percent of the faculty members opted for the correct option (a). About 43.59 percent of the faculty members said that a teacher should be sympathetic towards his students whereas about 17.95 percent of the faculty members remained neutral (Fig. 2.62).

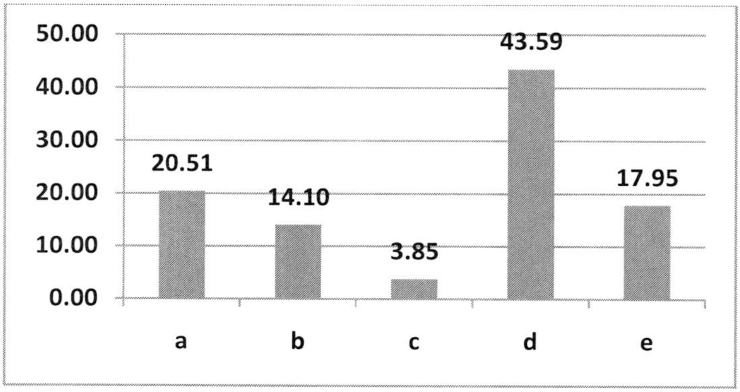

Fig. 2.62: Teacher Behaviour towards Students

45. It's your first day in a class, what would you do?

(a) Evaluate the subject, (b) Introduce yourself to the students, (c) Smile at everyone, (d) Ask the students to stay disciplined

It is a natural process that in a first day in any class, teachers should introduce themselves to the students. About 46.15 percent of the faculty members were correct. However, about 43.59 percent of the faculty members opted for the option (a) which is wrong whereas about 10.26 percent of the faculty members remained neutral (Fig. 2.63).

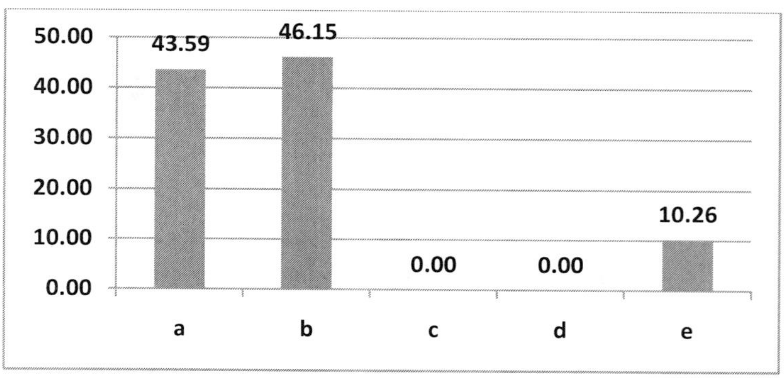

Fig. 2.63: Teacher on First Day in Class

46. The assignment questions are useful for

(a) Teaching students, (b) Testing students, (c) Making students aware, (d) None of the above

Assignments are having teaching values. That is why, the assignment questions are set in such a way that they help the students in teaching and learning rather than to test them. Thus, the right option was (a), i.e. teaching students and only about 14.10 percent of the faculty members gave the right answer. About 55.13 percent of the faculty members gave the wrong option (c) whereas about 15.38 percent of the faculty members remained neutral (Fig. 2.64).

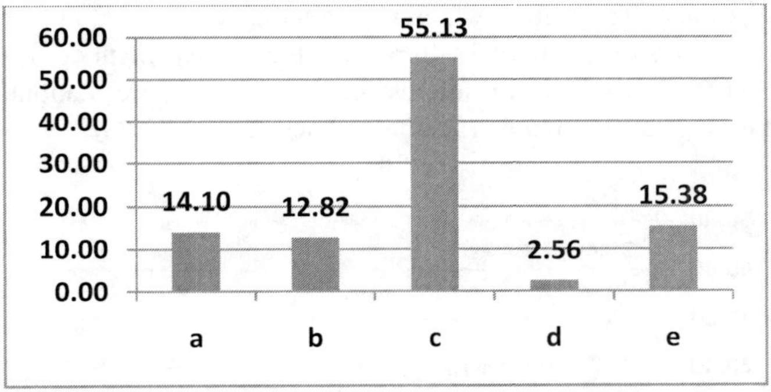

Fig. 2.64: Assignments Questions

47. CBCS stands for

(a) Credit Based Course System, (b) Choice Based Credit System, (c) Course Based Credit System, (d) Curriculum Based Course System

Majority of the faculty members (71.79 percent) gave the correct option (b) and about 24.36 percent of the faculty members opted for the option (a) as shown in Fig. 2.65.

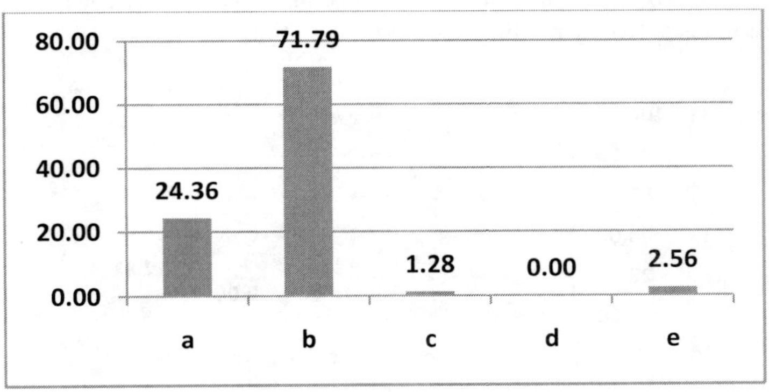

Fig. 2.65: CBCS Meaning

48. What is the most important contribution that a teacher can make in the classroom?

(a) Develop interest in the lesson, (b) Impart knowledge of the subject, (c) Reduce tension and make learning creative, (d) Set high achievement levels

This was most difficult question to be asked and all the options seem to be correct. However, option (c) i.e. reduce tension and make learning creative is the correct option which was opted by about 15.38 percent the faculty members only. About 38.46 percent the faculty members opted for the option (a) i.e. to develop interest in the lesson whereas about 23.08 percent of the faculty members remained neutral (Fig. 2.66).

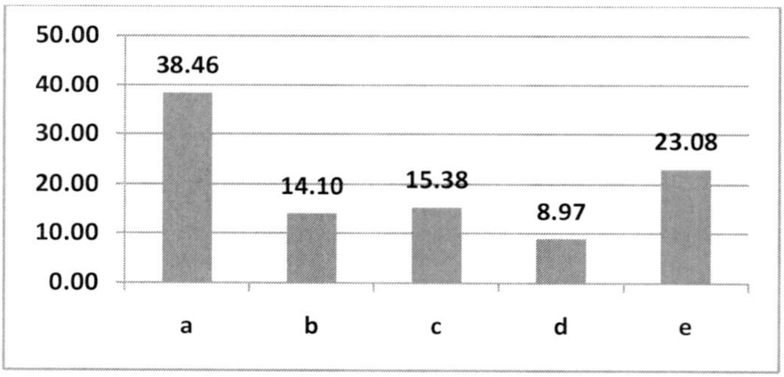

Fig. 2.66: Teacher's Contribution in Class

49. How would you improve student participation in classroom activity?

(a) By giving assignments, (b) By group activity and reporting, (c) By holding tests, (d) By reading textual information

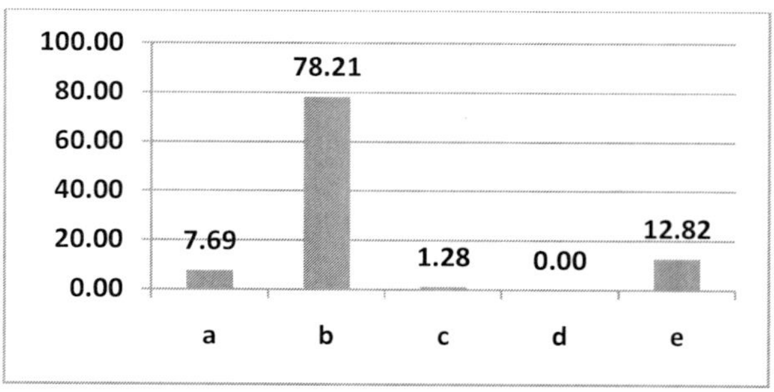

Fig. 2.67: Students Participation in Classroom

The student participation in the classroom could be improved by group activity and reporting, i.e. option (b). About 78.21 percent the faculty members opted for this whereas about 23.08 percent of the faculty members remained neutral (Fig. 2.67).

50. Lecture and tutorial are different. Do you agree?

(a) Fully agree, (b) Partially agree, (c) Not agree, (d) Undecided

Lectures and tutorials are different and this was shared by majority of the faculty members (89.74 percent). This is shown in Fig. 2.68.

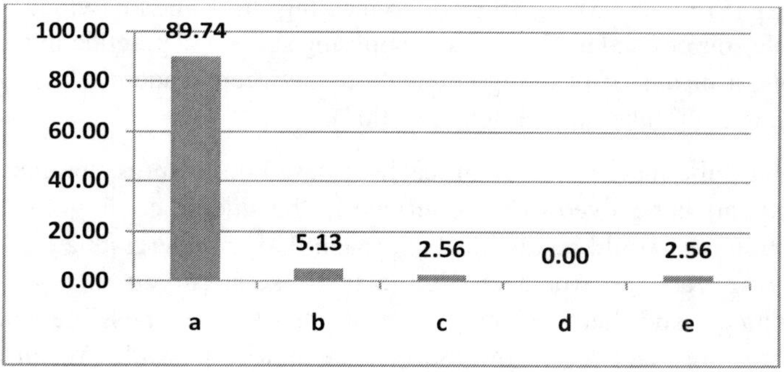

Fig. 2.68: Lecture and Tutorial

Innovation in Examination and Evaluation in Universities

The examinations and evaluations of students are the human face of any university. The universities should have proper guidelines for all associated activities like Semester End Examination (SEE), On Demand Examination (ODE), Practical Examination (PE), Setting of Questions Papers, Conduct of Examination and Evaluation of the answer scripts.

The authors have reviewed the system of examinations and evaluations in many universities including Cavendish group of universities and have observed many gaps which greatly affects the quality of education. In this paper, we have developed necessary guidelines for all aspects of examination and evaluations. The guidelines so developed and implemented in the Cavendish group of Universities are presented in this paper. It is expected that these guidelines may be adopted by any university for the betterment of the students as well as teachers.

The world has become a global village. Higher education has become a prime mover in bringing students and teachers at the one common plate form. This in turn has initiated a strong competition among higher education institutions and universities to provide quality education and research. The quality education has become a subject of concern in the diverse areas of university education like creditisation of programmes, teaching and learning, examination, evaluation and certification. The universities are making continuous efforts not only to maintain the set quality standards but to continuously improve upon them.

There are many advances in scientific knowledge and innovations in educational field that necessitates constant changes in course curricula and include self directed learning, problem based learning and integrated teaching (Smith 2005). The way of connecting skills and knowledge from multiple sources and experiences or applying skills and practice in various settings, a means of bridging connections between academic knowledge and practical (Huber and Hutchings 2004).

Thus, alternative method of teaching based on lectures, seminar, and assignments is believed to be beneficial to the student community at the institution and would be the ideal approach. Large undergraduate courses in any university offer a challenge to those involved in both their development and their delivery, to ensure that the best possible learning outcomes are achieved in the most efficient way possible. When these students represent a combination of internal and distance students, and domestic and international, the challenge to achieve these outcomes become even more complex. Kehoe et.al. (2004) have analysed the challenge of flexible and non- traditional learning and teaching methods.

It has been observed that not all students learn at the same pace. Students are unique in their own ways, including the way they learn. Since not all students learn in the same style, it is essential that teachers recognize the learning style differences of their students and teach in a manner in which all learning styles are considered. The characteristics of teachers are just as diverse as those of the students. The learning style, teaching style, and personality style of teachers have implications for student learning.

The problem-solving strategy must consider at least three dimensions: knowledge domain, problem-solving methods, and characteristics of learners. They have observed that the first two dimensions (knowledge domain and problem-solving methods) were widely accepted as essential for problem-solving, but there were no theories of problem-solving which took into account systematic individual differences. They concluded that modification of problem-solving instructions in ways consistent with students' learning styles seems an inevitable consequence.

Higher education quality assurance in Sub-Saharan Africa has been studied in detail by Materu (2007). It has been indicated that tertiary education is increasing in the African continent. The number of tertiary students increased between 1985 and 2002 by 3.6 times (from 800 thousand to about 3 million), on average by about 15 percent yearly. This trend was led by Rwanda (55 percent), Namibia (46 percent), Uganda (37 percent), Tanzania (32 percent), Kenya (27 percent), Chad (27 percent), Botswana (22 percent), and Cameroon (22 percent). Quality assurance in examination and evaluation can play a key catalytic role in initiating reforms to revitalize weak tertiary education systems. Despite variations in cultural and political preferences, differences in leadership styles within universities as well as varying stages of development, there is emerging consensus that traditional academic controls are inadequate for responding to today's challenges and that more explicit assurances about quality are needed.

The quest for quality has always been a priority in higher education in Africa. However, the tension between political pressure to expand access and the desire by academics in HEIs to maintain quality did not allow a healthy culture of quality to evolve. Changes in quality assurance mechanisms over the years were driven by factors such as rapid enrolment growth to meet increasing social demand, significantly decreased public funding of higher education amid rising enrolment. With the arrival of private universities in the African continent has changed the scene dramatically. These universities are now allowing latest concepts of quality assurance in providing higher education so that the graduates are at par with the international universities.

Quality assurance within institutions of higher learning takes place throughout the teaching and learning process and examination and evaluation process. An academic review provides an opportunity for a university to:

- Review of academic programmes against the set quality standards, if available;
- Establish priorities to develop its curriculum and to improve quality Review of examination and evaluation system
- Provide information that is essential to quality assessment, the development and the enhancement of the impact and reputation of the programme and the university
- Encourage all concerned to be self-conscious about quality and its improvement.

Okebukola (2012) has analysed quality assurance in higher education and pointed out the achievements and outstanding needs. Smout and

Stephenson (2001) on the other hand have studied quality assurance in South African higher education. Ajayi and Akindutire (2007) have studied the quality assurance issues in Nigerian universities. The literature survey shows that a number of studies are available for quality assurance initiatives (Munzali 2006, Paschal 2006, Saffu 2006, Bloom et. Al 2006, Hall 2005, Hanushek and Wossmann 2007, Liu and Chang 2006). These studies, however, have not touched upon the basic issues of quality control and quality assurance in creditisation of programmes, teaching and learning, examination, evaluation and certification. This paper has addressed issues related to examination and evaluation.

Innovation in Examination system

The examinations are the human face of the University. Any university following semester system of teaching and examination should have proper system or guidelines for the following:

- Semester End Examination (SEE)
- On Demand Examination (ODE)
- Practical Examination (PE)
- Setting Questions Papers
- Conduct of Examination
- Issuing of Class Assignments (CAs) and their marking

The universities following semester system of teaching and examination have several combinations of teaching and examination activities in a semester as elaborated below:

(1) Continuous Assessment

- Two assignments, or
- One assignment and one class test, or
- Two class tests

(2) Examination

- Semester End Examination in June and December

After an extensive survey of several universities, we have come to conclusion that university can have two Class Assignments (CAs) having 40 percent weightage and Semester End Exam to be conducted only in June and December having 60 percent weightage. This requires that all issues related to CAs should to be dealt with the set guidelines. This is because the schedule of issue of assignments to the students is not followed, or, we can say that there is no schedule. It depends upon a particular teacher when he likes to give the CA. The operation of assignment related activities may be as outlined in Table 2.6. The table gives the following:

(1) The university conducts exam in June and December
(2) First CA is issued at the end of covering 25 percent of the course
(3) Second CA is issued at the end of covering 50 percent of the course
(4) If the students have not cleared the CAs, a third CA will be issued by the said date.
(5) Marks are sent by the respective teachers to the Exam Office by the designated date.

Table 2.6: Proposed Operation Schedule for CAs

Exam Session	*Issue of CA1 at the end of covering 25% of the course*	*Issue of CA2 at the end of covering 50% of the course*	*Marks to Exam Office of CA1 and CA2*	*Issue of CA3 in case students have not cleared CAs*	*Marks to Exam Office of CA3*
June	September 15	October 15	October 30	November 10	November 20
December	March 15	April 15	April 30	May 10	May 20

Examination Schedule and Guidelines

Semester End Examination (SEE)

The semester end examination time table should be prepared by the university well in advance. It should also be placed on the University Website. The following guidelines will be followed:

(1) Those students who have cleared all dues will be permitted.
(2) The students without ID card will not be permitted to write Exam. University should issue to all its students their ID cards.
(3) The students have to inform the University that they are appearing in the Exam for given number of courses. This has to be given in writing through an undertaking. The following procedure may be adopted:

- Step 1: The University will announce the Time Table for June/ December Exam and put it on the University Website/Faculty Notice Boards.
- Step 2: The Students will fill up the Exam Form indicating the Modules etc and after getting it cleared from Account section will submit it to the Academic Office latest by certain date. Students

who failed to submit the Exam Forms by due date can do so even after the last date but with the late fine. The Exam Forms will also be uploaded on the University Website and can also be collected from the offices of Deans and also from the Programme Leaders.

- Step 3: The University will issue the Dockets (Hall Tickets) well before the start of Exam.

This entire operation for SEE is summarized in the Table 2.7 for universities operating on semester basis and two intakes January and July.

Table 2.7: Proposed Operation for SEE

Exam Session	*University to Announce Time Table*	*Students to Fill Up Exam Form and Submit to Academic Office*	*Students to Fill Up Exam Form and Submit to Academic Office with late fine*	*Dockets to be issued by the University latest by*
June	April 15	May 15	May 30	May 25
December	October 15	November 15	November 30	November 25

On Demand Examination (ODE)

On demand examination may be treated as a substitute of supplementary examination. It is useful for face to face programmes, distance learning programmes, credit transfer schemes of the University. The steps include:

- On Demand Examination will be conducted on the 25th of January/ July in the respective semesters. The students will apply for appearing in ODE.
- The students who could not clear a module in SEE will be eligible for ODE.
- The students who could not write SEE for specific reasons may be allowed to write ODE if accepted by the University.
- The students willing to get credit transfer will have to appear in ODE.

Practical Examination (PE)

(1) The practical examination schedule for the concerned courses should be prepared well in advance and made available to all concerned like semester end examination schedule.

(2) The students who have attended 75 percent of the practical classes will be allowed to appear in the Practical Exam.

(3) Those students who have not completed 75 percent attendance will be asked to repeat the practical classes.

Guidelines for Setting Questions Papers

The setting of question papers (QP) should be standarised. This is because; we have observed as many types of question papers as the number of modules. For example, Cavendish University conducts exam for about 300 modules and each module has different design of question paper. Each QP will have two sections; Section A and Section B.

Section A will be compulsory and will have two questions as described below:

> Q.1: A case study and one question (containing only 4 sub questions) to be answered. The weightage is 20 percent .
>
> Q.2: A multiple choice question containing 10 sub questions each of 2 marks. Each sub question will have 4 choices with only one choice as correct answer. The weightage is 20 percent . This question will fulfill the requirement of Bloom's Taxonomy.

Section B will have 5 questions (containing only 2 sub questions each) and 3 questions are to be answered. This section has 60 percent weightage. The questions in Section B will be numbered as Q.3, Q.4, Q.5, Q.6, Q.7.

Since paper setting is a confidential activity, all paper setters should give an undertaking "I , the undersigned hereby certify that I have read the relevant guidelines and do understand them and will not go against the rules and regulations of the University procedures for paper setters as stipulated in the guidelines. I also state that I have not kept anything related to question paper set by me in any form, photo copy, scan copy etc".

Schedule of Submission of Question Papers to Exam Office

The schedule of submitting the question papers to Exam Office will be as given in Table 2.8.

Table 2.8: Proposed Schedule of Examination Activities

Exam Session	*Two sets of question papers as per the standard format to Exam Office*	*Papers to be Moderated by the date*	*Papers to be printed in the desired numbers and packed as per the Exam Schedule*
June	May 15	May 20	May 25
December	November 15	November 20	November 25

Types of Questions

The question paper setters should take adequate precaution in setting up the questions. The purpose should be to test the learning outcome rather than testing the memorising capacity of the students.

This can be done by framing the following types of questions:

(a) Questions based on Case Studies

(b) Long Answer Questions

(c) Short Answer Questions

(d) Multiple Choice Questions

The guidelines are given in Table 2.9.

Table 2.9: Guidelines for Setting Question Papers

Cognitive Domain	*Feature*	*Outcomes*	*Learning Outcome*
Knowledge	Passive	Recallof specificfacts	know common terms, know specific facts, know methods and procedures, know basic concepts, know principles
Comprehension	Passive	Graspingorunder standingmeaning of informational study materials	understand facts and principles, interpret verbal material, interpret charts and graphs, translate verbal material to mathematical formulae, estimate the future consequences implied in data, justify methods and procedures
Application	Passive	Makeuse of the knowledge	apply concepts and principles to new situations, apply laws and theories to practical situations, solve mathematical problems, construct graphs and charts, and demonstrate the correct usage of a method or procedure
Analysis	Active	Takingapartthek nown& identifyingrelatio nships amongthem	recognize unstated assumptions, recognises logical fallacies in reasoning, distinguish between facts and inferences, evaluate the relevancy of data, analyse the organizational structure of a work (art, music, and writing)
Synthesis	Active	Puttingthingstog etherin a creativemanner	write a well-organized theme, gives a well-organized speech writes a creative short story, propose a plan for an experiment, integrate learning from different areas into a plan for solving a problem, formulates a new scheme for classifying objects (or events, or ideas)
Evaluation	Active	Makesjudgments aboutthevalueof materialsor methods	judge the logical consistency of written material, judge the adequacy with which conclusions are supported by data, judge the value of a work (art, music, writing) by the use of internal criteria, judge the value of a work (art, music, writing) by use of external standards of excellence

Questions based on Case Studies: The case study should be interesting one and may be related to daily life scene. The questions based should be to judge the capability of the student to extract the answer from the case study.

Long Answer Questions: The long answer questions should be framed to judge the capability of the student to answer in innovative way rather than giving the answer after memorising.

Short Answer Questions: The short answer questions should be framed from the entire course curriculum.

Multiple Choice Questions: This is most important component and the questions will test the students' knowledge in the right perspectives. Bloom's Taxonomy can be used to frame the multiple choice questions. Here are some guidelines.

Bloom and Krathwohl (1956) has excellently described the link between strategies and learning objectives to assist the teachers in developing and directing students in logical steps of learning.

Knowledge, comprehension and application are passive modes where activities are more or less teacher centred. Knowledge and comprehension focus on a recall of facts that students can attain by reading the course material and attending lectures. The evaluation strategies are through true/false and multiple-choice questions for knowledge and short essays for comprehension. In the application category students use previously learned information in new and concrete situations to solve problems that have single or best answers.

The analysis, synthesis and evaluation are the characteristics of teaching and learning that most engage the students and faculty because they are active. These categories deal with the issues that inspire the students to learn and reveal the creative. The students assume responsibility for acquiring the knowledge necessary to respond creatively and evaluate outcomes. This is the basis for non-traditional teaching and learning strategies where less emphasis is placed on information transmission and greater emphasis placed on developing skills, attitudes and values. This will lead students to engage in higher order of thinking such as analysis, synthesis, and evaluation.

Evaluation and Certification

Another important aspect of quality assurance is a proper scheme of marking the answer scripts.

Guidelines for Marking Answer Scripts

- The answer scripts should be coded before handing over to the Dean/Programme Leaders/Teacher Evaluators.
- Once the scripts are evaluated, they will be decoded and the awards list will be sent to Exam Office for updating.
- There shall be centralized evaluation.

- Evaluators have to give an undertaking saying that they will do their job as per the University Guidelines.
- A sample monitoring should be done by a senior academician.
- No over writing will be permitted. If the marks are to be revised, then original marks are to be crossed, new marks written and initialed.

Compilation of Marks and Submission to Exam Office

The evaluator after evaluating the answer scripts of a course will enter the marks in the award list supplied by the Exam Office. The marks should be entered with high precaution and concentration so that no harm is done to the students. No external recording of the marks should be done by the evaluator. All Deans should ensure the return of the award list and answer scripts to the Exam Office.

Certification Guidelines

The certification from the University shall be as per the standard procedures across the world. This should be based on Semester Grade Point Average (SGPA) and Commulative Grade Point Average (CGPA).

Semester Grade Point Average (SGPA) is defined as

$$SGPA = \frac{\sum_{i=1}^{n} C_i P_i}{\sum_{i=1}^{n} C_i}$$

where

C_i = Number of Credits earned in the ith course of Semester.

P_i = Grade point earned in ith course.

i=1 .....n represent the number of courses in which a student is registered in the concerned semester.

Commulative Grade Point Average (CGPA) is defined as

$$CGPA = \frac{\sum_{j=1}^{m} C_j P_j}{\sum_{j=1}^{m} C_j}$$

where

C_j= Number of Credits earned in the jth course of semester.

P_j = Grade points earned in j[th] course; a grade lower than D (i.e. grade point less than (4) in a course shall not be taken into account

j=1... m represents the number of courses in which a student was registered and obtained a grade not lower than D up to the semester for which CGPA is to be calculated.

Guidelines for Clearing a Course

- A student has to obtain minimum 40 percent marks in continuous assessment
- A student has to obtain minimum 40 percent marks in practical, if any
- A student has to obtain minimum 40 percent marks in semester end examination
- A student has to obtain overall 50 percent marks for clearing the course

If students has obtained 30 percent marks in the assignment and overall say 70 percent marks, even then he has not cleared the course. He needs to clear the assignment after resubmission of the new assignments. In that case, the student has to obtain new assignments.

Innovation in Teaching and Learning

Innovation is the process of creating value by applying novel solutions to meaningful problems. Executing an idea which addresses a specific challenge and achieve value for both the company and customer (Nick Skillicorn 2019, ideatovalue.com). Innovation has different meaning to different people. Fig. 2.69 shows how the people understand the innovation based on the views of 15 innovators.

Innovation can be defined as the application of new ideas to the prod-ucts, processes, or other aspects of the activities of a firm that lead to increased "value." This "value" is defined in a broad way to include higher value added for the firm and also benefits to consumers or other firms. Two important definitions are:

• ***Product innovation***: the introduction of a new product, or a signif-icant qualitative change in an existing product. For exam-ple, the Apple iPod is an innovation compared with the Sony Walkman, which was an earlier portable device for playing music.

• ***Process innovation***: the introduction of a new process for making or delivering goods and services. For example, going to visit the doctor and recording that you have arrived for your appointment by touching a screen instead of talking to a receptionist.

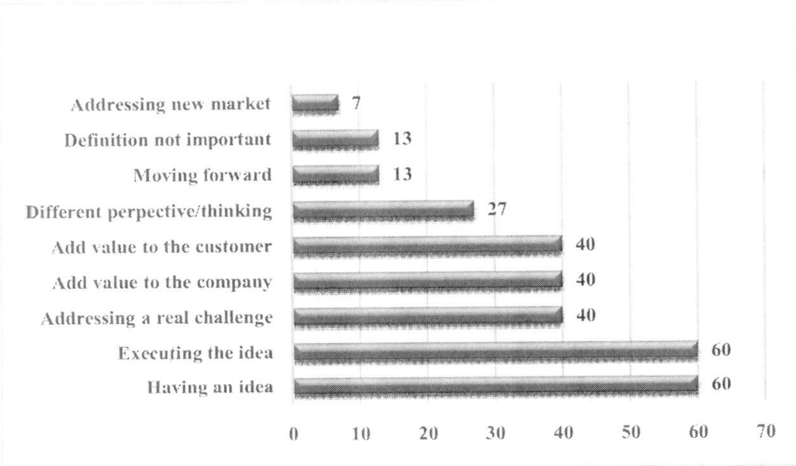

Fig. 2.69: Percentage of People with their views on Innovation

Webster's defines innovation as *"the introduction of something new."*

Peter Drucker said *"Innovation is the specific instrument of entrepreneurship... the act that endows resources with a new capacity to create wealth."*

Scott Berkun said *"Innovation is significant positive change."*

Tim Kastelle said innovation is *"not just having an idea—but executing it so that it creates value."*

A survey of 246 CEOs of the company's was published (http://www.pwc.com/gx/en/consulting-services/innovation.jhtml). A summary of the results is given in Table 2.10 and 2.11.

Table 2.10: Summary of Survey Results

Question	*Sub questions*	*Responses (%)*
Q. 1: Which of the following statements best describes your company's appetite for innovation?	Innovation is not a priority for us in the markets in which we operate.	3
	Innovation is our primary focus. We are creative and regularly pioneer cutting-edge ideas and approaches.	10
	We value innovation. We're good at recognising new ideas and approaches and adopting them quickly.	36
	Innovation is one of our priorities. We are good at generating new ideas and approaches.	51

(Contd...)

	Innovation is one of our priorities. We are good at generating new ideas and approaches.	51
Q.2: Which is more important to the success of your company – operational effectiveness or innovation?	Operational effectiveness is far more important to the success of my company than innovation.	2
	Innovation is far more important to the success of my company than operation effectiveness	3
	Operational effectiveness is more important to the success of my company than innovation.	23
	Innovation is more important to the success of my company than operational effectiveness.	8
	Innovation and operational effectiveness are equally important to the success of my company.	64
Q.3 Which of the following constraints is stopping you from being more innovative?	Financial resources	43
	Existing organisational culture	41
	Lack of talent	30
	Political and regulatory factors	21
	Inadequate technology	18
	Nothing is stopping me from being innovative	14
	Weak governance/leadership	9

Table 2.11: Summary of Survey Results

Question	***First Choice***		***Top 3 Mentions***	
	Sub Question	***Response (%)***	***Sub Question***	***Response (%)***
Q. 4: Which of the following do you see as your primary role in driving innovation within your organization?	Leader	37	Products	48
	Visionary	34	Technology	45
	Facilitator	16	Customer Experience	44
	Sponsor	7	System and Processes	43
	Advocate	5	Business Model	41
	Follower	1	Services	37
			Supply Chain and Channels to Market	33
			None/Don't Know	2
			Other	2
Q.5 What do you think are the most important ingredients for successful innovation at a company?	Strong visionary business leadership	26	Strong visionary business leadership	57

(Contd...)

	The willingness to challenge organizational norms and take risks	9	The willingness to challenge organizational norms and take risks	37
	Collaborating with customers	9	The ability to capture ideas throughout the organization	31
	Having a capacity and capability for creativity	9	Collaborating with customers	30
	The ability to capture ideas throughout the organizations	9	Being able to locate and train the right people	26
	The ability to capture ideas throughout the organizations	9	Use of new technology to support innovation	11
	Being able to locate and train the right people	5	Being able to secure the right levels of funding	9
	Collaborating with suppliers	2	None/Don't know	4
	Being able to secure the wright levels of funding	1		
	Use of new technology to support innovation	1		
	None/Don't know	4		

There could be five key questions any organization will need to address if it is to become genuinely innovative and generate full value from its investment:

1. Does the way you innovate (collaboration, employee empowerment, customer engagement, time horizons etc.) reflect your vision and appetite for innovation?
2. How effectively are you articulating your vision and appetite for innovation to employees, investors and business partners?
3. Do your employees see creating, promoting and executing new ideas as a crucial part of their job description?
4. Are the processes for decision making and organisational mobilisation quick enough to bring new innovations to market ahead of your competitors?
5. How effectively do you measure and track the return on investment and ability to meet customers' changing expectations?

In nutshell, innovation is simply the process of creating and implementing a new idea or ideas. Three main types of innovation exist:

(1) Process Innovation: Process innovation is achieved through the creation of a new means of producing, selling, and/or distributing an existing product or service. Some examples are: Online Banking, E-commerce etc.

(2) **Technical Innovation:** Technical innovation is simply the creation of a new product or service. Some examples: A new line of automobiles, the introduction of cellular telephones

(3) **Administrative Innovation:** Administrative innovation is the creation of a new organization design which better supports the creation, production and delivery of services or products. An example is: Virtual Teams: any task-focused group that meets without all members being in the same room or even working at the same time.

Learning Organizations

Learning organizations involve all of the employees in the process of identifying and solving problems. This enables the organization to continuously experiment, improve and increase its capacity to deliver its customers new and improved products and services. A learning organization, through continuous innovation and change, creates sustainable competitive advantage in its industry.

The Five Building Blocks of a Learning Organization

(1) **Shared Leadership**: All employees share at least some leadership responsibilities. Everyone is encouraged to find ways to improve products and services and to experiment with new methods to better serve the organization. This sharing of decision-making and leadership creates a culture that supports the efforts and goals of the organization

(2) **Culture:** The learning organization encourages these empowered employees to identify and experiment with new methods and approaches. Empowerment provides a way to integrate tasks and allows the employees to buy into an organization's goals.

(3) **Strategy:** This aspect addresses three key issues:

   (1) **Customer Focus:** reflects a clear understanding of how important customers are to success.

   (2) **Long-term Perspectives:** the process of learning and change simply take time.

   (3) **Internal Alignment:** the business strategy drives the design of all systems within the organization.

(4) **Organization Design;** In a learning organization, this emphasizes the use of teams and strategic alliances.

Teams: Team members take responsibility of aspects such as training, purchases, safety and. scheduling.

Strategic Alliances: suppliers, competitors and customers collaborate and communicate as a method of learning.

(5) Use of Information: This is the "lifeblood" of a learning organization. There are following three main aspects involving the use of information in a learning organization.

(1) Extensive scanning

(2) Measurement oriented

(3) Shared problems and solutions

3

Innovation in Integrated Model of Higher Education System

Introduction

The higher education institutions have a great responsibility to provide to the nation the innovative minds of graduates and postgraduates and scholars of eminence to accelerate growth and development to eliminate poverty, hunger, disease, unemployment and pollution. This has to be done by creativity and innovativeness to manifest the fullest of human potential.

The higher education should aim for a developed, prosperous and enlightened human society for peace, prosperity, harmony and happiness. This requires for a continuous effort on QRE (Quality, Relevance and Excellence) nurtured in an environment of Integration of Education with Values so that the research institutions could become partners in progress of nation's development and meet the global aspirations of human excellence (Sharma, 2018, Chandra et.al. 2014).

Growth of Higher Education

India's higher education has grown during the last 70 years. As per the UGC Annual Report 2015-16, the universities have increased to 40 times, colleges 100 times and the student's enrolment has gone up to the 165 times in the formal system of higher education in comparison to the figures at the time of independence (20 Universities and 500 Colleges in the country at the time of independence with 2.1 lakhs students in higher education). As on 22.12.2018, the number of Universities stood at 889 (48 Central, 394 State, 322 State Private and 125 Deemed to be Universities).

The University System

The concept of a university should target the following:

- providing a learning environment that promotes the spirit of enquiry
- providing a sense of commitment to find solutions to the pressing problems of the society
- a quest to discover the truth of being
- to unveil the secret of creation
- engage in pursuits of translating acquired knowledge and capabilities to create a better tomorrow.

The Govt. of India has initiated several innovative technological missions such as "Make in India", "Digital India", "Skill India" and "Start up India". This, however, requires a well-defined and well-articulated education policy, without which such novel missions would face the scarcity of talent pool and will lack continuous supply of innovations.

Our educational policies have revolved around increasing Gross Enrolment Ratio (GER), in higher education. The inclusive education being grossly misunderstood as driving every one towards university quality education. The net result being that we have achieved significant increase in GER (about 25 percent) but with low quality of graduates and low employability.

The Research and Development

Universities and Institutions of higher learning are supposed to be the lifeline of the local industries and drivers for change both at national and global levels to cause technology revolution and innovative new product development. The universities and institutions need to do research not only for industrial development but also for teaching and learning process. There is need to device mechanisms which supports the active participation of the industries for helping in changing the course curriculum and taking the research outcomes to their logical ends.

The innovations are a great creative power to make a better world but they are also a great disruptive power. Often the power of disruption is much more than what could be comprehended and assessed. Therefore, all the universities must be prepared to produce the manpower of tomorrow as also to retain the manpower of today to manage this disruption caused by new and excited innovations (Sharma 2018).

The need of the hour is, therefore, to have interdisciplinary education, need based research, and encourage creativity and innovations and take them to the level of commercially visible technologies and products.

When to Start and How to Start?

Our education policy has defined the usual journey of a student from 10+2 level to Ph.D degree as shown in Fig. 3.1.

The present system indicates that it takes minimum 8-9 years to complete Ph.D degree after 10 + 2 and we are not sure about the quality of the research and further academic choice of the student. This may be due to the fact that students are not made aware about the career in research.

Is it not possible to start a new programme, may be called Graduate Research Integrated Programme (GRIP)? The programme may have courses related to core courses, skill related courses and the courses based on OER/ MOOCs/SWAYAM platform.

The possible structure of 14 semesters (7 years) after 10 + 2 may be adopted as shown in Figs. 3.2-3.4. There are several advantages of this integrated structure as mentioned below:

During Integrated UG Programme

- The student is given exposure to undertake a research project at the end of 2nd semester during summer vacations.
- At the end of 4th semester, the student finalized the project and starts working on it.
- During 6th semester, the student does the research project, prepare a report and writes a research paper.

During Integrated PG Programme

- At the end of 2nd semester during summer vacations, the student further improves the research project and write a synopsis for the project.
- In the 4th semester, the student will undertake the following three courses (12 credits) which are required for a Ph.D. degree.

  Course 1: Subject specific related to the broad research area

  Course 2: Research Methodology

  Course 3: Computer Applications in Research
- The student will finalize the synopsis with objectives and research methodology and will also write a research paper.
- RDC will be held by the concerned university.
- Title of the thesis and the supervisor will be finalized.

Integrated Ph.D Programme

- The student will write a research paper and will submit for publication.
- Sem 3: Starts writing thesis, completes it and submit to the University for pre-submission viva-voce.
- Pre-Submission viva voce will take place.
- Sem 4: Once the evaluation reports are received, student will give final viva voce.
- The student will get the Ph.D Degree

Need of Proper Integrated Career Orientation including Research

In our education system, there is strong need for a clear policy such that each and every student is made aware about different career options available to their choice and capabilities. We have undertaken a survey in several schools (Private and Government) to see the responses of the teachers (100 from private and 100 from government schools) in NCR region on a five-point scale (1-strongly agree, 2-agree, 3-cannot say, 4- disagree, 5-strongly disagree) for the following four questions:

(1) The teachers teach in a way the learner understand

(2) School has a policy to allot teachers in vacant periods

(3) School orient the students about several career options

(4) The school pass outs have clear ideas about their future plans

The responses are shown in Fig. 3.5. We can observe the following:

(1) **The teachers teach in a way the learner understand**: About 37.5 percent of the teachers strongly agreed to it while about 22.5 percent agreed to it. About 22.5 percent of the teachers do not agree (disagree and strongly disagree put together).

(2) **School has a policy to allot teachers in vacant periods**: About 30 percent of the teachers strongly agreed to it while about 20 percent agreed to it. This shows that 50 percent of the teachers feel that schools have the policy to allot teachers in vacant periods. About 30 percent of the teachers do not agree (disagree and strongly disagree put together) and 20 percent are not aware of it. However, the policy is being implemented or not is a big question.

(3) **School orient the students about several career options**: About 25 percent of the teachers strongly agreed to it while about 17.5

percent agreed to it. This shows that 42.5 percent of the teachers feel that schools orient the students about several career options.

(4) **The school pass outs have clear ideas about their future plans**: About 22.5 percent of the teachers strongly agreed to it while about 20 percent agreed to it. This shows that 42.5 percent of the teachers feel that schools pass outs have clear ideas about their future plans. Thus about 57.5 percent of the teachers are of the opinion that students are not clear about their future plans.

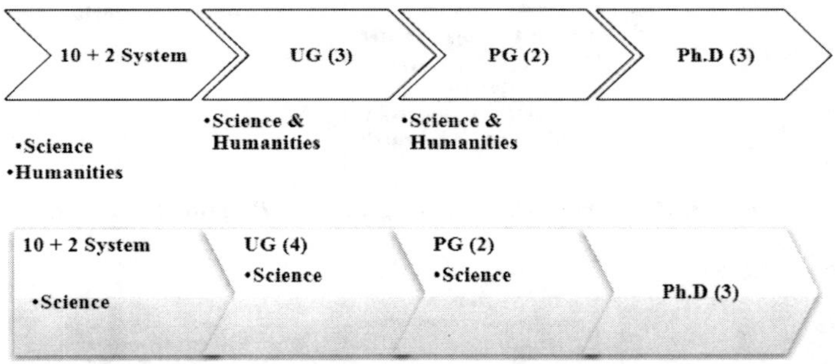

Fig. 3.1: Academic Journey of a Student

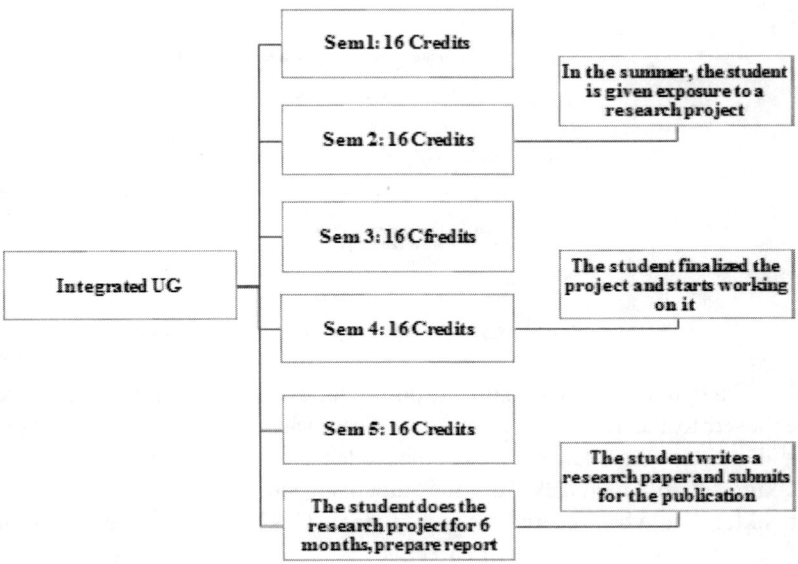

Fig. 3.2: Proposed System for Integrated UG Programme

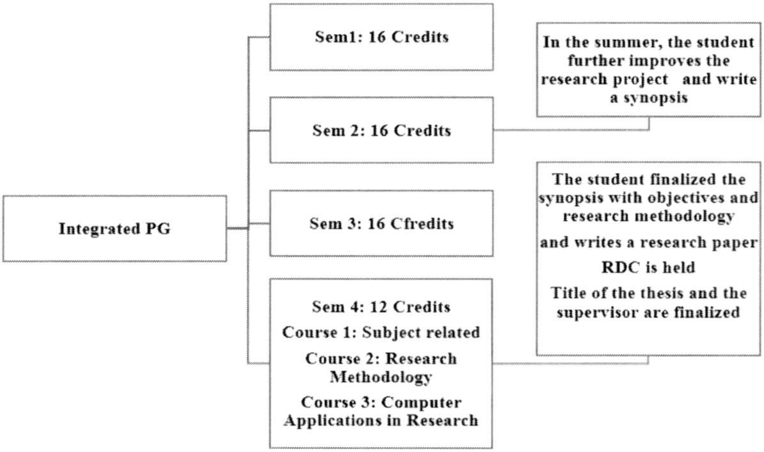

Fig. 3.3: Proposed System for Integrated PG Programme

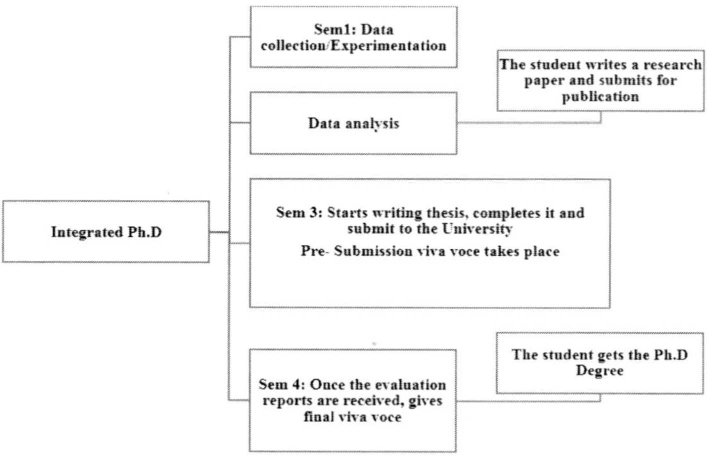

Fig. 3.4: Proposed System for Integrated Ph.D Programme

There must be a national/state policy for every school that students are exposed to the latest career options in the vacant periods through short audio/video films. The choices of the students should be strengthened after taking suitable feedback from the students/teachers/parents. Thereafter, a booklet should be prepared for each student. This booklet will be useful for the students in choosing their career.

The education in India does not come under priority sector like defense but it falls under state subject. That is why there is no uniform education

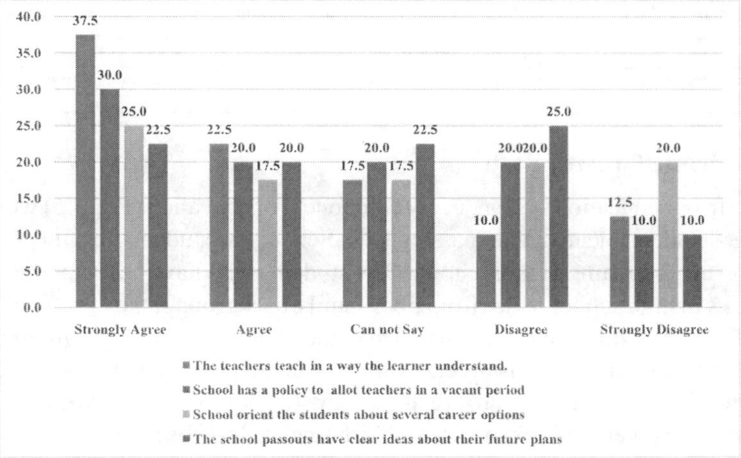

Fig. 3.5: Responses of the Teachers

structure across the country. When we look at our education structure, the pattern given in Table 3.1 emerges:

Table 3.1: Education Structure

Parameter	*Characteristics*
Structure of primary and secondary education	Different in every state
Evaluation and certification	Different in every state, controlled by the respective state board of education
Infrastructure in Schools	Different in every state; many schools are running in tents/fields
Infrastructure in Colleges	Different in every state; Lab facilities and no of teachers are highly inadequate in many colleges
Quality of teachers	Different in every state; untrained teachers are appointed in many institutions
Quality of teaching	Different in every state; un-oriented teachers
Quality of examination	Different in every state; not up to the mark; a toper of one state may get failed in another state in the same examination
Quality of evaluation	Different in every state; as many qualities as the no of teachers/evaluators
Guidance about the career	Very little guidance is given in public/convent schools only; others are ignorant about this
Higher education movement	Very insignificant; gross enrolment ratio in India is very low
University education	Highly substandard in many universities; here also no uniform curriculum, no quality control and no quality assurance; no choice of courses; everything is very rigid
Projects (summer and winter)	Is a part of the course curriculum in few universities only.
Training during course of study	Training during course of study is missing in several universities.

(Contd...)

Assignments Presentations	The concept of assignment preparation and their presentation in the class room in presence of fellow students and teachers is missing in several universities.
Laboratory Course Work	This vital component of learning is of highly substandard in many universities.

Academic Growth Path

In our education system, every component of education (Fig. 3.6) works almost independently. After passing High School, the students usually prefer to go to +2 streams of their choice. The students who have not scored good marks in high school or are from poor family background, they prefer to go to ITI. Until this stage, no student has the chance to see any equipment used in industries. That is precisely the reason that a 10+2 pass out student with science stream is unaware about how to fix a fuse wire. We need to reverse this scenario. Irrespective of the branch to be chosen by the students, they should be oriented towards skills needed in industrial applications.

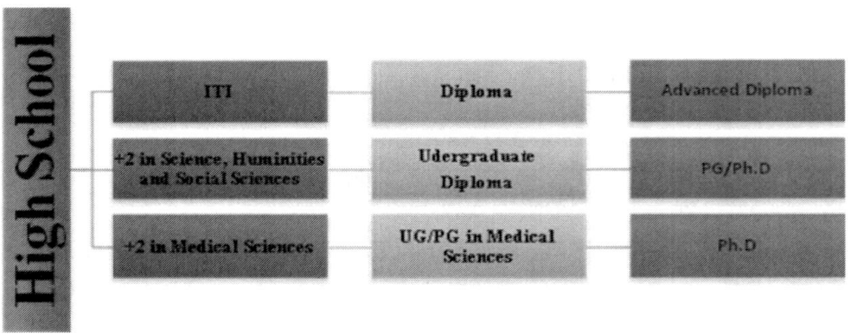

Fig. 3.6: Current Education Pattern

One of the serious limitation of the current educational system is that students hardly come across to a university before passing 10+2 system. Who stops the students of the primary, middle, high school or intermediate to have a feel of a university system and industrial application of the knowledge they are gaining. Thus, there is strong need for an integrated university system.

An Integrated University System

The proposed integrated university system is shown in Fig.3.7. It may be seen that all students, irrespective of their age will see all components of education starting from primary, High School, Intermediate, ITI, Diploma and University. All the labs at ITI and Diploma level will be placed in one enclosure. The advantages will be that primary students will see the lab components and the students working on them on daily basis. The students at ITI and diploma level will see daily various incubation centres at the university level. This will create a huge curiosity amongst the students and will create an atmosphere of learning while doing. Whenever, there is a vacant period, the students will be free to visit various labs/incubation centres.

Conclusion

- The students will start looking machines, equipment etc. from day 1 while going to their classes or coming out from the classes to go to their homes.
- The students can visit the labs, see the equipment while working in their vacant periods.
- They will start to have a feel of their career choice.

  Here, it is worth to mention a story how guru Drawn identified the interests of each Pandav. It is believed that when the five young Pandavas were brought to guru Drawn for teaching of weaponry system, he locked them in to a room full of all kinds of weapons and asked them to play with the weapons and choose the best suited to them. He further said that all the Pandavas will be taken out from the room after few days. They were instructed that they will come out from the room with the weapon of their choice. After the scheduled time, guru Drawn asked them to come out along with the weapon of their choice.

  - First came Yudhister with chariot
  - Second came Bhim with Fencer (Gada).
  - Third came Arjun with Archer
  - Fourth came Nakul with sword
  - Finally, Sahdev came with sword

  Thereafter, guru Drawn trained them in their chosen field and history tells us they became masters in their chosen discipline. Where is such an education system in our country? Our students continue to struggle to choose their career options.

Locations of Integrated University System

Earlier, there used to be seven IITs in the country (Delhi, Kanpur, Mumbai, Chennai, Kharagpur, Roorkee and Guwahati). They used to be our best educational institutions because of two main reasons:

(1) they used to admit students after a rigorous entrance exam, called JEE

(2) they were having better teachers and other infrastructure.

Sometime we used to wonder why we are so proud of these institutions because none of these IITs has admitted a student just having 55-60 percent marks and then made him a world class engineer. Why we don't have IITs for each category of students? Why can't we have a system where we test the knowledge rather than the memorising capacity of a student. The proposed system of IITs is shown in Fig. 3.8. It is believed that if we have at least one IIT in each state reserved for such students, it will add to the much-desired quality to the education.

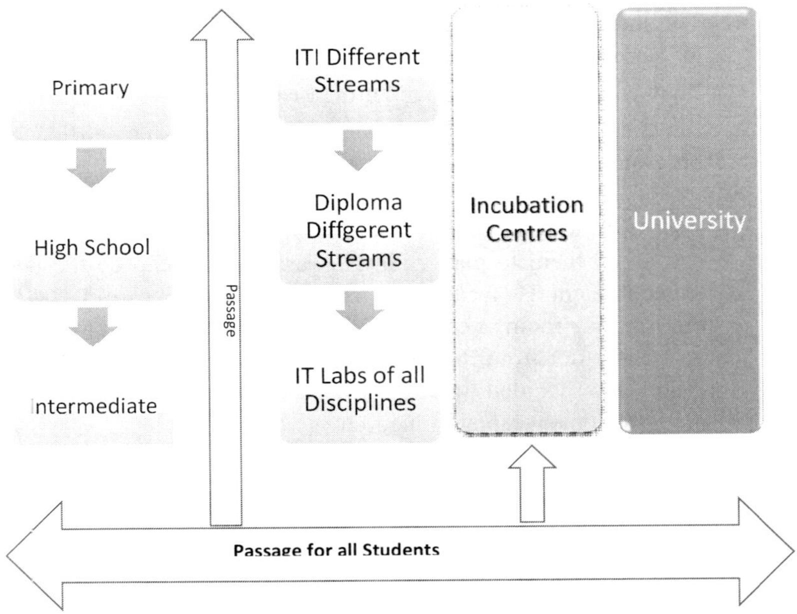

Fig. 3.7: The Proposed Integrated University System

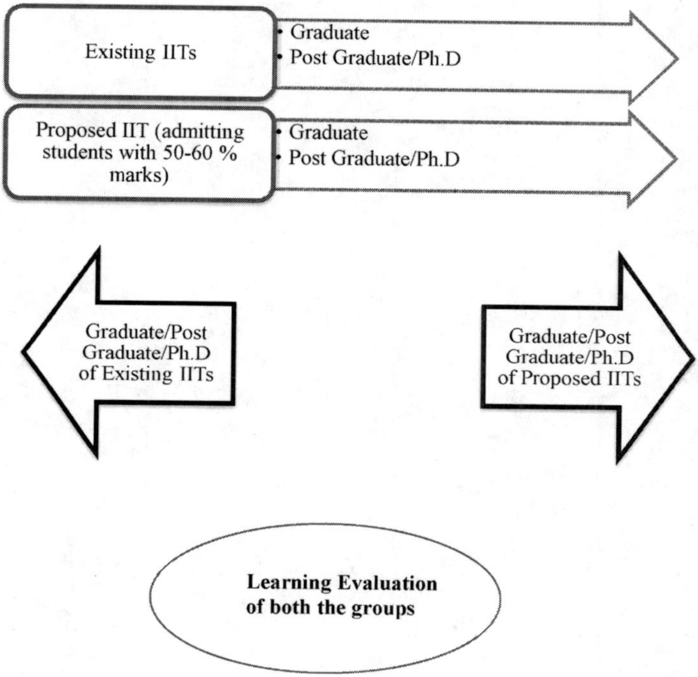

Fig. 3.8: The Proposed Systems of IITs

4

Innovations in Academia and Industry Interaction

Why Academia-Industry-University Interaction?

India is a developing nation with an estimated 65 percent of our population under 35 years of age. If suitably trained, this youth will offer great services not only for India but to the entire world. Govt. of India has set up a target of 500 million people to be skill trained by 2022 A.D. There are major constraints like lack of suitable infrastructure, experienced teacher trainers and quality resource material. On the other hand, our country has huge institutional as well as industrial infrastructure which is needs to be optimally utilized. We also, have plenty of industry experts settled across the nation (in service as well as retired) who could be persuaded to join in the mission.

It is worth mentioning here that the scheme of vocational education was revised in September 2011 by the Govt. of India for the dire need to generate high skilled human resource so as to sustain the high growth rate of Indian economy. The skilled manpower is also required in the context of growing international demand, changes in technologies and financial markets, growing international competition and increasing demand from various segments of population for job- oriented education.

Unfortunately, the vocational education at higher level is not given its due importance by the relevant regulatory bodies. Establishing new vocational universities or institutes will be a step amounting to reinventing the wheel. We have to reorient our policies and resources in such a way that existing infrastructure available in vocational training institutions as well as in the institutions of higher education is utilized to their full potential.

Academia and Industry

The world has changed or is changing at a fast rate, global challenges demand global collaborations. The population in cities id increasing, traffic is becoming unmanageable resulting into multiple problems like global warming, natural disasters and depleting natural resources. Security of water, food and energy, health care, education youth unemployment.

Universities have changed and are now powerhouses of R&D and training. Industries have changed. Strategic partnerships i.e. collaboration for mutual and societal benefits is the need of the hour.

Majority of higher educational institutions are not producing industry-specific manpower. They are simply producing bookish diploma holders, graduate, post- graduates, engineers without having the necessary skill or industry- specific knowledge. The result is a huge gap between demand and supply of skilled manpower, industry- specific manpower in the country. The universities have to come forward for meeting demand of skilled manpower.

The Resulting Gap and Possible Solution

Our universities and institutions have to develop graduates which are skilled and industry- specific. The vocational training institutions which are having world- class infrastructure may be allowed to join hands with the universities to produce industry- specific graduates. There is a clear gap between Academia-Industry-University.

There are institutions which may be providing best teaching; others may be concentrating on best practices in training while some may be concentrating on placement issues. But, there are very few universities/ institutions which are concentrating on all these aspects holistically. Only a handful of universities can be counted which are having course curriculum as per industry requirement. We do not have sufficient number of universities which can provide higher education as per the industry requirement. There are no clear-cut guidelines available from the regulatory bodies directing the universities to orient their course curriculum as per the need of the hour.

The possible solution could be that our universities start working hand-in- hand with industries and provide industry- specific education. This is only possible when universities go out from their campuses to the industries as well as those vocational training institutions which boast of world- class infrastructure. This will serve twin purpose. The universities will be able to provide industry-specific graduates on one hand, and on the other hand, the existing infrastructure available in such institutions will be utilized to their full potential.

Reasons behind the Gap between Academia and Industry

The gap between the needs of the industry and aspirations of academic community is very large. Academicians always have a strong feeling that unless these initiatives find a place in industrial sector, this interaction will be confined to only developmental activities. There is a strong mismatch in perceptions of the two on the issues related to technology development. At present, the academic community is not geared to face this challenge of translating an evolving idea into technology development (http:// www.reengineer.org/stevens/Harry-Sneed-CSMR2009-Stevens-Lecture-A4.pdf)

- Academics and Industrialists have a different mind-set; therefore, both are living in two different worlds.
- Both Academics and Industrialists are pursing different goals entirely. The Academic is striving for recognition from his or her peers. The Industrialist is striving to survive.
- Industry thinks in terms of short range goals whereas the Academic has a long-range perspective.
- Industry prefers proven solutions with a low risk, whereas Academia is interested in creating new solutions with a high innovation rate.
- Industry seeks the minimum solution to minimize their risk, whereas Academia strives for a maximum solution to maximize their recognition.
- Industry is mainly concerned with costs. Academia could care less about costs, it is mainly interested in the benefits (and prestige).

Industry Needs and Expectations

Large industrial companies have the resources to invest in technology development initiatives. Academic participation is often needed in minor technological innovation. Small scale industries often depend on support in the areas of design, process improvement and machinery performance, etc. They also rely on processes to yield a product which already exists. In some cases, problem solving may simply amount to product testing and production enhancement in terms of quantity and quality. In such interactions, industry's expected time frames have been immediate and investment is directed towards efforts that promise result oriented solutions.

Academia Expectations

An academician shows interest normally in problems that are intellectually challenging. His or her areas of interest lie in technology development initiatives and methods related to process and design improvement. Researchers have strong preference for working towards creation of knowledge in specialized areas. For industry-related problems, a researcher has to explore a variety of options which is time consuming. In academic institutions, the time frame of an academician is governed by research guidance and teaching assignments. Academicians are oriented towards R&D activities of the industry for funds which helps them to sustain their broader research interests.

The Seven Keys to Collaboration Success

1. Define the project's strategic context as part of the selection process.

- Use your company research portfolio to determine collaboration opportunities.
- Define specific collaboration outputs that can provide value to the company.
- Identify internal users of this output at the working level;
- Executive champions are not a substitute for this requirement.

2. Select boundary-spanning project managers with three key attributes

- In-depth knowledge of the technology needs in the field
- The inclination to network across functional and organizational boundaries
- The ability to make connections between research and opportunities for product applications

3. Share with the university team the vision of how the collaboration can help the company

- Select researchers who will understand company practices and technology goals.
- Ensure that the university team appreciates the project's strategic context.

4. Invest in long-term relationships.

- Plan multiyear collaboration time frames.
- Cultivate relationships with target university researchers, even if research is not directly supported.

5. Establish strong communication linkage with the university team.

- Conduct face-to-face meetings on a regular basis.
- Develop an overall communication routine to supplement the meetings.
- Encourage extended personnel exchange, both company to university and university to company.

6. Build broad awareness of the project within the company.

- Promote university team interactions with different functional areas within the company.
- Promote feedback to the university team on project alignment with company needs.

7. Support the work internally both *during* the contract and *after*, until the research can be exploited.

- Provide appropriate internal support for technical and management oversight.
- Include accountability for company uptake of research results as part of the project manager role.

The linking of Universities and the Economy

The linking of universities and the economy in the 21st century is going to be governed by the knowledge economy, a world-wide phenomenon. The knowledge of new material driving innovation, competitiveness and economic development is necessary. The economic success of a country is no longer determined by simply possession of raw material or physical power but by the capacity to generate new knowledge and by the ability of the manpower to apply this new knowledge for the betterment of the society.

Thus, there is strong need to develop effective and close cooperation between universities and industries. The following areas are important:

- Innovation in research and development
- Setting up new industries
- Promoting effective university-industry relationship

- Exploiting the results of research by the industry
- Evaluating the criterion of university functioning

Funding of University Research

The funding of university research is a win-win situation for all the three players i.e. University itself, Industry and the Government as shown in Fig. 4.1. It can be seen that funding of university research will give multiple advantages.

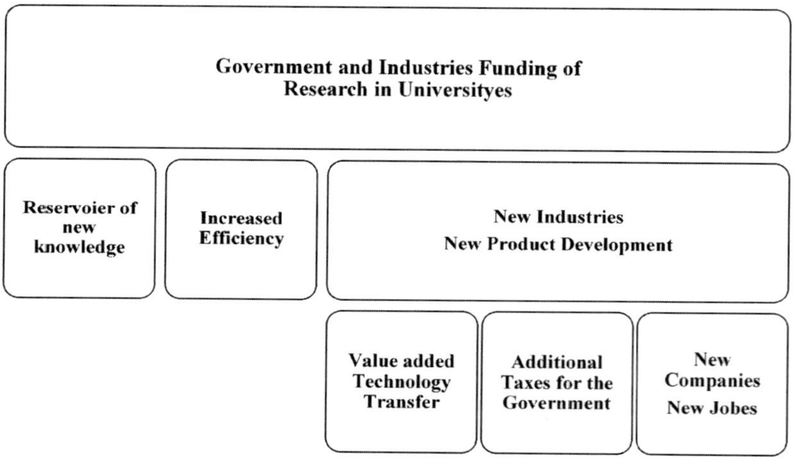

Fig. 4.1: Funding of Research in Universities

Conflicting Values and Common Interest

There are conflicting values and common interest between academia and industries as shown in Fig. 4.2. In addition to the scenario depicted in Fig. 4.2, there is complete freedom in universities while in industries there is some kind of confidentiality. This is further demonstrated in Table 4.1.

Table 4.1: University Research and Entrepreneurial Cultures

University	*Industry*	*How to bring two together*
Research priority set by the investigator	Research priority set by the management	Employment policy
Grant seeking	Profit seeking	Policy for intellectual property
Publications	Proprietary	Revenue sharing
Patenting driven by the publications	Patenting driven by the business decisions	Faculty involvement

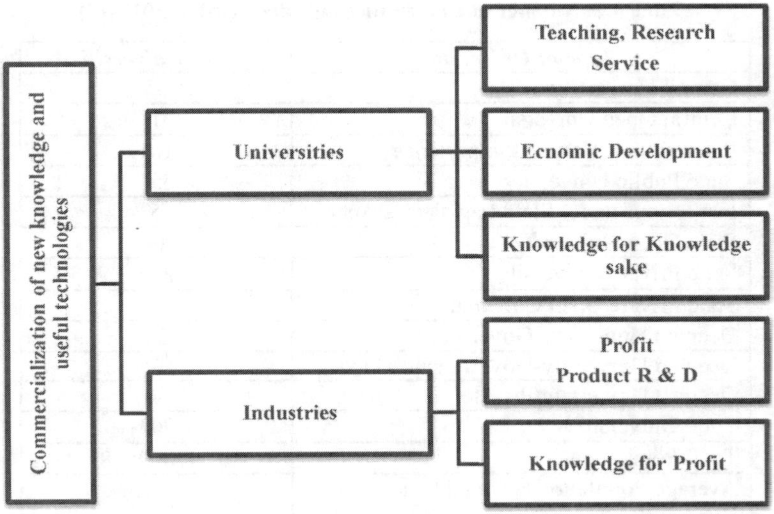

Fig. 4.2:Conflicting Values and Common Interest

Linking Universities with Gross Enrolment Ratio (GER)

Increasing enrolment, GER, employability are interrelated functions. The number of universities in 2017-18 are given in Table 4.2. There are 903 universities catering to the population (18-23 years) of 141829528 with GER 25.8. If we target a GER of 50, then there is need of about 1750 universities. If anyhow, this GER is achieved, where they will go after graduation because the employability market is uncertain.

The state wise number of universities along with GER is given in Table 4.3. The variation of GER among the states (2017-18) is shown in Fig. 4.3 (a). The 12 states which are below the all India average of 25.8 are Assam, Bihar, Chhattisgarh, Gujrat, Jharkhand, Meghalaya, Mizoram, Nagaland, Odisha, Rajasthan, Tripura, West Bengal. The state having lowest GER (13) is Bihar and highest GER (56.4) is Chandigarh. Only 4 States/UT are having GER greater than 40 (Chandigarh, Delhi, Puducherry and Tamil Nadu).

The variation of GER among some of the nations is shown in Fig. 4.3(b). It is seen that GER of India is 25.8 whereas for USA it is 85.8, for Russia it is 81.8.

The state wise population (18-23 years of age) is given in Table 4.4. We can link it with the number of universities and GER. It is shown in Fig. 4.4. The share of population of these 8 states is 64.05 percent . It is observed

Table 4.2: Number of Universities in India (AISHE 2017-18)

Type of University	*No of Universities*
Central University	45
Central Open University	1
Institution of National Importance	101
State Public University	351
Institutions under State Legislature Act	5
State Open University	14
State Private University	262
State Private Open University	1
Deemed University-Government	33
Deemed University-Government Aided	10
Deemed University-Private	80
Total Universities	903
Total Population	141829528
Average Population Covered by a University	157065
GER	25.8
Universities Needed for GER 50.0	1750
Average Population Covered by a University	81045

Table 4.3: State wise distribution of the Universities and Gross Enrolment Ratio (GER)

Sl. No.	*State/UTs*	*No*	*GER 2010-11*			*GER 2017-18*		
			Total	*Male*	*Female*	*Total*	*Male*	*Female*
1	Andhra Pradesh	34	30.9	34.7	27.1	28.4	32.1	24.4
2	Arunachal Pradesh	9	26.9	33.6	19.5	29.7	31.5	27.8
3	Assam	21	13.4	13.3	13.4	18.2	18.6	17.8
4	Bihar	24	10.5	11.8	9.1	13.0	14.5	11.5
5	Chandigarh	3	41.4	42.2	40.4	56.4	48.6	67.7
6	Chhattisgarh	24	13.6	15.8	11.4	18.4	18.5	18.3
7	Delhi	27	32.5	35.0	29.8	46.3	44.9	48.0
8	Goa	3	33.2	31.0	35.8	28.0	24.9	31.9
9	Gujarat	65	21.3	23.5	18.8	20.1	21.9	18.2
10	Haryana	40	24.1	27.2	20.7	28.7	27.0	30.7
11	Himachal Pradesh	25	26.0	25.9	26.0	37.9	34.0	42.2
12	Jammu and Kashmir	14	16.8	17.0	16.7	27.7	26.4	29.0
13	Jharkhand	21	8.1	8.8	7.5	18.0	18.4	17.6
14	Karnataka	60	25.5	26.6	24.3	27.8	27.2	28.5
15	Kerala	22	21.9	18.8	25.1	36.2	32.0	40.4
16	Madhya Pradesh	52	13.6	15.1	11.9	21.2	21.8	20.5

(*Contd...*)

17	Maharashtra	54	27.6	30.7	24.2	31.1	32.6	29.5
18	Manipur	5	35.9	38.5	33.3	31.8	31.3	32.3
19	Meghalaya	8	17.5	15.3	19.8	24.7	24.2	25.1
20	Mizoram	3	21.6	22.0	21.1	22.9	24.8	21.0
21	Nagaland	5	21.5	25.8	16.9	17.8	17.8	17.9
22	Odisha	25	16.1	18.1	14.1	22.0	23.8	20.1
23	Puducherry	14	31.2	32.6	29.9	45.4	42.9	48.1
24	Punjab	31	19.4	23.6	14.5	30.3	27.6	33.6
25	Rajasthan	79	18.2	20.9	15.2	21.7	22.7	20.6
26	Sikkim	7	24.2	26.0	22.2	37.4	33.9	41.1
27	Tamil Nadu	58	32.9	36.5	29.1	48.6	49.1	48.2
28	Telangana	24	33.1	36.9	29.3	35.7	37.1	34.2
29	Tripura	4	13.6	16.0	11.0	21.2	23.7	18.8
30	Uttar Pradesh	76	16.3	15.2	17.4	25.9	25.2	26.6
31	Uttarakhand	33	27.8	26.1	29.6	36.3	36.3	36.3
32	West Bengal	43	12.4	13.8	10.9	18.7	19.9	17.6
All India		903	19.4	20.8	17.9	25.8	26.3	25.4
Brazil						50.5		
Russia						81.8		
China						50.0		
South Africa						20.8		
USA						85.8		

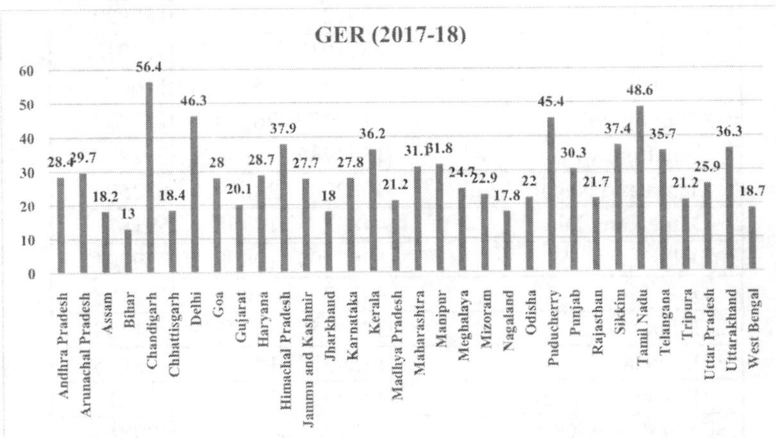

Fig. 4.3(a): Variation of GER Among the States (2017-18)

that Uttar Pradesh has the highest share of population (17.56 percent) and also has the highest number of universities (76), but GER is only 25.9 as against 48.6 of Tamil Nadu which has only 57 universities and 4.99 percent of population.

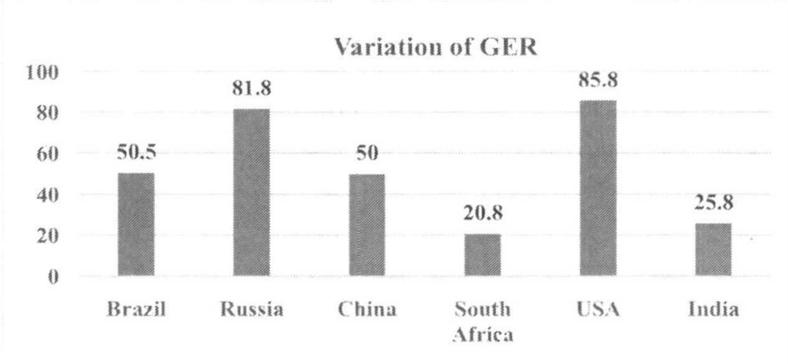

Fig. 4.3 (b): Variation of GER among the Nations (2017-18)

The status of enrolment during 2010-11 and 2017-18 among different programmes is given in Table 4.5 and 4.6. The percentage increase in enrolment during 2010-11 to 2017-18 is shown in Fig. 4.5. It is worth to mention that the increase in enrolment during 2010-11 to 2017-18 is maximum for Ph.D programme, followed by PG Diploma and Diploma.

Table 4.4: Population (18-23 Years) - 2017-18

1	Andaman and Nicobar Islands	24722	23917	48639
2	Andhra Pradesh	2728267	2766950	5495217
3	Arunachal Pradesh	79992	79930	159922
4	Assam	1811017	1918121	3729138
5	Bihar	6011917	5595537	11607454
6	Chandigarh	111207	76524	187731
7	Chhattisgarh	1553735	1574035	3127770
8	Dadra and Nagar Haveli	39623	23629	63252
9	Daman and Diu	44832	14355	59187
10	Delhi	1257204	1040813	2298017
11	Goa	99207	78091	177298
12	Gujarat	3784555	3432529	7217084
13	Haryana	1729377	1455176	3184553
14	Himachal Pradesh	377209	349405	726614
15	Jammu and Kashmir	670424	627732	1298156
16	Jharkhand	1925870	1904433	3830303
17	Karnataka	3567558	3415075	6982633
18	Kerala	1499642	1492924	2992566
19	Lakshadweep	3650	3619	7269

(Contd...)

20	Madhya Pradesh	4693864	4211674	8905538
21	Maharashtra	6969675	6300057	13269732
22	Manipur	163639	165779	329418
23	Meghalaya	167233	172603	339836
24	Mizoram	63997	64851	128848
25	Nagaland	124292	120037	244329
26	Odisha	2309432	2314497	4623929
27	Puducherry	84092	76814	160906
28	Punjab	1733665	1429163	3162828
29	Rajasthan	4643790	4286822	8930612
30	Sikkim	40090	37533	77623
31	Tamil Nadu	3543854	3531003	7074857
32	Telangana	1979708	2000154	3979862
33	Tripura	211914	220902	432816
34	Uttar Pradesh	13122748	11776057	24898805
35	Uttarakhand	618182	585806	1203988
36	West Bengal	5331100	5541698	10872798
All India		73121283	68708245	141829528

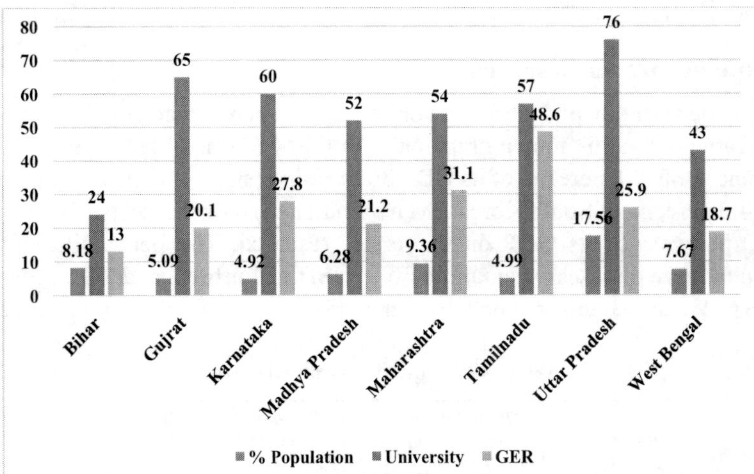

Fig. 4.4: Variation of Population, Number of Universities and GER

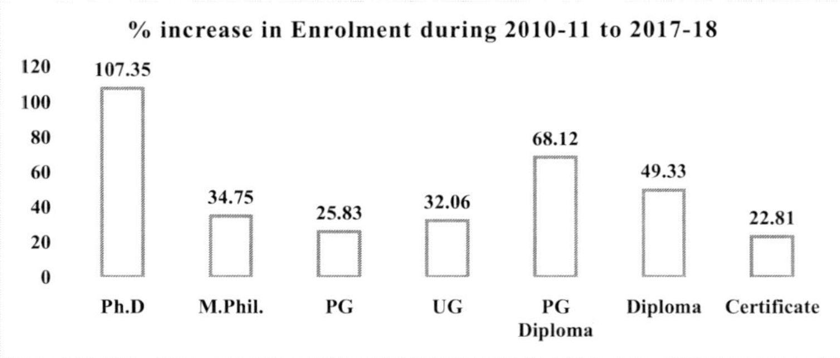

Fig. 4.5: Percent increase in Enrolment during 2010-11 to 2017-18

Table 4.5: Student Enrolment at various levels

State/UTs	*Ph.D.*			*M.Phil.*			*Post Graduate*		
	Male	*Female*	*Total*	*Male*	*Female*	*Total*	*Male*	*Female*	*Total*
2017-18	92570	68842	161412	12287	21822	34109	1891071	2223239	4114309
2010-11	48007	29837	77844	12687	12625	25312	1813992	1455677	3269669

Table 4.6: Student Enrolment at various levels

State/UTs	*Under Graduate*			*PG Diploma*			*Diploma*		
	Male	*Female*	*Total*	*Male*	*Female*	*Total*	*Male*	*Female*	*Total*
2017-18	15052304	13964045.6	29016349	126853	108410	235263	1838217	869717	2707934
2010-11	12117511	9854749	21972260	90412	49528	139940	1280668	532685	1813353

Expenditure on Research

The variation of expenditure on research as percentage of GDP is given in Table 4.7 and is shown graphically in Fig. 4.6. It is observed that India spends only 0.8 percent of its GDP on the university research as compared to 4.3 percent of South Korea. Even a small nation like Israel spends about 4.2 percent of its GDP on university research. The per capita Govt. expenditure on research at university is USD 12 for India and USD 256 for USA. We are lagging far behind in the university expenditure on research.

Table 4.7: Expenditure on Research

Country	*Expenditure on Research (% of GDP)*	*Per Capita Govt. Expenditure on Research at University Level*
India	0.8	USD 12
Israel	4.2	
South Korea	4.3	
China	2.0	
USA	2.7	USD 256

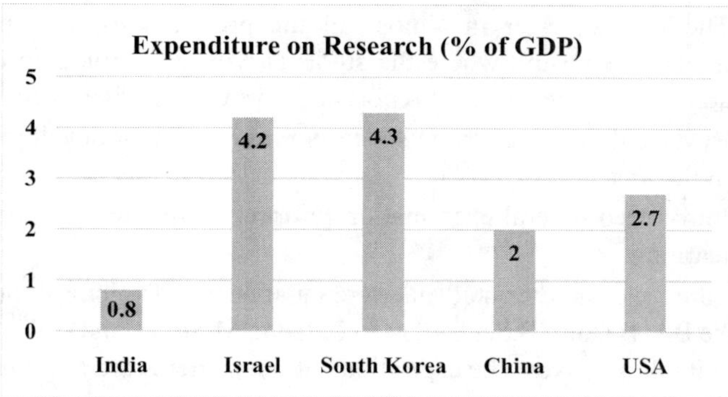

Fig. 4.6: Variation of Expenditure on Research (% of GDP)

Quality Research

All higher education institutions (universities/institutes) in order to stand on their own, have no option but to venture for quality research relevant to the society. The universities of tomorrow have to be the leaders in quality research. The research should not be for the sake of degree only but must be relevant for the society for all the time.

Need for Having Universities for Teacher Training

With an objective to impart best teaching to its students, Universities need to have well trained teachers. At present the scenario is as follows:

- There are no specific training institutes/universities which can train the teachers for teaching in higher educational institutes/universities.
- There are as many methodologies for teaching in higher education as the number of teachers.
- A fresh graduate is employed to teach the students at Diploma level.
- A fresh M.Sc/M.Tech/MBA is employed to teach the students at B.Sc/B.Tech/BBA level.
- A similar scenario is there in all areas.
- The end result is that quality of higher education always remains questionable.

What a University Should Do?

(1) Creditise all the programmes and courses as per UGC guidelines incorporating core courses, elective courses and skill based courses in almost all the programmes

(2) The last semester in almost all the programmes, is kept for industry exposure where the students will go, participate in the activities, write a project report and give project viva-voce.

(3) Revised the course contents incorporating the latest developments in the area

(4) Introduced several examination reforms leading to the enhanced learning

Gone are the days when students were satisfied with Diploma or normal Degree like BA, B.Com, B.Sc, B.E, MA, M.Com, M.Sc etc. and still lacking skill for suitable job. Now the aspirations of the students are to go for the latest job- oriented courses, obtain graduate/master degrees and simultaneously work in an appropriate job. It is the duty of all concerned to reorient the higher education for meeting this requirement.

Innovation in Academia-Industry Interaction

Innovation is crucial for long-run economic growth. Innovation tends to cluster in certain industries/sectors, which consequently grow more rapidly, leading to structural changes in production and demand and, eventually, organisational and institutional change. The capacity to undertake the latter is important for the ability to benefit from innovation. Innovation is a powerful explanatory factor behind differences in performance between firms, regions and countries. Firms that succeed in innovation prosper, at the expense of their less able competitors. Innovative countries and regions have higher productivity and income than the less-innovative ones. Countries or regions that wish to catch-up with the innovation leaders face the challenge of increasing their own innovation activities towards leader-levels (Jan Fagerberg 2004, Innovation: A Guide to the Literature, Presented in the workshop).

Sharma et. al. (2015) have studied academia-industry interaction. The industry academia interface mainly deals with knowledge experience and technology transfer. Universities and industry are rapidly coming closer to each other for their mutual benefits. Indian Industry has become more aware of the vital linkage between the education system and business and corporate productivity. There exists principal-agent relationship between institute and industry. In fact, input of one is critical for the other. In large firms, the formalization of the industrial Ph.D. studies, future Ph.D. programmes and academia-industry relationships can be used to enhance strategic competences. Internships, an example of successful cooperation between industry and academics, are designed to help students develop vocational self-concept, acquire job relevant skills and provide informed career decision making ability.

The various challenges currently facing Academia-Industry collaborations are awareness, identification, evaluation, protection and commercialization of ideas. The development of technology that allows the university to deliver quality coursework and manpower to the industries are needed. Some of the factors relevant to academia-industry interaction are:

- Organizing workshops, conferences and symposia on regular basis
- Promote Academia-Industry interaction in all areas
- MoU for the establishment of university industry collaboration centre, may be called University Industry Training Centre.
- Organising seminars, conferences, workshops at the University and at the Industry at regular intervals.
- Industry experts to be invited in curriculum design and subsequent revision
- Visit of faculty to the industry and vice-versa.
- Collaborative degree programmes; practical training and teaching during training
- Project/dissertation at the industry; industry expert acting as project joint supervisor
- Research and development facilities to be established by the industry at the university/institute

5

Innovations in Research Methodologies

Research Methodology

The word "Research" refers to search for knowledge; a search for truth, a prolonged, intensive and purposeful search. Research is by joining the two words: Re-Search. 'Re' means again and 'Search' stands for "to look at or examine carefully in order to find something concealed." Together they form a noun describing a careful, systematic, patient study and investigation in some field of knowledge, undertaken to establish facts or principles.

The goal of all research activities is to make a progress. This can be accomplished by raising several questions. Research is largely a matter of raising different questions and then trying to find an answer or solution to those questions.

Research methodology is a way to systematically solve the research problem. Research can be broadly defined as human activity based on intellectual application in the investigation of matter. The primary aim of research is discovering, interpreting and development of methods and systems for the advancement of human knowledge. We can generalize the definition of research as follows:

- Research is a way of thinking
- Research is one of the ways to find answers to our questions
- Research is critical examination of different aspects of professional work
- Research is as habit of questioning what we do, how we do, why we do.
- Research is a systematic examination of observed information.

The role of research in different areas has greatly increased in recent times. Research assumes significance in the context of the following:

- It enables to take decisions based on reliable and factual data.
- It is logical and objective.
- It foresees the implications of particular phenomenon.
- It promotes social welfare and scientific development.
- It facilitates prediction and helps in planning.
- It enables the researcher to be systematic and organized.

  Basic characteristics of research may be grouped as follows:
- By way of research, one can innovate or discover a certain thing. Innovation is the new ways of introducing something; whereas to discover is to be the first to find out something unknown.
- Management, statistics, commerce, economics, psychology etc. are the social science subjects, as here the study reveals the need of the society based on certain trends.
- It is important to begin with the understanding of research and its methodology by asking several questions like what is research? What is the importance of research? What are the meaning and benefits of research methodology?
- There are certain disciplines of research where we cannot simply develop any theory or where we cannot put our contribution into the development of certain basic concepts.
- Research unless it is understood in its right spirit cannot be taken into account with success. Research then becomes more of a passion to the researchers than just a mere source of career growth.

Meaning of Research

Research refers to a search for knowledge. Alternatively, we can also say that research is a scientific and systematic search for pertinent information on a specific subject. You can also say that research is an art of scientific investigation. When we say that we are undertaking a research study to find answers to a question, we are implying that the process:

- is being undertaken within a framework of a set of approaches;
- uses procedures, methods and techniques that have been tested for their validity and reliability;
- is designed to be unbiased and objective.

(1) Approaches means qualitative, quantitative and the academic discipline in which researchers have already been trained or are being trained.

(2) Validity means that correct procedures have been applied to find answers to a question. Reliability refers to the quality of a measurement procedure that provides repeatability and accuracy.

(3) Unbiased and objective means that we have taken each step in an unbiased manner and drawn each conclusion to the best of our ability and without introducing our own vested interest.

Thus, the process may be called 'research' provided it adheres to the above mentioned three criteria. However, the degree to which these criteria are expected to be fulfilled varies from discipline to discipline and so the meaning of 'research' differs from one academic discipline to another.

It becomes interesting to know the difference between research and non-research activities. The difference lies in the way we find answers: the process must meet certain requirements to be called research. We can identify these requirements by examining some definitions of research.

Definitions of Research

Research has been defined in various ways by different researchers. Some of the definitions are:

- Research is a structured enquiry that utilizes acceptable scientific methodology to solve problems and create new knowledge that is generally applicable. Scientific methods consist of systematic observation, classification and interpretation of data.
- Research is an active, meticulous and systematic process of inquiry in order to discover, interpret or revise facts, events, behaviours or theories or to make practical applications with the help of such facts and laws or theories.
- Research is a careful study to discover the correct information. It is a movement from the known to the unknown. It is actually a passage of discovery. Research is an innovative contribution to existing knowledge, making for its improvement. It is observed that most of us are interested in research to progress our career. In this manner, certain researches are carried out in a routine way.

  L.V. Redman and A.V.H. Mory: Research is defined as "systematized effort to gain new knowledge."

  D. Slesinger and M. Stephenson: Described research as "management of things, concepts or symbols for the purpose of generalizing to enlarge, correct or verify the knowledge, whether that knowledge aids in construction of theory or in the practice of an art."

Rusk: "Research is point of view, an attitude of inquiry or a frame of mind. It comprises defining and redefining problems, formulating hypothesis or suggesting solutions; collecting, organizing and evaluating data; making deductions and testing the conclusions to determine whether they fit the formulated hypotheses."

Crawford: "research is a systematic and refined technique of thinking, employing specialized tools, instruments and procedure in order to obtain a more adequate solution of a problem."

J. Francis Rummel: "Research is an endeavor / attempt to discover, develop and verify knowledge. It is an intellectual process that has developed over hundreds of years ever changing in purpose and form and always researching to truth."

P.M. Cook:"Research is an honest, exhaustive, intelligent searching for facts and their meanings or implications with reference to a given problem. The product or findings of a given piece of research should be an authentic, verifiable contribution to knowledge in the field studied."

W.S. Monroes: "Research may be defined as a method of studying problems whose solutions are to be derived partly or wholly from facts."

Every research is usually composed of two parts:

(1) Technical aspects

(2) Logical aspects

First one deals with collection of information and second comes at the time of generalization on the basis of the collected information.

John W. Best: "Research is considered to be the more formal, systematic intensive process of carrying on the scientific method of analysis. It involves a more systematic structure of investigation, usually resulting in some sort of formal record of procedures and a report of results or conclusion."

Clifford Woody: "Research comprises defining and redefining problems, formulating hypothesis or suggested solutions, collecting, organizing and evaluating data, making deductions and reaching conclusions and at last careful testing the conclusions to determine whether they fit the formulated hypothesis."

Redman & Mori: "Research is a systematic effort to gain new knowledge."

P.V. Younge: "Social research may be defined as a scientific undertaking which by means of logical and systematized techniques aims to discover new facts or verify and test old facts, analyze their sequences, interrelationships and casual explanation which were derived within an appropriate theoretical frame of reference, develop new scientific tools, concepts and theories which would facilitate reliable and valid study of human behavior."

Nature of Research

It is very important to know the nature of research. Nature of research is the way we do things. Nature of research is the way of life we take important decisions. Without it we are deluged with information. Nature of research is the very characteristics of collection of extensive information and modifying or transforming new ideas into reality. Each day of our life is research oriented and calls for an introspection of events for betterment. The studies may be in various fields e.g. business, industries, human life etc.

We research in many diverse ways. Some of them are:

- We research in book reviews before buying books
- We research the best buys in cars and appliances
- We research best B-Schools for studying
- We perform some kind of research in our jobs
- Our search for information may lead us to interview friends or other knowledgeable people
- Read articles in magazines, journals or newspapers
- Watch TV to explore the internet and World Wide Web for information.

Formal academic research differs from experiential research and may be more investigative in nature. For instance, it may require us to learn about an area where we have little knowledge or leaning to learn. It may be library oriented or field-oriented or laboratory oriented, depending on the nature of research as described below:

(a) **Systematic Way**: Research is a way of systematically solving the research problem. In management research, researcher always plans his step in systematic manner.

(b) Scientific Method: Research in management, serves as a scientific basis for solving new facts. Researcher attempt to achieve this by experimentation, observation, logical argumentation and a combination of three in different proportions.

(c) Verifiability: Conclusion of management research drawn through a scientific method is subject to verification at any time. Verifiability refers that the phenomena must be capable of being observed and measured.

(d) Tools for New Products Development: Research is a management tool for new product development and modification of existing products.

(e) Definiteness: Conclusion is arrived at as a result of research because of the study, observation and verification of data.

(f) Objectivity: In research, all things have to be objective and based on facts and internal conditions. There is no space for subjectivity.

(g) Helpful in Prediction: Conclusions that are drawn as a result of research are helpful in prediction and serve as an aid for decision making.

(h) Basis for Management Principles: Research serves as a basis for the development of new management techniques and principles.

(i) Aid in Decision Making: Research helps managers in decision making under different circumstances.

(j) Relies on Empirical Evidence: Research relies on empirical evidence and utilizes relevant concepts.

Objectives of Research

The main objective of research is to discover answers to questions through the application of scientific methods. The foremost objective of any research is to find out the truth which is hidden and which has not discovered yet.

The general objectives of research may be as mentioned below:

- To discover new facts
- To verify and test important facts
- To analyze an event or process or phenomenon to identify the cause and effect relationship
- To develop new scientific tools, concepts and theories to solve and understand scientific and non-scientific problems

- To find solutions to scientific, non-scientific and social problems
- To overcome or solve the problems occurring in our everyday life
- To test a hypothesis of a causal relationship between variables

Other Objectives are the following:

- **Development of Knowledge**: Research is the science that studies the business environment. It tries to collect a systematic body of knowledge about the subject-matter that it studies. It is to add knowledge.
- **New Product Development**: Research plays an important role in new product development or modification of existing products. It needs to conduct a research in order to find out something new.
- **Academic Purpose**: Management students are also use a research methodology for their academic purpose or for the compilation of their course.
- **Scientific Study of Business**: Research is an attempt. The researcher makes study of collective processes, environmental change, business structure and business processes etc.
- **Solution of Business Problems**: Research methodology helps improve understanding of particular business or management problem and result into solution to the problem.
- **Welfare Society**: Science is not an end itself. The knowledge that we acquire is intended at bringing about the welfare of society. No researcher makes study for the sake of study. He has to direct his study to some higher aim which invariably is welfare of society.
- **Control and Prediction**: Though research methodology we make study of phenomenon, events and factors that govern and guide business. Apart from that we present an analysis of social life and how to govern them in the scientific manner. It helps us in better control and prediction.

Types of Research

Research can be classified based on the following three perspectives as shown in Fig. 5.1.

- application of research study
- objectives in undertaking the research
- inquiry mode employed

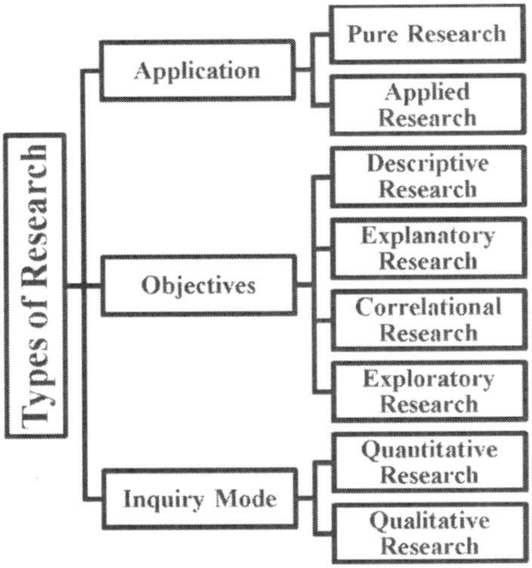

Fig. 5.1: Types of Research

Application: From the application point of view, there are two broad categories of research; pure research and applied research.

Pure research involves developing and testing theories and hypotheses that are challenging but may or may not have practical application. The knowledge produced through pure research is sought in order to add to the existing body of research methods.

Applied research is done to solve specific, practical questions; for policy formulation, administration and understanding of a phenomenon. It can be exploratory, but is usually descriptive. Applied research can be carried out by academic or industrial institutions. Often, an academic institution such as a university will have a specific applied research program which may be funded by an industrial partner interested in that program.

From the viewpoint of objectives, a research can be classified as descriptive research, correlational research, explanatory research and exploratory research.

Descriptive research attempts to describe systematically a situation, problem, phenomenon, service or programme, or provides information about, say, living condition of a community, or describes attitudes towards an issue.

Correlational research attempts to discover or establish the existence of a relationship/ interdependence between two or more aspects of a situation.

Explanatory research attempts to clarify why and how there is a relationship between two or more aspects of a situation or phenomenon.

Exploratory research is undertaken to explore an area where little is known or to investigate the possibilities of undertaking a particular research study (feasibility study / pilot study).

Inquiry Mode: In inquiry mode, two approaches are quantitative approach and qualitative approach.

Quantitative approach: The quantitative approach to inquiry is usually classified as structured research. Here everything that forms the research process- objectives, design, sample, and the questions that are asked from the respondents- is predetermined. It is more appropriate to determine the extent of a problem, issue or phenomenon by quantifying the variations.

Qualitative approach: The qualitative approach to inquiry is usually classified as unstructured research. This approach allows flexibility in all aspects of the research process. It is more appropriate to explore the nature of a problem, issue or phenomenon without quantifying it.

Tools of Research

The resources available to expedite the means by which a researcher endeavors to accomplish the research objectives are commonly grouped into five categories, called as tools of research. They are:

(a) Information Sources
(b) Statistical Tools
(c) Computers
(d) Measurement Techniques
(e) Languages

Applications of Research

The application areas of research are wide and contain almost all disciplines. The major areas could be:

- The professionals
- The consumers
- The administrators/Planners
- The service providers

Possible sub-areas are shown in Fig. 5.2.

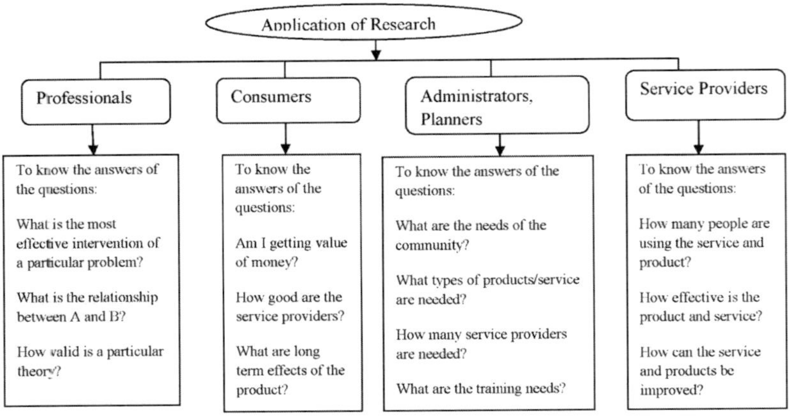

Fig. 5.2: Application Areas of Research

Characteristics of Research

Research is a process of collecting, analyzing and interpreting information to answer questions. But to qualify as research, the process must have certain characteristics: it must, as far as possible, be controlled, rigorous, systematic, valid and verifiable, empirical and critical as discussed below.

Controlled: The concept of control implies that, in exploring causality in relation to two variables (factors), you set up your study in a way that minimizes the effects of other factors affecting the relationship.

Rigorous: The procedures followed to find answers to questions should be relevant, appropriate and justified. Again, the degree of rigor varies markedly between the physical and social sciences and within the social sciences.

Systematic: The procedure adopted to undertake an investigation should follow a certain logical sequence. The different steps cannot be taken in a haphazard way. Some procedures must follow others.

Valid and verifiable: This concept implies that whatever you conclude on the basis of your findings is correct and can be verified by you and others.

Empirical: This means that any conclusion drawn is based upon hard evidence gathered from information collected from real life experiences or observations.

Critical: Critical scrutiny of the procedures used and the methods employed is crucial to a research enquiry. The process of investigation must be foolproof and free from drawbacks. The process adopted and the procedures used must be able to withstand critical scrutiny.

Research, thus, has many discrete characteristics which taken together, comprise the particular approach to probing for truth i.e. research. Some of them are:

- Research begins with the question in the mind of the researcher.
- Research demands the identification of the problem stated in clear unambiguous terms, which a researcher seeks to solve.
- Research requires a definite plan.
- Research deals with the main problem through appropriate sub-problems.
- Research seeks direction through appropriate hypotheses.
- Research deals with facts and their meaning (interpretation).
- Research is a cyclic process.

Criteria of Good Research

Whatever may be the types of research works and studies, one thing that is important is that they all meet on the common ground of scientific method employed by them. One expects scientific research to satisfy the following criteria:

- The purpose of the research should be clearly defined and common concepts be used.
- The research procedure used should be described in sufficient detail to permit another researcher to repeat the research for further advancement, keeping the continuity of what has already been attained.
- The procedural design of the research should be carefully planned to yield results that are as objective as possible.
- The researcher should report with complete frankness, flaws in procedural design and estimate their effects upon the findings.
- The analysis of data should be sufficiently adequate to reveal its significance and the methods of analysis used should be appropriate. The validity and reliability of the data should be checked carefully.
- Conclusions should be confined to those justified by the data of the research and limited to those for which the data provide an adequate basis.

- Greater confidence in research is warranted if the researcher is experienced, has a good reputation in research and is a person of integrity.

In other words, we can state the qualities of a good research as under:

- **Good research is systematic**: It means that research is structured with specified steps to be taken in a specified sequence in accordance with the well-defined set of rules. Systematic characteristic of the research does not rule out creative thinking but it certainly does reject the use of guessing and intuition in arriving at conclusions.
- **Good research is logical**: This implies that research is guided by the rules of logical reasoning and the logical process of induction and deduction are of great value in carrying out research. Induction is the process of reasoning from a part to the whole whereas deduction is the process of reasoning from some premise to a conclusion which follows from that very premise. In fact, logical reasoning makes research more meaningful in the context of decision making.
- **Good research is empirical**: It implies that research is related basically to one or more aspects of a real situation and deals with concrete data that provides a basis for external validity to research results.
- **Good research is replicable**: This characteristic allows research results to be verified by replicating the study and thereby building a sound basis for decisions.

Problems Encountered by Researchers in India

Researchers in India, particularly those engaged in empirical research, are facing several problems. Some of the important problems are as follows:

(1) The lack of a scientific training in the methodology of research

The lack of a scientific training in the methodology of research is a great impediment for researchers in our country. There is paucity of competent researchers. Many researchers take a leap in the dark without knowing research methods. Most of the work, which goes in the name of research is not methodologically sound. Research to many researchers and even to their guides, is mostly a scissor and paste job without any insight shed on the collated materials. The consequence is obvious, viz., the research results, quite often, do not reflect the reality or realities. Thus, a systematic study of research methodology is an urgent necessity. Before undertaking research projects, researchers should be well equipped with all the methodological aspects. As such, efforts should be made to provide short duration intensive courses for meeting this requirement.

(2) Insufficient interaction between different players

There is insufficient interaction between the university research departments on one side and business establishments, government departments and research institutions on the other side. A great deal of primary data of non-confidential nature remain untouched/untreated by the researchers for want of proper contacts. Efforts should be made to develop satisfactory liaison among all concerned for better and realistic researches. There is need for developing some mechanisms of a university—industry interaction programme so that academics can get ideas from practitioners on what needs to be researched and practitioners can apply the research done by the academics.

(3) Lack of confidence

Most of the business units in our country do not have the confidence that the material supplied by them to researchers will not be misused and as such they are often reluctant in supplying the needed information to researchers. The concept of secrecy seems to be sacrosanct to business organizations in the country so much so that it proves an impermeable barrier to researchers. Thus, there is the need for generating the confidence that the information/data obtained from a business unit will not be misused.

(4) Overlapping research studies

Research studies overlapping one another are undertaken quite often for want of adequate information. This results in duplication and fritters away resources. This problem can be solved by proper compilation and revision, at regular intervals, of a list of subjects on which and the places where the research is going on. Due attention should be given toward identification of research problems in various disciplines of applied science which are of immediate concern to the industries.

(5) Nonexistence a code of conduct

There does not exist a code of conduct for researchers and inter-university and interdepartmental rivalries are also quite common. Hence, there is need for developing a code of conduct for researchers which, if adhered sincerely, can win over this problem.

(6) Inadequate availability of infrastructure

Many researchers in our country also face the difficulty of adequate and timely secretarial assistance, including computer assistance. This causes unnecessary delays in the completion of research studies. All possible efforts be made in this direction so that efficient secretarial assistance is made available to researchers and that too well in time.

(7) Library facilities not up to the mark

Library management and functioning is not satisfactory at many places and much of the time and energy of researchers are spent in tracing out the books, journals, reports, etc., rather than in tracing out relevant material from them. There is also the problem that many of our libraries are not able to get copies of old and new Acts/Rules, reports and other government publications in time. This problem is felt more in libraries which are away in places from Delhi and/or the state capitals. Thus, efforts should be made for the regular and speedy supply of all governmental publications to reach our libraries.

(8) Non-availability of published data

There is also the difficulty of timely availability of published data from various government and other agencies doing this job in our country. Researcher also faces the problem on account of the fact that the published data vary quite significantly because of differences in coverage by the concerning agencies.

Road Map for Research Journey

A possible road journey for a good research is shown in Fig. 5.3. It is basically divided in to three phases. Each phase is further divided in to different steps till the research report (thesis) is written.

Research Process

The research process is similar to undertaking a tour. For a research tour, there are two important decisions to make:

- What research questions (problems) you want to find answers to?
- How to go about finding the answers?

There are well known practical steps through which you must pass in your research tour in order to find answers to your research questions. The path to finding answers to research questions constitutes research methodology. At each operational step in the research process you are required to choose from a multiplicity of methods, procedures and models of research methodology which will help you to best achieve your objectives.

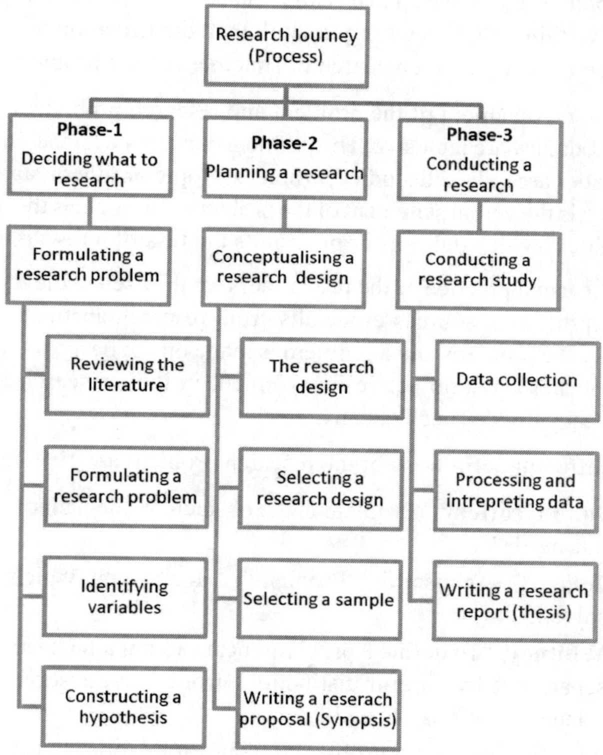

Fig. 5.3: Research Journey

Steps in Research Process

A research process follows multiple steps. Some of the important steps are given below:

- Formulating the Research Problem
- Literature Review
- Developing the Objectives
- Preparing the Research Design
- Collecting the Data
- Analysis of Data
- Generalization and Interpretation
- Presentation of Results

Formulating the Research Problem

Selection of problem is not the first step in research but identification of the problem is the first step in research. Selection of problem is governed by reflective thinking. It is wrong to think that identification of a problem means to select a topic of a research or statement of the problem.

A topic or statement of the problem and research problem are not the synonyms but they are inclusive. The problem concerns with the functioning of the broader area of field studied, whereas a topic or title or statement of the problem is the verbal statement of the problem. The topic is the definition of the problem which delimits or pin points the task of a researcher.

It is the usual practice of the researcher that they select the topic of the study from different sources especially from research abstracts. They do not identify the problem, but a problem is made on the basis of the topic. It results that they have no active involvement in their research activities, whatever, they do, do mechanically.

The different definitions of the research problem are given below:

John Geoffery: "Problem is the obstacle in the path of satisfying our needs."

John. G. Tornsand: "Problem is a question which is to be solved."

Whitney: "To define a problem means to put a fence around it, to separate it by careful distinctions from like questions found in related situations of need."

J.C. Townsend: "A problem is a question proposed for a solution generally speaking a problem exists when there is a no available answer to same question."

F.N. Kerlinger: "A problem is an interrogative sentence or statement that asks: What relation exists between two or more variables?"

Monero and Engelhart: "To define a problem means to specify it in detail and with precision each question and subordinate question to be answered is to be specified, the limits of the investigation must be determined. Frequently, it is necessary to review previous studies in order to determine just what is to be done. Sometimes it is necessary to formulate the point of view or educational theory on which the investigation is to be based. If certain assumptions are made, they must be explicitly noted."

The way you formulate a problem determines almost every step that follows. The sources of research problems are equally important. For example, research in social sciences revolves around 4 Ps:

- **People-** a group of individuals
- **Problems-** examine the existence of certain issues or problems relating to their lives; to ascertain attitude of a group of people towards an issue
- **Programs-** to evaluate the effectiveness of an intervention
- **Phenomena-** to establish the existence of regularity.

In practice, most research studies are based upon at least a combination of two Ps. Every research study has following two aspects:

(1) Study population

- People: individuals, organizations, groups, communities

(2) Subject area

- Problems: issues, situations, associations, needs, profiles
- Program: content, structure, outcomes, attributes satisfactions, consumers, Service providers, etc.
- Phenomenon: cause-and-effect relationships, the study of a phenomenon itself

You can examine the professional field of your choice in the context of the four Ps in order to identify anything that looks interesting.

Selecting a Research Problem

You need to consider some important steps that will help to ensure that your study will remain manageable and that you will remain motivated. Some of them are:

- **Interest**: a research endeavour is usually time consuming, and involves hard work and possibly unforeseen problems. One should select topic of great interest to sustain the required motivation.
- **Magnitude**: It is extremely important to select a topic that you can manage within the time and resources at your disposal. Narrow the topic down to something manageable, specific and clear.
- **Measurement of concepts**: Make sure that you are clear about the indicators and measurement of concepts (if used) in your study.

- **Level of expertise**: Make sure that you have adequate level of expertise for the task you are proposing since you need to do the work yourself.
- **Relevance**: Ensure that your study adds to the existing body of knowledge, bridges current gaps and is useful in policy formulation. This will help you to sustain interest in the study.
- **Availability of data**: Before finalizing the topic, make sure that data are available.
- **Ethical issues**: How ethical issues can affect the study population and how ethical problems can be overcome should be thoroughly examined at the problem formulating stage.

The necessary steps which must be followed in identifying a research problem are:

- Step 1: Determining the field of research in which researchers are keen to do the research work.
- Step 2: The researchers should develop the mastery on the area or it should be the field of their specialization.
- Step 3: The researchers should review the research conducted in area to know the recent trend and studies are being conducted in the area.
- Step 4: On the basis of review, the researchers should consider the priority field of the study.
- Step 5: The researchers should draw an analogy and insight in identifying a problem or employ their personal experience of the field in locating the problem. They may take help of supervisor or expert of the field.
- Step 6: The researchers should pin point specific aspect of the problem which is to be investigated.

You can find the sources of the problems in many situations. Some interesting situations are:

- The universities, institutions, community and other agencies of education are obvious sources.
- Social developments and technological changes are constantly bringing forth new problems and opportunities for research.
- Record of previous research such specialized sources as the encyclopedias of educational, research abstracts, research bulletins, research reports, journals of researches, dissertations and many similar publications are rich sources of research problems.

- Text book assignments, special assignments, reports and term papers will suggest additional areas of needed research.
- Classroom discussions, seminars and exchange of ideas with faculty members and fellow scholars and students will suggest many stimulating problems to be solved, close professional relationships, academic discussions and constructive academic climate are especially advantageous opportunities.
- A questioning attitude towards prevailing practices and research oriented academic experience will effectively promote problem awareness.
- The most practical source of problem is to consult supervisor, experts of the field and most experienced persons of the field. They may suggest most significant problems of the area. The researcher can discuss certain issues of the area to emerge a problem.

Although research problems should not be assigned or they should not be proposed and allotted by a guide but consultation with the more experienced faculty member or research worker is a desirable practice.

> **One of the most important functions of the research guide is to help the student clarify his thinking, achieve a sense of focus and develop a manageable problem from one that may be vague and too complex.**

Formulation of a Research Problem

Working through these steps presupposes a reasonable level of knowledge in the broad subject area within which the study is to be undertaken. The following points will be useful:

- Identify a broad field or subject area of interest
- Dissect the broad area into sub areas
- Select what is of most interest to your research
- Raise research questions
- Formulate objectives of your research
- Assess your objectives
- Re-check

Statement of Research Problem

Meeting some standard criteria for the problem statement will result, in a clear and concise idea of what the researcher wants to do. Kerlinger has identified following three criteria of good problem statements;

1. A problem should be concerned with relation between two or more variables.
2. It should be stated 'clearly and unambiguously in question form'.
3. It should be amenable to empirical testing.

Objectives of Assumptions about the Research Problem

The objectives of the assumptions about a research problem are very important and are given below:

1. To make the research work feasible.
2. To delimit the scope of the problem.
3. To establish the proper frame of reference.

This may require certain aspects for delimiting a problem. Some of these are elaborated below:

- Delimited to certain variables that should be mentioned clearly in the problem.
- Delimited to the area or level as primary level, secondary level, and college or university level.
- Delimited to size of sample, considering the time, energy and money.
- Delimited to the best method only.
- Delimited to the best available tool for measuring the variable.
- Delimited to the most appropriate techniques.
- Other delimitations particular to a problem.

As the above delimitations help the researcher for conducting the study, the findings of studies also confine to these delimitations.

Evaluation of the Research Problem

When considering a problem, the researchers are required to ask themselves a series of questions about it. These are helpful in the evaluation of the problem on the basis of personal suitability of the researcher and social value of the problem.

Following questions must be answered affirmatively before the study is under taken:

- Is the problem researchable?
- Is the problem relatively new?
- Is the problem significant to the society?
- Is the problem feasible for the particular researcher?

In order to be feasible, a problem should agree with the following:

- Research competencies of the researcher
- Interest and enthusiasm of the researcher
- Financial consideration in the research proposal
- Time requirement for the research project

Literature Review Concepts

Reviewing the existing literature is an essential preliminary task for acquainting yourself with the available body of knowledge in your area of interest. Literature review is integral part of entire research process and makes valuable contribution to every operational step. Reviewing literature can be time-consuming and frustrating, but is also rewarding.

The main functions of literature review are:

(1) Bring clarity to the research problem identified or to be identified
(2) Improve research methodology
(3) Broaden your knowledge base in the research area
(4) Contextualize your findings

Bring Clarity to the Research Problem

The process of reviewing the literature helps you to understand the subject area better and thus helps you to conceptualize your research problem clearly and precisely. It also helps you to understand the relationship between your research problem and the body of knowledge in the area.

A literature review tells you if others have used procedures and methods similar to the ones that you are proposing, which procedures and methods have worked well for them, and what problems they have faced with them. Thus, you will be better positioned to select a methodology that is capable of providing valid answer to your research questions.

Broaden your Knowledge base in the Research Area

It ensures you to read widely around the subject area in which you intend to conduct your research study. It also helps you to understand how the findings of your study fit into the existing body of knowledge.

Contextualize your Findings

How do answers to your research questions compare with what others have found? What contribution have you been able to make in to the existing body of knowledge? How are your findings different from those of others?

For you to be able to answer these questions, you need to go back to your literature review. It is important to place your findings in the context of what is already known in your field of enquiry.

Procedure for Reviewing the Literature

The following are the broad steps which should be included in the procedure for literature review.

(a) search for existing literature in your area of study
(b) review the literature selected
(c) develop a theoretical framework
(d) develop a conceptual framework

Search for Existing Literature

The search of existing literature is necessary to set parameters for your search. You must have in mind at least some idea of broad subject area and of the problem you wish to investigate. The next step is to compile a bibliography for this broad area from the existing sources like books and journals.

You should search for books in your area of interest and prepare a list, locate these books in the libraries or borrow from other sources. Examine their content relevant to your topic.

Journals provide you with the most up-to-date information, even though there may be a gap between the completion of a research project and the publication in a journal. Here also you need to prepare a list of journals for identifying literature relevant to your study. This can be done as follows:

- locate the hard copies of the journal that are appropriate to your study
- use the internet
- look at the index of research abstracts in the relevant field to identify and read the articles.

Select the latest issue, examine its content page to see if there is an article of relevance to your research topic. If you feel a particular article is of relevance to you, read it's abstract. If you think you are likely to use it, photocopy or prepare a summary and record it for reference for later use.

Review the Literature Selected

The next step is to start reading the selected books or journals or articles critically to pull together themes and issues that are associated. If you do not have a theoretical framework of themes in mind to start with, use separate sheets of paper for each article or book.

Once you develop a rough framework, slot the findings from the material so far reviewed into that framework, using a separate sheet of paper for each theme of that framework. As you read further, go on slotting the information where it logically belongs under the theme so far developed. You may need to add more themes as you go.

You should read critically while keeping the following aspects in mind:

- Observe whether the knowledge relevant to your theoretical framework is confirmed beyond doubt.
- Observe the theories put forward, the criticisms of these and their basis, the methodologies adopted and the criticisms of them.
- Examine to what extent the findings can be generalized to other situations.
- Ascertain the areas in which little or nothing is known-the gaps that exist in the body of knowledge.

Develop a Theoretical Framework

As you have limited time it is important to set parameters by reviewing the literature in relation to some main themes pertinent to your research topic. As you start reading the literature, you will realize that it deals with a number of aspects that have a direct 'and indirect bearing on your research topic. Use these aspects as a basis for developing your theoretical framework.

Until you go through the literature you cannot develop a theoretical framework and until you have developed a theoretical framework, you cannot effectively review the literature. Literature pertinent to your study may deal with two types of information:

In order to comply with the first function of literature review i.e. to provide theoretical background to your study:

- List the main themes that have emerged while reading literature.
- Convert them into subheadings. These subheadings should be precise, descriptive of the theme in question, and follow a logical progression.
- Now, under each subheading, record the main findings with respect to the theme in question, highlighting the reasons for and against an argument if they exist, and identify gaps and issues.

Systematically compare your findings with those made by others. Quote from these studies to show how your findings contradict, confirm or add to them. It places your findings in the context of what others have found out. This function is undertaken when writing about your findings i.e. after analysis of your data.

Developing the Research Objectives

The objectives are the goals you set out to attain in your study. They inform what you want to attain through the study. It is extremely important to word them clearly and specifically.

Generally, the objectives should be written under the following two headings:

- **Main objectives**: The main objective is an overall statement of the thrust of your study. It is also a statement of the main associations and relationships that you seek to discover or establish.
- **Sub-objectives**. The sub-objectives are the specific aspects of the topic that you want to investigate within the main framework of your study. The following points should be kept in mind:
  - Objectives should be numerically listed
  - Wording should clearly, completely and specifically
  - Each objective should contain only one aspect of the study.
  - Use action oriented words or verbs when writing objectives

The objectives should start with words such as 'to determine', 'to find out', 'to ascertain', 'to measure', 'to explore' etc. The wording of objectives determines the type of research (descriptive, correlational and experimental) and the type of research design you need to adopt to achieve them (Table 5.1).

Table 5.1: Wording of Objectives vis a vis Type of Research

Type of Research	*Wording of Objectives (Examples)*
Descriptive studies	• To describe the types of incentives to be given by a University to its employees • To find out the opinion of the employees about the teaching facilities provided by a University.
Correlatinal studies	• To ascertain the impact of training on employee retention. • To compare the effectiveness of different loyalty programmes on repeat clientele.
Hypothesis –testing studies	• To ascertain if an increase in working hours will increase the incidence of drug/alcohol abuse. • To demonstrate that the provision of company accommodation to employees in Mumbai hotels will reduce staff turnover.

Preparing the Research Design

Research design is the conceptual structure within which research would be conducted. The function of research design is to provide for the collection of relevant information with minimal expenditure of effort, time and money.

Meaning of Research Design

A research design is simply the framework or plan for a study that is used as a guide in collecting and analyzing the data. It is a blueprint that is followed in completing a study. Research design is the blue print for collection measurement and analysis of data. Actually, it is a map that is usually developed to guide the research.

Definitions of Research Design:

> **William Zikmund**: "Research design is a master plan specifying the methods and procedures for collection and analyzing the needed information."
>
> **Kerlinger**: "Research design is the plan, structure and strategy of investigation conceived so as to obtain answers to research questions and to control variance."

Thus, we can say that a research design is the arrangement of condition for collection and analysis of data in a manner that aims to generalize the findings of the sample on the population.

Purpose of a Research Design

Research designs are used for the following purposes:

- **To minimize the expenditure**: Research design carries an important influence on the reliability of the results attained It therefore provides a solid base for the whole research. This makes the research as effective as possible by providing maximum information with minimum spending of effort, money and time by preparing the advance plan of all about the research.
- **To facilitate the smooth scaling**: Research design is needed because it facilitates the smooth scaling of the various research operations, thereby making research as efficient as possible yielding maximal information with minimal expenditure of effort, time and money.
- **To collect the relevant data and technique**: Research design stands for advance planning of the methods to be adopted for collecting the relevant data and the techniques to be used in their

analysis, keeping in view the objective of the research and the availability of staff time and money. Poor preparation of research design upset the entire project.

- **To provide blue print for plans**: Research design is needed due to the fact that it allows for the smooth working of many research operations. It is like blue print which we need in advance to plan the methods to be adopted for collecting the relevant data and techniques to be used in its analysis for preparation of research project. Just as for better economical and attractive construction of a house need a blue print and a map of that, similarly we need a blue print or a design for the smooth flow of operation of research.
- **To provide an overview to other experts**: A research design provides an overview of all the research process and with the help of the design we can take the help and views of experts of that field. The design helps the investigator to organize his ideas, which helps to recognize and fix his faults.
- **To provide a direction**: A research design provides a proper or particular direction to the other executives and others who are helping us into the process. The researcher studies available, literature and learns about new (alternative approaches).

Characteristics of Good Research Design

Generally, a good research design minimizes bias and maximizes the reliability of the data collected and analyzed. The design which gives the smallest experimental error is reported to be the best design in scientific investigation. Similarly, a design which yields maximum information and provides an opportunity for considering different aspects of a problem is considered to be the most appropriate and efficient design.

A good research design possesses the following characteristics;

- **Objectivity**: It refers to the findings related to the method of data collection and scoring of the responses. The research design should permit the measuring instruments which are fairly objective in which every observer or judge scoring the performance must precisely give the same report. In other words, the objectivity of the procedure may be judged by the degree of agreement between the final scores assigned to different individuals by more than one independent observer. This ensures the objectivity of the collected data which shall be capable of analysis and interpretation.

- **Reliability**: It refers to consistency throughout a series of measurements. For example, if a respondent gives out a response to a particular item, he is expected to give the same response to that item even if he is asked repeatedly. If he is changing his response to the same item, the consistency will be lost. So, the researcher should frame the items in a questionnaire in such a way that it provides consistency or reliability.
- **Validity**: Any measuring device or instrument is said to be valid when it measures what it is expected to measure. For example, an intelligence test conducted for measuring the IQ should measure only the intelligence and nothing else and the questionnaire shall be framed accordingly.
- **Generalizability**: It means how best the data collected from the samples can be utilized for drawing certain generalizations applicable to a large group from which sample is drawn. Thus, a research design helps an investigator to generalize his findings provided he has taken due care in defining the population, selecting the sample, deriving appropriate statistical analysis etc. while preparing the research design. Thus, a good research design is one which is methodologically prepared and should ensure that generalization is possible.

  For ensuring the generalization we should confirm that our research problem has the following characteristics:
  - The problem is clearly formulated.
  - The population is clearly defined.
  - Most appropriate techniques of sample selection are used to form an appropriate sample.
  - Appropriate statistical analysis has been carried out.
  - The findings of the study are capable of generalizations.
- **Adequate Information**: The most important requirement of good research design is that it should provide adequate information so that the research problem can be analyzed on a wide perspective. An ideal design should take into account important factors like;
  - Identifying the exact research problem to be studied
  - The objective of the research
  - The process of obtaining information
  - The availability of adequate and skilled manpower and
  - The availability of adequate financial resources for carrying research.

Some other important features of a good research design are flexibility, adaptability, efficiency, being economic and so on. A good research design should minimize bias and maximize reliability and generalization.

Preparation of Research Design

he preparation of research design, appropriate for a particular research problem, involves the consideration of the following points:

- Objectives of the research study
- Method of data collection
- Sample design
- Tool for data collection
- Data analysis (qualitative and quantitative)

Objectives identified to answer the research questions have to be listed making sure that they are numbered and statement begins with an action verb.

Data Collection

In order to complete the section of preparation of research design, we are discussing data collection in brief. The detailed procedures will be discussed in the later part of this chapter. There are two types of data usually encountered in research.

- **Primary Data**: collected for the first time
- **Secondary Data**: those which have already been collected and analyzed by someone else.

Primary Data Collection

There are several methods of primary data collection.

Observation Methods for Data Collection

This method is commonly used in behavioural sciences. It is the gathering of primary data by investigator's own direct observation of relevant people, actions and situations without asking from the respondent. Observation can yield information which people are normally unwilling or unable to provide. There are several types of observation methods. These are given in Table 5.2.

Determining Sample Design

Researchers usually draw conclusions about large groups by taking a sample. A sample is a segment of the population selected to represent the population as a whole. Ideally, the sample should be representative and allow the researcher to make accurate estimates of the thoughts and behaviour of the larger population.

Table 5.2: Observation Methods for Data Collection

Type of Observations	***Advantages***	***Limitations***
• Structured • Unstructured	• Useful for descriptive research • Useful for exploratory research	• Feelings, beliefs and attitudes that motivate buying behaviour and infrequent behaviour cannot be observed. • Expensive method
Survey Method Approach most suited for gathering descriptive information. **Structured Surveys**: use formal lists of questions asked of all respondents in the same way. **Unstructured Surveys**: let the interviewer probe respondents and guide the interview according to their answers. **Survey research may be Direct or Indirect.** **Direct Approach**: The researcher asks direct questions about behaviours and thoughts. **Indirect Approach**: The researcher might ask questions: "What kind of people eat at MacDonald's?" From the response, the researcher may be able to discover why the consumer avoids MacDonald's. It may suggest factors of which the consumer is not consciously aware.	• Can be used to collect many different kinds of information • Quick and low cost as compared to observation and experimental method.	**Limitations:** • Respondent's reluctance to answer questions asked by unknown interviewers about things they consider private. • Busy people may not want to take the time • May try to help by giving pleasant answers • Unable to answer because they cannot remember or never gave a thought to what they do and why • May answer in order to look smart or well informed.
Contact Methods: Information may be collected by Mail Telephone Personal interview	**Mail** • can be used to collect large amounts of information at a low cost per respondent. • respondents may give more honest answers to personal questions on a • mail questionnaire • no interviewer is involved to bias the respondent's answers. • convenient for respondent's who can	**Mail** • not flexible • take longer to complete than telephone or personal interview • response rate is often very low • researcher has no control over who answers.

(*Contd...*)

	• mail questionnaire • no interviewer is involved to bias the respondent's answers. • convenient for respondent's who can answer when they have time • good way to reach people who often travel **Telephone Interviewing:** • quick method • more flexible as interviewer can explain	• researcher has no control over who answers. **Telephone Interviewing:** • Cost per respondent higher
Contact Methods: Information may be collected by Mail Telephone Personal interview	**Mail** • can be used to collect large amounts of information at a low cost per respondent. • respondents may give more honest answers to personal questions on a • mail questionnaire • no interviewer is involved to bias the respondent's answers. • convenient for respondent's who can answer when they have time • good way to reach people who often travel **Telephone Interviewing:** • quick method • more flexible as interviewer can explain questions not understood by the respondent • depending on respondent's answer they can skip some Qs and probe more on others • allows greater sample control • response rate tends to be higher than mail	**Mail** • not flexible • take longer to complete than telephone or personal interview • response rate is often very low • researcher has no control over who answers. **Telephone Interviewing:** • Cost per respondent higher • Some people may not want to discuss personal Qs with interviewer • Interviewer's manner of speaking may affect the respondent's answers • Different interviewers may interpret and record response in a variety of ways

(Contd...)

	Personal Interviewing: It is very flexible and can be used to collect large amounts of information. Personal interview can be used in any type of questionnaire and can be conducted fairly quickly.	• Under time pressure ,data may be entered without actually interviewing
Mail Questionnaires: This takes two forms Individual: Intercept interviewing Group: Focus Group Interviewing	**Intercept interviewing:** Widely used in tourism research. Allows researcher to reach known people in a short period of time. Only method of reaching people whose names and addresses are unknown Involves talking to people at homes, offices, on the street, or in shopping malls. Interviewer must gain the interviewee's cooperation Time involved may range from a few minutes to several hours	**Intercept interviewing:** Room for error and bias on the part of the interviewer who may not be able to correctly judge age, race etc. Interviewer may be uncomfortable talking to certain ethnic or age groups.
Focus Group Interviewing	It is rapidly becoming one of the major research tool to understand people's thoughts and feelings. It is usually conducted by inviting six to ten people to gather for a few hours with a trained moderator to talk about a product, service or organization.	Cost: may cost more than telephone survey Sampling: group interview studies keep small sample size to keep time and cost down, therefore it may be difficult to generalize from the results.
Experimental Method	It is a data-based research, coming up with conclusions which are capable of being verified with observation or experiment. Experimental research is appropriate when proof is sought that certain variables affect other variables in some way.	It may be costly and time consuming

Designing the sample calls for the following three decisions:

1. The researcher must determine what type of information is

needed and who is most likely to have it. How many people will be surveyed usually called Sample Size?

2. Large samples give more reliable results than small samples. However, it is not necessary to sample the entire target population. How should the sample be chosen? (Sampling)
3. Sample members may be chosen at random from the entire population (probability sample)

The needs of the research project will determine which method is most effective

Types of Samples

- **Simple random sample**: Every member of the population has a known and equal chance of being selected.
- **Stratified random sample**: Population is divided into mutually exclusive groups such as age groups and random samples are drawn from each group.
- **Cluster (area)sample**: The population is divided into mutually exclusive groups such as blocks, and the researcher draws a sample of the group to interview.
- **Convenience sample**: The researcher selects the easiest population members from which to obtain information.
- **Judgment sample**: The researcher uses his/her judgement to select population members who are good prospects for accurate information.
- **Quota sample**: The researcher finds and interviews a prescribed number of people in each of several categories.

Tool for Data Collection

The data collection is the most important aspect of a research project because anything you say by way of findings or conclusions is based up to the type of information you collect, and the data you collect is entirely dependent upon the questions that you ask of your respondents. The research tool provides the input into a study and therefore the quality and validity of the output (the findings), are solely dependent on it.

Guidelines to Construct a Research Tool

The guidelines consist of the following four steps:

- Step 1: Clearly define and individually list all the specific objectives or research questions for your study.

- Step 2: For each objective or research questions, list all the associated questions that you want to answer through your study.
- Step 3: Take each research question listed in step II and list the information required to answer it.
- Step 4: Formulate question(s) to obtain this information.

The Questionnaire

Structured surveys/ interviews employ the use of a questionnaire. A questionnaire consists of a set of questions presented to a respondent for answers. The respondents read the questions, interpret what is expected and then write down the answers themselves. It is called an Interview Schedule when the researcher asks the questions (and if necessary, explains them) and records the respondent's reply on the interview schedule. Because there are many ways to ask questions, the questionnaire is very flexible.

Questionnaire should be developed and tested carefully before being used on a large scale.

There are three basic types of questionnaire:

- Closed-ended
- Open-ended
- Combination of both

1. Closed-ended Questionnaire

- Closed ended questions include all possible answers/prewritten response categories, and respondents are asked to choose among them.
- Type of questions used to generate statistics in quantitative research.
- As these follow a set format, and most responses can be entered easily into a computer for ease of analysis, greater numbers can be distributed.

2. Open-ended Questionnaire

- Open-ended questions allow respondents to answer in their own words.
- Questionnaire does not contain boxes to tick but instead leaves a blank section for the respondents to write in an answer.
- Whereas closed-ended questionnaires might be used to find out how many people use a service open-ended questionnaires might be used to find out what people think about a service.

- As there are no standard answers to these questions, data analysis is more complex.
- As it is opinions which are sought rather than numbers, fewer questionnaires need to be distributed.

3. Combination of both

- This way it is possible to find out how many people use a service and what they think of the service in the same form.
- Begins with a series of closed-ended questions, with boxes to tick or scales to rank, and then finish with a section of open-ended questions or more detailed response.

Collecting Data

Having formulated the research problem, developed a study design, constructed a research instrument and selected a sample, you then collect the data from which you will draw inferences and conclusions for your study. Depending upon your plans, you might commence interviews, mail out a questionnaire, conduct experiments and/or make observations.

Collecting data through any of the methods may involve some ethical issues in relation to the participants and the researcher:

- Those from whom information is collected or those who are studied by a researcher become participants of the study.
- Anyone who collects information for a specific purpose, adhering to the accepted code of conduct, is a researcher.

Ethical issues concerning research participants

There are many ethical issues in relation to participants of a research activity.

- **Collecting information**: Your request for information may put pressure or create anxiety on a respondent. Is it ethical? Research is required to improve conditions. Provided any piece of research is likely to help society directly or indirectly, it is acceptable to ask questions, if you first obtain the respondents' informed consent. If you cannot justify the relevance of the research you are conducting, you are wasting your respondents' time, which is unethical.
- **Seeking consent**: In every discipline, it is considered unethical to collect information without the knowledge of the participant, and their expressed willingness and informed consent. Informed consent

implies that subjects are made adequately aware of the type of information you want from them, why the information is being sought, what purpose it will be put to, how they are expected to participate in the study, and how it will directly or indirectly affect them. It is important that the consent should be voluntary and without pressure of any kind.

- **Providing incentives**: Most people do not participate in a study because of incentives, but because they realize the importance of the study. Is it ethical to provide incentives to respondents to share information with you because they are giving their time? Giving a present before data collection is unethical.
- **Seeking sensitive information**: Certain types of information can be regarded as sensitive or confidential by some people and thus an invasion to their privacy, asking for such information may upset or embarrass a respondent. For most people, questions on drug use, pilferage, income, age, marital status etc are intrusive. In collecting data, you need to be careful about the sensitivities of your respondents. It is not unethical to ask such questions provided that you tell your respondents the type of information you are going to ask clearly and frankly, and give them sufficient time to decide if they want to participate, without any major inducement.
- **The possibility of causing harm to participant**: When you collect data from respondents or involve subjects in an experiment, you need to examine carefully whether their involvement is likely to harm them in any way. Harm includes l research that might include hazardous experiments, discomfort, anxiety, harassment, invasion of privacy, or demeaning or dehumanizing procedures. If it is likely to, you must make sure that the risk is minimal i.e. the extent of harm or discomfort is not greater that ordinarily encountered in daily life. If the way information is sought creates anxiety or harassment, you need to take steps to prevent this.
- **Maintaining confidentiality**: Sharing information about a respondent with others for purposes other than research is unethical. Sometimes you need to identify your study population to put your findings into context. In such a situation, you need to make sure that at least the information provided by respondents is kept anonymous. It is unethical to identify an individual's responses. Therefore, you need to ensure that after the information has been collected, the source cannot be known.

Ethical issues relating to the researcher

- **Avoiding bias:** Bias on the part of the researcher is unethical. Bias is a deliberate attempt to either to hide what you have found in your study, or highlight something disproportionately to its true existence.
- **Provision or deprivation of a treatment:** Both the provision and deprivation of a treatment/ intervention may pose an ethical dilemma for you as a researcher. Is it ethical to provide a study population with an intervention/ treatment that has not yet been conclusively proven effective or beneficial? But if you do not test, how can you prove or disprove its effectiveness or benefits? There are no simple answers to these dilemmas. Ensuring informed consent, 'minimum risk' and frank discussion as to the implications of participation in the study will help to resolve ethical issues.
- **Using inappropriate research methodology:** It is unethical to use a method or procedure you know to be inappropriate e.g. selecting a highly biased sample, using an invalid instrument or drawing wrong conclusions.
- **Incorrect reporting:** To report the findings in a way that changes or slants them to serve your own or someone else's interest, is unethical.
- **Inappropriate use of the information:** The use of information in a way that directly or indirectly adversely affects the respondents is unethical. If so, the study population needs to be protected. Sometimes it is possible to harm individuals in the process of achieving benefits for the organizations. An example would be a study to examine the feasibility of restructuring an organization. Restructuring may be beneficial to the organization as a whole bur may be harmful to some individuals. Should you ask respondents for information that is likely to be used against them? It is ethical to ask questions provided you tell respondents of the potential use of the information, including the possibility of it being used against some of them, and you let them decide if they want to participate.

Analysis of Data

Processing and analyzing data involves a number of closely related operations which are performed with the purpose of summarizing the collected data and organizing these in a manner that they answer the research questions (objectives).

The data processing operations are:

1. **Editing**- a process of examining the collected raw data to detect errors and omissions and to correct these when possible.
2. **Classification**- a process of arranging data in groups or classes on the basis of common characteristics. Depending on the nature of phenomenon involved

Classification according to attributes: Here data is analyzed on the basis of common characteristics which can either be : descriptive such as literacy, sex, religion etc. or : numerical such as weight, height, income etc. Such classification can be either: Simple classification: where we consider only one attribute, and divide the universe into two classes—one class consisting of items possessing the given attribute and the other class consisting of items which do not possess the given attribute.

(a) It facilitates the process of comparison.

(b) It facilitates the summation of items and the detection of errors and omissions.

(c) It provides the basis for various statistical computations. Tabulation may also be classified as simple and complex tabulation. Simple tabulation generally results in one-way tables which supply answers to questions about one characteristic of data only. Complex tabulation usually results on two-way tables (which give information about two inter-related characteristics of data), three –way tables or still higher order tables, also known as manifold tables.

Qualitative Data Analysis

Qualitative data analysis is a very personal process with few rigid rules and procedures. For this purpose, the researcher needs to go through a process called Content Analysis. Content Analysis means analysis of the contents of an interview in order to identify the main themes that emerge from the responses given by the respondents. This process involves a number of steps:

- **Step 1. Identify the main themes:** The researcher needs to carefully go through the descriptive responses given by respondents to each question in order to understand the meaning they communicate. From these responses, the researcher develops broad themes that reflect these meanings People use different words and language to express themselves. It is important that researcher select wording of the theme in a way that accurately represents the meaning of the responses categorized under a theme. These themes become the basis for analyzing the text of unstructured interviews.

- **Step 2. Assign codes to the main themes:** If the researcher wants to count the number of times a theme has occurred in an interview, he/she needs to select a few responses to an open- ended question and identify the main themes. He/she continues to identify these themes from the same question till a saturation point is reached. Write these themes and assign a code to each of them, using numbers or keywords.
- **Step 3. Classify responses under the main themes:** Having identified the themes Next step is to go through the transcripts of all the interviews and classify the responses under the different themes.
- **Step 4. Integrate themes and responses into the text of your report:** Having identified responses that fall within different themes, the next step is to integrate into the text of your report. While discussing the main themes that emerged from their study, some researchers use verbatim responses to keep the feel of the response. There are others who count how frequently a theme has occurred, and then provide a sample of the responses. It entirely depends upon the way the researcher wants to communicate the findings to the readers.

Quantitative Data Analysis

This method is most suitable for large well designed and well administered surveys using properly constructed and worded questionnaire. Data can be analyzed either manually or with the help of a computer. Manual Data Analysis: This can be done if the number of respondents is reasonably small, and there are not many variables to analyze. However, this is useful only for calculating frequencies and for simple cross tabulations. Manual data analysis is extremely time consuming. The easiest way to do this is to code it directly onto large graph paper in columns. Detailed headings can be used or question numbers can be written on each column to code information about the question.

To manually analyze data (frequency distribution), count various codes in a column and then decode them. In addition, if you want to carry out statistical tests, they have to be calculated manually. However, the use of statistics depends on your expertise and the desire/need to communicate the findings in a certain way.

Data Analysis Using a Computer: If you want to analyze data using computer, you should be familiar with the appropriate program. In this area, knowledge of computer and statistics plays an important role. The most common software is SPSS for windows. However, data input can be long and laborious process, and if data is entered incorrectly, it will influence the final results.

Presentation of Research Report/Research Paper

Writing the report is the last, and for many, the most difficult step of the research process. The report informs the world what you have done, what you have discovered and what conclusions you have drawn from your findings. The report should be written in an academic style. Language should be formal and not journalistic.

Written Research Report Format

Traditional written reports tend to be produced in the following format.

- Title Page
- Title of the Research Project,
- Name of the researcher,
- Purpose of the research project, e.g. "A research project submitted in partial fulfillment of the requirements of Master of Technology
- Date of Publication

Formulation of Hypothesis

The word hypothesis consists of two words Hypo+Thesis. 'Hypo' means tentative or subject to the verification. 'Thesis' means statement about solution of the problem. Thus, the literal meaning of the term hypothesis is a tentative statement about the solution of the problem. Hypothesis offers a solution of the problem that is to be verified empirically and based on some rationale. Again, 'hypo' means the composition of two or more variables which are to be verified and 'thesis' means position of these variables in the specific frame of reference.

Definitions of Hypothesis

- **J.S. Mill**: "Any supposition which we make in order to endeavor to deduce conclusions in accordance with facts which are known to be real under the idea that if the conclusions to which the hypothesis leads are known truths, the hypothesis itself either must be or at least likely to be true."

- **Lundberg**: "A hypothesis is a tentative generalization the validity of which remains to be tested. In its most elementary stage the hypothesis may be any hunch, guess, imaginative idea which becomes basis for further investigation."
- **John W. Best**: "It is a shrewd guess or inference that is formulated and provisionally adopted to explain observed facts or conditions and to guide in further investigation."
- **Barr and Scates**: "A hypothesis is a statement temporarily accepted as true in the light of what is, at the time, known about a phenomenon, and it is employed as a basis for action in the search for new, truth, when the hypothesis is fully established, it may take the form of facts, principles and theories."
- **Gorge J. Mouly**: "Hypothesis is an assumption whose testability is to be tested on the basis of the compatibility of its implications with empirical evidence and previous knowledge."

Nature of Hypothesis

The following points should be taken into consideration:

- **Conceptual**: Some kind of conceptual elements in the framework are involved in a hypothesis.
- **Verbal statement in a declarative form**: It is a verbal expression of ideas and concepts. It is not merely mental idea but in the verbal form, the idea is ready enough for empirical verification.
- It represents the tentative relationship between two or more variables.
- **Forward or future oriented**: A hypothesis is future-oriented. It relates to the future verification not the past facts and information.
- **Pivot of a scientific research**: All research activities are designed for verification of hypothesis.

Functions of Hypothesis

H. H. Mc Ashan has mentioned the following functions of hypothesis;

- It is a temporary solution of a problem concerning with some truth which enables an investigator to start his research works.
- It offers a basis in establishing the specifics what to study for and may provide possible solutions to the problem.
- It may lead to formulate another hypothesis.
- A preliminary hypothesis may take the shape of final hypothesis.

- Each hypothesis provides the investigator with definite statement which may be objectively tested and accepted or rejected and leads for interpreting results and drawing conclusions that is related to original purpose.
- It delimits field of the investigation.
- It sensitizes the researcher so that he should work selectively, and have very realistic approach to the problem.
- It offers the simple means for collecting evidences for verification.

Importance of a Hypothesis

- **Investigator's eyes**: Carter V. Good thinks that by guiding the investigator in further investigation hypothesis serves as the investigator's eyes in seeking answers to tentatively adopted generalization.
- **Focuses research**: Without hypothesis, a research is unfocussed research and remains like a random empirical wandering. Hypothesis serves as necessary link between theory and the investigation.
- **Clear and specific goals**: A well thought out set of hypothesis places clear and specific goals before the research worker and provides him with a basis for selecting sample and research procedure to meet these goals.
- **Links together**: According to Barr and Scates, "It serves the important function of linking together related facts and information and organizing them into wholes."
- **Prevents blind research**: In the words of P.V. Young, "The use of hypothesis prevents a blind search and indiscriminate gathering of masses of data which may later prove irrelevant to the problem under study."
- **Guiding Light**: "A hypothesis serves as powerful mechanism that lights the way for the research work."
    - It provides direction to research and prevent the review of irrelevant literature and the collection of useful or excess data.
    - It sensitizes the investigator certain aspects of situation which are irrelevant from the standpoint of problem at hand.
    - It enables the investigator to understand with greater clarity his problem and its ramification.

- It is an indispensable research instrument, for it builds a bridge between the problem and the location of empirical evidence that may solve the problem.
- It provides the investigator with the most efficient instrument for exploring and explaining the unknown facts.
- It provides a frame work for drawing conclusion.
- It stimulates the investigator for further research.

Forms of Hypothesis

According to Bruce W. Tuckman, the following are the forms of hypothesis:

- **Question form**: A hypothesis stated as a question represents the simplest level of empirical observation. It fails to fit most definitions of hypothesis. It frequently appears in the list. There are cases of simple investigation which can be adequately implemented by raising a question, rather than dichotomizing the hypothesis forms into acceptable / reject able categories.
- **Declarative Statement**: A hypothesis developed as a declarative statement provides an anticipated relationship or difference between variables. Such a hypothesis developer has examined existing evidence which led him to believe that a difference may be anticipated as additional evidence. It is merely a declaration of the independent variables effect on the criterion variable.
- **Directional Hypothesis**: A directional hypothesis connotes an expected direction in the relationship or difference between variables. This type of hypothesis developer appears more certain of anticipated evidence. If seeking a tenable hypothesis is the general interest of the researcher, this hypothesis is less safe than the others because it reveals two possible conditions. First that the problem of seeking relationship between variables is so obvious that additional evidence is scarcely needed. Secondly, researcher has examined the variables very thoroughly and the available evidence supports the statement of a particular anticipated outcome.
- **Non-Directional Hypothesis or Null Hypothesis**: This hypothesis is stated in the null form which is an assertion that no relationship or no difference exists between or among the variables. Null hypothesis is a statistical hypothesis testable within the framework of probability theory. It is a non-directional form of hypothesis.

There is a trend to employ or develop null hypothesis in research in most of the disciplines. A null hypothesis tentatively states that on the basis of evidence tested there is no difference. If the null hypothesis is rejected, there is a difference but we do not know the alternative or the differences. In this the researcher has not to anticipate or give the rational for the declaration or directional form. It does not make researcher biased or prejudiced. He may be objective about the expected outcomes of the research or findings.

Actually, this is a statistical hypothesis which is self- explanatory. Null hypothesis means zero hypotheses. A researcher has not to do anything in developing it. A null hypothesis in an appropriate form is order to accommodate the object of inquiry for extracting this information. It does not necessarily reflect the expectations of the researcher so much as the utility of the null form as the best fitted to the logic of chance in statistical knowledge or science.

It is the no difference form, i.e. there is no difference or relationship between or among variables under certain conditions. Statistical tests of significance are used to accept and reject the null hypothesis. If it is rejected, the general hypothesis is accepted.

Non-directional hypothesis is known as null hypothesis because it 'nullifies' the positive argument of the findings or non-directional statement of the generalization. It is also termed as statistical or zero hypothesis because it denies the existence of any systematic principles apart from the effect of chance. It assumes that none or zero difference exists between the two population means or the treatments.

Formulation of Testable Hypothesis

A hypothesis is a tentative assumption drawn from knowledge and theory. It is used as a guide in the investigation of other facts and theory that are as yet unknown. Its formulation is one of the most difficult and most crucial step in the entire scientific process. A poorly chosen or poorly worded hypothesis can prevent the following:

- The obtaining of enough pertinent data,
- The drawing of conclusions and generalizations, and
- The application of certain statistical measures in the analysis of the result.

Hypothesis is the central core of study that directs the selection of the data to be gathered, the experimental design, the statistical analysis and the conclusions drawn from the study.

A study may be devoted to the testing of one major hypothesis, a number of subsidiary hypothesis, or both major and subsidiary hypotheses. When several hypotheses are used, each should be stated separately in order to anticipate the type of analysis required and in order to definitely accept or reject each hypothesis on its own merit. Irrespective of number or type used each hypothesis should be testable and based upon a logical foundation.

Fundamental Basis of Hypothesis

The researcher deals with reality on two levels;

1. **The Operational Level**: On the operational level researcher must define events in observable terms in order to operate with the reality necessary to do researches.
2. **The Conceptual Level**: On the conceptual level the researcher must define events in terms of underlying communality with other events. Defining at a conceptual level, the researcher can abstract from single specific to general instance and begin to understand how phenomena operate and variables interrelate. The formulation of a hypothesis very frequently requires going from an operational or concrete level to the conceptual or abstract level. This movement to the conceptual level enables the result to be generalized beyond the specific conditions of a particular study and thus to be of wider applicability.

Research requires the ability to move from the operational to the conceptual level and vice–versa. This ability is required not only in constructing experiments but in applying their findings as well. The process of making conceptual contrasts between operational programme is called conceptualization or depersonalization.

Difficulties in the Formulation of Useful Hypothesis

Moving from the operational to the conceptual level and vice –versa is a critical ingredient of the research to demonstration process. The following are the difficulties in the formulation of hypothesis:

- Absence of knowledge of a clear theoretical framework.
- Lack of ability to make use of the theoretical framework logically.
- Lack of acquaintance with available research technique resulting in failure to be able to phrase the hypothesis properly.

Testing of a Hypothesis

Testing a hypothesis requires following three steps:

(1) Constructing a hypothesis

(2) Gathering appropriate evidence

(3) Analyzing evidence to draw conclusions as to its validity.

Fig. 5.4 shows testing process of a hypothesis of three phases.

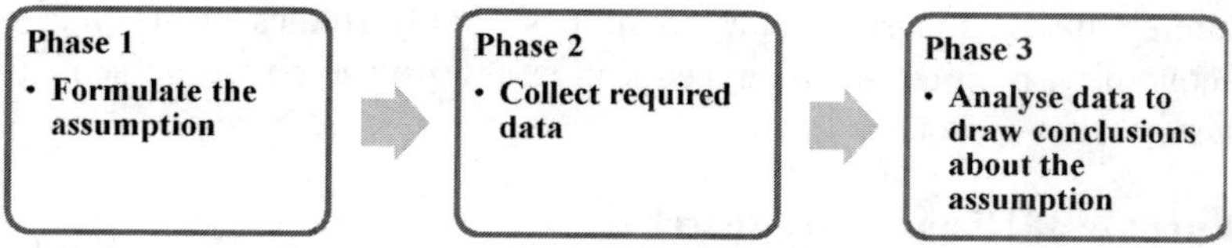

Fig. 5.4: Testing Process of a Hypothesis

Research Methods

Research methods may be classified broadly into the following three categories:

- Historical Research Methods
- Descriptive or Survey Research Method
- Experimental Research Method

Historical Research Method

We all know that history is the record of the changing processes. History consists of changes which social structures undergo. Social scientists study the past to gain a better understanding of the present state of affairs. History is the meaningful record of man's achievement. It is not merely a list of characteristics of chronological events, but an integrated account of the relationship between persons, events, times and places. Some of the definitions are as follows:

- **John W. Best**, "Man uses history to understand the past, and try to understand the present in the light of past events and developments."
- **F. N. Kerlinger**, "Historical research is the application of the scientific method of inquiry to historical problems."
- **Whitney**, "Historical research deals with the past experiences….its aim is to apply the method of reflective thinking of social problems , still unsolved , by means of discovery of past trends of event, fact and attitude. It traces the lines of development in human thought and action in order to reach some basis for social activity."

- **Redcliff Browne**, "Historical method may be defined as a system in which present day events are studied with reference to the events that took place in the past."

Historical method seeks to find explanation of questions of current interest by an intensive study of the past. Many studies in the field of economics, politics, sociology, education and psychology are essentially historical in approach.

Purpose of Historical Research

The purpose of the historical research may be the following:

- Historical researches provide important information concerning the effects of certain past practices and may suggest plans for future actions.
- It also offers explanation of the how and why of many of the theories and practices that has developed and now prevails in the school/college.
- It contributes to an understanding of the significance of the phenomenon studied.
- It helps to gain an accurate account of the past.
- It helps to gain a clear perspective of the present.

Sources of Historical Research

There are many sources for collection of historical data like; Autobiographies, Diaries, Confessions, Memories, Personal letters, Accessible documents, news-papers and literature, books and Magazines, Cultural and Analytical history material, Artistic materials, historical paintings, Portraits, charts etc.

These sources can be divided into two categories i.e. Primary sources and Secondary sources.

Primary Sources

The original documents are termed as Primary sources. These are solid basis of historical research and are highly prized by a historian. According to Kerlinger, "A primary source is the only repository of an historical datum, like an original record kept of an important occasion, an eye witness description of an event, a photograph, minutes of organization meeting and so on."

(i) Document or Records

These are maintained and written by actual participant or witness of an event. These sources are produced for the purpose of transmitting information to be used in the future. Documents classified as primary sources are constitution, charters, laws, court decisions, diaries, deeds, genealogies, contracts, wills, autobiographies, letters, official minutes or records, permits, licenses, affidavits, depositions, declarations, proclamations certificates, lists, bills, handbills, receipts, newspapers, magazines, accounts, maps, diagrams, books, pamphlets, catalogues, films, pictures, paintings, recordings, transcriptions and research reports.

(ii) Remains or Relics

These are associated with a person, group, period, fossils, skeletons, tools, weapons, food utensils, clothing, buildings, furniture, coins, art objects, pictures and paintings are examples of relics.

(iii) Oral Testimony

These are spoken account of witness or participant in an event. It is obtained in a personal interview. It may be recorded or transcript as the witness relates his experiences.

Secondary Sources of Data

In the words of Kerlinger, "A secondary source is an account or record of an historical event or circumstance one or more steps removed from an original history." Secondary sources are the reports of a person who relates the testimony of actual witness of, or participant in an event. The writer of the secondary source who was not on the scene of the event, merely reports what the person who was there said or wrote. Most history books and encyclopedias are the examples of secondary source.

Characteristics of Historical Method

The main characteristics of the historical research are as follows:

- Historical method is universal.
- Historical method involves very deep and intensive investigation of material that already exists.
- Historical facts cannot be repeated in an accurate fashion as can be done in laboratory observation.
- Only such problems which are based on historical records can be investigated by following this approach.

- Historical approach to research is the application of scientific method to historical problems.
- In Historical Method hypothesis may or may not be formulated depending upon the nature of the research.
- The interpretation of data entirely depends upon the topic of research.

Approaches to Historical Research

(a) **Perspective Approach**: It means to study the events from the past towards present. It is ancient approach. Ancient approach was to study the political personality approach.

(b) **Retrospective Approach**: It means to study the events of present and proceed to past events. It is a recent approach to study the phenomena in social milieu.

Types of Historical Research

- **Approach:** An example is the pragmatic approach used by Karl max to arrange facts of history to support his concept of socialism.
- **Subject**: It includes the bibliography of a given person, monography of a town, state, nation or civilization or slightly higher level the history of ideas, institutions or trends.
- **Technique**: It is based either on documents or relics.
- Classical studies
- Documentary research: It considers only documents.
- Bibliographical research: It includes history of a unit. (nation, person, culture)
- Legal Research

The Steps of Historical Research

- **Identification and Definition of the Problem**: It involves not only the location of the problem, which has a historical significance, but also the availability of adequate data.
- **Collection of Data**: It may involve anything from digging up ancient ruins to stumbling on old documents or remains. Most educational data have to be gathered in the routine fashion by giving minutes of meetings, diaries etc. Data are collected by two sources: primary or secondary.
- **Criticism of Data**: The establishment of the validity of data involves a dual process, of first establishing the authenticity of the sources and then the validity of its content.

- **Interpretation of Data**: This should be made from the standpoint of a hypothesis or theory of the data. Data should be considered in relation to one another and synthesized into a generalization or conclusion which places the overall significance in focus.

Limitations of Historical Research

- It is very difficult to study historical events on the basis of cause-effect relationship.
- Many obstacles hinder the objectivity of the study.
- The investigator must have a special historical perspective.
- The importance of historical research has declined due to use of scientific method in social sciences.

Guidelines of Historical Research

- Primary sources should be used as extensively as possible.
- Personal bias should not be allowed to influence research procedure.
- Proper recognition should be given to the inter-relationship of education with other social institutions and forces.
- Words and expressions should be interpreted in the light of their usages in earlier times.
- Various facts should be synthesized and integrated into meaningful generalization.
- Significant facts must be distinguished from trivial facts in a situation.

Descriptive or Survey Method

The term survey is used for the techniques of investigation by a direct observation of a phenomenon or a systematic gathering of data from population by applying personal contact and interviews when adequate information about certain problem is not available in records, files and other sources. The survey is an important tool to gather evidences relating to certain social problems. The term social survey indicates the study of social phenomena through a survey of a small sampled population and also to broad segments of population. It is concerned with the present and attempts to determine the status of the phenomenon under investigation.

Definitions

- **F. Well**: "A social survey is a process by which quantitative facts are collected about the social aspects of a community composition and activities."

- **S. Herman**: "The survey is in briefly a method of analysis in scientific and orderly form for defined purpose of given social situation of problem and population."

Objects of Social Survey

- Direct and close contact of researcher to the phenomenon under study.
- To collect general information.
- A basis for hypothesis.
- To explain cause and effect relationship.
- To know opinion and attitudes of the people

Purposes of Social Survey

- It provides necessary information which helps the administrator for making decisions.
- It provides necessary information and plan for improvement so it is forward-looking.
- It interprets, synthesizes and integrates data and points out their implications.
- It is more realistic because investigation is done in this method in natural setting.
- It is the only method through which the researcher can obtain the opinions, attitudes and suggestions for improvement.
- It is useful in the development of research tools such as checklists, questionnaires etc.

Characteristics of Survey Method

- Social survey is confined to the study of specific current problems of society eg poverty, unemployment etc.
- A survey research is planned collection of data for prediction of relations between the variables.
- Survey is concerned with large or widely dispersed group of peoples contrasted with the lab experiments.
- Under this method observation, interviews, attitude scales, projective techniques, small scale experiments etc. are used to collect data.

- The facts collected here may form the basis of further social researches.

Planning a Survey Method

The following are the steps which are involved in survey methods;

- Select a problem.
- Preliminary or pilot study should be done.
- General and Specific objectives of the study are to be framed.
- It should be determined that for which of the variables, identified in the problem whether; adequate techniques for data collection are available, and if not then is it possible for the researcher to design them.
- Population should be identified and representative sample should be selected.
- Data collection design should be prepared.
- The data should be collected.
- The data should be analyzed.
- The report should be prepared which should have descriptive past, comparative or evaluative past and findings.

Merits of Survey Methods

- Direct and close contact between researcher and respondents.
- Create objectivity.
- Testing the validity of theories.
- Formulation and testing of hypothesis.
- Social surveys are based on actual observation.
- It has universal application.

Limitations of Survey Methods

- Survey method is costly, time consuming and wasteful in certain cases where the objectives are limited.
- The survey method is unsuitable if the numbers of persons to be surveyed are very large or if they spread over a large geographical area.
- In this method, personal bias may vitiate the result.
- It lacks the flexibility.
- In this method, it is very difficult to verify the accuracy of the data collection.

- Only useful for current problems.
- It does not permit more comprehensive and dynamic study of the society but deals with the problems of immediate importance only.
- Under this method most of the surveys are conducted on sample basis. If the sample is not carefully planned, inferences drawn may be inaccurate and misleading.

Experimental Method

It may be defined as the study of the relationships among variables those manipulated and those measured. It simply enables the researcher to improve the conditions under which the researcher observes and thus to arrive at a more precise result. It enables him to relate a given consequent to a specific antecedent rather than to a vague conglomeration of antecedents.

It is a scientific method; give more precise, accurate and reliable results. It is just like an observation under controlled conditions. It acts on the law of single variable and causing factors. It studies cause and effect relationship. It is a systematic and logical method for answering the questions. In this the researcher seeks to evaluate something new. It leads to contribution to the already acquired fund of knowledge.

The essential elements in an experiment are; control, manipulation, observation and replication. In this, experimenter has to imagine that research conditions are entirely new, they were not existing previously and recently. It is a method in which we study the effect of d dependent variable on independent variable. Whatever we know about the environment, is possible only by observation. All types of experiments are related with observation and generalization of these observed facts and it is also possible to test the internal validity.

Definitions

- **Jhoda**: "It is a method of testing hypothesis."
- **F. S. Chapin**: "An experiment is an observation under controlled conditioned."
- **John W. Best**: "Experimental research is the description and analysis of what will be or what will occur, under carefully controlled condition."
- **Green Wood**: "Experiment is a means of providing the hypothesis whereby the causal relations between two facts is studied."

- **Festinger**: "The essence of an experiment may be described as observing the effect on a dependent variable of the manipulation of an independent variable."

Characteristics of Experimental Method

- Based on the law of single variable.
- This method of research is maximum in use in educational / social researches where the factors can be controlled.
- Experimental method is a method of testing of clear specific hypothesis of different intensions.
- It is a bias free estimation of the true effect.
- It emphasizes control of conditions and the experimentation of certain variables in controlled conditions.
- It sets out more or less of the causal type relationship between the phenomenon.
- It uses standardized tool for experimentation and makes the evidences very much objective.
- The sample is selected with great precaution and very care is taken to safe guard extraneous factors.
- This method helps in developing laws, postulate and theories.
- It allows for precision and definiteness.

Elements of Experimental Method

(1) Control

The extent to which different factors are accounted for

(a) Purposes of Control

- Intervening variables are isolated so that they may affect the dependent variable.
- Not only intervening variables are to be isolated from independent variables but it is also to be ascertained how much it contributed.
- The magnitude is not only ascertained terms of larger or small but also in quantitative terms.

(b) Degree of Control

It has to be remembered that in social researches high degree of control is not possible as in laboratory situation.

(c) Methods of Control

The researcher directs efforts towards controlling the variables which are related to the independent variable otherwise it will be difficult to ascertain which is responsible for effect on dependent variable.

The following methods are used for controlling;

- Random assignment of subjects to groups: It means that subjects are assigned in such a way that every member has an equal opportunity of being chosen.
- Matching subjects with random assignment: The subjects are assigned to groups to match individual's subjects on as many extraneous variables as the researcher can identify.

  They may be:

  (a) Subject to subject matching,

  (b) matching for mean and standard deviation,

  (c) Ranking of subjects on matching variable.
- Random assignment on the basis of homogeneous selection: It is done to make groups comparable on an extraneous variable so as to select groups those are as homogenous as possible on the variable. The variable may be like socio-economic –status and sex etc.
- Techniques of analysis of Co-variance: It is attempted to control the variation within the groups. A co-variate is a variable which the researcher has not been able to control.
- Methods of using subjects as their own controls: It is done to assign the same subjects to two experimental treatments and then to obtain measurements of the subjects under one treatment and then on the other. But there is practical difficulty in this method in some cases.

(2) Manipulation

In the experimental method manipulation is done to set the stage for the occurrence of the factor whose performance is to be studied under conditions in which all other factors are controlled. Variables which can be manipulated may be personality characteristics, attitudes, teaching methods, type of motivation etc.

(3) Observation

Another element of the experimental method is that the effect of the manipulation of independent variable on the dependent variable is studied or observed. The technique of observation is applied if measurement is not possible.

(4) Replication

In spite of attempts of controlling extraneous variables, some extraneous variable and some discrepancies remain and influence the results. Thus replication is a matter of conducting a number of sub experiments within the frame work of an overall experiment design.

Features of Experimental Method

- It is based on law of the single variable. It means if one element is added or subtracted in one of the two situations and other situation is kept as it is, the change in the two situations is the result of that single variable.
- It is applicable when significant factor or conditions can be controlled.
- It is not a perfectly precise method in educational research as in scientific method.
- Control group and experimental group are never identical as they should be for an exact experiment.

Experimental Validity

Two types of validity are involved;

(i) Internal Validity

It is the minimum without which an experiment is useless. The crucial point is whether the independent variable created the effect on the dependent variable. It means that some uncontrolled extraneous factors do not affect the dependent variable. The following eight extraneous factors are to be controlled for obtaining internal validity;

- Contemporary confounding factor.
- Maturation of the subject with the passage of time,
- Experience in pre-test reflecting itself in the post test,
- Change in the calibration of the measuring instruments,
- Tendency for extreme scores to regress towards the mean,
- Difference in the selection of subject in the pre-test and posttest,
- Differential loss of subjects from the experimental and control groups tend to bias the results of the experiment.
- Interaction of selection and maturation and selection and history.

(ii) External Validity

The crucial point is what is the applicability of the findings beyond the limits of particular experiment. Are the results valid in general for students? The following factors are to be controlled for obtaining external validity;

- Selections of sample with some special characteristics make the application restrictive.
- Pre-testing may sensitize the subject to the experimental factor.
- Effects of experimental procedures restrict the generalize ability of the findings.
- Effects of a treatment on a subject previously exposed to other treatments cannot be generalized to other subjects who have not undergone the same sequence of treatments.

Types of Experimental Designs

It is to the researcher what a blue –print is to an architect. The following are the factors upon which the selection of designs depends;

- What is the nature of the experiment?
- What is the main purpose of the experiment?
- What types of the variables are to be manipulated?
- What is the nature of data?
- What is the competence level of the experimenter?

The experimental designs are classified as follows;

(a) **Pre-experimental designs**: In this type of design there is no control over extraneous or situation variables.

(b) **True-experimental designs**: In these designs, the researcher attempts to control the effects of history, maturation, testing, measuring instruments etc.

(c) **Factorial Design**: This design enables the experimenter to evaluate or manipulate two or more experimenters to evaluate or manipulate two or more variables simultaneously in order to study the effects of number of independent factors singly as well as the effects due to interactions with one another.

In this design, the impact of more than one variable can be studied simultaneously. In this not only the significance of difference of different levels is studied but interaction effect can also be studied. However, if too many variables and too many levels are studied, the experiment and statistical analysis becomes too difficult to manage.

Steps of Experimental Research Methods

The procedures of the experimental method are to be executed under the following steps;

- **Identifying, defining and delimiting the problem**: The problem that can be verified or refuted by the experimental data should be selected first. The variables to be investigated are defined in operational terms.
- **Reviewing the literature**: After selecting the problem, the related literature and experiments should be reviewed and the method of approach or experimental design to be pursued should be planned or outlined.
- **Formulating the hypothesis and deducing their consequences:** The problem has to be converted into a hypothesis that can be verified or refuted by experimental method.
- **Drawing up the experimental design:** This section should place primary emphasis on the question of control, randomization, replication, place of the experiment, duration of the experiment, selecting or constructing and validating instruments to measure the outcomes of the experiment and conducting pilot for trial run tests to perfect instrument.
- **Defining the population:** It is necessary to define the population precisely so that there can be no question about population to which the conclusions are to apply. It may consist of selecting a sample of subjects to represent a given population and pairing of subjects to secure homogeneity.
- **Administration of test / Carrying out the study:** It is necessary to insist on close adherence to plans and experimental design. This will involve controlling variable or non-experimental factors, applying the experimental factors and keeping the careful record of steps in the procedure.
- **Measuring the outcomes / Collection of Data:** Careful consideration must be given to the selection of the criterion on the basis of which the results are measured.
- **Analyzing and interpreting the outcomes:** The result pertaining to the factors under study should be clearly noted. The analysis of data demands expert use of statistical procedures. Only then the analysis becomes the basis for valid interpretation.
- **Drawing the conclusions:** The conclusions of the study must be restricted to the population actually covered; care must be taken

not to over generalize the results. The result also pertains to the conditions under which they were derived. Care must be taken to restrict the conclusions to the conditions actually present in the experiment.

- Reporting the results:

The study must be reported in sufficient details.

Variables and their Types

Variable is a concept which can take on different quantitative values. For example; height, weight, income, age etc. The main focus of the scientific study is to analyse the functional relationship of the variables. A variable is a quantity which can vary from one individual to another.

Types of Variables

It is any feature or aspect of an event, function or process that, by its presence and nature, affects some other event or process, which is being studied. The different types of variables are as follows:

- **Continuous Variable**

  It is that which can assume any numerical value within a specific range.

- **Discrete Variable**

  A variable for which the individual values fall on the scale only with distinct gaps is called a discrete variable.

- **Dependent Variable or Criterion variable**

  If one variable depends or is a consequence of other, it is termed as dependent variable. Criterion variable is the basis on which the effectiveness of the experimental variable is studied.

- **Independent Variable or Experimental Variable**

  The variable that is antecedent to the dependent variable is termed as an independent variable. The variable whose effect is going to be known is known as experimental variable.

- **Controlled Variable**

  The effectiveness of an experimental variable is examined by comparing with another variable, known as controlled variable.

- **Confounding Variable**

  Those aspects of study or sample, that might influence the dependent variable (outcome measures), and whose effect may be confused with the effects of the independent variable. They are of two types; Intervening and extraneous variable.

- **Intervening Variable**

  There are a number of abstract variables in educational/social experiments, which intervene the effect of experimental or criterion variable. For controlling intervening variable appropriate research design should be used. Intervening variables are hard if not impossible, to observe because they usually have to do with an individual's feelings like boredom, stress, fatigue, excitement etc. Extraneous variable on the other hand, are more readily observed or measured and thus are more easily controlled.

- **Extraneous Variable**

  Independent variables that are not related to the purpose of the study, but may affect the dependent variable are termed as extraneous variables. Suppose the researcher wants to test the hypothesis that there is a relationship between children's gain in social studies achievement and their self-concept. Here self-concept is independent variable and achievement in social study is dependent variable. Intelligence may as well affect the social studies achievement; but since it is not related to the purpose of the study undertaken by the researcher, it will be termed as extraneous variable. Whatever effect is noticed on dependent variable as a result of extraneous variable(s) is technically described as an 'experimental error.'

  Study must always be so designed that the effect upon the dependent variable is attributed entirely to the independent variables and not to some extraneous variable(s). When the dependent variable is not free from the influence of extraneous variable(s), the relationship between the dependent and independent variable is said to be confounded by an extraneous variable(s). Extraneous variable can be controlled by removing the variable causing distraction. It may be eliminated by selecting cases with uniform characteristics and through randomization.

- **Organismic Variable**

  There are some variables which cannot be manipulated. They are accepted by the researcher as they are. They are levels of intelligence, sex, class levels, and the like. The researcher can classify the subjects by sex but he cannot modify to suit his research condition. If a researcher attempts to compare boys and girls on some learning task, any differences might be attributed to sex differences but not necessarily so. The differences between boys and girls could be due to differences in intelligence, training, motivation or a myriad of other conditions present in all human beings and not necessarily to biological differences between sex. Those variables which cannot be manipulated and cannot themselves point out causal relations are called organismic variables.

Sampling Design

Sampling

Sampling is the process of selecting a sample from the population. For this purpose, the population is divided into a number of parts called sampling units. Sampling designs means the joint procedure of selection and estimation. Sampling is a part of the strategy of research. Sampling should be such that the error of estimation is minimum.

Assumptions of Sampling

Homogeneity amidst complexity

Social phenomenon is very complex in nature and every unit appears to be different from another. But at the same time, they also possess similarities in many respects. It is, therefore, assumed that there is the possibility of such representative types in the whole population that makes sampling possible.

Possibility of Representative Selection

Sampling has its origin in the mathematical theory of probability and law of statistical regularity. The law of statistical regularity lays down that a group of objects chosen at random from a large group tend to possess the characteristics of that large group. Absolute accuracy is not essential but relative or significant accuracy is needed in case of large scale observations.

Need of Sampling

For a research, a survey may be needed and is conducted by either of two methods

1. Census method or Parametric method
2. Sampling method or Non-parametric method

Census Method

It deals with the investigation of the entire population. Here the data are collected for each and every unit of the universe. This method provides more accurate and exact information as no unit is left out.

Sampling Method

Here a small group is selected as representative of the whole universe. It works with the objective to obtain accurate and reliable information about the universe with minimum of cost, time and energy and to set out the limits of accuracy of such estimates. It makes exhaustive and intensive study possible with much less time, money and material. It is more popular in research work.

Population or universe means, the entire mass of observations, which is the parent group from which a sample is to be formed. The term population or universe conveys a different meaning than a traditional one. In census survey, the count of individuals (men, women and children) is known as population.

But in Research Methodology population means characteristics of a specific group. For example, secondary school teachers, who have some specific features like teaching experience, teaching attitudes etc. Sampling means selecting a given number of subjects from a defined population as representative of that population. One type of population distinguished by educational researchers is called the target population. By target population distinguished by educational researchers is called the target population. By target population, also called universe, we mean all the members of a real or hypothetical set of people, events or objects to which we wish to generalize the results of our research. The first step in sampling is to define the target population.

Sampling is indispensable technique in behavioral research and not so common in physical sciences. It is fundamental to all statistical methodology of behavioral and social research. It makes research findings economical and accurate. Sampling means selection of individuals from the population in such a way that every individual has equal chance to be taken into the sample.

Some definitions are as follows:

- **Frank Yates**, "Sample is set of units of an aggregate."
- **Good and Hatt**, "A sample as the name implies, is a smaller representation of a larger whole."

- **W. G. Cocharn**, "In every branch of science we lack the resources, to study more than a fragment of the phenomenon that might advance our knowledge." i.e. fragment is sample and phenomenon is population. The sample observations are applied to the phenomenon i.e. generalization.
- **David S. Fox**, "In the social sciences, it is not possible to collect data from every respondent relevant to our study but only from some fractional part of the respondents. The process of selecting the fractional part is called sampling."
- **P. Y. Young**, "A statistical sample is a miniature picture or cross – section of the entire group or aggregate from which the sample is taken."

The need, advantages, limitations and essentials of sampling are given in Table 5.3.

Table 5.3: Need, Advantages, Limitations and Essentials of Sampling

Need	*Advantages*	*Limitations*	*Essentials*
Economy of time. Economy of money. True detailed knowledge. Utility in experimental study. It has reliability because it is based on probability theory.	It has a greater adaptability. It is an economical technique. It has high speed for generalization. According to W.G. Cocharan, "It has greater precision and accuracy in the observation". This technique has great accuracy. It has a greater speed in conducting a research work. It has a greater scope in the field of research. It reduces the cost of observation or data collection.	Scope of biasness. (Less accuracy) Problem of representative sample- Difficulty in selecting a truly representative sample. Need of eligible researchers. Instability of sample subjects or changeability of units i.e. in heterogeneous population. There are certain situations where sampling is possible.	Homogeneity: The units included in sample must be as likeness with other units. Adequacy: A sample having 10% of the whole data is adequate. Independence: Every unit should be free to be included in the sample. Representativeness: An ideal sample must be such that it represents the whole data adequately

Characteristics of a Good Sample

- A good sample is the true representative of the population corresponding to its properties.

- The population is known as aggregate of certain properties and sample is called sub-aggregate of the universe.
- A good sample is free from bias; the sample does not permit prejudices, the learning and pre-conception, imaginations of the investigator to influence its choice.
- A good sample is an objective one; it refers objectivity in selecting procedure or absence of subjective elements from the situation.
- A good sample maintains accuracy. It yields an accurate estimates or statistics and does not involve errors.
- A good sample is comprehensive in nature. This feature of a closely linked with true-representativeness. Comprehensiveness is a quality of a sample which is controlled by specific purpose of the investigation. A sample may be comprehensive in traits but may not be a good representative of the population.
- A good sample has the practicability for research.

Types of Sampling Designs/Methods of Sampling

The sampling methods are classified as probability sampling and non-probability sampling. The difference is given in Table 5.4.

Table 5.4: Difference between Probability and Non-Probability Sampling

S.No.	*Probability Sampling*	*Non-probability Sampling*
	Random Sampling Systematic Sampling Stratified Sampling Multistage Sampling Purposive Sampling Cluster Sampling Multiple Sampling or Double Sampling	Incidental or Accidental Sampling Judgment Sampling Purposive Sampling Quota Sampling
1	It is a method of sampling which gives the probability that a sample is representative of population.	In the absence of any idea of probability the method of sampling is known as non-probability sampling.
2	Probability sampling is generally used in fundamental research in which the purpose is to generalize the results.	It is generally used in action researches in which one studies a class without any generalization purpose.
3	It refers from the sample as well as the population.	There is no idea of population.
4	Every individual of the population has equal probability to be taken into the sample.	There is no probability of selecting any individual.
5	It may be representative of the population.	It has free distribution.
6	Its observations (data) are used for the inferential purpose.	The observations are not used for generalization purpose.

(*Contd...*)

7	Inferential or parametric statistics are used.	Non-inferential or non-parametric are used.
8	There is a risk of drawing conclusion.	There is no risk for drawing conclusions.
9	It is based on Law of probability sampling i.e. Law of Statistical Regularity and Law of Inertia of the Large Sample.	It is not based on law of probability sampling.

Probability Sampling

A probability sample is one that has been used selected in such a way that every element chosen has a known probability of being included. Probability sampling is of different types:

(1) Simple Random Sampling

It is one in which each element of the population has an equal and independent chance of being included in the sample i.e. a sample selected by randomization method is known as simple random sample and this technique is simple randomizing. The techniques, merits and demerits of randomizations are given in Table 5.5.

Table 5.5: Techniques, merits and demerits of randomizations

Techniques of Randomization	*Merits of Randomization*	*Demerits of Randomization*
• Tossing a coin • Throwing a dice • Lottery method • Blind folded method • Tippett's table method	• It requires the minimum knowledge of population. • It is free from subjectivity and free from personal error. • It provides appropriate data for one's purpose. • The observations of the sample can be used for inferential purpose.	• It cannot ensure the representativeness of a sample. • It does not use the knowledge about the population. • Its inferential accuracy depends upon the size of the sample.

(2) Systematic Sampling

Systematic sampling is an improvement over the simple random sampling. This method requires the complete information about the population. There should be a list of information of all the individuals of the population in any systematic way.

The size of the sample may be decided as follows:

Let the size of sample is = n and population size is = N

Now we select each N/n individual from the list and thus we have the desired size of sample which is known as systematic sample. Thus, for this technique of sampling population should be arranged in any systematic way. The merits and demerits of systematic sampling are given in Table 5.6.

Table 5.6: Merits and demerits of systematic sampling

Merits of systematic sampling	*Demerits of systematic sampling*
• This is a simple method of selecting a sample. • It reduces the field cost. • Inferential statistics may be used. • Sample may be comprehensive and representative of population. • Observations of the sample may be used for drawing conclusions and generalizations.	• This is not free from error, since there is subjectivity due to different ways of systematic list by different individuals. • Knowledge of population is essential. • Information of each individual is essential. • This method can't ensure the representativeness. • There is a risk in drawing conclusions from the observations of the sample.

(3) Stratified Sampling

It is an improvement over the earlier methods. When we employ this technique, the researcher divides his population into strata on the basis of some characteristics and from each of these smaller homogenous groups (strata) draws at random a predetermined number of units. Researcher should choose that characteristic as criterion which seems to be more relevant in his research work.

Stratified sampling is of three types:

1. **Disproportionate**: Means that the size of the sample in each unit is not proportionate to the size of the unit but depends upon considerations involving personal judgement and convenience. This method of sampling is more effective for comparing strata which have different error possibilities. It is less efficient for determining population characteristics.
2. **Proportionate**: It refers to the selection from each sampling unit of a sample that is proportionate to the size of the unit. Advantages of this procedure includes representativeness with respect to variables used as the basis of classifying categories and increased chances of being able to make comparisons between strata. Lack of information on proportion of the population in each category and faulty classification may be listed as disadvantages of this method.
3. **Optimum allocation**: Stratified sampling is representative as well as comprehensive than other stratified samples. It refers to

selecting units from each stratum. Each stratum should be in proportion to the corresponding stratum the population. Thus, sample obtained is known as optimum allocation sample.

The merits and demerits of stratified sampling are given in Table 5.7.

Table 5.7: Merits and demerits of Stratified sampling

Merits of Stratified sampling	*Demerits of Stratified sampling*
• It is a good representative of the population. • It is an improvement over the earlier technique of sampling. • It is an objective method of sampling. • Observations can be used for inferential purpose.	• Serious disadvantage of this method is that it is difficult for the researcher to decide the relevant criterion for stratification. • Only one criterion can be used for stratification, but generally it seems more than one criterion relevant for stratification. • It is costly and time-consuming method. • Selected samples may be representative with reference to the used criterion but not for the other. • There is a risk of generalization.

(4) Multiple or Double Repetitive Sampling

Generally, this is not a new method but only a new application of the samplings. This is most frequently used for establishing the reliability of a sample. When employing a mailed questionnaire, double sampling is sometimes used to obtain a more representative sample. This is done because some randomly selected subjects who are sent questionnaires may not return them.

Obviously, the missing data will bias the result of the study, if the people who fail to reply the query differ in some fundamental way from the others in respect to the phenomenon being studied.

To eliminate this bias, a selected sample may be drawn at random from the non-respondents and the people interviewed to obtain the desired information. Thus, this technique is also known as repeated or multiple sampling.

This double sampling technique enables one to check on the reliability of the information obtained from first sample. Thus, double sampling, where in one sample is analyzed and information obtained is used to draw the next sample to examine the problem further.

The merits and demerits of multiple sampling are given in Table 5.8.

(5) Multi Stage Sampling

This sample is more comprehensive and representative of the population. In this type of sampling primary sample units are inclusive groups and secondary units are sub-groups within these ultimate units to be selected which belong to one and only one group.

Table 5.8: Merits and demerits of multiple sampling

Merits of multiple sampling	*Demerits of multiple sampling*
• The sampling procedure leads to the inferences of free determine precision based on a number of observations. • This technique of sampling reduces the error. • This method maintains the procedure of the finding evaluate the reliability of the sample.	• This technique of sampling cannot be used for a large sample. It is applicable only for small sample. • This technique is time consuming and costly. • Its planning and administration is more complicated.

Stages of a population are usually available within a group or population, whenever stratification is done by the researcher. The individuals are selected from different stages for constituting the multi stage sampling.

The merits and demerits of multi stage sampling are given in Table 5.9.

Table 5.9: Merits and demerits of multiple sampling

Merits of multi stage sampling	*Demerits of multi stage sampling*
• It is a good representative of the population. • Multistage sampling is an improvement over the earlier methods. • It is an objective procedure of sampling. • The observations from multi stage sample may be used for inferential purpose.	• It is a difficult and complex method of sampling. • It involves errors when we consider the primary stages. • It is again a subjective technique of sampling.

(6) Cluster Sampling

To select the intact group as a whole is known as a cluster sampling. In cluster sampling the sample units contain groups of element (cluster) instead of individual members or items in the population. Rather than listing all elementary school children in a given city and randomly selecting 15 percent of these students for the sample, a researcher lists all of the elementary schools in the city, selects at random 15 percent of these clusters of units, and uses all of the children in the selected schools as the sample.

The merits and demerits of Cluster stage sampling are given in Table 5.10.

Table 5.10: Merits and demerits of Cluster sampling

Merits of Cluster sampling	*Demerits of Cluster sampling*
• It may be a good representative of the population. • It is an easy method. • It is an economical method. • It is practicable and highly applicable in education. • Observations can be used for inferential purpose.	• Cluster sampling is not free from errors. • It is not comprehensive.

Non-Probability Sampling Method

Samples which are selected through non-random methods are called non-probability samples. Depending upon the technique used it may be;

(1) Incidental or Accidental Sampling

The term incidental or accidental applied to those samples that are taken because they are most frequently available i.e. this refers to the groups which are used as samples of a population because they are readily available or because the researcher is unable to employ more acceptable sampling methods.

The merits and demerits of Incidental sampling are given in Table 5.11.

Table 5.11: Merits and demerits of Incidental sampling

Merits of Incidental sampling	*Demerits of Incidental sampling*
• It is very easy method of sampling. • It is frequently used method in behavioural sciences. • It reduces the time, money and energy i.e. it is an economical method.	• It is not representative of the population. • It is not free from errors. • Parametric statistics cannot be used.

(2) Judgment Sampling

This involves the selection of a group from the population on the basis of available information assuming as if they are representative of the entire population. Here group may also be selected on the basis of intuition or on the basis of the criterion deemed to be self-evident. Generally, investigator should take the judgment sample so this sampling is highly risky.

The merits and demerits of Incidental sampling are given in Table 5.12.

(3) Purposive Sampling

The purposive sampling is selected by some arbitrary method because it is known to be representative of the total population, or it is known that it will produce well matched groups. The idea is to pick out the sample in relation to criterion which are considered important for the particular study. This method is appropriate when the study places special emphasis upon the control of certain specific variables.

Table 5.12: Merits and demerits of Judgment sampling

Merits of Judgment sampling	*Demerits of Judgment sampling*
• Knowledge of investigator can be best used in this technique of sampling. • This method of sampling is economical.	• This technique is objective. • It is not free from errors. • It includes uncontrolled variation. • Inferential statistics cannot be used for the observation of this sampling, so generalization is not possible.

The merits and demerits of Purposive sampling are given in Table 5.13.

Table 5.13: Merits and demerits of Purposive sampling

Merits of Purposive sampling	*Demerits of Purposive sampling*
• Use the best available knowledge concerning the sample subjects. • Better control of significant variables. • Sample groups data can be easily matched. • Homogeneity of subjects used in the sample.	• Reliability of the criterion is questionable. • Knowledge of population is essential. • Errors in classifying sampling subjects. • Inability to utilize the inferential parametric statistics. • Inability to make generalization concerning total population.

(4) Quota Sampling

This combines both judgment sampling and probability sampling: on the basis of judgment or assumption or the previous knowledge, the proportion of population falling into each category is decided. Thereafter a quota of cases to be drawn is fixed and the observer is allowed to sample as he likes. Quota sampling is very arbitrary and likely to figure in municipal surveys.

The merits and demerits of Quota sampling are given in Table 5.14.

Table 5.14: Merits and demerits of Purposive sampling

Merits of Quota sampling	*Demerits of Quota sampling*
• It is an improvement over the judgment sampling. • It is an easy sampling technique. • It is not frequently used in social surveys.	• It is not a representative sample. • It is not free from errors. • It has the influence of regional, geographical and social factors.

(5) Snowball Sampling

The term; snow ball sampling' has been used to describe a sampling procedure in which the sample goes on becoming bigger and bigger as the observation or study proceeds. The term snowball stems from the analogy of a snowball sample which would allow computation of estimates of sampling error and use of statistical test of significance.

For example, an opinion survey is to be conducted on smokers of a particular brand of cigarette. At the first stage, we may pick up a few people who are known to us or can be identified to be the smokers of that brand. At the time of interviewing them, we may obtain the names of other persons known to the first stage subjects. Thus, the subjects go on serving an informant for the identification of more subjects and the sample goes on increasing.

Merit

Snowball sampling which is generally considered to be nonprobabilistic can be converted into probabilistic by selecting subjects randomly within each stage.

Demerits

Sampling errors may creep in.

(6) Purposive or Expert Choice Sampling

Samples are sometimes expressly chosen because, in the light of available information, these mirror some larger group with reference to one or more given characteristics. The controls in such samples are usually identified as representative areas (city, country, state, and district), representative characteristics of individuals (age, sex, marital status, socio-economic status, and race) or types of groups (administrator, counselors, teachers etc.).

These controls may be further sub-divided by specified categories within classes such as amount of training, years of experience or attitudes towards a specific phenomenon. Up-to this stage, these controls are somewhat similar to those used in satisfaction. Purposive sampling differs from stratified random sampling in that the actual selection of the units to be included in the sample in each group is done purposively rather than by random method.

Methods of Data Collection

A researcher requires many techniques for data collection. Tests are used for measurement and it guides the researcher in data collection and also in evaluation. There are techniques which vary in complexity, interpretation, design and administration. Each technique is suitable for the collection of certain type of information. One has to select from the available techniques the most suitable one.

Frequently used techniques for data collection are:

- Questionnaires
- Interviews
- Schedules
- Observation Techniques

The collection of data means collection of numerical information related to the subject-matter coming under the preview of the investigation. It is the preliminary step of the statistical inquiry or investigation. Having determined the purpose and scope of statistical enquiry, a statistician or investigator has to determine the best method of collecting the data. The sources of data collection are classified, on the basis of the nature of data, into two groups primary and secondary.

Primary Data

Primary data are those data which are originally collected for the first time, for a specific purpose by an investigator. They are collected directly from the people to whom the inquiry is related. They are original in character. For example, if it is desired to conduct an inquiry into the cost of living of the workers in a certain mill, and if the facts pertaining to this inquiry are collected by the investigator or his representatives from the workers themselves such data would be termed as primary data. Data collected in the population census are also called primary data.

Secondary Data

Secondary data are those data which are already collected, processed and used by someone else for their own purpose. They are either published or unpublished. They are finished products. They are secondary to all those institutions except the one which has collected them. In other words, the term secondary data refers to that statistical material which is not originated by the investigator himself, but which he obtains from someone else's records. Thus, if instead of obtaining our data from the workers themselves we get them from the records of the trade union, or from some other source, the data will be called secondary data.

According to M.M Blair, "Secondary data are those already in existence and which have been collected for some other purpose than the answering of the questions at hand."

Distinction between Primary and Secondary Data

One should be careful while drawing the distinction between primary and secondary data. It may be observed that the distinction between primary and secondary data is a matter of degree or relatively only. The same set of data may be primary in the hands of one and secondary in the hands of others. The distinction between primary and secondary data can be determined on the basis of the different criteria, as given Table 5.15.

Table 5.15: The distinction between primary and secondary data

S.No.	*Basis*	*Primary Data*	*Secondary Data*
1	Originality	It is original because the investigator himself collect data	It is not original
2	Collection	It involves large expenses interm of time, energy and money.	It is relatively a less costly method
3	Suitability	If the data has been collected in asystematic manner, its suitability will be positive.	It may or may not suit the object of enquiry
4	Precautions	No extra precautions are needed	It should be used with great care

Methods of Collecting Primary Data

The methods commonly used for the collection of primary data are:

- Direct personal investigation
- Indirect oral investigation
- Information received through correspondents

Questionnaire method

- Mailed questionnaire method
- Schedules sent through enumerators

Direct Personal Investigation

This method consists of the collection of data personally for making observations or enquiries and soliciting information from the informants or respondents.

This method of collecting data is suitable for the following conditions:

- When the area of investigation is limited
- When a higher degree of accuracy is needed,
- When the results of the investigation are to be kept confidential,

- Where the area of investigation is complex and heterogeneous, and
- Where a greater degree of intellectual power, experience and labour are required.

The merits and demerits of direct personal investigation are given in Table 5.16.

Table 5.16: Merits and Demerits of Direct Personal Investigation

S.No.	*Merits*	*Demerits*
1	Original data are collected	unsuitable when the area of investigation is large
2	Correct and required information is gathered	It is more expensive and time-consuming
3	There is uniformity in collection of data.	The chances of personal bias are more
4	Due to personal presence of the investigator, there is flexibility in the enquiry, and necessary adjustments can easily be done.	It is more complex and places a heavy burden upon the resources of the investigator
5	Personal approach helps to overcome reluctance to respond.	
6	It permits probing to explore questions in depth	
7	Promptness is assured.	

Indirect Oral Investigation

When the informant is reluctant to supply information, the method of indirect oral investigation can be followed. Under this method the investigator approaches the witnesses or third parties, who are in touch with the informant. The enumerator interviews the people, who are directly or indirectly connected with the problem under study.

Imagine that an investigation is being conducted to study the habit of drugs among the students of an educational institution. The respondents may not give the true account of the situation. In such a case, the 'direct personal investigation' is not practicable because of the unwillingness or reluctance of the respondents to provide the required information. To get the information, the investigator has to contact the persons, who are close to the respondent like friends, neighbours, relatives, or the persons who know the information. The investigator takes these persons into confidence and interviews them. Through various questions he tries to find out the facts about the respondent.

This method is suitable in the following situations:

- When the area of investigation is large
- When the information cannot be obtained directly from the informants
- When expertise in collection of data is required to be used

The merits and demerits of indirect oral investigation are given in Table 5.17.

Table 5.17: Merits and demerits of indirect oral investigation

S.No.	*Merits*	*Demerits*
1	It can be used when the area of investigation is large.	As the information are obtained indirectly from other persons or parties, there remains possibility of getting false information.
2	It is a simple and convenient method of investigation	The careless attitude of the information according to their interests.
3	It is economical and saves time, money and labour.	Witnesses may colour the information according to their interests.
4	More complex data can also be analyzed.	If the information may not be collected. Hence, contacting many persons becomes necessary.
5	This method is free from the bias of the investigator as well of the informant.	
6	It is possible to obtain complete and adequate information regarding the enquiry	

Information through Correspondents

In this method, the investigator does not collect the information directly from the respondents. The task is handed over to a few persons or a group of persons who are known as correspondents. They do this according to their own ways and tastes.

The method is suitable in the following situations:

- When the area of investigation is very large
- When regular and continuous information is required
- When the degree of accuracy is only of secondary importance

The method is generally employed by newspapers, magazines, broadcasting agencies and various governmental agencies requiring information on regular basis:

The merits and demerits of information through Correspondents are given in Table 5.18.

Questionnaire Method

Questionnaire and schedules are widely used in collection of primary data. In practice, these two words are used in the same sense but technically they differ.

Table 5.18: Merits and Demerits of Information through Correspondents

S.No.	*Merits*	*Demerits*
1	It is the most economical and extensive method of investigation.	There is a lack of originality in data.
2	It is a very convenient method of collecting information from far-off areas.	The information can be biased.
3	It is useful where the information is needed from time to time.	Degree of accuracy is generally very low.
4		Information made available may be out-of-date.
5		There may not be uniformity in the collected data.

Definition of Questionnaire: In a statistical enquiry, the necessary information is generally collected in a printed sheet, which is known as questionnaire. This sheet contains a set of questions which the investigator intends to ask the informant, and the answers are noted down against the respective questions on the sheet.

Some important definitions of questionnaire are as follows:

"A questionnaire may be defined as set of questions to be answered by the informants without personal aid of an investigator or enumerator."

- **P.V.Young**: "The questionnaire is defined as a form used in self-enumeration, usually mailed to the respondents…In which the content is aimed at finding out facts or opinions or both, and the questions are directed to persons about themselves or their families or their business."
- **Goode and Hatt:** "In general the word questionnaire refers to advices for securing answers to questions by using a form which this respondent fills in himself."
- **Barr, Davis & Johnson**: "A questionnaire is a systematic compilation of questions that are submitted to a sampling of population from which information is desired."
- **W. J. Goode & K. Hall**: "In general, the word questionnaire refers to a device for securing answers to questions by using a form which the respondent fills in himself."

A distinction is often made between a questionnaire and a schedule. Questionnaire refers to a device for securing answers to questions to by using a form which the respondent fills in himself. Schedule is the name usually applied to a set of questions which are asked and filled in face-to-face situation with another person.

The main differences are as follows:

- Questionnaire is filled in the informants themselves whereas the schedule is filled in by the enumerators on the basis of information obtained from informants.
- In questionnaire, there may or may not be blank space along with questions, while in a schedule blank space is positively provided for giving answer of each question.
- Generally, we use normal language in a schedule, while in a questionnaire we use the language in the form of questions.
- The questionnaire is generally mailed to informants, while in schedule system the investigator or enumerator personally approach the informants with a prepared questionnaire.
- The questionnaire method can be adopted only when informants are educated, while the schedule method can be applicable equally to both types of informants educated or uneducated.
- Questionnaire method is relatively cheap, while the schedule method is the costliest.

The questionnaire is probably most used and most abused of the data gathering devices.

Characteristics of a Good Questionnaire

- It deals with an important or significant topic.
- Its significance is carefully stated on the questionnaire itself or on its covering letter.
- It seeks only that data which cannot be obtained from the resources like books, reports and records.
- It is as short as possible, only long enough to get the essential data.
- It is attractive in appearance, nearly arranged and clearly duplicated or printed.
- Directions are clear and complete, important terms are clarified.
- The questions are objective, with no clues, hints or suggestions.
- Questions are presented in a order from simple to complex.
- The questionnaire is a form prepared and distributed to secure responses to certain questions.
- It is a device for securing answers to questions by using a form which the respondent will fill by himself.
- It is a systematic compilation of questions.

- It is an important instrument being used to gather information from widely scattered sources.
- Normally used where one cannot see personally all of the people from whom he desires responses or where there is no particular reason to see them personally.

The merits and demerits of Questionnaire method are given in Table 5.19.

Table 5.19: Merits and demerits of Questionnaire Method

S.No.	*Merits*	*Demerits*
1	It's very economical.	Through this we get only limited responses
2	It's a time saving process.	Lack of personal contact
3	It covers the research in wide area.	Greater possibility of wrong answers
4	It's very suitable for special type of responses.	Chances of receiving incomplete response are more
5	It is most reliable in special cases.	Sometimes answers may be illegible
6		It may be useless in many problems.

Essential of a Good Questionnaire

Questionnaire method is the most popular method of collecting data. A questionnaire should be prepared and drafted with utmost care, since the success of any statistical investigation is determined by the quality of the questionnaire and the response it evokes from the informants. Apart from the care and caution, a lot of expertise and experience of the phenomenon under investigation are required in its preparation. Though there are no hard and fast rules for drafting a questionnaire, still following points be given due consideration. These points are:

(1) **Covering Letter**: In this letter, the investigator should introduce himself and make the objectives of the survey clear to the informant. In this the informant should be assured that the information provided by him will be kept secret. A self-addressed stamped envelope should also be sent so that the informant can return the questionnaire.

(2) **Limited Questions**: The number of questions should be as less as possible keeping in view the nature of information desired. Generally, 15 to 20 questions can be asked in one good questionnaire should be divided into various parts. This results in time saving and is convenient to both, i.e., to the enumerator and the respondent.

(3) **Simplicity and Clarity**: The questions should be clear, unambiguous and precise. As far as possible, highly technical

word or words having multiple meaning and vague concept should be avoided. The language should be very simple so that informants can easily understand.

(4) **Logical Sequence of the Questions**: The questions should be arranged in a logical order. When there are few related questions they should be arranged in a way as to initiate a chain of systematic answers. The sequence of the questions should be such that there should be a logical flow of thought. The logical arrangement of questions will facilitate work of classification.

(5) **Selection of Nature of Questions**: The nature of questions may be of different types. Hence, while framing a questionnaire, the nature of questions should also be determined carefully.

On the basis of nature, the questions may be broadly classified into two parts:

- Shut Questions
- Open Questions

(a) Shut Questions: Shut Questions are those questions in which possible answers are suggested in the Questionnaire and the respondent is required to select from these answers. Shut questions may also be of two types:

- **Simple Alternative Questions**: Such Questions can be answered in 'Yes' or 'No', 'True' or 'False'. In other words, in such Questions, the respondent has to choose between two alternatives. For Example, a Question, "Do you smoke?" can only be answered in 'Yes' or 'No'.
- **Multiple Choice Questions**: Such questions may be answered in a number of ways. The answers should be printed in the questionnaire itself, and the informant should be requested to mark against any one of them.

(b) Open Questions: Open questions are those questions where different opinions can be gathered or obtained from the answers given by different respondent. In other words, open questions are those questions which leave the door open to any answer. Such questions are to be answered by the informants in their own words.

Mailed Questionnaire Method

This method consists in preparing a 'Questionnaire' (a list of questions) relating to the field of enquiry and providing space for the answers to be filled by the respondents or informants or addressee to whom the questionnaire is mailed with a request for quick response within the specified time. A very polite covering note or letter explaining the aims and objects of enquiry is attached. Respondents are also requested to extend their full co-operation by furnishing information and returning the questionnaire duly filled in. Respondents are taken into confidence by ensuring them that the information so supplied by them will be kept strictly confidential and secrete. In order to ensure quick and better response, the return postal expenses are usually borne by the investigating organization by sending the self-addressed stamped envelope. This method is usually used by the research workers, private individuals, non-official agencies and government departments.

This method is suitable in the following situations:

- when the area under investigation is very large
- when the informants are educated and are likely to co-operate.

The merits and demerits of this method are given in Table 5.20.

Table 5.20: Merits and demerits of Mailed Questionnaire Method

S.No.	*Merits*	*Demerits*
1	It can conveniently be used when the area of investigation is very large.	It is not possible to determine the degree of accuracy of data.
2	It is economical and involves less labour and time.	Informants may prove un-cooperative, and hence may refuse to depart with proper information.
3	Collected information may be more reliable.	Information may be biased.
4	Original data can be obtained directly from the informants.	Informants may not like to provide written information.
5		If the questionnaire is complex, it may not be information.
6		(vi) It may involve a long time-lag in answering the questionnaire.

Selection of Suitable Method for the Collection of Primary Data

In the context of various methods of collection of primary data an important question arises that which of these methods is best? The fact is that none of these methods can be best for all types of investigations. If will have to be decided for each investigation as to which of the methods is the best for it. Generally, the following factors are considered while taking this decision:

Nature of Investigation

What method should be adopted for collecting primary data, depends upon the nature of investigation. If it is essential to establish a personal contact with the informants, the methods of direct personal investigation will be appropriate. For getting information from educated persons or institutions, 'mailing the questionnaire' will be appropriate. Where the scope of enquiry is very wide, and information is to be gathered on a number of subjects, it will be better to engage enumerators for filling in the schedules. Thus, the nature of investigation is one of the main determining factors in selecting the method of enquiry.

Object and Scope of Enquiry

Object and scope of enquiry also plays a vital role while a method for collecting primary data. If the scope of enquiry is limited and information sought is of confidential nature, direct personal investigation method should be adopted. The method of indirect personal investigations is more appropriate in enquiries conducted by a committee or commission. If data are to be collected on regular basis from widely scattered areas, then the information through correspondents should be adopted.

Degree of Accuracy

It depends upon the desired degree of accuracy as to which method should be adopted for collecting primary data. If the enquiry is such where more degree of accuracy is necessary, the method of direct personal investigation should be adopted. If more degree of accuracy is not necessary then the method of indirect oral investigation may be suitable. When the degree of accuracy is only of secondary importance, information through correspondent's method will be appropriate. If questionnaires are filled in by the informants the degree of accuracy will be less as compared to when they are got filled in through enumerators.

Financial Resources

Financial resources also determine as to which of the methods of data collection will be suitable. If more finance is available, methods of direct personal investigation or schedules to be filled in by the enumerators can be followed. On the other hand, in case of limited financial resources mailing the questionnaire method may be adopted.

Time Factor

If results are to be obtained within a very short period, then information can be collected through correspondents or schedules can be got filled-in by the enumerator. If there is no time limit, other methods can be followed.

Observation Method

Observation is one of the methods of collecting data. It is used to get both past and current information, for example, instead of asking respondents about their current behaviour, we may observe it and record and observations. Although it is not possible to observe past behaviour, we may observe the results of such behaviour. In a way, secondary data reflect the results of the past behaviour of people as also of past occurrences.

There are several methods of observation of which any one or a combination of some of them can be used by the observer. Thus, there are structured or unstructured methods, disguised or undisguised methods, or observations made in a natural setting, direct-in direct observation, or human-mechanical observation. These are briefly discussed below.

Structured-unstructured Observation

Structured observation is used when the research problem has been formulated precisely and the observers have been told especially what is to be observed. They may be given a simple form to record their observations. Unstructured observation implies that observe whatever they think is relevant and important. While structured observations are free from subjective bias, unstructured observations are subject to this limitation. The extent of the bias may vary to the extent an observation is unstructured.

Disguised-undisguised Observation

In the case of disguised observation, the subjects do not know that they are being observed. In some cases, disguised observation may be made by the observer by posing as one of the shoppers who are being observed. This type of observation if often preferred because it is feared that people may behave differently when they are being observed. It may be difficult to completely disguise an observation, through this apart; it poses an ethical question of its desirability when those who are being observed are kept in the dark.

Observation under Natural Setting-laboratory Setting

Another way to classify observations is on the basis of their setting, i.e. natural or laboratory. Observations in field studies are in their natural setting and are, therefore, undertaken in extremely realistic conditions. Sometimes, an experimental manipulation may be introduced in a field study. Observation in a laboratory setting, on the other hand, enables the enables the observer to control extraneous variables which influence the behaviour of people. Observational studies in laboratory settings have certain advantages over field studies. They enable the collection of data promptly and economically and in addition, permit the use of more objective measurements.

Direct-indirect Observation

In the case of direct observation, the event or the behaviour of a person is observed as it occurs. In contrast, indirect observation implies that some record of past behaviour is observed. In other words, the behaviour itself is not observed, rather its effects are observed. An observer engaged in indirect observation generally looks for physical traces of behaviour or occurrence of an event. Suppose, he is interested in knowing about the liquor consumption of a household, he would like for empty liquor bottles in the garbage. Similarly, the observer may seek the permission of the housewife to see the pantry. He may carry out a pantry audit to ascertain the consumption of certain types of products. It may be noted that the success of an indirect observation largely depends on how best the observer is able to identify physical traces of the problem under study. Direct observation is far more common than indirect observation.

Human Mechanical Observation

Another way of classifying observations is whether they are made manually or by machines. Most of the studies in marketing research based on human observation where in trained observers are required to observe and faithfully record their observations. In some cases, mechanical devices such as eye cameras and audiometers are used for observation.

One of the major advantages of electrical/ mechanical devices is that their recordings are free from subjective bias. As against this advantage, such observations may be less valid than human observations. This is because the observer's power of integration can lead to a more valid evaluation of the observation.

Collection of Secondary Data

Secondary data are those data which are already collected, processed and used by other persons or institutions for their own purpose. In most of the studies the investigator finds it impracticable to collect first-hand information on all related issues and as such he makes use of the data collected by others. The sources of secondary data can broadly be classified under two heads:

- Published sources
- Unpublished sources

Published Sources

There are certain international, national and local agencies which publish statistical data on a regular basis. Certain periodicals are published regularly. Moreover, there are certain research organizations which publish magazines or other periodicals. These sources can be summed up as follows:

International Publications

Foreign governments and international agencies publish regular and occasional reports on economics and other related matters of significance, e.g. U.N.O. statistical year book, demography year book, annual reports of the international labour organization and annual reports of the economic and social commission for Asia and Pacific (ESCAP), international monetary fund (IMF), world bank etc.

Official Publications of Central and State Governments

The central government and the State Governments and their different departments publish reports on current problems. They gather information which is generally more reliable and authentic. Some of the important publications are census of India, Reserve bank of India bulletins, statistical abstracts of the states; report on currency and finance, etc.

Semi-official Publications

Semi government institutions like municipalities, corporations, district boards, etc., publish reports and data regarding birth and death, health and sanitation and other related subjects. These sources supply rich original materials to the researchers and other persons interested in data.

Reports of Committees and Commissions

At times state and central governments appoint committees and commissions with a specific reference to study a phenomenon. The reports of these committees and commissions provide important secondary data.

Private Publications

The private research and commercial institutions also supply data on the current economic and other issues. Some of them are as follows:

a. **Commercial and Financial Institutions**: These institutions also publish occasional reports and statistical data of common and specific interest, e.g., the reports of Stock Exchanges, Trade Unions, FICCI, etc.

b. **Research Institutions**: The different departments of Indian universities, Indian Statistical Institute, National Council of Applied Economic research, Institute of Economic growth, etc., are engaged in research work and publish their findings in the form of research papers and small monographs. These are perennial sources of information.

c. **Journals and Newspapers**: Eastern Economists, monthly statistics of trade, Financial Express, Economic times, business standard, etc., are some of the journals and newspapers which regularly collect and publish data on various aspects of business, economics, commerce and trade.

Unpublished Sources

In some cases, data are collected but these are not put in published form. For example, research scholars in the institutes and universities, trade associations and labour bureaus do collect data but they never put it in published form. Still, the data from these sources may be used when needed.

Precautions in the use of Secondary data

The collection and use of secondary data is simple and economical. However, a secondary data may not be suitable, adequate and competent for the purpose of the enquiry. Also, such data may have errors because of bias, improper sampling procedures, errors of definition, etc. Therefore, before using the secondary data, the investigators should consider the following factors:

(1) **Reliability of Data**: The determination of the reliability of secondary data is very important but a difficult job. The reliability of data can be tested y finding out the agency that collected such data. If the agency has used proper methods in collecting data, statistics may be relied upon.

(2) **Suitability of the Data**: Before using secondary data, the investigator should make sure the data are suitable for the purpose of the enquiry. The nature and scope of investigation may help in judging suitability of data. For example, if the object of the present enquiry is to study the trend in retail prices, while the data provide only wholesale prices, such data are unsuitable.

(3) Adequacy of the Data: This means whether the secondary data available is sufficient for the purpose and scope of the enquiry. Adequacy of the data is to be judged in the light of the requirements of the survey and the geographical area covered by the available data. We must consider the time for which the data are available. In the above example, if our object is to study the retail price trend of India, and if the available data cover only the retail price trend in the state of Haryana, then if would not serve the purpose. Further, for a monthly study of phenomenon, yearly figures are inadequate.

Choice between Primary and Secondary Data

The investigator must decide at the outset whether he will use primary data or secondary data in an investigation. The choice between the two depends on the following considerations:

- Nature and scope of the inquiry.
- Availability of financial resources.
- Availability of time.
- Degree of accuracy desired, and
- The status of the investor, i.e., individual, corporation, government, etc.

It may be pointed out that most statistical analyses rest upon secondary data. Primary are generally used in those cases where the secondary data do not provide an adequate basis for analysis. In certain cases, both primary as well as secondary may be used. The reason why secondary data are being increasingly used in that published statistics are now available covering diverse fields so that an investigator finds required data readily available to him in many cases.

Synopsis and Thesis Writing

Research Proposal (Synopsis)

All researchers have to write a research proposal, usually referred to as Synopsis, before they undertake any research work. For a new researcher, it presents a great problem because he does not know the components of any research proposal. Even an experienced research worker is required to write a research proposal if he proposes to obtain financial assistance for a research project from any research organization.

Title of the Proposal

The first part of any research proposal is its title. If the title is not clearly stated it will not help the researcher in his work. A good title should clearly identify the research proposal and must clearly state about the following:

- What variables are included in the research proposal?
- What is the relationship between the different variables?
- Which is the population to which the results may be generalized?

Research Problem

The second part of any research proposal is the research problem. The problem should define and delimit the specific area of the proposed research. It should begin with the general background of the problem and end with a specific statement of the problem.

The research problem should be so structured that it should begin with a broad base of general problems and explanations. It should be followed by a survey of related research literature. It should end with the problem statement. The background of the research should identify the variables of the research problem, discuss the variables which are selected for the research study. Other important variables which are not included in the research study should also be briefly discussed. It should also be made clear that which criteria were used for the selection of the variables. This part of the research proposal should be written in simple language and should also be précised. The significance of the problem should also be written. It should meet the following requirements:

- Only such areas should be selected which are of crucial importance.
- The research proposal should be related with practical problems. It should provide solution to any existing social / behavioral / educational /institutional/library related problem etc.
- The research problem should not have small target population, because its result cannot be verified.
- Target population of any research problem should be related to a popular population.

If the research proposal is to be submitted for financial assistance it should also be seen that what the areas of priority of the funding agency are. Each agency grants financial assistance to those research studies which it considers as central to its area of concern and others as peripheral. The statement of the problem is the last stone in the pyramid of the research problem. It specifies the variate and criterion variables in non-experimental studies and independent and dependent variables in an experimental study, the type of relationship between variables and target population. Another criterion of a good problem statement is that it can be measured. A research problem in which the relationship between variables cannot be measured empirically cannot be categorized a research problem. The statement which seeks to answer the question of value judgment should not be included in research problem. Such questions cannot be answered by a research study. They should be avoided in a research proposal.

Statement of Hypothesis

The third part of a research proposal is statement of Hypotheses. It is done more sophistically than the statement of problem. The research hypothesis is presented in an affirmative form rather than in the interrogative form. They state what is expected to occur if various conditions are evoked or presumed.

The researcher should review the related literature thoroughly before formulating hypotheses. All the terms which are used in any hypothesis should be carefully defined. The hypothesis should be unambiguous and testable. Since the quantum of achievement is difficult to predict at the time of statement of hypothesis, researchers prefer 'null hypothesis' which assumes that only a chance difference is expected to occur between the groups.

The following criteria should be used for the formulation of testable and significant hypothesis;

- The hypothesis must be clearly stated in operational terms.
- The hypothesis must be specific and testable.
- Research problems should be selected which are directly related to previous research or theoretical formulations.

Methodology

The fourth part of a research proposal is called Methodology. It comprises of the following;

Target Population

It is also called universe. The salient characteristics of the population should be thoroughly described so that it should be definite that what is the target population for which sample is to be drawn and to which the results of the study could be generalized.

Sampling Plan

The method of sampling should be specified in the research proposal. If the sample is not thoroughly analyzed and precisely described, faulty generalizations may be made. The sample should be made the true representative of the population. The sampling plan should also be described in the proposal. It should describe how the units in the target population will be selected and used. A good sampling plan should meet the following criteria; a. Obtaining or constructing an accurate, current list of the target population units. b. Method of drawing the sample. c. Number of subjects or population units to be selected.

Research Design

The research design should indicate how the research setting will be arranged in order to yield the desired data with the least possible contamination/ error by intervening variables. There is no single design that can be applied in all the cases. It depends upon individual researcher to devise his design. The design should ensure the answer of every hypothesis designed in the proposed research work.

A well-prepared research design should contain the following characteristics:

- Specifications of its relationship to each research hypothesis.
- Description of the methods of proposed control of confounding variables and threats to validity.
- Description of the design in statistical terms.
- Identification of the types of interferences that may be made.

Stimulus Materials

It should also be specified in the research proposal that what stimulus materials will be used in the study. Kinds and ways of stimuli should be described. Most commonly used stimuli are printed instructional materials. Instructional materials should include the following elements:

- Title
- Author/Editor
- Publisher
- Year of publication
- Intended population
- Time required for administration
- Cost of material

Response Measures

The researcher should specify clearly what raw data are required by the research design and how they will be collected. Each instrument should be described including the following items of information:

- Title
- Author/Editor
- Publisher
- Population
- Forms
- Test Objectives
- Description of test, items, scoring procedures
- Traits represented in score
- Predictive / Concurrent validity
- Reliability data
- Normative data
- Internal consistency of tests
- Time required for administration
- Cost of material
- Data of publication

Data Collection Methods

The research proposal should identify the schedules and procedures to be used for acquiring the data and recording it accurately. If they are lengthy, they should be placed in an appendix and reference be given in the body of the proposal.

Data Analysis

The researcher should specify how the data will be ordered and reduced to relate directly to the research problem. The statistical procedure to be used in the analysis of data they should be described. It will be done hypothesis wise or not, it should be indicated in the research proposal.

If a complex design or obscure statistical test is to be used, it should be indicated in the proposal. If the research proposal is to be submitted to a Funding agency, the following information should also be provided in the research proposal;

Logistics

It consists of the following:

- Time Schedule
- Facilities, equipment and supplies
- Travel expenses
- Publication costs and other direct costs
- Budget forms

Research Report (Thesis)

A detailed account of the research experience from selection and definition of the problem, formulation of hypotheses, gathering, analyzing and interpreting data, testing of hypotheses, making conclusion and suggesting further research in the related problem area is called a research report (Thesis).

The basic components of a research report (thesis) are as follows:

Introduction of the research problem

The researcher will write in it the following:

- What is the problem?
- What is its importance?
- What is the relation of the problem with previous theory and research,
- What are the objectives of the study?
- What are the hypotheses?

Description of the procedure of the research

The researcher will write in it the following:

- How did he select the subjects?
- How many subjects were used?
- How were the subjects assigned to groups?
- What was done to the subjects?
- How was it done?
- When was it done?
- How long was it done?
- How was the reliability of the measuring instruments measured?
- How was the validity of the measuring instruments measured?

Description and presentation of the results

The researcher will write in it the following:

- Which statistical procedures he used to test the hypotheses?
- What were the outcomes of those procedures?
- What were the subsidiary findings of the research?

Discussion of the study findings

The researcher will write in it the following:

- Why did the results manifest themselves in a particular way?
- What did these results signify?
- What was the relationship between this research and the previous research upon which it was based?

Features of Thesis

The following are the essential features of a good thesis:

- Clarity
- Conciseness
- Veracity
- No place for figures of speech, lyrical prose and in using anecdotes.
- No lengthy digressions
- Only necessary details
- Absolute uncompromising honesty
- Serious attempt and not a game

Mode of Communications

The researcher may use any of the following modes for communicating his research results:

- **A research monograph**: The researcher may publish a research monograph on the basis of his research results through a research journals or a reputed research publisher.ph depends upon the standard of the research work and the reputation of the researcher.
- **A research journal**: The researcher may publish a research paper in a reputed research journal. But this requires that the paper should be acceptable to the Editor of the journal. The prestigious journals send these papers to reviewers who are conversant with the research area in which the research paper has been written.

- **Presenting in the meeting of the Association/ Society /Congress**: There are annual conferences of the associations, societies and Congress in each subject area. They provide opportunities to the researchers to present their research results in the form of a research paper before the members of the association or the society or the delegates of the Congress which are followed by the discussions. The journals of those organizations publish these papers in the form of the proceedings of the Association / Society / Congress.

Format of Thesis

The thesis may be divided into the following parts:

(a) **Preliminary Section**: It consists of the following:
  - Title Page
  - Preface
  - Table of Contents
  - List of Tables
  - List of figure, maps and illustrations

(b) **Introduction**: It consists of the following:
  - Importance of the problem under investigation.
  - A review of related literature
  - Statement of Hypotheses or relationships being studied
  - Delimitations of the study (v) Assumptions of the study
  - Definition of important terms

(c) **Methods**: It consists of the following;
  - How was the study conducted?
  - From which population was the sample selected?
  - How many subjects were selected?
  - What were the demographic characteristics of the subjects? (male/female, average age)
  - Was there any characteristic which make the sample a typical to the population?
  - How were the subjects assigned to groups?
  - What instructions were given to the subjects?
  - How conditions were controlled?
  - What was the treatment of variables?
  - How, when and on what were subjects measured?

- What data collection instruments were used?
- What was the format of items?
- What was the reliability of the instrument?
- What was the validity of the instrument?
- What are the details of the instruments which was prepared by the researcher?

(d) **Results:** It consists of the following:

- What statistical procedure was used to study the hypotheses?
- What was the probability level of each hypotheses test?
- What was the probability level of each statistics?
- What was the attendant degree of freedom?
- What was the strength of the relationship of the variables? (vii) What were the group means and standard deviation?
- What were principle finding?

(e) **Discussion**: It consists of the following;

- What were the original purposes of the study?
- How were these purposes met?
- Why the obtained occurred?
- What were the conclusions of the researcher for practice, theory and future research?
- What is the contribution of the study to the research literature?
- What are the strengths and weaknesses of the study?

(f) **Reference Section**: It consists of the following:

- Bibliography
- Appendices: Questionnaires, Copies of letters used, evaluation sheets, checklists etc

A Thesis Format

1. General

The purpose of this sample is to provide broad guidelines to the Ph.D. candidates for the preparation of their thesis. It lists the general and specific requirements for the thesis preparation including guidelines for structuring the contents. Further, for style, structure and presentation of a very special type of work specific to a particular field, the scholar may refer to additional style manuals or reference guides and to the published literature in their respective fields of study.

2. Arrangement of The Contents of Thesis

The sequence in which the thesis contents should be arranged and bound should be as follows:

- o Cover Page and Colour
- o Inner Cover Page
- o Candidate Certificate for Self-Declaration
- o Certificate by Supervisors
- o Plagiarism Report
- o Copy Right Transfer Certificate
- o Acknowledgements
- o Table of Contents
- o List of Symbols, Figures and Tables, if any
- o Preface of the thesis
- o Introduction
- o Literature Review
- o Chapters covering the work
- o Conclusions
- o References
- o Appendices
- o List of Publications
- o Copies of Manuscript/reprints of Papers

3. Manuscript Preparation

- **Cover Page/ Title Page**

  A specimen of the cover/title page is given in the Annexure-I. It carries the pattern and font size required for cover page. The colour of cover page should be blue.
- **Inner Cover Page**

  Colour print of front page in normal paper.
- **Candidate Certificate for Self-Declaration**

  The Certificate from Candidate is should be there as per format available in Annexure-II. The heading Certificate Times New Roman font size 14 bold in the center should start about 60mm - 70mm from the top of the page.
- **Certificate by Supervisor/ Supervisors**

  The Certificate of Supervisor/supervisors of the thesis by the supervisor(s) should be there as per the format shown in Annexure-

III. The heading Certificate Times New Roman font size 14 bold in the center should start about 60mm -70mm from the top of the page. The certificate shall carry the supervisor's signature in original and shall be followed by the supervisor's name, academic designation as per format.

- **Plagiarism Report**

  The scholars must check and scan his/her thesis completely with an authenticate plagiarism software before final submission and submit a certificate regarding same duly signed by scholar along with supervisor and co-supervisor.

- **Copy Right Transfer Certificate**

  The copy right transfer certificate should be there as per format available in Annexure-IV duly signed by Research Scholar/ candidate.

- **Acknowledgements**

  Acknowledgements shall be brief and should not exceed one page when typed in single spacing Times New Roman with font size 12 within the specified margin of the page. The signature of the candidate shall be made at the bottom right end above his/her name typed in title case.

- **Table of Contents**

  The table of contents should list all the contents of the research report.

- **List of Symbols, Figures and Tables, if any**

  The list of symbols, figures and tables should be placed in thesis as per format available in Annexure-VI.

- **Preface of the Thesis**

  Preface should be an essay type of narration not exceeding four pages outlining the research problem, the methodology used, summary of the findings, possible applications of the research and suggestions/directions for future research.

- **Introduction**

  It should cover the background, statement of problems, definition, purpose of study, theoretical basis, and contribution of the study along with future perspectives.

- **Literature Review**

  It covers the chronological, categorical or related theoretical viewpoints related to topic or area of research.

- **Chapters covering the work**

  This part of thesis includes the research design and approach, methodology, experimental details, analytical study including data analysis with procedures, results and discussion of findings along with limitations.

- **Conclusions**

  This part summarizes the whole research efforts, purpose of study and research, importance of work along with future application and suggestions for further research and development in concern area. This must leave an impression on the reader/expert/examiners.

- **References**

  References should be followed by any standard International organization pattern such as Apa/Ieee/ Chemical Abstract/ Currentcontents/Physicsabstract/Mla etc.

- **Appendices**

  Appendices in thesis are provided to give supplementary information, which if included in the main text may serve as a distraction and could tend to dilute the central theme under discussion. It includes maps, questionnaires, raw data etc.

- **List of Publications**

  The candidate must provide a list of papers published, accepted and communicated by the research findings of the thesis and attach copy of reprint of published papers.

Innovations in Research Methodologies

Zhao (2003) have compared the research processes, specially research supervision, to a knowledge management process as shown in Fig. 5.5. The knowledge management consists of the preserving, embedding and enhancing the knowledge. The researchers develop new knowledge, theory and methodology (knowledge creation) through integrating, synthesizing and valuing existing knowledge (knowledge transfer), and then develop new insight into their area of investigation (knowledge embedding).

Bryman and Bell (2011) concluded that qualitative research provides a great deal of descriptive detail based on their findings. They identified four traditions of qualitative research as shown in Fig. 5.6.

Emerging Innovative Methodologies

The innovative research methodologies do not mean designing a completely new methodology but rather using tested methods in novel ways in an effort to share methodological expertise.

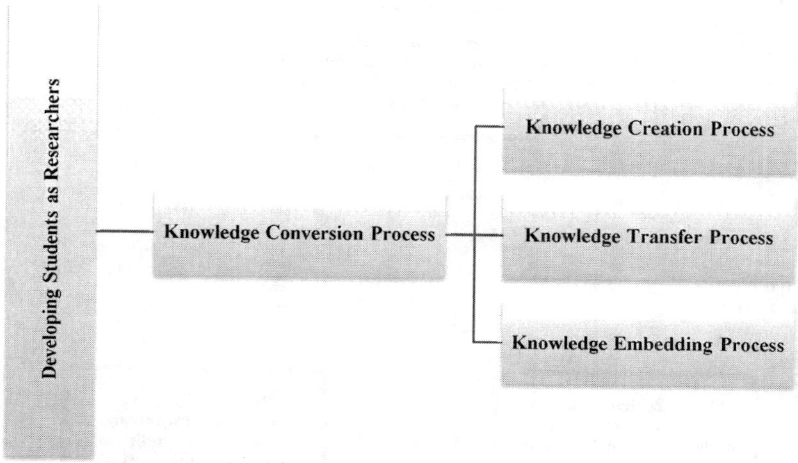

Fig. 5.5: Knowledge Management Model

Wiles et. al. (2011) have identified three main reasons for innovative research methodologies as shown in Fig. 5.7. These are theoretical reasons, ethical reasons and practical reasons. A further discussion of these reasons is beyond the scope of this book.

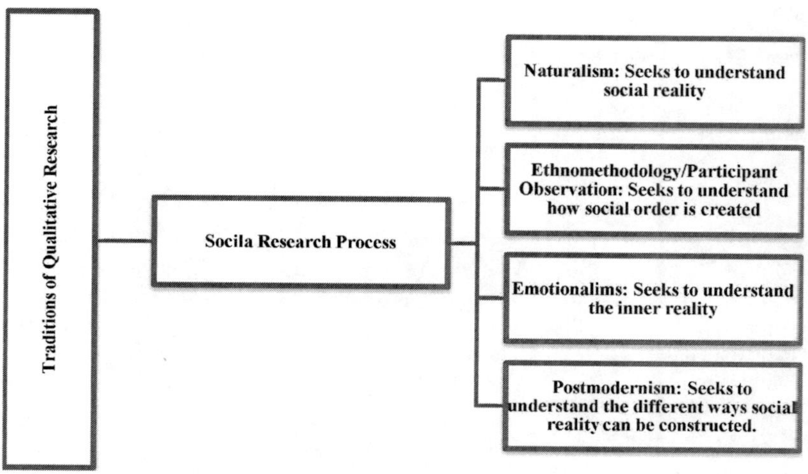

Fig. 5.6: Qualitative Research Traditions

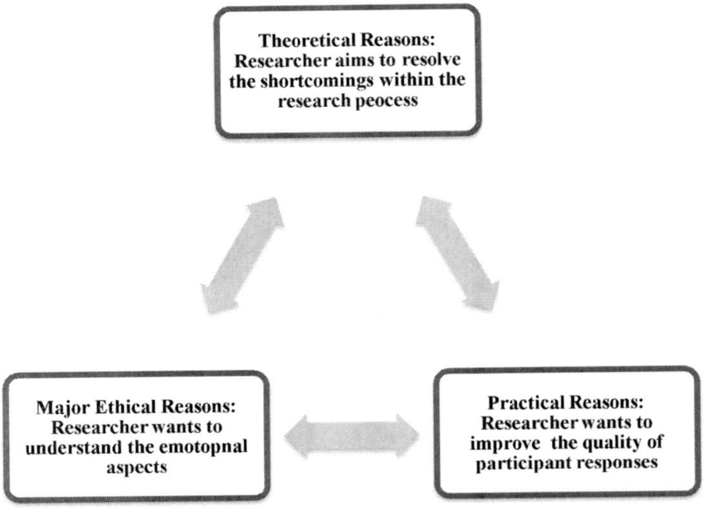

Fig. 5.7: Innovative Research Methodologies

6

Innovations in Project Management

Project

The word 'project' has diverse meaning. A project is accomplished by performing a set of activities. The construction of a shopping mall is a project. It consists of many activities like digging of foundation pits, construction of foundation, construction of walls, construction of roofs, fixing of doors and windows, fixing of sanitary fittings, wiring, fixing of air conditioning system, fixing of fire safety equipment etc. A shopping mall project is complete provided all the above-mentioned activities are complete. A project completion mission will require different types of resources like men, money, material and time. These resources are limited and managers have to adopt changing technologies while keeping environment in mind.

Project management and Programme management

Generally, there is confusion between project management and programme management.

Project management is concerned with detailed planning, scheduling, monitoring and adjusting the processes involved in implementing a specific project.

Programme management is concerned with evaluating and then managing a series of related projects using common processes and evaluation

The production of goods is a project. There are two factors in today's business environment which have become very common. These are change and complexity. The nature of business has incorporated these factors into everyday lives. The managers work in an environment of constant change and increasing complexity and must be competitive, productive, customer-focused, and profitable.

All the needed strategies like marketing strategies, manufacturing strategies, service strategies must accept the realization that as soon as the details are spelled out, factors in the marketplace will demand that these strategies be reexamined. Managing change has become a key component for today's successful business which has become extremely complicated. This complexity is related to the number of factors involved in the effort.

Projects can be defined in many different ways. However, there are some traits that all projects have in common. Typically, these traits are used to identify what a project is. The most distinguishing feature is a specific time frame. All projects have a beginning and an end. Many efforts are called "projects" but actually become programs as they extend indefinitely and cover broader, less specific business objectives. Projects must have a clear, definitive goal or objective. The objective is specific, identifiable, and can be accomplished.

All these statements could be combined as shown in Fig. 6.1.

The project is defined by many people in different ways.

- **Harison**: 'Project is a non-routine, non-repetitive, one-off under taking, with well defined time, financial and technical performance goal.'
- **Project Management Institute (PMI)**: 'Project can be defined as a temporary endeavour undertaken to accomplish a unique objective at a goal'
- **Little & Missless:** 'A project is any scheme or part of a scheme for investing resources which can be reasonably analyzed and evaluated as an independent unit.'

Thus, we can define project as a complex of non-routine activities that must be completed with a set amount of resources and with a set time frame.

Some of the well-known examples of projects are:

- Designing renewable energy device
- Designing a solar green house
- Determine technology parameter
- Construction of a mall
- Construction of a house

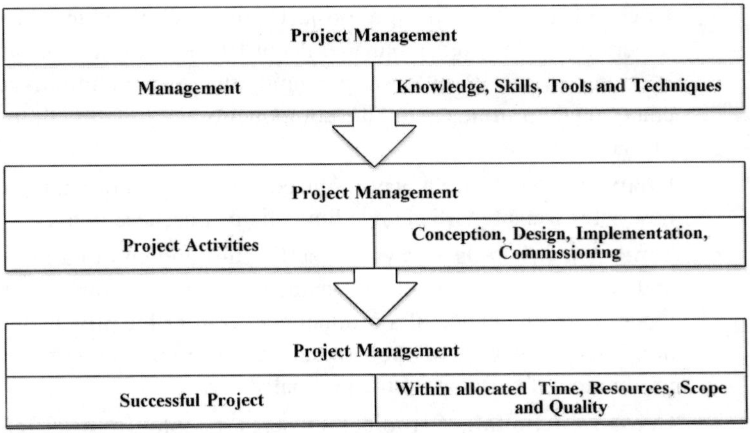

Fig. 6.1 Project Defined

- Writing a book
- Construction of a dam
- Construction of road and bridges
- Manufacturing of cars
- Developing a new product or service
- Constructing a facility
- Renovating the kitchen
- Designing a new transportation vehicle
- Acquiring a new or modified data system
- Organizing a meeting
- Implementing a new business process

Characteristics of Projects

Some of the key characteristics of projects are as follows:

- **Objectivity:** Each and every project has well defined project. The project comes to an end once objectives are met. For example, construction of a house is a project. The objective is to have a house in which we can live. As soon as house comes in shape, project will come to an end.
- **Uniqueness:** The activities involved in projects are unique. Example: Building a fiftieth school is different from building the forty-ninth one. The location is different, the design is different, and there are different categories of students.

- **Uncertainty**: Parts of the project are unique, which brings uncertainty. The project manager is not 100 percent sure how this is going to work out. For example, the owners might keep changing their minds about the components and functionalities of the sales software.
- **Change**: Projects are a way to introduce change. For example, a new sales website will change how clients purchase items.
- **Temporary:** here is always a specific start and end to a project, and it should cease once the mandatory products are created. Ongoing maintenance of a product occurs after the project and is not considered part of the project. An example for this is the production of software to manage sales.
- **Cross-Functional**: A project engages people from different seniority and business departments that work together for the period of the project. For example, to develop sales software, people from marketing and sales departments should work closely with the IT department.
- **Specific:** The project must be specific. Being specific includes detailing out the project's structure, goals, benefits, milestones and costs. All these requires careful planning and inputs from the project team members involved and if necessary the external consultants or experts.
- **Measurable**: A clearly defined project must be measurable in terms of its benefits and achievements. This should not only be in terms of monetary benefits but also other tangible and intangible benefits derived from the project's execution. A clear and precise plan devised during the project's planning stage will enable objective measurements be executed to analyse the project's achievements.
- **Achievable:** A project will only be meaningful if it is achievable. Being too ambitious in planning for the project will not be helpful and may result in the project being unachievable.
- **Relevant**: The project needs to bring relevant benefits to the entity concerned. This may be in the form of reducing its overall production costs, increasing its operational efficiency or other specific purposes relevant to the entity.
- **Time Bound:** A project has boundaries, so its extent is defined. It means that the project should come with a time frame for its completion including its planning, development, execution, fine

tuning before its full run instead of taking forever to be completed. Any adjustments to this time table should be clearly justified by the parties involved bearing in mind the costs involved in the project's execution, opportunity costs and finance costs related to the project.

- **Progressive Elaboration:** With the progress of a project, continuous investigation and improvement become available, and all this allows producing more accurate and comprehensive plans. This key characteristic means that the successive iterations of planning processes result in developing more effective solutions to progress and develop projects.
- **Well Planned:** Obviously you need to keep your eye on the project plan as the work progresses but if you get it done well at the start then it will be a lot easier for you further down the line.
- **A Strong Team:** Even the best project manager in the world isn't likely to be able to deliver completed projects on time without the support of a strong team. Part of your role is to make sure that everyone in the team understands the project, has the skills and resources to contribute and feels happy and motivated.
- **Clear Communication:** One of the features of a well-run project is that it involves clear communication all the way through it. Obviously, this doesn't just depend on the project manager but when you work in this role it is something which you will want to focus on. The smartest way of dealing with this is to put your communication strategy in place at the start and stick to it.
- **Good Change Control:** Projects change as they go on, and the things you end up delivering could be very different from what you started out looking at. This means that a robust change control process is vital.
- **A Clear Vision:** You should keep a clear vision what you want to achieve. The best way to make sure that you do this is to be clear in your initial project documentation about the goals. If you do this then you will always have this to look back on if things get too confusing.
- **Risk Control:** There are many different types of risk which could affect your projects and you will want to have an effective way of managing them. Again, you need to identify them at the start and then get your stakeholders to sign off the document containing them. Project risks have a habit of getting out of hand if you let them.

- **Project Management Life Cycle**: Every project, small or large, passes through four compulsory phases in life span. These are conceptualization, design, implementation and commissioning. The process each manager follows during the life of a project is called the Project Management Life Cycle (PMLC). A proven methodical life cycle is necessary to repeatedly implement and manage projects successfully.

During the life cycle of any project, proven and tested project management processes or best practices should be initiated. The types and extent of processes initiated depend on the nature of the project, i.e. size, probability of failure and its consequences. Strong and effective leaders apply process to protect all projects. Every project has a life cycle, with a beginning, a life and an end (defined by accomplishing the objective).

Project Management

Project management has been practiced for thousands of years. However, it has been about half a century ago that organizations start applying systematic project management tools and techniques to complex projects. In the 1950s, Navy employed modern project management methodologies in their Polaris project. During the 1960s and 1970s, Department of Defense, NASA, and large engineering and construction companies utilized project management principles and tools to manage large budget, schedule-driven projects. In the 1980s, manufacturing and software development sectors started to adopt and implement sophisticated project management practices. By the 1990s, the project management theories, tools, and techniques were widely received by different industries and organizations.

The origin of the modern project management concept started between 1900s and 1950s. During this time, technology advancement shortened the project schedule. Automobiles allowed effective resource allocation and mobility. Telecommunication system increased the speed of communication.

Project management can be considered both as an art and a science. The science consists of a systematic approach using a standard methodology. The art consists of "soft skills" including leadership, trust, credibility, problem solving, and managing expectations. The art of project management is developed through experience, practice, and intuition. A project manager who is skilled in the art instinctively knows how and when to react to project problems. Project management is equally divided between the art and science and a successful project manager utilizes and refines both skill sets to effectively manage projects.

Project management is the process of achieving project objectives (schedule, budget and performance) through a set of activities that start and end at certain points in time and produce quantifiable items. Successful project management is the art of bringing together the tasks, resources and people necessary to accomplish the business goals and objectives within the specified time constraints and within the monetary allowance. Projects and programs are linked directly to the strategic goals and initiatives of the organization supported.

Project management is a management method that is used to plan, organize and control project activities. The project is initiated by executive committee that will initiate project work. The basic concept of project management is the delegation of general management authority to the project leader.

Scope of Project Management

The primary aim of the project is to deliver a product or service to a client within the specified time, with all kinds of resources and quality measures. Thus, project managers are required to use all resources efficiently to achieve the project objectives (Fig. 6.2). The factors like scope, quality, time cost and resources are very important.

- **(a) Project Scope:** It is simply a brief and accurate description of the end products or deliverables expected from the project. It includes all the activities that are to be performed as end product from the successful completion of the project.
- **(b) Quality:** The quality is very important. The quality standards should be specified at the time of deciding scope of the project.
- **(c) Time:** The completion of the project in the scheduled time is very important.
- **(d) Cost:** Cost is another important parameter in managing the project.
- **(e) Resources:** Resources include the human resource, finance, and other physical resources.

Classification of Projects

The projects are classified in many ways. Some of the examples are given in Table 6.1. Some of the prominent categories are agriculture, research, service sector, techno-economic, business etc.

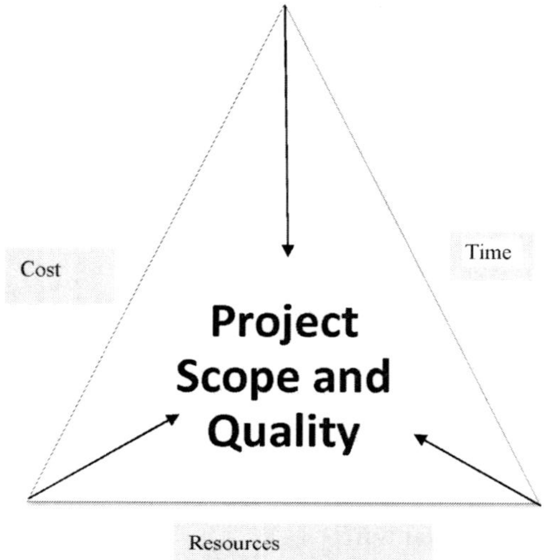

Fig. 6.2: Scope Triangle of Project Management

Table 6.1: Classification of Projects

S.No.	*Category of the Projects*	*Types of the Projects*
1	Agricultural Projects	Agricultural projects are related to: • Land development • Irrigation • Soil- conservation • Fertilizers • Seeds etc.
2	Research Projects	These projects generate new knowledge which may be represented as models, patterns as patents or else knowledge may be embedded in a working process. The examples are: • Business modeling • Developing a model of the Indian economy • Developing a new species of agricultural products • Developing an innovative education system which can make India as knowledge centre • Developing a new methodology of constructing roads
3	Quantifiable Projects	• Quantifiable assessment of benefits can be made. • Are concerned with industrial development, power generation, and mineral development.
4	Non- quantifiable Projects	• Here quantitative assessment is not possible. • Concerned with health, education, defense etc.

(Contd...)

5	Sectoral Projects	The sectoral basis may be used as the criterion for classification of projects. Some of the examples are: • Agriculture & allied sector • Irrigation and power sector • Industry and mining sector • Transport and communication • Social service sector • Miscellaneous
6	Techno- Economic Projects	These are based on their techno- economic characteristics. Techno-economic classification facilitates the process of project feasibility appraisal. (a) Factor intensity- oriented classification • Capital intensive • Labour intensive (b) Causation-oriented classification • Demand based • Raw materials based (c) Magnitude- oriented classification- based on the size of the investment. • Large- scale • Medium- scale • Small- scale
7	Financial Institution Classification	All India and state financial institutions classify projects according to their age, experience and the purpose. These projects are invariably profit- oriented. Examples are: • New projects • Expansion projects • Modernization projects • Diversification projects
8	Services Projects	• Welfare projects • Service projects • Research and development projects • Educational projects
9	Business Implementation Projects	The project produces an operationally effective process. The value generated by the project is embedded in the process. The examples are: • Developing a new business process • Installing e-commerce

Knowledge Areas of Project Management

There could be several areas of the project management. Some of the prominent knowledge areas of project management are given below:

1. **Scope Management**: Scope management includes initiating, planning, definition, verification, change and control
2. **Communications Management**: Project communications management includes the processes required to ensure timely and appropriate generation, collection, dissemination, storage, and ultimate disposition of project information
3. **Risk Management**: Project risk management includes the processes concerned with identifying, analyzing, and responding to project risk.
4. **Human Resources Management**: Project human resource management includes the Processes required to make the most effective use of people involved with the project.
5. **Procurement Management**: Project procurement management includes the processes required to acquire goods and services from outside the performing organization
6. **Time Management**: Project time management includes the processes required to ensure timely completion of the project.
7. **Cost Management**: Project cost management includes the processes required to ensure that the project is completed within the approved budget
8. **Quality Management**: Project quality management includes the processes required to ensure the Project will satisfy the needs for which it was undertaken
9. **Integration Management**: Project issues management includes the processes required to identify, resolve, and control in a timely manner factors which could influence the overall scope, time, cost, risk, and quality of the project.

Elements of Successful Project Management

There is no single process that could make a project successful. It is the careful implementation of a number of different elements.

The factors that lead to successful projects include:

- Clearly defined goals and objectives
- A well-defined project management process

- A proven set of project management tools
- A clear understanding of the role of project management.

Every project manager has a broad array of behavioral and management techniques from which to choose. The objective of the selection process is to choose techniques that ensure high-quality, on-time deliverables that are accepted by the business and that fit the conditions and environment.

Project Management Basic Steps

The basic steps for a project management are the following:

(a) The initiation phases

(b) The project planning phase

(c) Project execution and control phase

(d) Project close-out phase

A brief summary of these phases is given in Table 6.2.

Table 6.2: Basic Steps for a Project Management

Steps/Phase		*Purpose*	*Project Manager Role*	*Inputs*	*Outputs*
1	The Initiation Phase	To develop a high-level plan and risk assessment for a proposed project To provide information for portfolio assessing strategic viability of the project. Emphasis is placed on analyzing the project sponsor's strategic requirements as well as immediate needs.	Assist the account representative with formulating a solution. Assist with identifying scope that will be produced to complete the solution. Assist with a high level estimate of work to be performed. Assist with determining project scope Assist with developing a high-level estimation of the project size in hours and cost. Assist with proposal development. Assist in developing a high-level work breakdown structure.	Interviews with customer and other key personnel Strategic documentation Customer literature Lessons learned from previous projects performed for project sponsor	Project proposal document with all necessary inputs like cost estimates, risk, problem etc

(Contd...)

2	The Project Planning Phase	To establish an accurate plan and schedule. To plan for the infrastructure To fix the responsibilities To establish communications and reporting expectations To establish tracking systems To develop a Risk Management Plan	Obtain staff Assign roles & responsibilities Develop organization chart Prepare project notebook and project files Develop communications plan Establish reporting frequencies Conduct due diligence or risk assessment	High level project charter (with attachments) High level risk Assessment requirements document	Responsibility matrix Risk management guide Project notebook Developing task worksheet Project schedule
3	Project Execution and Control Phase	The project manager must monitor the project team at all times. Executing, monitoring and controlling project progress is important to detecting issues, problems and solutions early enough to quickly get the project back on schedule so the objectives are still met. Project managers can regulate work as the project progresses, and still deliver a finished product that meets the objectives and requirements laid out in the initiation and planning phases.	The project manager is responsible for controlling the project. Project manager implements tracking and reporting processes, tracks the plan as it progresses and reschedules when needed to keep the project on track. Project manager is responsible for scope management. Project manager is responsible for quality assurance of the products. Project manager is responsible for executing the risk management plan and ensuring that risks have little or no unexpected impact on the project.	Project team Communication plan Risk management plan Organization chart Responsibility matrix Project notebook Status reports Project schedule	Change management Quality management

(Contd...)

4	Project Close-Out Phase	All project activities are completed and all deliverables are finalized. The project sponsor reviews the project and all testing is completed. Final reviews and documentation are completed and the customer accepts the final project deliverable. The continuous improvement on both team and personal levels is practiced.	The project manager is responsible for archiving project documentation, obtaining deliverable sign-off, assessing customer satisfaction, capturing lessons learned, debriefing team members, and completing performance evaluations.	Completed, up-to-date project schedules All project documentation Quality checklists	Post implementation review Performance evaluations Lessons learned Project evaluation Delivery of final documentation Project sign-off Customer satisfaction survey

Project Planning and Implementation

We need to consider a detailed planning, scheduling, monitoring and adjusting the processes involved in implementing a specific project.

Project Planning

An important decision of any project is to decide upon the organization and composition of the team. The project manager should be appointed at this stage and the responsibilities of all the members should be fixed. The selection of the team members should be based on the skills required by the project. The first step is to set up the objectives and then define the project, breaking it down into set of activities and related costs. Project scheduling is concerned with attaching a time scale and sequence to the activities to be considered within the project.

Stages of Project Management

The various stages of project management are:

1. Preparing to implement the project
2. Managing construction
3. Managing the transition from construction to operation
4. Completing the project
5. Assessing or auditing the project

Preparing to Implement the Project

A project requires many tasks for the successful implementation. Some of the important tasks are:

- Financing
- Acquisition of land
- Public approvals
- Construction strategy
- Marketing
- Transition planning

There are some constraints which may be faced by the project manager during implementation of the project. As a result of general economic conditions, any difficulty in obtaining required financing may cause delay or cancellation. Inability to acquire the necessary land may require restructuring of the project. A major client may back out of a lease, so that it becomes impossible to get a construction loan.

Project Management Techniques

There are several techniques for the project management. Some of the necessary techniques are:

(1) Statement of work
(2) Work breakdown structure
(3) Network diagrams
(4) Schedules for activities
(5) Cost estimation and budgets

Statement of Work

The statement of work includes the following:

- Part of the contractual agreement between the owner and the builder or the basic objective for the project manager
- What is to be done, using what resources, within what timetable
- Changes to the statement of work may be needed:
  - Owner: change in scope of project
  - Contractors: changes in costs, time or processes may be needed
  - Trade-off: time required to complete project vs. cost of completion

Work Breakdown Structure (WBS)

It consists of the following:

- Break down a complex project into manageable activities

- Identify and categorize all of the steps that will be required
- Can be shown as a table or as an organizational chart

Network Diagram

The network diagram should have:

- Show how the activities in the WBS are related
- Some activities can start immediately; others must wait until prerequisite activities are completed
- Interdependencies among activities may reflect logic, regulations, choice of technology or contractor preferences

Schedules for Activities

The schedule of activities should have the following:

- Earliest start date
- Latest start date
- Critical path of activities (the minimum time for completion of the project)
- Slack time
  - The difference between the earliest and latest start date for an activity
  - Equals zero for activities on the critical path

Cost Estimation and Budgets

This should have the following components:

- Rough estimates will be sufficient at first
- More accurate costs will be needed as the number of options dwindles,
- Eventually, once the project is approved, a budget should be accurate to within a few percent

Basic Skills for Project Managers

Project managers are a very special people. They are in much demand and will be increasingly so as the need for effective technologists continues to soar. Good technology helps the project managers to get trained. They develop skills through experience and education. They become better project managers each time they successfully implement and deliver a project. They learn new techniques and apply them on their upcoming projects. They learn necessary lessons to be better managers for the future projects.

Actions of a Project Manager

Managers need to fulfill the following broad requirements:

- Define and review the business case and requirements by regular reviews and controls to ensure that the client receives the system that he or she wants and needs.
- Initiate and plan the project by establishing its format, direction, and base lines that allow for any variance measurements and change control.
- Partner with the end users, work with project sponsors and other management to establish progress and direction of the project by achieving goals, reaching targets, solving problems, mitigating risks.
- Manage the technology, people, and change in order to achieve goals, reach targets, and deliver the project on time and within budget.
- Manage the project staff by creating an environment conducive to the delivery of the new application in the most cost-effective manner.
- Be able to manage uncertainty, rapid change, ambiguity, surprises, and a less defined environment.
- Manage the client relationship by using an adequate direct yet complete and formal reporting format that compliments a respected and productive relationship.
- Drive the project by leading by example, and motivating all concerned until the project accomplishes its goal.

Now let us examine the skills and qualities needed to meet these requirements.

Necessary Skills

The skills of a good project manager are many and varied, covering the entire spectrum of the human personality. We can divide these skills into a number of specific categories, namely:

Personal Skills

Project managers must be able to motivate and sustain people. Project team members will look to the project manager to solve problems and help with removing obstacles. Project managers must be able to address and solve problems within the team, as well as those that occur outside the team. There are numerous ways, both subtle and direct, in which project managers can help team members.

Some examples include the following:

- **Manage by example (MBE)**: Team members will be closely watching all actions of the project manager. Therefore, project managers must be honest, direct, straightforward, and knowledgeable in all dealings with people and with the project. A good manager knows how to work hard and have fun, and this approach becomes contagious.
- **A positive attitude:** Project managers must always have a positive attitude, even when there are substantial difficulties, problems, or project obstacles. Negative attitudes erode confidence, and a downward spiral will follow.
- **Define expectations**: Managers must clearly define what is expected of team members. It is important to do this in writing and get agreement from the individual team members. This leaves no room for problems later, when someone states "It's not my job." Performance expectations must be defined at the start of the project.
- **Be considerate**: Project management is a demanding job with a need for multiple skills at many levels. Above all, be considerate and respectful, and give people and team members the time and consideration they deserve. Make people aware that their efforts are appreciated and the work that they do is important. A letter, personal word, or e-mail of appreciation goes a long way.
- **Be direct**: Project managers are respected if they are direct, open, and deal with all types of problems. Never conceal problems or avoid addressing them. If a problem is bigger than the project manager or the team can deal with, escalate it to senior management. Never make commitments that cannot be delivered.

Technical Skills

Some project managers prefer to have little technical knowledge about the projects they manage, preferring to leave the technical management to other junior managers, such as programming managers or network managers. Others have detailed technical skills of computer languages, software, and networks.

There is no hard and fast rule. It really depends on the type and size of projects, their structure, resources available, and the project environment.

Questions that project managers should ask include the following:

- What types of technical problems are required by the management?
- Who is going to solve them?
- Is it to be done with quality and satisfaction?
- Who are going to be in the project team?
- What are outside resources, if any, which can be made available?

As with all employees, project managers should have the technical knowledge and skills needed to do their jobs. If managers lack these skills, they should be given proper training. Technical training that provides breadth may be useful for the project managers handling big projects. For smaller projects, the project manager may also be a key technical contributor. In this case, technical training may enhance the abilities of project managers to contribute technically, but it is unlikely to improve their management skills.

The project manager is ultimately responsible for the entire management of the project, technical or otherwise, and will require solutions to the technical issues that will occur.

Management Skills

Project managers need other key skills besides those that are purely technical to lead and deliver on their projects successfully. A good project manager needs to understand many facets of the business aspect of running a project, so critical skills touch on expertise in the areas of organization, communication, finance, and human resources.

The following are examples of the management topics used in training effective project managers:

- Project planning, initiation, and organization
- Recruiting people and keeping them
- Effective project negotiation
- Software tools for project management
- Accurate estimating and cost control
- Project execution and control
- Developing powerful project presentations
- Personal and project leadership
- Managing risk and making decisions
- Effective problem management

- Performance management
- Managing the projects within the organization
- Growing and sustaining a high-performance team
- Managing change within an organization

Coping Skills

A good project manager has to acquire a number of skills to cope with different situations, conflicts and uncertainty. This requires the following:

- Being flexible
- Being persistent and firm when necessary
- Being creative, even when the project does not call for it
- Absorbing large volumes of data from multiple sources
- Being patient but able to differentiate between patience and action
- Being able to handle large amounts of continuous, often unrelenting stress

Additionally, good project managers have high tolerance for surprises, uncertainty, and ambiguity. Projects rarely progress the way that they are defined, and managers need to manage the uncertainty that comes with that.

Keys to a Successful Skills Management Endeavor

Three areas must be worked out for a skills management initiative to be successful:

1. Employees have to adopt the program as their own, rather than as a management dictate, including the employees assuming control of their own professional development
2. Supervisors have to surrender some control over employee development
3. Executives must ensure that employees use metrics as a tool for professional development, not as a weapon in cutthroat competition

As enterprises turn to technology to reach the next level of corporate performance, IT organizations should identify the skills they need to meet the corporate objectives. Through a program of skills identification, IT organizations can see the holes in their coverage, set priorities for projects, define which training is required, and determine which skills may need third-party coverage. A commitment to funding for training is essential.

Skills Necessary to Lead Projects

Some of the soft skills required to lead projects include:

- Leadership
- team building
- negotiation
- conflict management
- organization for self and others
- oral and written communication to technical and non-technical audiences
- change management; and active listening.

The technical skills necessary to lead projects include:

- project management software
- level of understanding of the technology being used in the project
- basic knowledge of the business; cost estimating and budgeting.

Project Market and Demand

Market and demand analysis provides a detailed analysis of all market conditions and helps in estimating revenue from the project. The objective of the market and demand analysis is to see if the idea of the project is feasible from the point of view of market potential. This requires the following activities:

- Objective specifications
- Collection of required data
- Market survey, description, forecasting
- Market planning

Fig. 6.3 may be used as the guidance for the market and demand analysis.

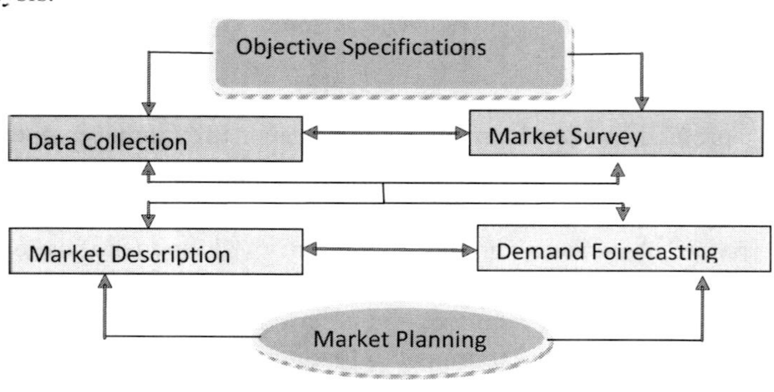

Fig. 6.3: Market and Demand Analysis

Project Technical Analysis

Technical analysis of a project includes an in-depth study of all technical aspects related to manufacturing operations, detailed design, assembling etc.

Objective of Technical Analysis

The following are the objectives of technical analysis:

- To see whether the project idea is feasible or not
- To find out the most optimal formulation of the project technology, size, location etc.
- To find out the cost of the product for determining the profitability

Activities in Technical Analysis

The following are the activities required:

- Technical selection
- Input (material etc.) requirements
- Plant capacity
- Location and site of the project
- Machinery and equipment

Structured Project Management Techniques

The benefits for organizations that use structured project management techniques are:

- improvement in customer satisfaction
- better cost performance, higher return on investment
- better schedule performance, better allocation of time commitments and better utilization of resources, higher productivity
- increased quality reducing re-work; and increase in delivering required features.

Scope for the Success of a Project

Scope is the list of customer requested requirements. It is assessed by the degree to which the system satisfies the requirements set forth and agreed upon by the customer and the development team. Functional requirements as well as non-functional requirements are defined at the beginning of the project. The development team uses this definition as the blue prints for building an acceptable product for the customer. The extent to which an activity in the development life cycle meets these requirements is a measure of the scope criteria.

Basic Functions to run Successful Projects

The basic functions are:

(1) The project manager must manage project scope, or make sure the team works on what is needed for the project and nothing else.

(2) The project manager must manage human resources - the team must work together, which doesn't just happen without directed effort.

(3) The project manager must manage communications; this occurs at many levels, such as team members, customers, managers, vendors, and others.

(4) The project manager manages schedule by keeping people on schedule to deliver work on time.

(5) The project manager must manage quality, or make sure that all work performed meets with customer expected levels of quality.

(6) The project manager manages cost by keeping an eye on the budget to make sure all the work can be done and not exceed the allocated budget.

Assignments Projects

The role of assignments/projects is very important for the continuous assessments of the students. The present system of setting assignment questions, writing assignments by the students and finally evaluating the assignments by the teachers needs improvements in many areas. A teacher uses assignments as one of method on teaching and learning process. It becomes one of steps or processes to students to learn more about a given topic, deepen it and finally expand their knowledge automatically. Their responses give teacher an opportunity to help them by commenting on their performance.

Usually, there are several types of assignments that are given.

- The first type is practice assignment. The students can improve newly acquired skills; they can learn a new method of solving a problem.

- The second is the preparation assignment. They help students to get ready for future classroom activities.
- The third is extension assignment. Here, the students can enjoy long-term homework that parallels class work.

The assignment should contain the following points:

- Objective of the assignment
- Presentation of the topic with examples
- Conclusions

Assignment given in the lesson concerned to the student must train them in self learning and to acquire the presentation skills of the learners. The assignment method inculcates the learning experiences and information retrieval and report writing skills.

The following objectives can be derived from the assignments.

- It provides good training for information seeking and retrieval behaviour.
- It inculcates the self-learning attitude among the students.
- It provides information analysis and research attitude to the learners.
- It develops the learning experiences from various sources.

Assignment Types

1. **Page or Paragraph Assignment**: This assignment deal with the frequently used topic / unit in Text books. Usually assignment confines with a page or few paragraphs only. It is the method of instant answering or reporting in learning activities.
2. **Chapter Assignment**: This is somewhat broader than the page or paragraph assignment. Its scope confines with a chapter in the text book or a specific topic / unit to be described in the Text books. Generally, this assignment based on the contents of the chapter of a lesson hence it is called as chapter assignment.
3. **Topical Assignment**: Such assignments are based on a chapter or more or a topic interrelated with the text book units. There may be ample opportunities the topical assignments may cross the boundaries of text books and its chapters. This assignment will be helpful in teaching and learning, the everyday problems can be correlated with science teaching and learning by the students.
4. **Problem Assignment**: In order to solve a problem through scientific method this type of assignments are given to the

students. The problem solving is its primary objective. The students are trained to learn the problem-solving process through this assignment method. This type of assignment is considered as exclusive one.

5. **Individual or Group Report Assignment**: This assignment has given to bring out the actual capabilities of a student or a group of students.
6. **Experiment Assignment**: This assignment has the best features from the problem assignment and project method. Basically, this assignment evolved from the laboratory experiments and its reports. But this assignment could not be used as a representative for testing hypothesis. This is a best tool for the learning and teaching process.

Tutor Marked Assignments

These assignments are marked/evaluated by the teacher/tutor and hence are called tutor marked assignments (TMA). These assignments comprise a variety of questions such as essay type, short answer type, problem solving exercises etc. These assignments are generally used to assess the higher order cognitive objectives such as analysis, synthesis, judgement, comprehension, application, etc.

Examples of TMAs

- o Essay type
- o Short answer type
- o Practical type exercises

The teachers may go through the assignment response and evaluate its organisational aspects covering the following:

- Introduction
- body or mid part
- ending/conclusion
- accuracy of information
- content density
- logical and critical analysis of concept
- clarity in expression, language and so on.

An Example of Retail Management: Field Project

Market research is for discovering what people want or need, or believes. It is for also discovering how they act. The market research is an effort to ascertain the worth or demand of the product in the market as well as the standing of the enterprise in the industry. It may be defined as the systematic and objective process of collecting, generating, analyzing, and interpreting information and communicating the findings for use in making marketing decisions. It furnishes all the relevant information about the existing products in the market and helps the firm to identify and solve problems related to launching of new products. It helps the firm to identify and evaluate the marketing opportunities and exploit them for the firm's profitability. Thus, market research is useful to a firm in a wide variety of activities, which include sales forecasting; measuring market share; identifying market trends; measuring brand images; developing consumers profiles; designing products and packaging; analyzing demand; measuring price perceptions and ascertaining advertising effectiveness.

Objectives of Market Research

The objectives of marketing research are listed below:

- To link the consumer with the company through information.
- To investigate the real needs and requirements of customers.
- To search and analyze information that can be used for selecting at the best alternative marketing decision.
- To suggest necessary changes in the goods and services in order to meet the market demands.
- To know in advance what kinds of target market exist in the economy, where, the company may launch its product.
- To know the reactions of the people in the market about the existing or newly introduced products of the company.
- To identify opportunities and threats in the external environment.
- To find out reasons for slowly losing market share, and identify ways and means for strengthening company's position in the market, within and outside the country.

Importance of Market Research

Following are the reasons, which will explain you the importance of marketing research.

- It facilitates planned production by forecasting probable sales.
- It helps in identifying the reasons for consumer resistance to existing or new products.

- It reveals the nature of demand for the product i.e. whether the product is in demand throughout the year or has a seasonal demand.
- It indicates the product utility as well as the effectiveness of existing channels of distribution.
- It may reveal certain new uses for the existing products.
- It provides information about potential or future markets.
- It helps in the discovery of new lines of production.

However, a research study will fail to serve its purpose, if you do not offer full perspective of the research problem; or allow inadequate time; or use research as a 'firefighting' device; or do not really appreciate the value of research. Hence every company irrespective of its size must have a full proof market research strategy which continuously monitors the performance of its product.

The strategy should also examine the competition for the product as well as the response of the customers on a regular basis. This research process is much easier for large scale businesses which generally have their own formal marketing networks, media campaigns and strong sales force.

Steps in Market Research Process

It is important for you to understand different steps in market research process.

- **Identification and definition of the objectives:** This is the first step in the process of marketing research. It is of crucial importance as it shows the direction of the research work. The research process begins by making a clear and concise statement of a problem or issues to be investigated. A clear definition of the problem helps the researcher in all subsequent research efforts including the setting up of proper research objectives, the determination of the techniques to be used, and the extent of information to be collected.
- **Statement of research objectives:** In the next step, the researcher makes a formal statement of the research objectives and states the reasons and aims for which the research is being undertaken. Such objectives may be stated in qualitative or quantitative terms and are expressed in the form of research questions, statement or hypothesis.
- **Planning the research design:** The next step is developing research design which is a master plan specifying the procedures

for collecting and analyzing the needed information. It represents a framework for the research plan of action. The objectives of the study are included in the research design to ensure that data collected are relevant to the objectives. The researcher also determines the sources of information needed; the data collection method such as survey, interview, etc; the methodology, timing and possible costs of research.

- **Planning the sample:** Sampling involves procedures whereby a small number of items or parts of the 'targeted population' are taken to represent the whole population. It involves several important decisions relating to : (i) defining the target population; (ii) selection of a sample which truly represents the population; (iii) the sample-size to be used for the purpose; and (iv) selection of various units to make up the sample.
- **Data collection:** It involves gathering of facts to be used in solving the problem. Data is two types – a) Primary & b) Secondary. Data is primary, if it is collected from the original base through empirical research by means of various tools such as observation, experiment and survey methods. It may be collected from salesmen, customers and dealers. Data is secondary, if it is collected from concerned reports, magazines and other periodicals, especially written articles, government publications, books, etc. The data sources may be internal or external. Internal sources exist within the firm itself like accounting data, salesmen's reports, etc. while, sources outside the firm are external sources.
- **Data processing and analysis:** The data collected from all the sources, is processed and analyzed. It is thus converted into a meaningful format so as to suggest answers to the initially identified and defined problems. Data processing begins with the editing or inspection of data for checking consistency in its classification and coding. The analysis of data represents the application of logic to the understanding of the data collected. It may involve determination of consistent patterns and summarizing of appropriate details by using various analytical techniques. The aim of this step is to check whether empirical findings support or refute the statements or hypothesis made earlier.
- **Formulating conclusions and preparing the report:** The final stage is that of interpreting the information and drawing conclusion to make business decisions. The research report should clearly and effectively communicate the research findings. If needed, the

researcher may bring out his appropriate recommendations or suggestions in the matter. The presentation of the report so prepared must be technically accurate and understandable.

Case Study

You are planning to open a retail outlet (say ABC Store) for convenient items such as food & grocery, staples, vegetables & fruits etc. You have planned to open ABC store under your proprietary ship at your hometown and start its operations in next three months' time.

In order to make it a success, students must plan each and every step properly. The first step being the market research, students are required to conduct a survey and find answers to the questions.

Introduction to Software Project Management

What exactly do we mean by 'software project management'? Software project management is the art and science of planning and leading software projects. It is a sub-discipline of project management in which software projects are planned, monitored and controlled. The software project management could have the following features:

- A Software Project is the complete procedure of software development from requirement gathering to testing and maintenance, carried out according to the execution methodologies, in a specified period of time to achieve intended software product.
- When the plan starts to involve different things happening at different times, some of which are dependent on each other, plus resources required at different times and in different quantities and perhaps working at different rates, the paper plan could start to cover a vast area and be unreadable.
- Nevertheless, the idea that complex plans could be analyzed by a computer to allow someone to control a project is the basis of much of the development in technology that now allows projects of any size and complexity.
- The original programs and computers tended to produce answers long after an event had taken place. Now, there are many project planning and scheduling programs that can provide real time information, as well as linking to risk analysis, time recording, and costing, estimating and other aspects of project control.
- But computer programs are not project management: they are tools for project managers to use. Project management is all that mix of

components of control, leadership, teamwork, resource management etc. that goes into a successful project.

- Project managers can be found in all industries. Their numbers have grown rapidly as industry and commerce has realized that much of what it does is project work. And as project-based organizations have started to emerge, project management is becoming established as both a professional career path and a way of controlling business.
- So, opportunities in project management now exist not only in being a project manager, but also as part of the support team in a project or program office or as a team leader for part of a project. There are also qualifications that can be attained through the professional associations.

Need of Software Project Management

Software development is a new type of business in world and there's very little experience in building software products. Most software products are developed to fit client's requirements. The most important is that the underlying technology changes and advances so frequently and rapidly that experience of one product may not be applied to the other one. All such business and environmental constraints bring risk in software development hence it is essential to manage software projects efficiently.

There are three essential part of software organization (as shown in Fig. 6.4):

1. Quality: deliver quality product
2. Cost: keeping the cost within client's budget
3. Time: deliver the project as per scheduled

Fig. 6.4 shows triple constraints for software projects. It is an essential part of software organization to deliver quality product, keeping the cost within client's budget constrain and deliver the project as per scheduled. There are several factors, both internal and external, which may impact this triple constrain triangle. Any of three factors can severely impact the other two.

Therefore, software project management is essential to incorporate user requirements along with budget and time constraints.

Software Project Vs Other Types of Project

There might be many differences between software project and other

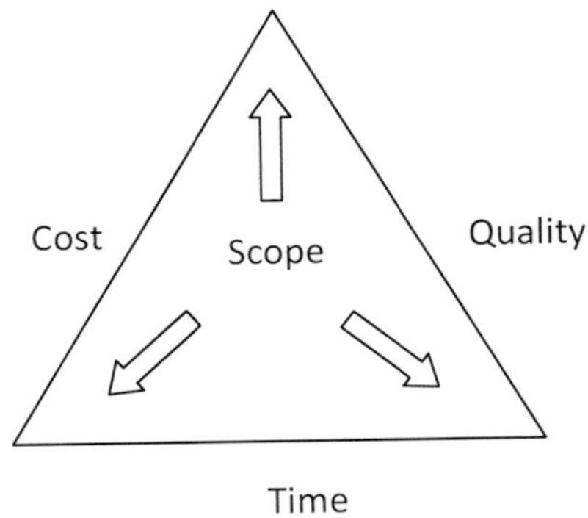

Fig. 6.4: Essential Part of Software Organization

types of project but according to my knowledge there are four basic differences between software project and other projects.

1. **Invisibility:** When a physical artifact such as a bridge or road is being constructed the progress being made can actually be seen. With software, progress is not immediately visible.
2. **Complexity:** Per rupees spent, software products contain more complexity than other engineered artifacts.
3. **Flexibility:** The ease with which software can be changed is usually seen as one of its strengths. However, this means that where the software system interfaces with a physical or organizational system, it is expected that, where necessary, the software will change to accommodate the other components rather than vice versa. This means the software systems are likely to be subject to a high degree of change.

Activity Covered by Software Project Management

A software project is not only the work of code writing. In fact, where a software application is bought in 'off the shelf', there may be no software writing as such, but this is still fundamentally a software project because so many of the other activities associated with software will still be present. There are mainly three processes (shown in Fig. 6.5) that used in developed a new system:

1. **Feasibility study:** The feasibility study assesses whether a project is worth starting that is has a valid business case. Information is gathered about the requirements of the proposed application. Requirements elicitation can, at least initially, be complex and difficult. The stakeholders may know the aims they wish to

pursue, but not be sure about the means of achievement. The development and operational costs, and the value of the benefits of the new system, will also have to be estimated. With a large system, the feasibility study could be a project in its own right with its own plan. The study could be part of a strategic planning exercise examining a range of potential software developments. Sometimes an organization assesses a program of development made up of a number of projects.

2. **Plan:** In the feasibility study we study that proposed system is feasible or not? If the feasibility study indicates that the prospective project appears viable, then project planning can start. For large projects, we would not do all our detailed planning at the beginning. We create an outline plan for the whole project and a detailed one for the first stage. Because we will have more detailed and accurate project information after the earlier stages of the project have been completed, planning of the later stages is left to nearer their start.
3. **Project Execution:** In this activity, the project can be executed. This activity contains design and implementation sub-phases. Students new to project planning often find that the boundary between design and planning can be hazy. Design is making decisions about the form of the products to be created. This could relate to the external appearance of the software, that is, the user interface, of the internal architecture. The plan details the activities to be carried out to create these products.

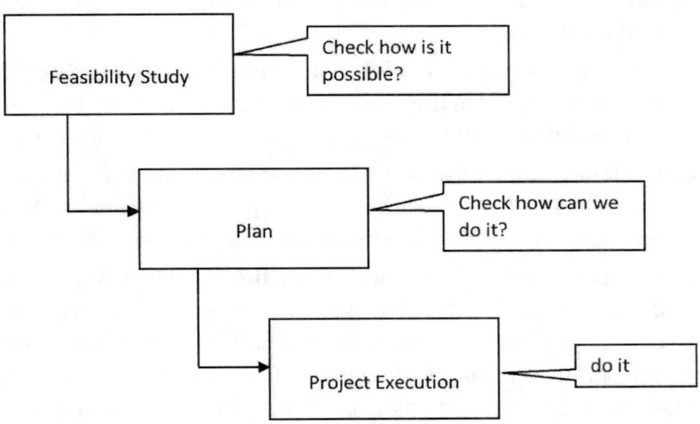

Fig. 6.5: Feasibility Study, Plan, Execution Cycle

Problems with Software Projects

It is not possible that every software project is a roaring success. But every so often, you'll find you've created something that turns out to be exactly what the market wanted. The customers love it, the sales team is selling new features faster than you can implement them, and you're rapidly expanding your development team to keep up with demand. Before you know it, you've released Version 8, and you have almost one million lines of code in source control.

Working on a product like this is exciting and rewarding, but as time goes on, serious problems can emerge that hinder development and threaten the long-term viability of your product. Let's take a look at some of the ways that this can happen.

1. **Not Assigning the Right Person to Manage the Project:** During resource allocation, most of the effort is focused on finding the right resources other than finding the right project manager. Indeed, too often "project managers get picked based on availability, not necessarily on skill set." However, an inadequately trained and/or inexperienced project manager can doom a project.
2. **Failing to Get Everyone on the Team Behind the Project.** Many projects are failed because they didn't get enough support from the departments and people affected by and involved in the project. Managers didn't make clear what everyone's role was. They didn't describe the personal payoff everyone would get when the project was completed successfully. Managers didn't tell how each person's contributions to the project would be evaluated.
3. **Putting too many Projects into Production at Once:** Most managers think that they can get more done by starting all projects at once, but in reality, it is big problem to deliver a project timely.
4. **Lack of Communication/Meetings:** Communication is the most important factor of successful project management. Without regularly and clearly communicating, the project will fall apart.
5. **Not Being Specific Enough with the Scope:** Any project that doesn't have an ultra-clear goal, it cannot be successes. Scope change is one of the most dangerous things that can happen to your project. If not handled properly it can lead to cost and time overrun. Even something small, like changing the color of a logo or adding a page to a website might cause unexpected delays.

6. **Providing Aggressive/Overly Optimistic Timelines:** The intentions are noble, as project managers are often trying to keep their clients happy. But missing deadline after deadline will only lead to distrust and aggravation on the part of your client.
7. **Your Client Gives You Vague, Ever-changing Requirements:** Fickle clients can be a huge hassle. If a client doesn't know what they want until a certain stage is complete, then schedule those decision points into the project as milestones. It is important to have a clear path mapped out from start to finish because it forces the client to be specific with their requirements, as well as keeping the project on track.
8. **Your Client is Slow with Communication:** People are busy, but it's tough for you to move forward on a project if you can never get answers from the person you're working with.
9. **Too Much Time is Spent Solving Problems After Projects Are "Live":** There are bound to be a few bugs here and there, but this is a classic problem caused by focusing too much on production, and not enough on testing. The continuity of this becomes an issue.

Importance of Managing Software and IT Projects

Project Management software can dramatically improve the productivity of any project whether large or small. There are a variety of Project Management software options available for use; all of which offer the following features:

- Scheduling
- Resource assignments (man-machine-material)
- Cost control and budget management
- Quality management
- Tracking progress
- Report generation

Scheduling

Scheduling is one of the most critical tools required to manage a project to its conclusion. By making use of this feature in 'Microsoft Project' you can schedule a project from the information you input about the overall project, the individual tasks required to see the project through to completion, and the resources (people, equipment, materials) necessary to complete those tasks. If there are changes that occur to the tasks or resources after the schedule has been created, you can update these and MS Project will update the schedule.

Resource Assignments

With the help of resource assignments, you create the association between specific tasks and the resources required to complete them. These resources include the work resources (people and equipment required to conclude a task) and material resources (materials or supplies).

Quality Management

It is the set of activities planned at the beginning of the project that help achieve quality in the project being executed, and which are defined on the basis of the quality standards set by the project manager and the company delivering the product.

Tracking Progress

For the project to finish on schedule the path of series of tasks must be completed on schedule. This critical path completion will dictate the project's finish date. Microsoft Project defines the critical path by determining the critical tasks and the tasks having 'slack', meaning which tasks will be finished early or late according to start date and scheduled duration.

By knowing and tracking the critical path of the project, as well as resources assigned to critical tasks, the finish date of the project can be determined. Keeping track of the completion and status of critical tasks is essential to keeping the project on course to being completed on time. It is important to understand that Microsoft Project is not a simple spreadsheet application, such as MS Excel. One has to get well trained from subject matter experts before starting to use it. Trying to learn by trial and error may require more time & at the same time one may not understand its context as well.

Report Generation

It is important to generate timely reports about 'completion of work, use of resources, cost expended, quality of work and the forecasts. It gives better picture to project stakeholders about the status and progress of the project. Various types of reports in variety of forms can be generated by using project management software such as "Status report, progress report, variance report, trend report, Forecasting reports, etc." These reports also help stakeholders to take proactive decisions to enhance opportunities and decrease threats about the project deliverables.

Software Project Planning

Project planning is concerned with activities involved in ensuring that software is delivered on time and on schedule and in accordance with the requirements of the organizations developing and procuring the software.

General Activities

Software project management comprises of a number of activities, which contains planning of project, deciding scope of software product, estimation of cost in various terms, scheduling of tasks and events, and resource management. Project management activities may include:

- Project Planning
- Scope Management
- Project Estimation

Project Planning

Project planning is an organized and integrated management process, which focuses on activities required for successful completion of the project. It prevents obstacles that arise in the project such as changes in projects or organization's objectives, non-availability of resources, and so on. Project planning also helps in better utilization of resources and optimal usage of the allotted time for a project. The other objectives of project planning are listed below.

- It defines the roles and responsibilities of the project management team members.
- It ensures that the project management team works according to the business objectives.
- It checks feasibility of the schedule and user requirements.
- It determines project constraints.

Software project planning is task, which is performed before the production of software actually starts. It is there for the software production but involves no concrete activity that has any direction connection with software production; rather it is a set of multiple processes, which facilitates software production. Project planning may include the following:

- Scope Management
- Project Estimation

Scope of Management

It defines the scope of project; this includes all the activities, process need to be done in order to make a deliverable software product. Scope management is essential because it creates boundaries of the project by clearly defining what would be done in the project and what would not be done. This makes project to contain limited and quantifiable tasks, which can easily be documented and in turn avoids cost and time overrun.

During Project Scope management, it is necessary to -

- Define the scope
- Decide its verification and control
- Divide the project into various smaller parts for ease of management.
- Verify the scope
- Control the scope by incorporating changes to the scope

Project Estimation

For an effective management, accurate estimation of various measures is a must. With correct estimation managers can manage and control the project more efficiently and effectively. Project estimation may involve the following:

- **Software Size Estimation:** Software size may be estimated either in terms of KLOC (Kilo Line of Code) or by calculating number of function points in the software. Lines of code depend upon coding practices and Function points vary according to the user or software requirement.
- **Effort Estimation:** The managers estimate efforts in terms of personnel requirement and man-hour required to produce the software. For effort estimation software size should be known. This can either be derived by managers' experience, organization's historical data or software size can be converted into efforts by using some standard formulae.
- **Time Estimation:** Once size and efforts are estimated, the time required to produce the software can be estimated. Efforts required is segregated into sub categories as per the requirement specifications and interdependency of various components of software. Software tasks are divided into smaller tasks, activities or events by Work Breakthrough Structure (WBS). The tasks are scheduled on day-to-day basis or in calendar months.

The sum of time required to complete all tasks in hours or days is the total time invested to complete the project.

- **Cost Estimation:** This might be considered as the most difficult of all because it depends on more elements than any of the previous ones. For estimating project cost, it is required to consider -
    - o Size of software
    - o Software quality
    - o Hardware
    - o Additional software or tools, licenses etc.
    - o Skilled personnel with task-specific skills
    - o Travel involved
    - o Communication
    - o Training and support

Project Selection

Project selection is the first important part of project portfolio management. The generic process of project selection looks as shown in Fog. 6.6.

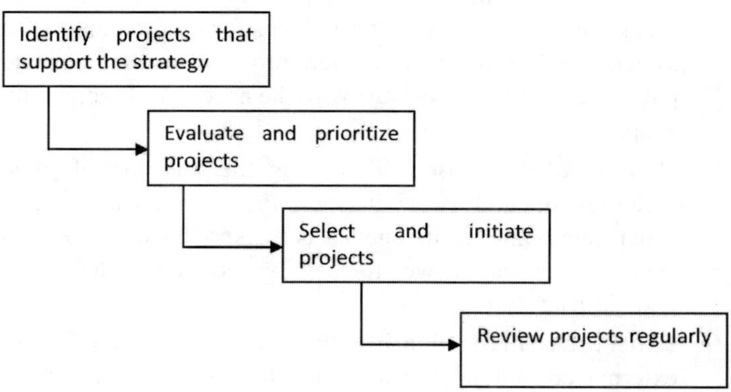

Fig. 6.6: Project Selection Process

Identification of Projects

The first step of this process, identification, requires a clearly defined and communicated strategy. The best option would be to set up a strategy development process that contains project identification and project selection as an integral part. In fact, we observe that most organizations identify investment projects within their strategy development process, but delegate the identification of customer projects to their key account and sales departments.

Like in strategy development, we find four different ways to identify projects. We categorize them as given in Table 6.3.

Table 6.3: Classification of Projects

	Implicit	*Explicit*
External: given from outside the organization	Intuitive	Expert Oriented
Internal: created by the organization, its parts, or its members	Incremental or Evolutionary	Holistic

The following examples may illustrate these four basic approaches.

1. **Intuitive Identification:** The family who owns our company wants to add a new product to our portfolio. Therefore, they tell our management to start a development project for this new product.
2. **Evolutionary Identification:** Quite a few of our colleagues in our engineering department find it necessary to have a more efficient knowledge management system. In their coffee and tea breaks, they discuss some basic ideas for requirements of such a system, and, some weeks later, propose to start a project to purchase a software package with the necessary functionality and adapt it to our needs.
3. **Holistic Identification:** Following the tradition of periodical meetings, all employees join beginning of this fiscal year again; as usual, one point on the agenda is the session with presentations and question and answer for new projects which have division-wide impact.
4. **Expert Oriented Identification:** Project manager invites an external consultancy firm to benchmark our customer service organization. Two months later, this firm proposes to start a project in order to change our service organization's structure.

Evaluation and Prioritization of Projects

Central part of the project selection process is evaluation and prioritization of identified projects. There are a couple of methods available:

- Net Present Value (NPV)

- Internal Rate of Return (IRR)
- Benefit / Cost Ratio (BCR)
- Opportunity Cost (OC)
- Payback Period (PP)
- Initial Risk Assessment

These methods require a certain minimum level of "planning" for each one of the projects to be evaluated. We need to know

- Project life cycle duration, in number of accounting periods,
- Expected project cost per accounting period,
- Expected project revenue per accounting period,
- Overall risk values of the projects to be evaluated.

Usually, we do this whole evaluation in definition or early planning phase. Then, we only have estimates of those values and should make sure that the estimation accuracies are comparable.

The Net Present Value (NPV) of a project is defined as the difference between present value of cash inflow and present value of cash outflow of that project over the project life cycle time.

Selection and Initiation of Projects

Project selection and initiation is the step that naturally follows evaluation and prioritization. A particularly delicate step of project initiation turns out to be the staffing of project teams. As mentioned earlier, resources are scarce, and in most organizations, appear to be the most limiting factor in project selection. If we take in too many projects we overload our resources, if we do not take in enough we do not utilize them economically enough. Sometimes staff members work in multi-tasking mode, i.e. on two or more projects at the same time, decreases overall productivity of the organization. On a medium / long term scale, it seems to be the better option to initiate projects in a way so that the teams can focus and work on one project at a time, thus, avoiding disturbances of one project by the others. Of course, that needs clear prioritization of the selected projects, based on evaluation done in the previous step.

Review of Projects

After project selection, we need to regularly review projects that are under way in order to find out if they are still in-line with our strategy. Thus, the first way of checking them is repeating the initial evaluation with more accurate estimates as they become available; the second way is holding regular project management review meetings in order to identify major problems on a per-project basis, via project status reports.

Decomposing of a Project

Decomposition is a technique used in project management that breaks down the workload and tasks before the creation of the work breakdown structure. This important step can save time in the long run.

A project can be breakdown in the following structure:

1. Work Breakdown Structure (WBS)
2. Product Breakdown Structure
3. Organizational Breakdown Structure (OBS)
4. Resource Breakdown Structure (RBS)
5. Product Breakdown Structure (PBS)
6. Risk Breakdown Structure (RBS)
7. Cost Breakdown Structure (CBS)

Work Breakdown Structure (WBS)

A work breakdown structure is a tool used to define and group a project's discrete work elements (or tasks) in a way that helps organize and define the total work scope of the project It provides the framework for detailed cost estimating and control along with providing guidance for schedule development and control.

Organization Breakdown Structure (OBS)

The organizational breakdown structure defines the organizational relationships and is used as the framework for assigning work responsibilities. The intersection of the OBS and WBS defines points of management accountability for the work called Control (or Cost) Accounts.

Resource Breakdown Structure (RBS)

The resource breakdown structure is a standardized list of personnel resources related by function and arranged in a hierarchical structure to facilitate planning and controlling of project work.

Product Breakdown Structure (PBS)

A product breakdown structure is an exhaustive, hierarchical tree structure of components that make up an item, arranged in whole-part relationship. In practice, there is very little difference between a PBS and a

WBS, both systems define the full extent of the work required to complete the project.

Risk Break Down Structure (RBS)

The risk breakdown structure is a hierarchically organized depiction of the identified project risks arranged by risk category. The risks are placed into the hierarchical structure as they are identified, and the structure is organized by source so that the total risk exposure of the project can be more easily understood, and planning for the risk more easily accomplished.

Cost Breakdown Structure (CBS)

The cost breakdown structure classifies the costs within project into cost units/cost centre and cost elements/cost types. The establishment of a cost structure aids efficient cost planning, controlling, and the introduction of measures to reduce costs.

Mile Stones

In a project management, a milestone is a significant event which is used to give visibility of progress in term of achievement of predefined milestone goals. Failure to meet a milestone indicates that a project is not proceeding to plan and usually triggers corrective action by management.

Milestones have no duration. They represent instantaneous events that occur throughout the project. Typical project events that are marked with milestones are:

- The completion of a project phase
- The approval of a deliverable
- The completion of a scheduled review
- The completion of an activity
- The commencement of an activity.

In software project management, you should describe your milestones in terms of the following attributes:

- **Milestone Name:** A short catchy phrase or acronym that describes the milestone (Example: Preliminary Design Review - PDR)
- **Project Event:** A description of the project event to which the milestone is tied (Example: formal approval of the Preliminary Design by the PDR team)
- **Milestone Goals:** The criteria that will be applied to determine if the milestone has been reached - the milestone goals (Example: Preliminary Design approval).

Your milestones should also be defined in terms of an absolute date or an elapsed time period from a previous milestone such as project commencement. Make sure your milestone goals are verifiable. You should be able to verify a goal with a yes or no answer. For example, the Software Requirements Specification is either complete or not complete, the Software Design Description has either passed or not passed peer review. The software product is or is not in commercial operation.

Classification of Milestones

Milestones are classified into following two categories:

1. Major Milestones

The major milestones give visibly or progress to people external to the project. Some examples of major milestones are as following:

- Concept approval
- Requirements review
- Preliminary design review
- Critical design review
- Test plan review etc.

2. Minor Milestones

Minor (or micro) milestones are the monitoring points you as project manager use to maintain control of day to day activities. They divide the elapsed time between major milestones into shorter intervals to give you the confidence that the major milestones will be met. They also give the team a sense of achievement by demonstrating progress on a daily or weekly basis. Some examples of major milestones are as following:

- Document outlines complete
- Document complete
- Technical investigation complete
- Compile complete etc.

Software Project Estimation

Software projects are notorious for going past their deadline, going over budget, or both. The problem lies in the estimation of the amount of effort required for the development of a project. The cost estimation is usually dependent upon the size estimate of the project, which may use lines of code or function points as metrics. There are several different techniques for performing software cost estimation, including expert judgments.

Cost Estimation

Cost estimation is a process which is used to calculate costs for a project. Cost estimation will never be an exact science because there are too many variables involved in the calculation for a cost estimate, such as human, technical, environmental, and political. Furthermore, any process that involves a significant human factor can never be exact because humans are far too complex to be entirely predictable. Furthermore, software development for any fair-sized project will inevitably include a number of tasks that have complexities that are difficult to judge because of the complexity of software systems.

Cost estimation is usually measured in terms of effort. The most common metric used is person months or years. The effort is the amount of time for one person to work for a certain period of time. It is important that the specific characteristics of the development environment are taking into account when comparing the effort of two or more projects because no two development environments are the same. Different variables can be used for cost estimation, which leads to a difficulty when comparing projects if standard models or tools are not used. For example, a cost estimate can include factors from management, development (e.g., training, quality assurance), and other areas specific to an organization.

Cost Estimation Process

In order to understand the end result or the outputs of the software cost estimation process we must first understand what is software cost estimation process. Software cost estimation process is a set of techniques and procedures that is used to derive the software cost estimate. There is usually a set of inputs to the process and then the process uses these inputs to generate or calculate a set of outputs. Software cost estimation process can be classified into two categories:

1. Classical View
2. Actual View

Classical View

Most of the software cost estimation models views the estimation process as being a function that is computed from a set of cost drivers. And in most cost estimation techniques the primary cost driver or the most important cost driver is believed to be the software requirements. As shown in Fig. 6.7, in a classical view of software estimation process, the software requirements are the primary input to the process and also form the basis for the cost estimation. The cost estimate will then be adjusted accordingly to a number of other cost drivers to arrive at the final estimate.

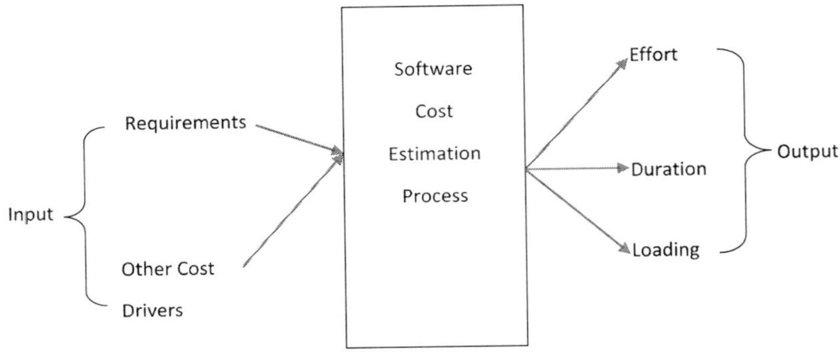

Fig. 6.7: Classical View of Software Estimation Process

Now question is that what is cost driver? Cost driver is anything that may or will affect the cost of the software. Cost drivers are things such as design methodology, skill-levels, risk assessment, personnel experience, programming language or system complexity. In a classical view of the estimation process, it will generate three outputs:

1. **Manpower Loading:** number of personnel (which also includes management personnel) that are allocated to the project as a function of time.
2. **Project Duration:** time that is needed to complete the project.
3. **Effort:** amount of effort required to complete the project and is usually measured in units as man-months (MM) or person-months (PM).

Actual Cost Estimation Process

In the actual cost estimation process, there are other inputs and constraints that needed to be considered besides the cost drivers (Fig. 6.8). One of the primary constraints of the software cost estimate is the financial constraint, which are the amount of the money that can be budgeted or allocated to the project. There are other constraints such as manpower constraints, and date constraints. Other input such as architecture, which defines the components that made up the system and the interrelationships between these components. Some company will have certain software process or an existing architecture in place; hence for these companies the software cost estimation must base their estimates on these criteria.

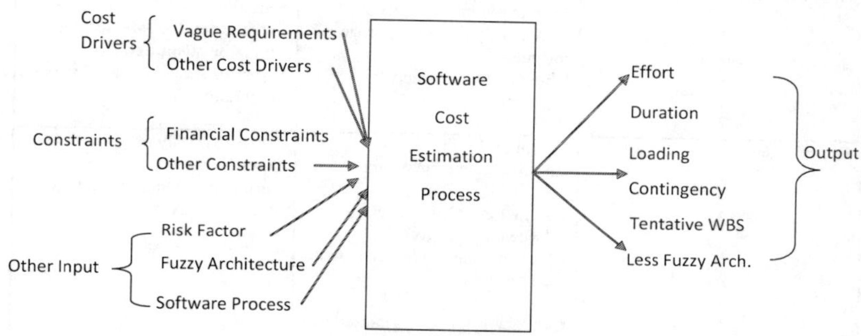

Fig. 6.8: Actual Cost Estimation Process

There are only very few cases where the software requirements stay fixed. Hence, how do we deal with software requirement changes, ambiguities or inconsistencies? During the estimation process, an experienced estimator will detect the ambiguities and inconsistency in the requirements. As part of the estimation process, the estimator will try to solve all these ambiguities by modifying the requirements. If the ambiguities or inconsistent requirements stay unsolved, which will correspondingly affect the estimation accuracy?

Methods of Cost Estimation

There is a lot of software cost estimation methods or techniques in the software industry some commonly used technologies are as follows:

- Algorithmic (Parametric) Model
- Expert Judgment (Expertise Based)
- Top - Down
- Bottom - Up
- Estimation by Analogy

The relative advantages and disadvantages of these estimation methods are given in Table 6.4.

Software Project Activity Planning

As project progresses it is unlikely that everything will go according to plan. Much of the job of project management concerns recognizing when

Table 6.4: The relative advantages and disadvantages of these estimation methods

Estimation Method	*Advantages*	*Disadvantages*
Algorithmic (Parametric) Model	Generate repeatable estimations Easy to modify input data Easy to refine and customize formulas Objectively calibrated to experience	Unable to deal with exceptional conditions Some experience and factors cannot be quantified Sometimes algorithms may be proprietary
Expert Judgment	Useful in the absence of quantified, empirical data. Can factor in differences between past project experiences and requirements of the proposed project Can factor in impacts caused by new technologies, applications and languages.	Estimate is only as good expert's opinion Hard to document the factors used by the experts
Top-Down	Requires minimal project detail Usually faster and easier to implement Focus on system level activities	Tend to overlook low level components No detailed basis
Bottom-Up	More stable More detailed Allow each software group to hand an estimate	May overlook system level costs More time consuming
Estimation by Analogy	Based on actual project data	Impossible if no comparable project had been tackled in the past. How well does the previous project represent this one

something has gone wrong, identifying its causes and revising the plan to mitigate its effects. The activity plan should provide a means of evaluating the consequences of not meeting any of the activity target dates and guidance as to how the plan might most effectively be modified to bring the project back to target. We shall see that the activity plan may well also offer guidance as to which components of a project should be most closely monitored.

Activity Planning and Scheduling

Project time management includes two high-level groups of processes for planning and scheduling project activities and tasks necessary for timely completion of the project.

- Project activities planning and scheduling is the first process group of project time management.
- Developing the project implementation schedule is the second group.

To plan and schedule project activities and tasks the project manager needs to take the next four steps:

- Set up activities.
- Define relationships between activities.
- Estimate resources required for performing activities.
- Estimate durations for activities.

Set up Activities

The first step of project activities planning and scheduling requires the project manager to define what amount of actions and tasks are necessary for producing project deliverables in a timely manner. The input for this process will be the project deliverables statement. The project manager can use this document to define high-level activities that will be used later in creating the project implementation schedule. The project manager should also work on developing *project activities templates* that help simplify the process of project scheduling and planning.

This process starts with the WBS and identifies the activities required to produce the various project deliverables. Activities are viewed from the perspective of the work packages. The resulting information from this process is used next to organize the activities into a specific sequence. The inputs, tools, techniques, and outputs for the activity definition process are as given in Table 6.5.

Table 6.5: Activity Definition Inputs, Outputs, Tools, and Techniques

Inputs	*Outputs*	*Tools and Techniques*
Enterprise environmental factors	Activity list	Decomposition
Organizational process assets	Activity attributes	Templates
Project scope statement	Milestone list	Rolling wave planning
Work breakdown structure	Requested changes	Expert judgment
WBS dictionary		Planning component

Sometimes it is difficult to know everything about a project during the planning stage. It is common to learn more about the project as you work through the project life cycle. This is called progressive elaboration and it affects the planning process. If you don't know everything about the project, you can't plan the whole project to the level of detail necessary. For large projects, it is common to plan the entire project at a high level. The project starts with detailed plans in place for the work packages that are near the beginning of the project. As the time draws near to begin additional work, the more detailed, low-level plans for those work packages are added to the project plan. The planning process is revisited multiple times to ensure that the detailed plans contain the latest information known about the project. This practice is called *rolling wave planning* because the planning wave always moves to stay ahead of the work execution wave.

Define Relationships

The next step for planning project activities and tasks requires the project manager to make a sequence of all the activities identified at the previous step. The manager will use project activities lists, the milestones list and the product scope statement to define relationships among the activities. With help of project management software that person can set up priorities for each of the project activities and make task sequences organized and sorted by importance and urgency. There is also a need to define dependencies between the activities.

For example, when building a car, you cannot install the engine until the engine has been built and delivered to the main assembly line. This is just one simple example of how activities may be dependent on one another. This process is one that can benefit from the use of computer software to assist in noting and keeping track of inter-activity dependencies.

Risk Analysis

The proactive management of risks throughout the software development lifecycle is important for project success. In this unit, we will explain the risk management practice, which involves risk identification, analysis, prioritization, planning, mitigation, monitoring, and communication.

Risk Management

"Risks are future uncertain events with a probability of occurrence and a potential for loss". Risk identification and management are the main concerns in every software project. Effective analysis of software risks will help to effective planning and assignments of work. Risk management in software engineering is related to the various future harms that could be possible on the software due to some minor or non-noticeable mistakes in software development project or process. "Software projects have a high probability of failure so effective software development means dealing with risks adequately. Risk management is the most important issue involved in the software project development. This issue is generally managed by Software Project Management (SPM). During the life cycle of software projects, various risks are associated with them. These risks in the software project is identified and managed by software risk management which is a part of SPM. Some of the important aspects of risk management in software engineering are software risk management, risk classification and strategies for risk management.

Software Risk Management

Since there could be various risks associated with the software development projects, the key to identify and manage those risks is to know about the concepts of software risk management. Many concepts about software risk management could be identified but the most important are risk index, risk analysis, and risk assessment.

1. **Risk Index:** Generally risks are categorized into two factors namely impact of risk events and probability of occurrence. Risk index is the multiplication of impact and probability of occurrence. Risk index can be characterized as high, medium, or low depending upon the product of impact and occurrence. Risk index is very important and necessary for prioritization of risk.
2. **Risk Analysis:** There are quite different types of risk analysis that can be used. Basically, risk analysis is used to identify the high-risk elements of a project in software engineering. Also, it provides ways of detailing the impact of risk mitigation strategies. Risk analysis has also been found to be most important in the software design phase to evaluate criticality of the system, where risks are analyzed and necessary counter measures are introduced. The main purpose of risk analysis is to understand risks in better ways and to verify and correct attributes. A successful risk analysis includes important elements like problem definition, problem formulation, data collection.
3. **Risk Assessment:** Risk assessment is another important case that integrates risk management and risk analysis. There are many risk assessment methodologies that focus on different types of risks. Risk assessment requires correct explanations of the target system and all security features. It is important that a risk referent levels like performance, cost, support and schedule must be defined properly for risk assessment to be useful.

Risk Classification

The key purpose of classifying risk is to get a collective viewpoint on a group of factors. These are the types of factors which will help project managers to identify the group that contributes the maximum risk. A best and most scientific way of approaching risks is to classify them based on risk attributes. Risk classification is considered as an economical way of analyzing risks and their causes by grouping similar risks together into classes. Software risks could be classified as internal or external. Those risks that come from risk factors within the organization are called internal risks whereas the external risks come from out of the organization and are difficult to control. Internal risks are project risks, process risks, and product risks. External risks are generally business with the vendor, technical risks, customers' satisfaction, political stability and so on. In general, there are many risks in the software engineering which is very difficult or impossible to identify all of them. Some of most important risks in software engineering project are categorized as software requirement risks, software cost risks, software scheduling risk, software quality risks, and software business risks. These risks are explained detail below:

Resource Risk

This risk mainly arises from outsourcing and personnel related issues. A big project might involve dozens or even hundreds of employees and it is essential to manage the attrition issues and leaving of key personnel. Bringing in a new worker at a later stage in the project can significantly slow down the project.

Apart from attrition, there is a skill related risk too. For instance, if the project requires a lot of website front end work and your team doesn't have a designer skilled in HTML/CSS, you could face unexpected delays there. Another source of the risk includes lack of availability of funds. This could happen if you are relying on an external source of funding (such as a client who pays per milestone) and the client suddenly faces a cash crunch.

Operational Risks

Operational risks are the risks of loss due to improper process implementation, failed system or some external events risks. Causes of Operational risks:

- Failure to address priority conflicts
- Failure to resolve the responsibilities
- Insufficient resources
- No proper subject training
- No resource planning
- No communication in team.

Software Scheduling Risks

Project schedule get slip when project tasks and schedule release risks are not addressed properly. Schedule risks mainly affect on project and finally on company economy and may lead to project failure. Schedules often slip due to following reasons:

- Wrong time estimation
- Resources are not tracked properly. All resources like staff, systems, skills of individuals etc.
- Failure to identify complex functionalities and time required to develop those functionalities.
- Unexpected project scope expansions.

Technical Risks

This risk includes delays arising out of software & hardware defects or the failure of an underlying service or a platform. For instance, halfway through the project you might realize the cloud service provider you are using doesn't satisfy your performance benchmarks. Apart from this, there could be issues in the platform used to build your software or a software update of a critical tool that no longer supports some of your functions.

Technical risks generally lead to failure of functionality and performance. Causes of technical risks are:

1. Continuous changing requirements
2. No advanced technology available or the existing technology is in initial stages.
3. Product is complex to implement.
4. Difficult project modules integration.

Programmatic Risks

These are the external risks beyond the operational limits. These are all uncertain risks are outside the control of the program. These external events can be:

- Running out of fund.
- Market development
- Changing customer product strategy and priority
- Government rule changes.

Risk Identification

In the risk identification step, the team systematically enumerates as many project risks as possible to make them explicit before they become problems. There are several ways to look at the kinds of software project risks, as shown in Fig. 6.9. It is helpful to understand the different types of risk so that a team can explore the possibilities of each of them.

Each of these types of risk is described below.

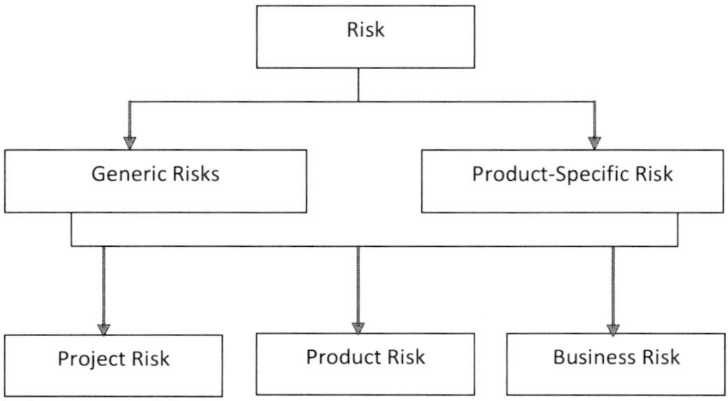

Fig. 6.9: Software Project Risks

Generic Risks

Generic risks are potential threats to every software project. Some examples of generic risks are changing requirements, losing key personnel, or bankruptcy of the software company or of the customer. It is advisable for a development organization to keep a checklist of these types of risks. Teams can then assess the extent to which these risks are a factor for their project based upon the known set of programmers, managers, customers, and policies.

Product-Specific Risks

Product-specific risks can be distinguished from generic risks because they can only be identified by those with a clear understanding of the technology, the people, and the environment of the specific product. An example of a product-specific risk is the availability of a complex network necessary for testing.

Generic and product-specific risks can be further divided into:

1. **Project Risks:** Project risks are those that affect the project schedule or the resources (personnel or budgets) dedicated to the project.

2. **Product Risks:** Product risks are those that affect the quality or performance of the software being developed.
3. **Business Risks:** Business risks are those that threaten the viability of the software, such as building an excellent product no one wants or building a product that no longer fits into the overall business strategy of the company.

Resource Allocation

Resource allocation is used to assign the available resources in an economic way. It is part of resource management. In project management, resource allocation is the scheduling of activities and the resources required by those activities while taking into consideration both the resource availability and the project time.

By the word resources can be referred to all the resources required for a project such as financial resources, natural resources, human resources etc. Resource allocation involves the planning of all the resources required for the project. It helps you to utilize only that much resources which are required. We all know that economy is going down these days which have resulted in a tough competition especially with regard to financial resources. The operating cost of doing business has increased. Companies have limited budget for projects so there is no margin for you to waste or misuse any material.

Project managers have to work in limited or even tight budgets. Everyone can perform well within huge budgets but only a professional and experienced project manager can manage to work in every situation. If you do resource allocation efficiently then it means your half project is already completed as resource allocation is the most important yet difficult part of project management. Being a project manager, you should know its importance so that you may not do any mistake while allocating the resources. One simple tip is to make the list of all the resources needed for project and then shortlist them to select only those which are most important.

Resources are always limited—not just in software development projects, but for projects all over. Pressure mounts on resource managers who work in software project management to complete any given project ASAP. Human resources and computer resources are always limited as they service multiple projects. Therefore, the onus is on a software project manager is to marshal his resources carefully and use them diligently to achieve the objectives set for the project. The feasibility of deploying more resources to reduce the calendar time has limited applicability in software development projects. What we really need to do is manage the available resources effectively.

Consider the use the following resources in software development:

- Time
- Human Resources – the most crucial of all the resources
- Computer Resources
- Money

Classification of Resources

Resources can classify into four categories:

1. **Availability**
    - **Recurring** – such as human resources that are available in the same quantity day-after-day – spending these resources does not deplete them.
    - **Depleting** – like time and money – spending these resources depletes them.
2. **Place of Availability**
    - **Immovable** – available wherever they are situated – they cannot be moved from place to place, such as computer resources.
    - **Movable** – these resources can be moved from place to place – such as human resources and money.
3. **Elasticity**
    - **Elastic Resources** – their supply can be increased or decreased – such as human resources and money.
    - **Plastic Resources** – their supply cannot be extended, such as time.
4. **Shared and Dedicated**
    - **Dedicated resources** – these should be dedicated to the project for the required duration – such as computer systems and programmers.
    - **Shared resources** – these are resources that are needed for short durations but would not be utilized for the entire duration of the project – such as DBAs (*Database Administrators*), programming language experts, functional specialists, etc.

Identifying Resource Requirements

Once the Work Breakdown Structure (WBS) has been applied and the project activities have been identified, you are ready to identify the types (labor, equipment, material) and quantities of the resources needed to implement the project.

In order to identify the resource requirements, the following steps should be followed:

1. **Review the project scope and activities/ tasks list** in order to identify the project's requirements for people, equipment and material resources.
2. **Gather historical information** from old project files, databases and from people who have worked on similar projects, regarding what types and numbers of resources were required for performing similar work on previous projects, as well as the duration of the relative tasks.
3. **Consider how resource quantities, capabilities and quality affect the duration of the activities/ tasks**. The duration of most tasks is influenced by the number of resources assigned to them. In most cases, particularly for production tasks, two resources can complete a task in half the time it would take for a single resource. Similarly, a resource working half time on a task will typically take about twice as much time as the same resource working full time. However, in other instances, for example for design tasks, adding resources does not guarantee that the duration will decrease. The duration of most tasks is also influenced by the capabilities and experience of the resources assigned to them. For example, a team member with five years' experience can typically be expected to complete a task in less time than one with two years' experience.
4. **Identify the resource types and quantities needed**. Once you have collected all the necessary information, identify the types of resources and the quantities needed for each. Generally, the resources are distinguished in three main categories:
   (a) **Labor (or Human Resources)**: It is not necessary at this stage of the project to be identified by name, but the professional qualifications and the type of skills required for carrying out an activity/ task should be identified. For example, there is no need to specify that Mr. X will be used to elaborate the detail design for the construction of a bridge, but you

could say that one civil engineer with relative experience in bridge construction projects is required. Do not forget to identify the necessary resources required to perform the project management tasks, such as the Project Manager, Quality Manager, etc.

(b) **Equipment**: You have to list the equipment that will be used for the performance of works (e.g. excavators, cranes), the delivery of services or supplies (e.g. classrooms for the conduction of training seminars, lorries for carrying supplies and warehouses for storing supplies), as well as for carrying out supportive actions like project and procurement management (e.g. computers, software packages, photocopiers).

(c) **Material**: You have to list the material that will be used for the production of the deliverables. For example, in case of a building construction project, materials like bricks, cement, steel, cables, paints will be used. Or in case of a training delivery project, materials like paper for printing the training material and blank CDs for distributing the training material to participants will be used. In addition, material that will be used for project management and procurement management activities should also be listed (e.g. paper for printing the tender documents, posters to be used for publicity actions of the project, etc.)

5. **Ask for an expert's judgment**. Once you have identified the types and quantities of resources you should present the resource requirements to an individual expert or a group of experts in order to assess them and advise you for their suitability and appropriateness. Such expertise and specialized knowledge may be acquired either from other units within the agency (e.g. technical unit, HR unit) or/and by external consultants or/and by professional and technical associations or/and by industry groups.

6. **Examine the adequacy of resources**. Regardless of whether the project will be implemented with own resources (in-house production) or it will be contracted out to an economic operator through a tendering process, you have to examine the sufficiency of the internal resources, because even in the second case (outsource production) you will need to involve internal resources for performing the project management tasks in order to monitor and control the contractor. The sufficiency of internal resources (i.e. those resources owned by the Implementing Agency) should be

examined both in terms of quantity, as well as in terms of skills, experience and expertise with relation to project requirements. Taking into account the result of adequacy examination, as well as the organizational policies regarding staffing and the rental or purchase of supplies and equipment you should decide whether there is a need to acquire external resources. If for example there is a need to use a legal advisor in performing some activities and there is not such an expert in the Agency's staff, you will need to hire an external advisor, or if for example there is a need of classrooms for conducting training seminars and the Agency doesn't own any classroom or the classrooms it owns are used for another project that given period, it will have to rent them either from another agency or from a private entity.

Resource Allocation and Contingency Planning

Allocating resources and smoothing resource histograms is relatively straightforward where all resources of a given type can be considered more or less equivalent. When allocating laborers to activities in a large building project we need not distinguish among individuals- there are likely to be many laborers and they may be treated as equals so far as skills and productivity are concerned.

This is seldom the case with software projects. Because of the nature of software development skill and experience play a significant part in determining the time taken and, potentially, the quality of the final product. With the exception of extremely large projects it makes sense to allocate individual members of staff to activities as early as possible, as this can lead us to revise our estimate of the duration.

In allocating individual to tasks, a number of factors need to be taken into account.

1. **Availability**: We need to know whether a particular individual will be available when required. Reference to the departmental work plan determines this but the wise project manager will always investigate the risks that might be involved – earlier projects might for example, over-run and affect the availability of an individual.
2. **Critically**: Allocation of more experienced personnel to activities on the critical path often helps in shorting project durations or at least reduces the risk of overrun.
3. **Risk**: Identifying those activities posing the greatest risk and knowing the factors influencing staff to the highest risk activities

is likely to have the greatest effect in reducing overall project uncertainties. More experienced staff are however, usually more expensive.

4. **Training**: It will benefit the organization if positive steps are taken to allocate junior staff to appropriate non-critical activities where there will be sufficient slack for them to train and develop skills. There can even be direct benefits to the particular project since some may be allocated to the training budget.
5. **Team Building**: The selection of individuals must also take account of the final shape of the project team and the way they will work together.

Monitoring and Quality Assurance

Once work schedules have been published and the project in under way, attention must be focused ensuring progress. This requires monitoring of what is happening, comparison of actual achievement against the schedule and, where necessary, revision of plans schedules to bring the project as far as possible back on target.

We have already read the importance of producing plans that can be monitored for example, ensuring the activities have clearly defined and visible completion points. Now we will discuss how information about project progress is gathered and what actions must be taken to ensure a project meets its targets.

Project Monitoring and Control

The Monitoring and Control Process consists of those processes performed to observe project execution so that potential problems can be identified in a timely manner and corrective action can be taken, when necessary, to control the execution of the project.

Project Monitoring and Control activities take place in parallel with Project Execution Process Group activities so that, while the project work is being executed, the project is being monitored and controlled by implementing the appropriate level of oversight and corrective action.

The project is observed and measured regularly against the project plan to ensure that the project is within acceptable variances of cost, schedule and scope, and that risks and issues are continually monitored and corrected as needed.

The main purpose of monitoring and controlling activities is to be proactive in finding issues ahead of time and taking corrective action.

Corrective action can require revisiting Planning Process and updating the Project Management Plan as needed with the ultimate goal of bringing the project back in line with project objectives and constraints and improving future execution to avoid repeating the same issues.

The various monitoring and control processes are as follows:

- Monitoring and Controlling Project Work
- Integrated Change Control
- Scope Verification and Scope Control
- Schedule Control
- Cost Control
- Managing the Project Team
- Performance Reporting
- Managing Stakeholders

Monitoring and Controlling Project Work

The Monitoring and Controlling Project Work process collects, measures and disseminates performance information, and assesses measures and trends to forecast potential items requiring corrective action. This includes monitoring project risks and ensuring that they are being managed according to the project's risk plans.

The outputs of this process are as follows:

- Recommended corrective actions
- Recommended preventive actions
- Forecasts
- Recommended defect repair
- Requested changes

Integrated Change Control

The Integrated Change Control process ensures that changes as a result of project corrective actions and other controlling factors are managed across the project knowledge areas. Integrated change control takes place throughout the project, from project initiation through project closure.

The outputs of this process are as follows:

- Approved change requests
- Rejected change requests
- Updates to the Project Management Plan

- Updates to the Project Scope Statement (and requirements)
- Approved corrective and preventive actions
- Approved defect repair
- Validated defect repair
- Deliverables

Scope Verification and Scope Control

The scope verification process ensures that project deliverables are formally accepted. The Scope Control process ensures that changes to project scope are controlled.

The outputs of this process are as follows:

- Accepted deliverables
- Requested changes
- Recommended corrective actions
- Updates to the Project Scope Statement
- Updates to the Work Breakdown Structure (WBS) and the WBS Dictionary
- Requested changes
- Recommended corrective actions
- Updates to organizational process assets
- Updates to the Project Management Plan

Schedule Control

The Schedule Control process monitors and controls changes to the project schedule.

The outputs of this process are as follows:

- Updates to the schedule model data and baseline
- Performance measurements
- Requested changes
- Recommended corrective actions
- Updates to organizational process assets
- Activity list and activity attribute updates
- Updates to the Project Management Plan

Cost Control

The Cost Control process monitors and controls costs and changes to the project budget.

The outputs of this process are as follows:

- Cost estimate updates
- Cost baseline updates
- Performance measurements
- Forecasted completion
- Requested changes
- Recommended corrective actions
- Updates to organizational process assets
- Updates to the Project Management Plan

Managing the Project Team

This process tracks team member performance, provides feedback, resolves issues and coordinates changes to maintain and improve project performance.

The outputs of this process are as follows:

- Requested changes
- Recommended corrective and preventive actions
- Updates to organizational process assets
- Updates to the Project Management Plan

Performance Reporting

The Performance Reporting process collects and distributes performance information — including status reports, progress reports and forecasts.

The outputs of this process are as follows:

- Performance reports
- Forecasts
- Requested changes
- Recommended corrective actions
- Updates to organizational process assets

Managing Stakeholders

This process manages stakeholder communications and works with stakeholders to ensure that requirements are satisfied and issues are proactively resolved.

The outputs of this process are as follows:

- Resolved issues
- Approved change requests
- Approved corrective actions
- Updates to organizational process assets
- Updates to the Project Management Plan

Visualizing Progress

Having collected data about project progress, a manager needs some way of presenting that data to greatest effect. In this section, we look at some methods of presenting a picture of the project and its future.

Earned Value Analysis

Earned value analysis (EVA) is the only project management tool that can objectively status schedule and cost performance in real time. EVA creates a "dollars in time" paradigm tracking costs and schedule in an objective, reliable and easy to use model replacing the complex and confusing project deliverables dependent-milestone-antecedent subjective model. EVA creates a "project at a glance" paradigm with readily understood visual display of quantitative information.

EVA compares the calculated value of work performed, what you have earned, to the actual cost and to a projected cost of work performed. Deviations are cost, time, or both, and can be expressed in dollars, time or calculated further as progress, per cent complete or a performance index. EVA is primarily a schedule tracking tool, determining schedule from cost and earned value of individual WBS tasks performed in time: the project management trinity of scope, cost and schedule

Three fundamental concepts to effective EVA:

1. Understand the difference between the value of work performed and the cost of work performed.
2. Tracking dollars in time is more effective and predictable, simpler and objective than the traditional project deliverables precedent-milestone-antecedent hierarchical model as it unlinks tracking subjective assessment of technical deliverables from tracking the cost and time to perform that work.
3. Take a long view while also being aware of short term anomalies or early problem identifiers: believe it when the data looks bad.

Common problems with EVA

1. Not believing it when the data looks bad because EVA is a real time performance metric tool, schedule or cost slippage will be presented graphically for all to see and the common response is to explain it away as a local anomaly, known and expected.
2. Not updating the EVA tool with regular cost and percent complete work assessments. Typically followed by playing catch-up later on and entering data all at once. Hides early problem identification, sometimes used as explanation for #1 problem.
3. Incomplete WBS activities and budget and improper mid-project updates. Moving dollar amounts around immediately affects all earned value calculations. This is ok if an error was made, or scope creep is agreed to.
4. EVA used with other project tracking tools and trying to link or equate them. EVA is a standalone tool for complex, large multi discipline projects. It allowing the PM to track the project performance in time and the technical discipline leads to track deliverables performance in time. The dollars in time paradigm and unlinking of technical deliverable tracking is a key how EVA is a light weight tool with incredible data density control. Attempts to link back these two separated activities are a waste of time and never work well.

Corrective Actions and Maintaining Control

The process of maintaining control over projects is the same: you track project-plan details and expenditures, deal with team members, and monitor performance.

Follow this list of activities to maintain control over your project, ensure that it proceeds according to plan, and produces the desired results:

1. **Reconfirming the Plan:** At the beginning of each performance period, reaffirm with team members the following project responsibilities and commitments they made for the coming period:
   - Activities they agreed to perform
   - Dates they agreed they will start and end these activities
   - Amount of person-effort they agreed they'll need to perform these activities.
2. **Assessing Performance:** During the performance period, have team members record information on the following:

- o Completed intermediate and final deliverables
- o Dates they reached milestones
- o Dates they started and ended activities
- o Number of hours they worked on each activity
- o Amount of nonpersonnel resources they used for each activity
- o Expenditures they made for each activity

Collect this information at the end of the performance period, compare it with the plan, and determine the reasons for any differences.

3. **Taking Corrective Action:** If necessary, take steps to bring your project's performance back into conformance with your plans, or if doing so isn't possible, change the plans to reflect new expectations.
4. **Keeping People Informed:** Share your achievements, problems, and future plans with your project's audiences.

Choose the periods for monitoring your project's performance based on the overall length of the project, the risk of unexpected occurrences, and your proximity to major milestones. Although you may choose to monitor selected project activities on a daily basis in certain situations, plan to assess your project's overall performance at least once a month to identify promptly any unexpected occurrences or performance problems that must be addressed.

Initially, you may be uncomfortable reconfirming commitments people have made for an upcoming performance period because you feel that by doing so, it

- **Suggests that you don't trust the person.** After all, the person has made a commitment to do the specified work; wouldn't she tell you if she were unable to live up to that commitment?
- **Increases the likelihood that she'll say she can't live up to the original promise.** You're concerned that raising the topic may actually encourage her to say she can't honor her commitments.

Software Quality

Quality is a rather vague term and we need to define carefully what we mean by it. For any software system, there should be three specifications:

- **Functional Specification:** A functional specification describing what the system is to do.
- **Quality Specification:** A quality specification concerned with how well the functions are to operate.

- **Resource Specification:** A resource specification concerned with how much is to be spent on the system.

There have been several attempts to identify specific product qualities that are appropriate to software. James A. McCall, for instance, grouped software qualities into three sets:

1. Product Operation Qualities
2. Product Revision Qualities
3. Product Transition Qualities

Product Operation Quality Factors

1. **Correctness:** The extent to which a program satisfies its specifications and fulfils the user's objectives.
2. **Reliability:** The extent to which a program can be expected to perform its intended function with required precision.
3. **Efficiency:** The amounts of computer resources required by the software.
4. **Integrity:** The extent to which access to software or data by unauthorized persons can be controlled.
5. **Usability:** The effort required to learn, operate, prepare input and interpret output.

Product Revision Qualities Factors

1. **Maintainability:** The effort required to locate and fix an error in an operational program.
2. **Testability:** The effort required to test a program to ensure it performs its intended function.
3. **Flexibility**: The effort required to modify an operational program.

Product Transition Quality Factors

1. **Portability**: The effort required to transfer a program from one hardware configuration and/or software system environment to another.
2. **Reusability**: The extent to which a program can be used in other applications.
3. **Interoperability**: The effort required to couple one system to another.

The Importance of Software Quality

We would expect quality to be a concern of all producers of goods and services. However, the special characteristics of software, and in particular its intangibility and complexity, make special demands.

1. **Increasing Criticality of Software:** The final customer or user is naturally anxious about the general quality of software, especially its reliability. This is increasingly the case as organizations become more dependent on their computer systems and software is used more in areas that are safety-critical, for example control aircraft.
2. **The Intangibility of Software:** This makes it difficult to know that a particular task in a project has been completed satisfactorily. The result of these takes can be made tangible by demanding that the developer produces 'deliverables' that can be examined for quality.
3. **Accumulating Errors during Software Development**: As computer system development is made up of a number of steps where the output from one step is the input to the next, the errors in the earlier deliverables will be added to those in the later steps leading to an accumulating detrimental effect. In general, the later in a project that an error is found the more expensive it will be to fix. In addition, because the number of errors in the system is unknown, the debugging phases of a project are particularly difficult to control.

Product Vs. Process Quality

When we talk about software quality assurance, we often discuss process measurements, process improvements, productivity increase, quality improvement etc. And when we talk about quality improvement, mostly people think about product quality improvement. Most of the time people forget about process quality improvement. In fact, people find it difficult to differentiate between product quality and process quality.

During software development, we have work products like requirement specifications, software design, software code, user documentation, etc. Quality of any of these work products can be done by measuring its attributes and finding of they are good enough. For instance, a requirement specification may be ambiguous or even wrong. In that case, quality of that requirement specification is bad. So during quality assurance audit (peer review, inspection etc.), this defect can be caught so that it can be rectified.

During software development project, a lot of processes are followed. The top processes are the project processes like project initiation, project planning, project monitoring, and project closure. Then we have development processes like requirement development, software design, software coding, software testing and software release.

All of these processes are not executed perfectly on any project. Improvement in these processes can be achieved if we have audits of these processes. For instance, these audits are done by using standards like CMM (Capability Maturity Model). These standards dictate as to how any project or development process needs to be executed on any project. If any process step is deviating too much from these standards then that process step needs to be improved. The most important job of any software quality assurance department is to audit and ensure that all processes on projects being executed in that organization adhere to these standards and so quality of these processes (project & development) is good enough.

Project Evaluation Measures for Quality Assurance in India

IGNOU offers many programmes including Certificate, Advanced Certificate, Diploma, Advanced Diploma, Degree, Master and Ph.D. programmes. Majority of these programmes are offered through a network of Regional Centres and Study Centres. Quality education has always been on the priority of IGNOU. In the professional programmes like Computer Programmes, Health Programmes, Educational Programme, Science Programmes, it has become more important. In Computer Programmes (BCA and MCA), in addition to practical components, there is a project work (CS-76 for BCA and CS-17 for MCA).

A large number of these projects are submitted at Regional Centres across the country. The quality issues like copying the project, making fake guides, hiring proxy writers and purchasing the projects from the market etc. are some of the issues which need adequate attention of all concerned. The students submit their projects proposals at the respective Regional Centres. The project proposals are approved or disapproved by the approved evaluators. The students write the full projects and submit at the Regional Centre. Thereafter, the students are asked to report for the viva-voce at the Regional Centre. The approved evaluators evaluate the project and conduct the viva voce.

We have analyzed large numbers of projects proposals (Synopsis) and final projects, the reasons for the rejections of the project proposals, similarity of the projects guided by the same evaluator, the comments given by the evaluators since 2007 covering about 3000 projects that were submitted at Regional Centre Delhi-I. We have observed that there are large number of projects which are of similar contents and title, variations in evaluation and comments vis-à-vis marks awarded by the evaluators. We have recommended some corrective measures to improve upon these issues for overall improvement in the quality of projects.

The quality education in all possible modes is of utmost important. It has been addressed by several authors (Powar et.al, 2000, Chandra, R. and Singh, S. 2004, Kumar, A. and Dixit, J. 2006, Panda, S. 1999. IGNOU is the only Open University at the national level in India and is mandated to carry out two functions; (1) to design, develop and offer programmes through open and distance education at the national and international level and (2) to coordinate and maintain standards as an apex body of the open and distance education systems in the country (Panda 1996). The quality concerns of the University are quite explicit in its outlined functions.

MCA and BCA are two important professional programmes offered by the University which were launched in 1994 and 1996 respectively (Kumar and Dixit, 2006). The lab components are essential, apart from the theoretical sessions. The application skills of the students are tested through the project course (CS-17 for MCA and CS-76 for BCA) in the terminating semester of the programme duration. The project course is undertaken by the students at any industry /company after a brief orientation at the respective study centres/programme study centres.

The main objective of the BCA/MCA project work is to give the students an opportunity to develop quality software solution. The student should involve in all the stages of software development life cycle (SDLC) like requirements analysis, system design, software development/coding, testing and documentation, with an overall emphasis on the development of the reliable software systems. The primary emphasis of the project work is to understand and gain the knowledge of the principles of software engineering practices and develop good understanding of SDLC.

The topics selected should be complex and large enough to justify as a BCA/MCA project. The project should be genuine and original in nature and should not be copied from anywhere else. We have tried to analyse the BCAMCA projects submitted and evaluated by keeping all these factors in mind. The main emphasis is, however, is for BCA projects.

The following issues for BCA/MCA projects were considered:

(1) Similarity of the projects
(2) Copying of the projects
(3) Contents of the projects

(4) Large variations among the evaluators for awarding marks of projects

In IGNOU, BCA/MCA projects guidelines indicate that the projects should be evaluated and commented on various aspects such as analysis, design, testing, coding and security. A brief discussion of these items is given below:

- **Analysis**: A specification regarding the concerned system on which the project is based is to be given here. It is basically a requirement gathering process, specifying on the software to understand the nature of the programme to be built.
- **Design**: The programme structure of the project is to be given and explained through flowcharts and pseudo codes / algorithms.
- **Coding**: It performs the task of translating design into a machine-readable form.
- **Security**: It covers the aspects of risk, exposure and costs and specifies measures such as passwords and encryption to safeguard the software.
- **Testing**: The test method and the test levels are introduced here along with the future scope of modifiability, portability and the reusability.
- **Report organization**: It relates to the overall systematization and presentation of the project.

We recommend the following:

- There seems to be no correlation between the comments made by the evaluators and the marks given. The evaluator should have given the meaningful comments. Many evaluators have left the comment column "Blank" and have used the terms like ok, poor, very poor, good, very good, average, below average, satisfactory etc.
- Since large numbers of projects are turning bogus, copied from each other, the teaching value of these projects is almost nil. It is therefore, recommended that BCA projects should be withdrawn and instead a new course may be introduced.
- If the projects are to be continued then the following points may be considered: a. Major industries in the country may be approached to provide facility for live projects. The project guides from the industries may also act evaluators. b. The approved as project academic counsellors and guide of MCA programme may be

allowed to guide the BCA projects c. An orientation of evaluators for both project proposal and final project should be made compulsory at all Regional Centres before the start of the activities.

- There has to be an intensive workshop-cum-training programme for the evaluators so that they understand the basic needs of the project components and evaluation process.
- The evaluators who are not serious should not be allowed to evaluate the projects.

Innovation in Project Management

Harold Kerzner (2018) under the IIL Blog observed that some researchers argue that project management and innovation management should be treated as separate disciplines. This is because requirement for innovations and project management are not the same. Innovation requires many things. Some of them are the following:

- an acceptance of significant risk, more so than in traditional project management
- a great deal of uncertainty
- a focus on strategic goals and possibly no business case exists
- unknown constraints and assumptions that continuously change
- decision making in an unfamiliar landscape
- a creative mind-set
- collaboration across all enterprise organizational boundaries
- significant interfacing with customers in every market segment
- a different leadership style than with traditional project management and
- a set of tools different than what is being taught in traditional project management courses.

Innovation management is a combination of the management of innovation processes and change management. It refers to products, services, business processes, and accompanying transformational needs, whereby the organization must change the way they conduct their business. Sergey Filippov and Herman Mooi (2010), Innovation Project Management: A Research Agenda (RISUS. Journal on Innovation and Sustainability ISSN 2179-3565 – http://revistas.pucsp.br/risus) discussed "Innovation", "Research and Development (R&D)" and "Project Management" in detail.

Innovative research leads to new technologies, new industries, and new business models leading to impressive gain in productivity and GDP growth.

R&D is one component of innovation activities and knowledge creation among others. Innovation emerges as a pervasive and complex force, not only in the high-tech sectors in advanced economies, but also as a phenomenon existing in low-tech industry of developing, or catching-up economies. Innovation is a non-linear process, innovation is the exploration and exploitation of new ideas and recombination of existing knowledge in the pursuit of sustained competitive advantage. Besides, both innovation and R&D projects by their nature differ from conventional projects.

Fagerberg and Verspagen (2009) provide a comprehensive analysis of the cognitive and organizational characteristics of the emerging field of innovation studies. They observed that as society develops and changes, needs for new types of knowledge emerge. Responding to such challenges, entrepreneurs within the university/institute from time to time try to develop new bodies of knowledge and establish institutions and organizations that facilitate the continuing progress of the emerging eld. 'Innovation studies' is such a case a fairly successful one. The different cultures and mind-sets are significant hurdles to be removed in obtaining useful cooperation between academia and industry. The innovation process creates value and includes social corporate responsibility.

7

Field Training

Training, Education & Development

The education world is changing at an alarming rate. The ever-rising higher skill expectations and changing structure of the employment sector have posed numerous challenges for higher education providers. This has become more important and relevant because of increasing competitive environment in business and service sectors. This has resulted a mismatch between students seeking employment and industries requiring skilled employees. Therefore, there is no other way to resolve this, but to align education especially higher education with necessary skills. The industries and academic institutions need to join hands and develop suitable course curriculum where training, research and projects are an integral part of the education.

Training is short term, task oriented and targeted on achieving a change of attitude, skills and knowledge in a specific area. It may be job related or a step for becoming an expert entrepreneur. The students are required to go for training as a part of their course curriculum and also to become industry ready once they get graduated. Education is a lifetime investment. It tends to be initiated by a person in the area of his/her interest. The development is a long-term investment in human resources. Economic growth requires that the supply of high-skilled labour continues to rise. The main role of the educational system is to deliver skilled students to the workforce.

Industrial Training is important for making an engineering student work ready. To graduate from an engineering programme at any university, the students must complete a minimum duration of approved Industrial Training/ practical training. It means, not only do you graduate with some real on-the-job experience, you also qualify as per the requirement of statutory bodies.

Training may also be considered a means to use activities to fill the gaps of performance between the actual results and the expected results. The anticipated gaps can be separated into 3 main themes:

1. Attitude of the person
2. Skills already have and to be gained during training
3. Knowledge acquisition and perfection

During the training programme, one should remember the following concepts:

- **Participation**: The participation involves trainees and a mechanism of learning by doing.
- **Repetition**: It involves repeat ideas and concepts to help people learn.
- **Relevance**: The relevance helps to learn better when training material is meaningful and related.
- **Transference**: It helps to real world using simulations.
- **Feedback**: The feedback is very important and adjust training methods to suit trainee.

After that, the following nine steps in the training process be considered.

1. Assessing training needs as per the programme
2. Preparing training plan as per the course requirement
3. Specifying training objectives
4. Designing the training programme
5. Selecting the instructional methods for the training
6. Completing the training plan
7. Implementing the training programme
8. Evaluating the training outcome
9. Planning future training if needed

Benefits of Industrial Training

The main reason engineering students need to do Industrial Training (IT) is so that they are well-prepared for a graduate job in their chosen field. It also provides the opportunity to put what you have learned at university to work in real-life situations. The major benefits of industrial training are:

- First-hand experience working as an engineering professional

- Apply your technical knowledge and engineering methods to real-life situations
- Work with other engineering professionals
- Experience what it's like to work in a professional organisation.
- Witness the functioning and organisation of business and companies
- Increase your technical, interpersonal and communication skills, both oral and written
- Observe interactions of engineers with other professional groups
- Gain contacts for future networking opportunities

Many employers also use Industrial Training to assess their potential future employees, you will also have the opportunity to determine if this is where you want your future career to be.

Some Common Types of Industrial Training

Any of these types of placements will have to demonstrate how they reflect in your competencies, as you will be required to write on these in your report.

- **Company R&D** – involves Research and Development departments of companies.
- **Technical Engineering** (Both office and field) – involve working in an office or hands-on field activities to solve engineering problems.
- **Engineering Consulting** – professional engineering service firms who provide independent services, expertise and technical advice to companies who require specialised engineering tools and support to solve problems.
- **Research & Development** – all projects associated with the company
- **Student-led Projects** – some projects approved by the university as part of the course curriculum.

Some other areas of training are given in Table 7.1. This is a selective list only. There could be many more areas as per the changing needs of the industries. The need of these training programmes and skilled manpower can be seen from Fig. 7.1. It can be seen that the percentage of skilled manpower in India is very poor (2 percent) as compared with other countries like Korea, Japan and Germany where is more that 75 percent as reported in University News.

Table 7.1: Common Areas of Training

Major Head	*Sub Areas where training should be done*
CAD	Computer-aided design (CAD) technicians use their engineering, IT and mathematical knowledge and skills to design buildings, machinery, products and parts. CAD technicians usually work in engineering, manufacturing and construction industries and specialise in a certain technical field, such as mechanical, electrical, structural, control and instrumentation or piping design. You'll also be able to use CAD skills in a range of creative industry jobs, such as set and interior design. Your training should be to get first-hand experience on these systems.
Control and instrumentation engineer	Control and instrumentation (C&I) engineers are responsible for designing, developing, installing, managing and maintaining equipment which is used to monitor and control engineering systems, machinery and processes. Your training should be to make sure that these systems and processes operate effectively, efficiently and safely.
Design Engineer	As a design engineer you're involved in the initial concept, design, development and management of projects in a range of sectors such as construction and the built environment, materials, software, components, machinery and vehicles. In your training programme, you should get strong technical knowledge, as well as problem solving, communication, leadership and project management skills.
Electrical Engineer	As an electrical engineer, you'll design, develop and maintain electrical control systems and components to required specifications. Your training work should focus on: • economy • quality • reliability • safety • sustainability. The electrical equipment that you'll use, design and manufacture is used across many sectors, including: • the building industry and services, including lighting, heating and ventilation • transportation and transport networks • manufacturing and construction • production and distribution of power. Electrical engineers are involved in projects from the concept and detail of the design, through to implementation, testing and handover. You may also be involved in maintenance programmes.
IT Consultant	Your role as an IT consultant will be to work in partnership with clients, advising them how to use information technology in order to meet their business objectives or overcome problems. You'll work to improve the structure and efficiency of IT systems in various organisations. Your training should include all these components.
Management Consultant	Management consultants help organisations to solve issues, create value, maximise growth and improve business performance. They use their business skills to provide objective advice and expertise, and help an organisation to develop any specialist skills that it may be lacking. You'll be concerned primarily with the strategy, structure, management and operations of a company. Your role is to identify options for the organisation and suggest recommendations for change, as well as advising on additional resources. The training programme should have all such components.

(Contd...)

Project Manager	As a project manager, you'll need to track work to be completed, set deadlines and delegate tasks to your project team, identifying any potential risks. Ultimately, you're responsible for completing the project work in line with the plan and will often report progress to senior managers. Your training should cover the areas falling under the jurisdiction of the following cadre: • assistant project manager • business change manager • junior/senior project manager • project coordinator • project officer.
Nano Technology	The training on nano-technologies is highly competitive but highly job oriented.
E-learning and Production of e-learning material	E-learning is going to solve many problems of learning and evaluation. The training on contents development is very important.
E-business	E-business is the future business trend. Training on e-business becomes more important.
Energy Management	In future, energy conservation and environment protection will require many personnel and training in these areas is very important.
Event Management	The cope of event management is tremendous and hence the training scope is also very broad.
Hospitality Industry	The students can take training in several hospitality areas like hotels, hospitals, call centres etc.
Tourism and Travel Industry	This sector offers several areas of training and jobs.
Audio/Video Industry	Audio and Video content generation is an important area for training purposes.
Mobile and Communication Technology	This is emerging as an impressive field for teaching and learning. The training could be in all possible areas related to this.
Convergent Thinking Skills Areas	Critical thinking, productive thinking, positive thinking, independent thinking
Divergent Thinking Skills Areas	Originality, flexibility, sensitivity to new problems, Ability to analyse, synthesize, organize ideas
Generic Skills Areas	Leadership qualities, communication skills, management skills, problem solving skills
Entrepreneurial Skills Areas	Calculated risk taking, independent thinking, information seeking, problem solving attitude, goal setting
Business Management	Training could be planned for all the five major functions: Planning, Organising, Staffing, Directing and Controlling

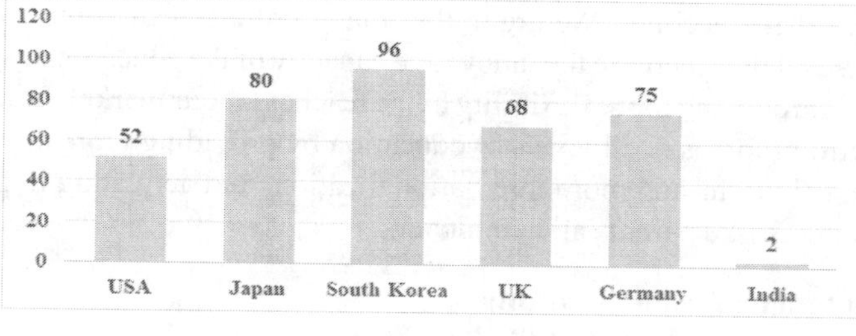

Fig. 7.1: Skilled Manpower in Different Nations

With the world constantly evolving, it is important to keep up with it. Technology, learning and teaching must constantly evolve an innovative education system including training. Innovation is creating success, innovation is what's now and is the process of improving lives. Our cutting-edge in education includes keeping up with the latest technologies that provide skills to students to use in life. Self-managed learning makes the student feel comfortable to stay. Using an engaging, humorous and easy to understand approach by teachers, will convey information to learners in a way that will make them want to listen, absorb and apply what is being taught. This is what is precisely required to be done in training.

Innovation is a driver of growth and well-being not only for individuals but for the entire nation. New technologies, products, services and organisations create jobs and rejuvenate industries. To reap the gains of innovation, policy makers need to understand how the way we innovate is changing and what this implies for education and training policies. We need effective and evidence-based governance mechanisms are needed to encourage, facilitate and help measure innovation in education systems.

Innovations in teaching methodology towards a more intensive use of computers and e-learning have not universally increased student achievement. The evidence also clearly suggests that ICT skills themselves are not rewarded in the labour market. Instead, the labour market mainly rewards basic skills in mathematics and science, in addition to non-cognitive skills like personal traits and character. Cognitive skills seem to be of major importance for advanced and innovative economies, and can be fostered by more intensive teaching. A more open question is how non-cognitive skills can be stimulated in an educational setting.

Innovations in teaching methods require teachers that are able to innovate. Excellent teachers are able to motivate students and to choose the most productive teaching method for each specific topic. A challenge for many countries is to provide incentives for high- ability students to choose the teaching profession, and to incentivize teachers in schools to improve their teaching. We argue that many policies can stimulate such changes and thus increase the innovative capacity of the educational system, such as introducing more flexibility in the teacher labour market, increasing competition forces at all levels of education by providing more autonomy to the institutions and more internationalization, and activating important stakeholders like parents and employers.

Importance of Field Training

The field training is another important component for skill development and innovative research. You come across the real problems faced by the society. The expected outcome of the field training is many folds as elaborated below:

1. You will improve your subject skills by undergoing the field training at an industry in your chosen stream or training institute or any service provider.
2. You will learn the entrepreneurial aspects for setting up a small business unit by participating in the live operations of such business unit during the field training.
3. You will come across the real problems being faced by the industries.

You should get a broad training schedule prepared with the help of your local guide who will be chosen from the organization where you are going for training. It will cover many areas, some of them are the following:

- Raw material procurements
- Production process
- Quality control mechanism
- Customer satisfaction of the product or services
- Marketing and sales procedures
- Stock and inventory mechanism
- Feedback from the people
- Nature of problems faced by the people

You are advised to undergo the field training as per the schedule prepared by the local supervisor. If you are inclined to start some kind of business after your training, then you should also consider issues related to business start-up, management and promotion.

There are various methods you can adopt to start a business. The first step to establish a small business unit (SBU) is to decide on the product or services. After deciding the product or service, you have to decide the location of your business. This could be your home or outside in a rented or self-owned premises. Some of the important parameters which you have to consider before starting a business are infrastructure, technology, manpower, raw materials and production and finally distribution.

Infrastructure Needed

Infrastructure is the most important parameters in any business. Infrastructure requirement includes transportation, communication, power, raw material, trained and skilled manpower and building and equipment. Lack of any of these facilities may affect any business. You may face many problems with respect to infrastructure. The problems faced by the small and medium scale entrepreneurs are as follows:

- ***Inadequate infrastructural facilities:*** Inadequate storage space leads to shortages of basic raw materials, especially those which are scare and need to be imported from distant places.
- ***Difficulty in distribution:*** Incomplete construction or non-existence of basic roads and highways may restrict the growth prospects of your firm.
- ***Shortage of power supply:*** Small and medium scale enterprises may face a shortage of power supply. In such case, the enterprise may not be able to make full utilization of plant capacity. Usually, new entrepreneurs don't have sufficient funds to install their own power generating plants so as to ensure uninterrupted operations.
- ***Difficulty in communication:*** If your business is located in rural or remote areas, you may face problems in telecom network. It may be difficult for the entrepreneurs to communicate with people outside the region. These affect the long run profit earning capacity of your business as well as prevent the chances of survival.

Technology Needed

While choosing the process technology, you should consider the following factors:

- The level of skilled workers or complex machines required by the process.
- The quantity of water and/or power required.
- Whether any process or product patent is needed in order to utilise the selected process technology.
- Any special pollution or environmental regulation that is to be followed.

Manpower Needed

There is strong need to assess the kind and number of staff needed, and then select them. Simultaneously, efforts have to be made for the training arrangements for preparing the selected people to handle their jobs efficiently. Selecting a right person to do a specific job is not an easy task. You have to do series of exercises before and after selecting a person.

Training and Development

Systematic and scientific training involves imparting technical knowledge, skills, and enhanced problem-solving abilities of the employee. Through this process, the knowledge, skills, aptitude and abilities of an employee for doing the specific job in an efficient manner are increased. The main advantages of training are:

- ***Higher Performance**:* Training helps to improve the quantity and quality of work output by increasing knowledge, skills and productivity of both employees and an organisation as a whole.
- ***Shorter learning period**:* Training helps to reduce the learning time and cost required for reaching the acceptable level of performance.
- ***Uniformity of procedures**:* The best available methods of performing a job can be standardised and taught to all employees, which helps to improve the quality of performance.
- ***Manpower development**:* Training enables an organisation to fill manpower needs. The promising employees can be spotted and trained for higher job-levels. Training thus provides a reservoir of competent replacements and prevents managerial obsolescence.
- ***Economy of materials and equipment**:* Training helps employees to make better and more economical use of materials and equipment. The rate of industrial accidents and damages to machinery and equipment will be minimised. This in turn will lead to lower costs of production per unit.
- ***Less supervision**:* Training reduces the need for detailed and constant supervision as they know what to do and how to do it.
- ***Better morale**:* Training helps to improve the employees' job satisfaction and, therefore, morale. It enables them to utilize and develop their full potential.
- ***Participative management**:* Training facilitates delegation and decentralisation of authority. Trained employees accept new and challenging assignments which improves the stability and flexibility of the organisation.

Raw Material for Production Process

An understanding of different issues related to raw material and production of the goods is very important. Proper planning for raw materials is essential for your business. If the quality and quantity of raw material are not managed properly, you may face problems. For example, production may be held up, resulting in idle machinery and manpower. On the other hand, if you order more than what you require, you will lock up much of your working capital. Proper planning is required for imported raw material whose lead times are long. Proper care can increase your manufacturing process by smooth and cost-effective production.

Production Process

Manufacturing is a process of putting together different components either purchased from outside or made in your own factory and making the required finished products. Varieties of products are manufactured by using different methods. Production is a process of the transformation of all inputs into outputs to meet the needs of customers. This is shown in Fig. 7.2.

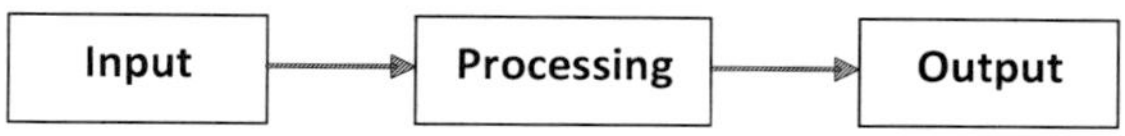

Fig. 7.2. Production Process

This is referred to as the Conversion Process. Production incorporates many tasks that are interdependent.

Quality Control

Quality control (QC) is the method used to manage quality of the product or service (education is a service). It is concerned with checking and reviewing work that has been done. Quality control is to make sure that what's being produced is meeting the required standard or not. Quality control can be done at three main points during the production process when inspection is performed:

(1) When raw materials are received prior to entering production.
(2) When products are going through the production process.
(3) When products are finished. Here inspection for quality takes place before products are stored for sales or dispatched to customers.

The quality control may lead to the following disadvantages:

- Working capital is tied up in stocks which cannot be sold.
- Inspection is costly, in terms of materials, labour, time, and employee morale, customer goodwill, lost sales.
- It is usually done by a separate "quality control inspection team" rather than by the workers themselves.

- It is sometimes done too late in the production process. This often results in defective or non-acceptable goods actually being received by the customer.
- The inspection process does not add any value.
- Inspection is often not compatible with more modern production techniques which do not allow time for much inspection.

Market Consideration

The important factor influencing the choice of distribution channel is the nature of the target market. Some of the important features in this respect are:

- Direct selling is more suitable when the number of prospective customers is small or the market for the product is geographically located in a limited area. For a large number of potential customers, however, the use of middlemen becomes necessary.
- Direct selling is also preferred if the customers place orders for the product in big lots. If the product is sold in small quantities, middlemen are used to distribute such products.
- If the market for the product is for industrial users, the channel of distribution will not need any middlemen. In the case of goods meant for domestic consumers, middlemen may have to be involved.

Business Management

You can become a successful entrepreneur provided before doing any business you learn how to run it successfully. Good management helps utilise the resources of an organisation optimally. It comprises several interconnected elements for achieving its goals. These are the most important elements in the whole business management process and include:

- Promoting and marketing the product
- Making its product available to prospective consumers through proper distribution channels
- Managing the accounts and finances
- Protecting its intellectual property
- Creating harmony among the firm's working of various departments and divisions
- Managing human resources and relationship with the customers.

Your good managerial skills can convert the disorganised resources of men, money, material and machinery into a productive business enterprise. In a modern business, you have to possess different types of skills to manage your organisation. These skills are:

- ***Human skills:*** These are the ability to work effectively with other people, individually and in a group. Such skills enable you to gain the co-operation of other and build the base for a successful team work.
- ***Technical skills:*** These are the ability with knowledge to use equipment, techniques and procedures to perform specific tasks. You must understand both the role of each skill employed and the inner-relationship between the skills.
- ***Conceptual skills:*** These skills include the ability to understand a problem faced by the organisation in all its aspects and solving it.

Management Functions

Business administration is creative problem-solving mechanism through the following management functions:

- Planning
- Organising
- Staffing
- Directing
- Controlling

Planning: You can develop your business mission through continuous and careful planning and objectives. You should make sure that your planning covers both the broadest view of your organisation i.e., its mission and the narrowest i.e., any tactic for accomplishing a specific goal.

Organising: When you organise properly, you can establish your company's internal organisation structure. Your focus should be on division, coordination, control of tasks, and the flow of information within your organisation. This is how managers distribute authority to job holders.

Staffing: You must fill positions in your business with qualified people. Recruiting, hiring, training, evaluating and compensating are parts of intelligent staffing.

Directing: You must influence your staff behaviour through motivation, communication, group dynamics, leadership and discipline. This will channalise the behaviour of your staff to accomplish your organisation's mission and objectives while helping them accomplish their own career objectives.

Controlling: You can control your staff by establishing performance standards based on your firm's objectives, measuring and reporting actual performance.

Finance

An important aspect of managing your business is the efficient management of your finances. Once you have estimated your financial requirements for fixed and working capital, you must identify the sources of finance.

You have to control and manage your firm's financial resources which involve managing the flow of money into and out of your business in a systematic form cash-flow management. A cash-flow statement is a financial tool for measuring cash receipts and disbursements over a period of time. It lists cash to and cash from operating, investing and financing activities along with the net increase or decrease in cash for the period.

Business Promotions

Business promotion is a process of informing and convincing prospective customers about the products or services of the firm. It creates and maintains the demand for the product.

The functions of promotion are:

1. Establishing the contact with the members of society
2. Showing how the products will satisfy their needs
3. Creating the desire to buy the products

Promotion also helps customers in differentiating the product of a particular firm from the competing products of other firms; assure the customers about the quality and price of the product. This will prevent the shifting from a particular brand of product to another brand of product.

You can sell your products only if you undertake various promotional activities effectively. In today's globalised world with the widening of market, stiff competition, rapid advancement in technology and continuous changes in tastes and preferences of customer, it is important to increase the promotional activity.

Advertising happens to be the most important promotional tool. It involves non-personal dissemination of information about a firm's product on a large scale to potential customers. Salesmanship is the oldest form of promotion used by the firms to directly and verbally communicate with the customers. Sales promotion is another promotion technique used to supplement the other selling efforts of the firm.

Innovative Practices for Higher Education Institutions Training Programmes

The higher education institutions should concentrate on the following points for making education relevant to the society and making students knowledgeable about various innovations.

- To introduce need based courses
- To introduce skill based vocational courses
- To introduce Choice Based Credit programmes
- To promote international as well as national collaboration for academic programmes, faculty and student exchange
- To introduce joint research programmes
- To introduce in house training in the areas of communication, creativity and innovation, stress management, time management
- To introduce e-learning, MOOCs and SWAYAM courses
- To introduce faculty development programmes
- To have last semester of each programme reserve for project work
- To introduce training programmes during summer vacations
- To introduce assignments as a teaching, learning and evaluation tool.

References

Abbad, M. M., Morris, D., & de Nahlik, C. (2009). Looking under the Bonnet: Factors Affecting Student Adoption of E-Learning Systems in Jordan. The International Review of Research in Open and Distance Learning.

Ajay, A.I and Akindutire, I.O. (2007). The Unresolved Issues of Quality Assurance in Nigerian Universities, Journal of Sociology and Education in Africa, Vol. 6, No. 1, January.

Akkoyuklu, B. & Soylu, M. Y. (2006). A study on students views on blended learning environment. Turkish Online Journal of Distance Education, 7(3), ISSN 1302-6488.

Algahtani, A.F. (2011). Evaluating the Effectiveness of the E-learning Experience in Some Universities in Saudi Arabia from Male Students' Perceptions, Durham theses, Durham University.

Almosa, A. & Almubarak, A. (2005). E-learning Foundations and Applications, Saudi Arabia: Riyadh.

Arya, Umesh (2017), The Rise of MOOCs (Massive Open Online Courses) and Other Similar Online Courses Variants –Analysis of Textual Incidences in Cyberspace, Journal of Content, Community & Communication, Vol. 6, pp. 26-35.

Arroyo, I., Woolf, B. P., Cooper, D. G., Burleson, W., Muldner, K. (2011). The Impact of Animated Pedagogical Agents on Girls and Boys Emotions, Attitudes, Behaviors and Learning. 11th IEEE International Conference on Advanced Learning Technologies, 506-510.

Armony H and Vuilleumier P, (2013). The Cambridge Handbook of Human Affective Neuroscience, Cambridge Univ. Press, N.Y.

Astleitner, H. (2000). Designing emotionally sound instruction: The FEASP-approach. Instructional Science, 28, 169-198.

Astleitner, H., and Leutner, D. (2000). Designing instructional technology from an emotional perspective. Journal of Research on Computing in Education, 32, 497-510.

Bloom, B.S., and Krathwohl, D.R. (1956). Taxonomy of Educational Objectives: The Classification of Educational Goals: Handbook I, Cognitive Domain. New York: Longmans, Green.

Bloom, David, David Canning, and Kevin Chan. (2006). "Higher Education and Economic Development in Africa." Africa Region Human Development Working Paper Series No. 102. Washington, D.C.: The World Bank.

Borstorff, P. C., & Lowe, S. L. (2007). Student perceptions and opinions toward e-learning in the college environment. Academy of Educational Leadership Journal, 11 (2), 13–30.

Brennan, J., S. Ryan, M. Ranga, S. Broek, N. Durazzi and B. Kamphuis (2014). Study on innovation in higher education: final report. European Commission Directorate for Education and Training Study on Innovation in Higher Education, Luxembourg.

Brymah A and Bell F (2011), Business Research Methods, New York, Oxford University Press.

Butcher, (2011), A Basic Guide to Open Educational Resources, Vancouver, Canada & Paris: COL and UNESCO.

Callahan, J. L. (2004). Breaking the cult of rationality: Mindful awareness of emotion in the critical theory classroom. New Directions for Adult and Continuing Education, 102, 75-83.

Cadle, J. & D. Yeates, D., (2008). Project management for information systems (5th ed., Harlow: Pearson – Prentice Hall). ISBN: 978-0-13-206858-1.

Cano. J., Carton, B.I and Raven, M.R. (1991), An assessment of selected teacher characteristics of pre-service teachers of agriculture education, Proceedings of the 45th Annual Central State Conference.

Chandra R and Singh S (2004), Open and Distance Education System: New Vistas in Higher Education, Rajdhani Book Service, New Delhi.

Chandra R and Moni Sahay (2008). Quality Issues in IGNOU's BCA and MCA Projects: A Case Study of Regional Centre, Patna, Indian Journal of Open Learning, 17(2), 145-153.

Chatzara, K., Karagiannidis, C., Stamatis, D. (2010). Student's attitude and learning effectiveness of emotional agents. 10th IEEE International Conference on Advanced Learning Technologies, 558-559.

Chaffar S and Frasson C (2004). Using an emotional intelligent agent to improve the learner's performance, www.iro.umontreal.ca

Conole, G. (2013). MOOCs as disruptive technologies: strategies for enhancing the learner experience and quality of MOOCs. Retrieved from http://www.um.es/ead/red/39/conole. pdf

Cranton, P.(1994). Understanding and promoting transformative Learning: A Guide to Educators of Adults. San Francisco: Jossey-Bass.

Dawson, Catherine, (2002). Practical Research Methods, New Delhi, UBS Publishers 'Distributors

Delaney, J.G. (2002). Educational (2000). Policy Studies: A Practical Approach. Calgary, Alberts: Detselig Enterprises Ltd.,

Dirkx, J. M. (2006). Engaging emotions in adult learning: A jungian perspective on emotion and transformative learning. New Directions for Adult and Continuing Education, 109, 15-26. San Francisco.

Do, A. T., King, S. A. (2011). Creating Emotional Speech for Conversational Agents. Workshop on Digital Media and Digital Content Management, 107–110.

Dowling, C., Godfrey, J. M. & Gyles N. (2003). "Do Hybrid Flexible Delivery Teaching Methods Improve Accounting Students' Learning Outcomes," Accounting Education: An International Journal, 12 (4), 373-391.

Fagerberg J and Verspagen B (2009). Innovation Studies-The emerging structure of new scientific field, Research Policy, Vol. 38, pp. 218-233.

Fatahi, S and Aghaee, N. G. (2010). Design and implementation of an intelligent educational model based on personality and learner's emotion, Int. J. Computer Science and Information Security, 7(3), 1-13.

Fry, K. (2001). E-learning markets and providers: some issues and prospects. Education Training, 233-239.

Gadiya, A. K. and Chandra, R. (2014). Teaching and Learning Skills in University System, Mewar University Press, 2014.

Garger, S and Guild, P. (1984). Learning Styles: The crucial differences, Curriculum Review, pp. 9-12.

Gotschall M. (2000). E-learning strategies for executive education and corporate training. Fortune 141(10): 5–59.

Griffiths, R., M.M. Chingos, C. Mulhern and R. Spies (2014). "Interactive online learning on campus: Testing MOOCs and other platforms in hybrid formats in the university system of Maryland."

Hall, Martin. (2005). "Quality Assurance at UCT." Version 5, undated. www.ched.uct.ac.za/ qaprojects. htm (2005).

Hameed, S. Badii, A. & Cullen, A. J. (2008). Effective e-learning integration with traditional learning in a blended learning environment. European and Mediterranean conference on information system, (25-26).

Hanushek, E.A., and L. Wossmann. (2007). "The Role of Education Quality in Economic Growth." World Bank Policy Research Working Paper No. 4122, The World Bank, Washington, D.C.

Heimlich, J.E. (1990). Measuring teaching styles: a co-relational study, Ohio State University.

Heidig, S., Clarebout, G. (2011). Do pedagogical agents make a difference to student motivation and learning? Educational Research Review, 6, 27-54.

Hill, Peter R., (2001). Practical software project estimation: A toolkit for estimating software development effort & duration (McGraw-Hill). ISBN: 978-0-07-171791-5

Huber, M. T., P. Hutchings (2004). Integrative Learning: Mapping the Terrain. The Academy in Transition. Washington, DC.: Association of American Colleges and Universities.

Hughes, B. & M. Cotterell, (2009). Software project management (5th ed., Maidenhead: McGraw Hill). ISBN: 978-0-07-712279-9.

Hoxby, C. (2014). "The economics of online postsecondary education: MOOCs, nonselective education, and highly selective education." American Economic Review, vol. 104, pp. 528–533.

Ivanoviæ, M., Mitroviæ, D., Budimac, Z., Vidakoviæ, M. (2011). Metadata harvesting learning resources – an agent-oriented approach. In Proceedings of the 15th International Conference on System Theory, Control and Computing, 306-311.

Jackson, G. E. (1990). Evaluating learning technology: Methods, Strategies, and Examples in Higher Education, The Journal of Higher Education, Vol. 61, No. 3, pp. 294.

Jung, S. J. (2006). Investigating the relationships among students' emotional intelligence, achievement, satisfaction and amount of interaction in online learning. Unpublished master ìs thesis, Ewha Womans University, Seoul, Korea.

Kajaste, Matti (2018), Quality management of research, development and innovation activities in Finnish universities of applied sciences, Journal of Quality in Higher Education, Vol. 24, Issue 3.

Kanwar, Kodhandaraman, & Umar, (2010), Towards Sustainable Open Educational Resources: A Perspective from the Global South, American Journal of Distance Education, 24 (2), 65-80.

Kang, D.S., Kim, J.K., and Chong, H-I. (2011). The structural relationship among affective characteristics, learning presence, learning flow, learning satisfaction in distance education. The Journal of Educational Information and Media, 17(1), 133-152.

Kang, M., and Goo, N. (2007). Predictive validity of emotional intelligence on various achievement in blended learning environment. Korean Journal of Curriculum and Instruction, 11(1), 235-255.

Kehoe, J; Tennent, B; Windeknecht, K. (2004), The challenge of Flexible and non-traditional learning and teaching methods: Best practice in every situation, Studies in Learning Evaluation Innovation and Development, Vol. 1(1), pp. 56-63.

Keller, C. & Cernerud, L. (2002). Students' perception of e-learning in university education. Learning, Media and Technology, 27(1), 55-67.

Kim, M. (2008). Processes of emotional experiences in online discussions: Emotional changes through interacting with other students. The Korean Journal of Educational Psychology, 22(4), 697-722. IJEMT, 6(1), 14-22 ISSN 1882-1693.

Kothari, C.R., (1985), Research Methodology- Methods and Techniques, New Delhi, Wiley Eastern Limited.

Kort, B; Reilly, R. and Picard. R. (2001). External representation of learning process and domain knowledge: Affective state as a determinate of its structure and function, 10nth International conference on artificial intelligence in education, San Antonio, Texas.

Koppleman, K. (1980), The relationship of cognitive style to teaching style. Paper presented to the Midwest Educational Research Association, Toledo, OH. (ERIC Document Reproduction Service No. ED 194 609).

Kumar, Ranjit, (2005), Research Methodology-A Step-by-Step Guide for Beginners, (2nd.ed.), Singapore, Pearson Education.

Kumar, A. and Dixit, J. (2006) Computer Hands-on and Lab Practicals in Distance Education. In S.C. Garg, V.Venkaiah, C.Puranik and S. Panda (eds.), Four Decades of Distance Education in India: Reflections on Policy & Practice. New Delhi: Viva Books Private Ltd.

LaRose, R., Gregg, J., & Eastin, M. (1998). Audio graphic tele-courses for the Web: An experiment. Journal of Computer Mediated Communications, 4(2).

Lawther, P. M., and Walker, D. H. T. (2001), An evaluation of a distributed learning system. Education and Training, 43(2), 105-116.

Lee, I.S. (2012). Research Trends on Emotional Factors in the e-Learning Context, International Journal of Educational Media and Technology, 6 (1), 14-22.

Lee, I. S. (2011). Emotion, emotional intelligence, and e-learning. Online proceeding of the 9th International Conference for Media in Education (1-4). Sungkyunkwan University, R. of Korea (pdf. semantic scholar. org).

Lee, S-M., and Song, K.S. (2007). The effects of affective feedbacks according to the learner's emotions in e-learning. Journal of the Korea society of computer and information, 10(4), 125-133.

Liaw, S.S., Huang, H.M. (2003). Exploring the World Wide Web for on-line learning: a perspective from Taiwan. Educational Technology 40(3): 27–32.

Light, V., Nesbitt, E., Light, P., and Burns, J. R. (2000). "Let's you and me have a little discussion": Computer mediated communication in support of campus-based university courses. Studies in Higher Education, 25(1), 85-96.

Liu, Y., & Wang, H. (2009). A comparative study on e-learning technologies and products: from the East to the West. Systems Research & Behavioral Science, 26(2), 191–209.

Liu, N.C., and Y. Cheng. (2005). "Academic Ranking of World Universities—Methodologies and Problems." Higher Education in Europe 30 (2).

Love, N. & Fry, N. (2006). "Accounting Students' Perceptions of a Virtual Learning Environment: Springboard or Safety Net?" Accounting Education: An International Journal, 15 (2), 151-166.

Loizou, M., Hartley, T. Slater, S., Newman, R., Pannese, L. (2012). Emotions for intelligent agents in crisis anagement simulations: A survey. CGAMES-The 17th International Conference on Computer Games, 219.

Materu (2007). Higher Education Quality Assurance in Sub-Saharan Africa Status, Challenges, Opportunities and Promosing Practices, World Bank Working Paper No. 124.

Mishra, S. (2017). Promoting Use and Contribution of Open Educational Resources, CEMCA.

Maltz, L., Deblois, P. & The EDUCAUSE Current Issues Committee. (2005). Top Ten IT Issues. EDUCAUSE Review, 40 (1), 15-28.

Mikko Alasarrela, (2017). Machinelearning.com

Mostafa, S; Masum Al and Ishizuka M (2005). An effective role of software agent for effective agent-based e-learning by interplaying between emotions and learning, Proceedings of the first international conference on web information systems and technology (pdfs.semantischolar.org).

Munzali, J (2006). "Quality Assurance and Accreditation in Higher Education in Nigeria."

Oblinger, D. G., & Hawkins, B. L. (2005). The myth about E-learning. Educause review.

OECD (2014). Measuring Innovation in Education. A New Perspective. Paris, OECD.

OECD (2005). E-learning in tertiary education [Online]. Available at http://www.cumex.org. (Accessed 27 /02/ 2014). Organization for Economic Co-Operation and Development

(OECD). (2005). "E-learning in Tertiary Education".Policy Briefs. http://www.oecd.org/dataoecd/27/35/35991871.pdf accessed 8 January 2006.

Okebukola P (2012). Quality Assurance in Higher Education: The African Story of Achievements and Outstanding Needs, CHEA.

Okebukola, P. (2006). "Quality Assurance in Higher Education: The Nigerian Experience." Paper presented at the Quality Assurance in Tertiary Education Conference, Sevres, France, June 18–20.

Osuji, S. N (2009). Teacher Education Curriculum in Nigeria in the Perspective of Lifelong Education. The Journal of International Social Research, Volume 2/8 Summer 2009. Available online: http://www.sosyalarastirmalar.com/cilt2/sayi8pdf/osuji.pdf.

Paschal, M.(2006). "Quality Assurance and Accreditation in Higher Education in Tanzania."

Panda, S. (1999). (ed.) Open & Distance Education: Policy Practices and Quality Concerns. New Delhi: Aravali Books International Private Ltd.

Powar, K.B., Panda, S. and Bhalla, V. (2000) Performance Indicators in Distance Higher Education, New Delhi: Aravali Books International Private Ltd.

Perryman, L. A. & Seal, T., (2015). Open Educational Practices and Attitudes to Openness Across India: Reporting the Findings of OER Research Hub Pan-India Survey, OER 15 Conference, Cardiff, UK.

Mezirow, J. And Associates (2000). Learning as Transformation: Critical Perspectives on a Theory in Progress, San Francisco: Jossey-Base Publishers.

Niyozov, S. (2008). Understanding Pedagogy: Cross-cultural and Comparative Insights form Central Asia. In Mundy, K:Bickmore, K:Hayhore, R., Madden, M. and Madjidi, K.(eds). Comparative and International Education: Issues for Teachers. Toronto: Canadian Scholars' Press.

Palmer, P.J. (1998). The courage to teach: Exploring the inner landscape of a teacher's life. San Francisco: Jossey-Bass Publishers.

Park, J.H., Kim, I.O., Jung, S.M., Song, K.S., and Kim, J.B. (2008). Enhancing e-learning interactivity via emotion recognition computing technology. Journal of the Korea society of computer and information, 11(2), 89-98.

Pasquier G and Paulmaz E, (2004). The Notebooks of the Academy of Nantes, 31, 17-21.

Pekrun, R. (2006). The control-value theory of achievement emotions: Assumptions, corollaries, and implications for educational research and practice. Educational Psychology Review, 18, 315-341.

Pekrun, R., Gortz, T., Titz, W., and Raymond, P. P. (2002). Academic emotions in students' self-regulated learning and achievement: A program of qualitative and quantitative research. Educational Psychologist, 37(2), 91–105.

Petrides, L. A. (2002). Web-based technologies for distributed (or distance) learning: Creating learning-centred educational experiences in the higher education classroom. International Journal of Instructional Media, 29(1), 69-77.

Peilin Li (2016) Innovation in higher education: the effectiveness of disruptive technology in e-learning (pdfs. semantischolar. org).

Rha, I., and Sung, E. (2005). Emotional expression factors and the dimensions of interactive messages in online learning community. Journal of Life long Learning Society, 1 (1), 1-22.

Richard, H., & Haya, A. (2009). Examining student decision to adopt web 2.0 technologies: theory and empirical tests. Journal of computing in higher education, 21(3), 183-198.

Rowe, J. (2005). Since feeling is first: Narrative inquiry toward understanding emotion in online teaching and learning. University of Wisconsin-Madison Doctoral dissertation.

Rodrigo, M. M. T., Baker, R. S. J. D., Agapito, J., Nabos, J., Repalam, C., Reyes Jr., S. S., San Pedro, M. O. C. Z. (2012). The Effects of an Interactive Software Agent on Student Affective Dynamics while Using an Intelligent Tutoring System. IEEE Trans. on Affective Computing, 3 (2), 224-236.

Rriya, J.J. (2017). University News, Vol. 55, No.4, pp.8-11.

Rosenberg J.M. (2001). E-learning: Strategies for Delivering Knowledge in the Digital Age. McGraw-Hill: New York.

Rossi. P. G. (2009). Learning environment with artificial intelligence elements. Journal of e-learning and knowledge society, 5(1), 67-75.

Ronning, R.R., McCurdy, D., and Ballinger, R. (1984). Individual differences: A third component in problem-solving instruction. Journal of Research in Science, 71-82.

Saffu, Y. (2006). "Quality Assurance and Accreditation in Higher Education in Ghana."

Salati, K.M. and Chandra, R. (2014). Quality Assurance in Higher Education: Creditisation, Examination, Evaluation and Certification, Journal of Indian Research, Vol. 2, No. 2, pp. 183-205.

Salati K.M. and Chandra, R. (2014). "Innovation in Examination and Evaluation in Universities" Presented in the 32ndAnnual Conference of the Association for Educational Assessment in Africa (AEAA), held in Livingstone, 11-15 August 2014.

Shabani, J. (2006). Higher Education in French Speaking Sub-Saharan Africa. UNESCO Harare Cluster Office, Zimbabwe.

Sharma, S, Ekta Sharma, Yatendra Sharma, (2015). Academia industry interaction: A 'win-win' partnership, National Journal of Advanced Research, Vol. 1, Issue 1, pp. 26-28.

Sharma, P.B. (2018). Presidential Address, 92nd Annual Meet, AIU 2018).

Smith, S. R. (2005). Toward an Integrated Medical curriculum. Med Health R I, 88(8): 258-61.

Smout and Stephenson (2001). Quality Assurance in African Higher Education: A New Beginning, The Sixth QHE Seminar, Birmingham.

Smith, S. R. (2005), Toward an Integrated Medical curriculum. Med Health R I, 88(8): 258-61.

Sommerville, I. (2010). Software engineering (9th Intnl ed., Harlow: Pearson Education). ISBN: 978-0-13-705346-9

Skillicorn, N (2019). ideatovalue.com.

Tang, T. Y. and Mccalla, G. (2002). Smart recommendation for an Evolving e-Learning System, researchgate.net

Tao, Y. H., Yeh, C. R., & Sun, S. I. (2006). Improving training needs assessment processes via the Internet: system design and qualitative study. Internet Research, 16 (4), 427-49.

Tavangarian, Djamshid, Markus E. Leypold, Kristin Nölting, Marc Röser, Denny Voigt (2004). e-Learning the Solution for Individual Learning? , Electronic Journal of e-Learning Volume 2 Issue 2 2004 (273-280)

Tierney, W.G. and Michael Lanford, Conceptualizing Innovation in Higher Education (https://www.researchgate.net/publication/303208037)

Valentina Arkorful and Nelly Abaidoo (2015). The role of e-learning, advantages and disadvantages of its adoption in higher education, International Journal of Instructional Technology and Distance Learning, Vol. 12, No. 1, pp. 29-42.

Virginio, C; Massimo, C and Marco. P. (2004). Perspectives and challenges in e-learning towards natural interaction paradigms, Journal of Visual Languages and Computing, 15, 333-345.

Waldrop, M. (2013). "Campus 2.0." Nature, vol. 495, pp. 160–163.

Wang, Y. S., Wang, Y. M., Lin, H. H., & Tang, T. I. (2003). Determinants of user acceptance of Internet banking: An empirical study. International Journal of Service Industry Management, 14, 501–519.

Wentling T.L, Waight C, Gallagher J, La Fleur J, Wang C, Kanfer A. (2000). E-learning - a review of literature. Knowledge and Learning Systems Group NCSA 9.1–73.

Willett, H. G. (2002), Not one or the other but both: Hybrid course delivery using WebCT. The Electronic Library, 20(5), 413-419.

Willes R, Crow G and Pain H (2011). Innovation in qualitative research methods: A narrative review, Innovative Research, 11(5), 587-604.

Yang. M-H. (2009). Emotion as moderator on the relations between achievement goal orientation and academic outcomes. The Korean Journal of Educational Psychology, 23(1), 51-71.

Yang. M.H., and Kim. E.J. (2010). The influence of emotional regulation on learning strategy: Mediated by emotionality. The Korean Journal of Educational Psychology, 24(2), 449-467.

Zhao F (2003), Transforming quality in research supervision: A knowledge management approach, Quality in Higher Education, 9(2), 187-197.

Zeitoun, H. (2008). E-learning: Concept, Issues, Application, Evaluation, Riyadh: Dar Alsolateah publication.

Subject Index

A

B

C

D

T

U